Cambridge IGCSE™

Mathematics
Core
Fifth edition

Ric Pimentel
Frankie Pimentel
Terry Wall

Cambridge International copyright material in this publication is reproduced under licence and remains the intellectual property of Cambridge Assessment International Education.

Endorsement indicates that a resource has passed Cambridge International's rigorous quality-assurance process and is suitable to support the delivery of a Cambridge International syllabus. However, endorsed resources are not the only suitable materials available to support teaching and learning, and are not essential to be used to achieve the qualification. Resource lists found on the Cambridge International website will include this resource and other endorsed resources. Any example answers to questions taken from past question papers, practice questions, accompanying marks and mark schemes included in this resource have been written by the authors and are for guidance only. They do not replicate examination papers. In examinations the way marks are awarded may be different. Any references to assessment and/or assessment preparation are the publisher's interpretation of the syllabus requirements. Examiners will not use endorsed resources as a source of material for any assessment set by Cambridge International. While the publishers have made every attempt to ensure that advice on the qualification and its assessment is accurate, the official syllabus, specimen assessment materials and any associated assessment guidance materials produced by the awarding body are the only authoritative source of information and should always be referred to for definitive guidance. Cambridge International recommends that teachers consider using a range of teaching and learning resources based on their own professional judgement of their students' needs. Cambridge International has not paid for the production of this resource, nor does Cambridge International receive any royalties from its sale. For more information about the endorsement process, please visit www.cambridgeinternational.org/endorsed-resources

Photo credits: pp,2-3 © chaoss/stock.adobe.com; p.3 © Inv. Id P. Lund. inv. 35, reproduced with the kind permission of Lund University Library, Sweden; pp.100-1 © denisismagilov/stock.adobe.com; p.101 © Eduard Kim / Shutterstock; pp.156-7 © Microgen/stock.adobe.com; p.157 © Georgios Kollidas - Fotolia; pp.176-8 © tampatra/stock.adobe.com; p.178 © Alexey Pavluts - Fotolia; pp.226-7 © ardely/stock.adobe.com; p.227 © uwimages - Fotolia; pp.270-1 © Marina Sun/stock.adobe.com; p.271 © Dinodia Photos / Alamy Stock Photo; pp.294-5 © ohenze/stock.adobe.com; p.295 © Matěj Baťha via Wikipedia Commons (https://creativecommons.org/licenses/by-sa/2.5/deed.en); pp.310-1 © あんみつ姫/stock.adobe.com; p.311 © Bernard 63 - Fotolia; pp.328-9 © J BOY/stock.adobe.com; p.329 © caifas/stock.adobe.com

Every effort has been made to trace all copyright holders, but if any have been inadvertently overlooked, the Publishers will be pleased to make the necessary arrangements at the first opportunity.

Although every effort has been made to ensure that website addresses are correct at time of going to press, Hodder Education cannot be held responsible for the content of any website mentioned in this book. It is sometimes possible to find a relocated web page by typing in the address of the home page for a website in the URL window of your browser.

Hachette UK's policy is to use papers that are natural, renewable and recyclable products and made from wood grown in well-managed forests and other sustainable sources. The logging and manufacturing processes are expected to conform to the environmental regulations of the country of origin.

Orders: please contact Hachette UK Distribution, Hely Hutchinson Centre, Milton Road, Didcot, Oxfordshire, OX11 7HH. Telephone: +44 (0)1235 827827. Email education@hachette.co.uk Lines are open from 9 a.m. to 5 p.m., Monday to Friday. You can also order through our website: www.hoddereducation.com

© Frankie Pimentel, Ric Pimentel and Terry Wall 2023

First edition published 1997
Second edition published 2006
Third edition published 2013
Fourth edition published 2018
This fifth edition published 2023 by

Hodder Education,
An Hachette UK Company
Carmelite House, 50 Victoria Embankment, London EC4Y 0DZ

www.hoddereducation.com

Impression number	10 9 8 7 6 5 4 3 2 1
Year	2027 2026 2025 2024 2023

All rights reserved. Apart from any use permitted under UK copyright law, no part of this publication may be reproduced or transmitted in any form or by any means, electronic or mechanical, including photocopying and recording, or held within any information storage and retrieval system, without permission in writing from the publisher or under licence from the Copyright Licensing Agency Limited. Further details of such licences (for reprographic reproduction) may be obtained from the Copyright Licensing Agency Limited, www.cla.co.uk

Cover photo © Real Moment - stock.adobe.com

Typeset by Integra Software Services Pvt. Ltd., Pondicherry, India

Printed in Italy

A catalogue record for this title is available from the British Library.

ISBN: 978 1 3983 7393 8

Contents

Introduction		v
TOPIC 1	**Number**	**2**
Chapter 1	Number and language	4
Chapter 2	Accuracy	16
Chapter 3	Calculations and order	24
Chapter 4	Integers, fractions, decimals and percentages	32
Chapter 5	Further percentages	45
Chapter 6	Ratio and proportion	51
Chapter 7	Indices and standard form	61
Chapter 8	Money and finance	70
Chapter 9	Time	84
Chapter 10	Set notation and Venn diagrams	89
	Mathematical investigations and ICT 1	95
TOPIC 2	**Algebra and graphs**	**100**
Chapter 11	Algebraic representation and manipulation	102
Chapter 12	Algebraic indices	109
Chapter 13	Equations	112
Chapter 14	Sequences	126
Chapter 15	Graphs in practical situations	133
Chapter 16	Graphs of functions	140
	Mathematical investigations and ICT 2	153
TOPIC 3	**Coordinate geometry**	**156**
Chapter 17	Coordinates and straight line graphs	158
	Mathematical investigations and ICT 3	175
TOPIC 4	**Geometry**	**176**
Chapter 18	Geometrical vocabulary	178
Chapter 19	Geometrical constructions and scale drawings	188
Chapter 20	Symmetry	198
Chapter 21	Angle properties	202
	Mathematical investigations and ICT 4	224
TOPIC 5	**Mensuration**	**226**
Chapter 22	Measures	228
Chapter 23	Perimeter, area and volume	234
	Mathematical investigations and ICT 5	269

CONTENTS

TOPIC 6	**Trigonometry**		**270**
Chapter 24	Bearings		272
Chapter 25	Right-angled triangles		275
	Mathematical investigations and ICT 6		291
TOPIC 7	**Vectors and transformations**		**294**
Chapter 26	Transformations		296
	Mathematical investigations and ICT 7		307
TOPIC 8	**Probability**		**310**
Chapter 27	Probability		312
	Mathematical investigations and ICT 8		325
TOPIC 9	**Statistics**		**328**
Chapter 28	Mean, median, mode and range		330
Chapter 29	Collecting, displaying and interpreting data		335
	Mathematical investigations and ICT 9		352
Glossary			354
Index			364

Answers can be found at www.hoddereducation.com/CambridgeExtras

Introduction

This book has been written for students studying the Core content of the Cambridge IGCSE™ and IGCSE (9–1) Mathematics syllabuses (0580/0980) for examination from 2025. It carefully and precisely follows the syllabus from Cambridge Assessment International Education. It provides the detail and guidance that are needed to support you throughout the course and help you to prepare for your examinations.

How to use this book

To make your study of mathematics as rewarding and successful as possible, this book, endorsed by Cambridge International, offers the following important features:

Learning objectives
Each topic starts with an outline of the subject material and syllabus content to be covered.

Organisation
Topics follow the order of the syllabus and are divided into chapters. However in some cases, the order of chapters is determined by continuity of the mathematics they cover, rather than the order of the syllabus. All instances where students should refer to other chapters are clearly explained in the text. Within each chapter there is a blend of teaching, worked examples and exercises to help you build confidence and develop the skills and knowledge you need. In particular, there is an increased emphasis on non-calculator methods as well as suggestions for the use of scientific calculators.

At the end of each chapter there are comprehensive student assessment questions. You will also find sets of questions linked to **Boost eBook** on our Boost platform (boost-learning.com), which offer practice in topic areas that students often find difficult.

ICT, mathematical modelling and problem-solving
Problem-solving is key to mathematical thinking, and ICT can play a crucial role in this. Therefore, each topic ends with a section involving investigations and the use of ICT. The ICT investigations go beyond the requirements of the syllabus, but are included for interest and to encourage students to explore the context of the mathematics in real-life situations.

Diagrams and working

Students are encouraged to draw diagrams when tackling questions where appropriate, and to show their full worked solutions. This is helpful for checking your own work, and also applies to any questions where use of a calculator is allowed.

Calculator and non-calculator questions

All exercise questions that should be attempted without a calculator are indicated by ❌. Students should do as many calculations as possible without using a calculator. This will help understanding and confidence.

Some areas of mathematics, such as those using powers & roots, π, trigonometry and calculations with decimals, are more likely to require a calculator.

Additional material

There are a few instances where we consider it to be appropriate to include some additional content that lies beyond the scope of the syllabus but is useful in supporting the syllabus content and helpful in deepening understanding. Where any content beyond the scope of the syllabus, this is indicated by a note.

Core worksheets

Additional worksheets covering all topics in this book and answers are free available on www.hoddereducation.com/CambridgeExtras. These worksheets have not been through the Cambridge International endorsement process.

Key terms and glossary

It is important to understand and use mathematical terms; therefore, all key terms are highlighted in bold and explained in the glossary.

Answers and worked solutions

Answers to all questions are available and can be downloaded free on hoddereducation.com/cambridgeextras

Worked solutions for the Student Assessment questions are available in *Cambridge IGCSE Core and Extended Mathematics Teacher's Guide with Boost Subscription.*

Callouts and Notes
These commentaries provide additional explanations and encourage full understanding of mathematical principles. Notes give additional clarifications and tips.

Worked examples
The worked examples cover important techniques and question styles. They are designed to reinforce the explanations, and give you step-by-step help for solving problems.

Exercises
These appear throughout the text, and allow you to apply what you have learned. There are plenty of routine questions covering important mathematical techniques.

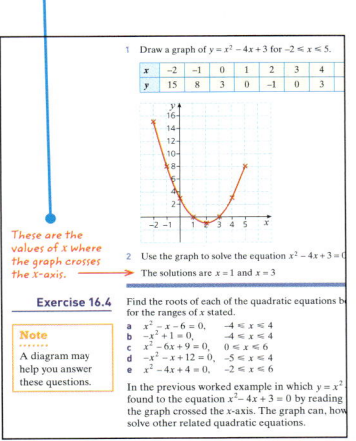

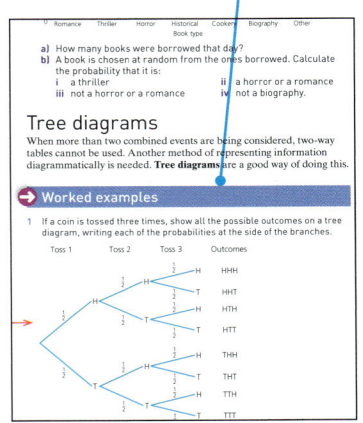

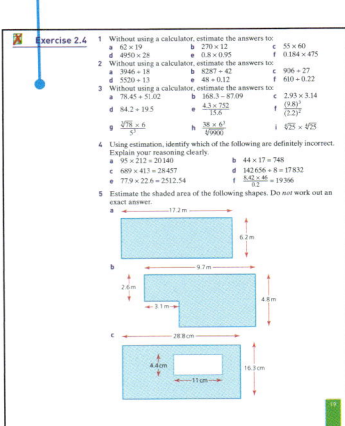

Mathematical investigations and ICT
More real-world problem-solving activities are provided at the end of each section to put what you've learned into practice.

Student assessments
End-of-chapter questions to test your understanding of the key topics and help to prepare you for your exams.

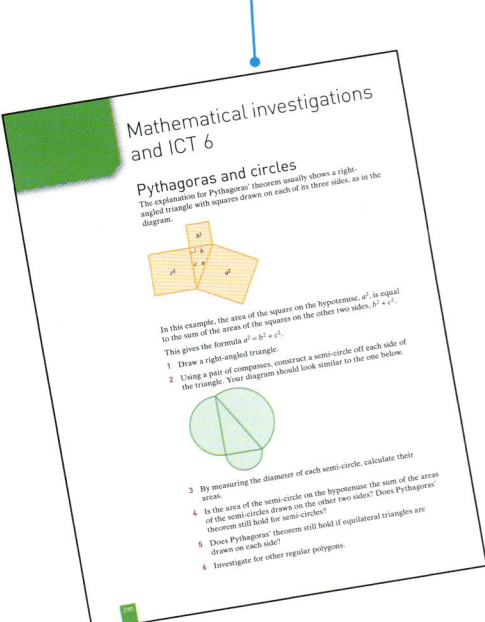

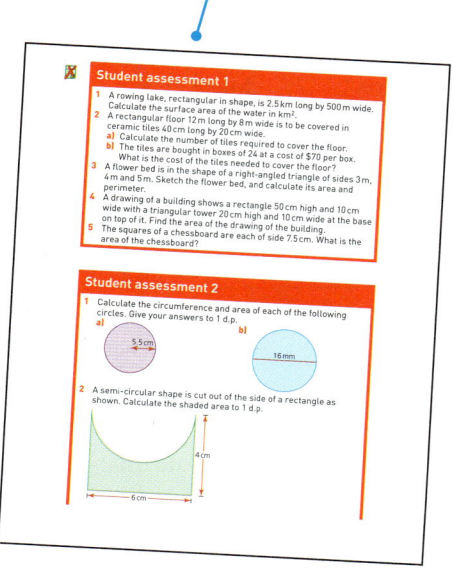

Assessment

The information in this section is based on the Cambridge International syllabus. You should always refer to the appropriate syllabus document for the year of examination to confirm the details and for more information. The syllabus document is available on the Cambridge International website at www.cambridgeinternational.org

For Cambridge IGCSE™ Mathematics you will take two papers. For the Core syllabus, you will take Paper 1 and Paper 3. You may use a scientific calculator only for Paper 3. Paper 1 is a non-calculator paper.

Paper	Length	Type of questions
Paper 1 Non-calculator (Core)	1 hour 30 minutes	Structured and unstructured questions
Paper 3 Calculator (Core)	1 hour 30 minutes	Structured and unstructured questions

Examination techniques

Make sure you check the instructions on the question paper, the length of the paper and the number of questions you have to answer.

Allocate your time sensibly between each question. Be sure not to spend too long on some questions or this might mean you do not have enough time to complete all of them.

Make sure you show your working to show how you've reached your answer.

Command words

The command words that may appear in examinations are listed below. The command word will relate to the context of the question.

Command word	What it means
Calculate	Work out from given facts, figures or information
Construct	Make an accurate drawing
Describe	State the points of a topic / give characteristics and main features
Determine	Establish with certainty
Explain	Set out purposes or reasons/make the relationships between things clear / say why and/or how and support with relevant evidence
Give	Produce an answer from a given source or recall/memory
Plot	Mark point(s) on a graph
Show (that)	Provide structured evidence that leads to a given result
Sketch	Make a simple freehand drawing showing the key features
State	Express in clear terms
Work out	Calculate from given facts, figures or information with or without the use of a calculator
Write	Give an answer in a specific form
Write down	Give an answer without significant working

From the authors

Mathematics comes from the Greek word meaning *knowledge* or *learning*. Galileo Galilei (1564–1642) wrote 'the universe cannot be read until we learn the language in which it is written. It is written in mathematical language.' Mathematics is used in science, engineering, medicine, art, finance, etc., but mathematicians have always studied the subject for pleasure. They look for patterns in nature, for fun, as a game or a puzzle.

A mathematician may find that his or her puzzle solving helps to solve 'real life' problems. However, trigonometry was developed without a 'real life' application in mind, before it was then applied to navigation and many other things. The algebra of curves was not 'invented' to send a rocket to Jupiter.

The study of mathematics is across all lands and cultures. A mathematician in Africa may be working with another in Japan to extend work done by a Brazilian in the USA.

People in all cultures have tried to understand the world around them, and mathematics has been a common way of furthering that understanding, even in cultures which have left no written records.

Each topic in this textbook has an introduction that tries to show how, over thousands of years, mathematical ideas have been passed from one culture to another. So, when you are studying from this textbook, remember that you are following in the footsteps of earlier mathematicians who were excited by the discoveries they had made. These discoveries changed our world.

You may find some of the questions in this book difficult. It is easy when this happens to ask the teacher for help. Remember though that mathematics is intended to stretch the mind. If you are trying to get physically fit, you do not stop as soon as things get hard. It is the same with mental fitness. Think logically. Try harder. In the end you are responsible for your own learning. Teachers and textbooks can only guide you. Be confident that you can solve that difficult problem.

Ric Pimentel

Terry Wall

Frankie Pimentel

TOPIC 1

Number

Contents

Chapter 1 Number and language (C1.1, C1.3)
Chapter 2 Accuracy (C1.9, C1.10)
Chapter 3 Calculations and order (C1.5, C1.6, C1.14, C2.6)
Chapter 4 Integers, fractions, decimals and percentages (C1.4, C1.6)
Chapter 5 Further percentages (C1.4, C1.13)
Chapter 6 Ratio and proportion (C1.11, C1.12)
Chapter 7 Indices and standard form (C1.7, C1.8)
Chapter 8 Money and finance (C1.13, C1.14, C1.16)
Chapter 9 Time (C1.14, C1.15)
Chapter 10 Set notation and Venn diagrams (C1.2)

Learning objectives

C1.1
Identify and use:
- natural numbers
- integers (positive, zero and negative)
- prime numbers
- square numbers
- cube numbers
- common factors
- common multiples
- rational and irrational numbers
- reciprocals.

C1.2
Understand and use set language, notation and Venn diagrams to describe sets.

C1.3
Calculate with the following:
- squares
- square roots
- cubes
- cube roots
- other powers and roots of numbers.

C1.4
1 Use the language and notation of the following in appropriate contexts:
- proper fractions
- improper fractions
- mixed numbers
- decimals
- percentages.
2 Recognise equivalence and convert between these forms.

C1.5
Order quantities by magnitude and demonstrate familiarity with the symbols $=$, $\neq$, $>$, $<$, $\geq$ and $\leq$.

C1.6
Use the four operations for calculations with integers, fractions and decimals, including correct ordering of operations and use of brackets.

C1.7
1 Understand and use indices (positive, zero and negative integers).
2 Understand and use the rules of indices.

C1.8
1. Use the standard form $A \times 10^n$ where n is a positive or negative integer and $1 \leq A < 10$.
2. Convert numbers into and out of standard form.
3. Calculate with values in standard form.

C1.9
1. Round values to a specified degree of accuracy.
2. Make estimates for calculations involving numbers, quantities and measurements.
3. Round answers to a reasonable degree of accuracy in the context of a given problem.

C1.10
Give upper and lower bounds for data rounded to a specified accuracy.

C1.11
Understand and use ratio and proportion to:
- give ratios in simplest form
- divide a quantity in a given ratio
- use proportional reasoning and ratios in context.

C1.12
1. Use common measures of rate.
2. Apply other measures of rate.
3. Solve problems involving average speed.

C1.13
1. Calculate a given percentage of a quantity.
2. Express one quantity as a percentage of another.
3. Calculate percentage increase or decrease.
4. Calculate with simple and compound interest.

C1.14
1. Use a calculator efficiently.
2. Enter values appropriately on a calculator.
3. Interpret the calculator display appropriately.

C1.15
1. Calculate with time: seconds (s), minutes (min), hours (h), days, weeks, months, years, including the relationship between units.
2. Calculate times in terms of the 24-hour and 12-hour clock.
3. Read clocks and timetables.

C1.16
1. Calculate with money.
2. Convert from one currency to another.

C2.6
Represent and interpret inequalities, including on a number line.

The development of number

In Africa, bones have been discovered with marks cut into them that are probably tally marks. These tally marks may have been used for counting time, such as numbers of days or cycles of the Moon, or for keeping records of numbers of animals. A tallying system has no place value, which makes it hard to show large numbers.

The earliest system like ours (known as base 10) dates to 3100 BCE in Egypt. Many ancient texts, e.g. texts from Babylonia (modern Iraq) and Egypt, used zero. Egyptians used the word *nfr* to show a zero balance in accounting. Indian texts used a Sanskrit word, *shunya*, to refer to the idea of the number zero. By the fourth century BCE, the people of south-central Mexico began to use a true zero. It was represented by a shell picture and became a part of Mayan numerals. By CE 130, Ptolemy was using a symbol, a small circle, for zero. This Greek zero was the first use of the zero we use today.

Fragment of a Greek papyrus, showing an early version of the zero sign

The idea of negative numbers was recognised as early as 100 BCE in the Chinese text *Jiuzhang Suanshu* (*Nine Chapters on the Mathematical Art*). This is the earliest known mention of negative numbers in the East. In the third century BCE in Greece, Diophantus had an equation whose solution was negative. He said that the equation gave an absurd result.

European mathematicians did not use negative numbers until the seventeenth century, although Fibonacci allowed negative solutions in financial problems where they could be debts or losses.

1 Number and language

Natural numbers

A child learns to count 'one, two, three, four, …' These are sometimes called the counting numbers or whole numbers.

The child will say 'I am three', or 'I live at number 73'.

If we include the number zero, then we have the set of numbers called the **natural numbers**.

The set of natural numbers = {0, 1, 2, 3, 4, …}.

Integers

On a cold day, the temperature may drop to 4 °C at 10 p.m. If the temperature drops by a further 6 °C, then the temperature is 'below zero'; it is −2 °C.

If you are overdrawn at the bank by $200, this might be shown as −$200.

The set of **integers** = {…, −3, −2, −1, 0, 1, 2, 3, …}.

Integers are therefore an extension of natural numbers. Every natural number is an integer.

Prime numbers

1 is not a prime number. →

A **prime number** is one whose only factors are 1 and itself.

Reciprocal

The **reciprocal** of a number is obtained when 1 is divided by that number. The reciprocal of 5 is $\frac{1}{5}$, the reciprocal of $\frac{2}{5}$ is $\frac{1}{\frac{2}{5}}$, which simplifies to $\frac{5}{2}$.

 Exercise 1.1

1 In a 10 by 10 square, write the numbers 1 to 100.
   Cross out number 1.
   Cross out all the even numbers after 2 (these have 2 as a factor).
   Cross out every third number after 3 (these have 3 as a factor).
   a Continue with 5, 7, 11 and 13, then list all the prime numbers less than 100.
   b What do you notice about the numbers that are left?

2 Write the reciprocal of each of the following:
   a $\frac{1}{8}$
   b $\frac{7}{12}$
   c $\frac{3}{5}$
   d $1\frac{1}{2}$
   e $3\frac{3}{4}$
   f 6

4

Prime factors

Square numbers

 Exercise 1.2 In a 10 by 10 square, write the numbers 1 to 100.
Shade in 1 and then 2 × 2, 3 × 3, 4 × 4, 5 × 5, etc.
These are the **square numbers**.

The ² is called an index; plural indices.

3 × 3 can be written 3^2 (you say 'three squared' or 'three raised to the power of two')

7 × 7 can be written 7^2

Cube numbers

3 × 3 × 3 can be written 3^3 (you say 'three cubed' or 'three raised to the power of three')

5 × 5 × 5 can be written 5^3 ('five cubed' or 'five raised to the power of three')

2 × 2 × 2 × 5 × 5 can be written $2^3 × 5^2$

 Exercise 1.3 Write the following using indices:
- a 9 × 9
- b 12 × 12
- c 8 × 8
- d 7 × 7 × 7
- e 4 × 4 × 4
- f 3 × 3 × 2 × 2 × 2
- g 5 × 5 × 5 × 2 × 2
- h 4 × 4 × 3 × 3 × 2 × 2

Factors

The **factors** of 12 are all the whole numbers which will divide exactly into 12:

   1, 2, 3, 4, 6 and 12.

 Exercise 1.4 List all the factors of the following numbers:
- a 6
- b 9
- c 7
- d 15
- e 24
- f 36
- g 35
- h 25
- i 42
- j 100

Prime factors

The factors of 12 are 1, 2, 3, 4, 6 and 12.

Of these, 2 and 3 are prime numbers, so 2 and 3 are the **prime factors** of 12.

 Exercise 1.5 List the prime factors of the following numbers:
- a 15
- b 18
- c 24
- d 16
- e 20
- f 13
- g 33
- h 35
- i 70
- j 56

An easy way to find prime factors is to divide by the prime numbers in order, smallest first.

5

1 NUMBER AND LANGUAGE

> **Worked examples**

1 Find the prime factors of 18 and express it as a product of prime numbers:

	18
2	9
3	3
3	1

$18 = 2 \times 3 \times 3$ or 2×3^2

2 Find the prime factors of 24 and express it as a product of prime numbers:

	24
2	12
2	6
2	3
3	1

$24 = 2 \times 2 \times 2 \times 3$ or $2^3 \times 3$

3 Find the prime factors of 75 and express it as a product of prime numbers:

	75
3	25
5	5
5	1

$75 = 3 \times 5 \times 5$ or 3×5^2

Exercise 1.6 Find the prime factors of the following numbers and express them as a product of prime numbers:

a 12   b 32   c 36   d 40   e 44
f 56   g 45   h 39   i 231   j 63

Highest common factor

The factors of 12 are 1, 2, 3, 4, 6, 12.

The factors of 18 are 1, 2, 3, 6, 9, 18.

As can be seen, the factors 1, 2, 3 and 6 are common to both numbers. They are known as **common factors**. As 6 is the largest of the common factors, it is called the **highest common factor** (HCF) of 12 and 18.

The prime factors of 12 are $2 \times 2 \times 3$

The prime factors of 18 are $2 \times 3 \times 3$

So the highest common factor can be seen by inspection to be 2×3, i.e. 6.

Rational and irrational numbers

 Exercise 1.7 Find the HCF of the following numbers:
a 8, 12
b 10, 25
c 12, 18, 24
d 15, 21, 27
e 36, 63, 108
f 22, 110
g 32, 56, 72
h 39, 52
i 34, 51, 68
j 60, 144

Multiples

Multiples of 2 are 2, 4, 6, 8, 10, etc.

Multiples of 3 are 3, 6, 9, 12, 15, etc.

The numbers 6, 12, 18, 24, etc. are **common multiples**, as these appear in both lists.

The **lowest common multiple** (LCM) of 2 and 3 is 6, since 6 is the smallest number divisible by 2 and 3.

The LCM of 3 and 5 is 15. The LCM of 6 and 10 is 30.

 Exercise 1.8
1 Find the LCM of the following numbers:
a 3, 5
b 4, 6
c 2, 7
d 4, 7
e 4, 8
f 2, 3, 5
g 2, 3, 4
h 3, 4, 6
i 3, 4, 5
j 3, 5, 12

2 Find the LCM of the following numbers:
a 6, 14
b 4, 15
c 2, 7, 10
d 3, 9, 10
e 6, 8, 20
f 3, 5, 7
g 4, 5, 10
h 3, 7, 11
i 6, 10, 16
j 25, 40, 100

Rational and irrational numbers

A **rational number** is any number which can be expressed as a fraction. Examples of some rational numbers and how they can be expressed as a fraction are:

$$0.2 = \tfrac{1}{5} \quad 0.3 = \tfrac{3}{10} \quad 7 = \tfrac{7}{1} \quad 1.53 = \tfrac{153}{100} \quad 0.\dot{2} = \tfrac{2}{9}$$

An **irrational number** cannot be expressed as a fraction. Examples of irrational numbers include:

$$\sqrt{2}, \quad \sqrt{5}, \quad 6 - \sqrt{3}, \quad \pi$$

In summary, rational numbers include:

- whole numbers
- fractions
- recurring decimals
- terminating decimals.

Irrational numbers include:

- the square root of any number other than square numbers
- a decimal which neither repeats nor terminates (e.g. π).

1 NUMBER AND LANGUAGE

Exercise 1.9

1. For each of the numbers shown below, state whether it is rational or irrational:
   a. 1.3
   b. $0.\dot{6}$
   c. $\sqrt{3}$
   d. $-2\frac{3}{5}$
   e. $\sqrt{25}$
   f. $\sqrt[3]{8}$
   g. $\sqrt{7}$
   h. 0.625
   i. $0.\dot{1}\dot{1}$

2. For each of the numbers shown below state whether it is rational or irrational:
   a. $\sqrt{4} \times \sqrt{3}$
   b. $\sqrt{2} + \sqrt{3}$
   c. $\sqrt{2} \times \sqrt{3}$
   d. $\frac{\sqrt{8}}{\sqrt{2}}$
   e. $\frac{2\sqrt{5}}{\sqrt{20}}$
   f. $4 + (\sqrt{9} - 4)$

3. Look at these shapes and decide if the measurements required are rational or irrational. Give reasons for your answer.

   a. 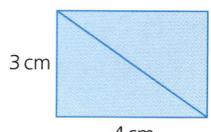 Length of diagonal
   3 cm
   4 cm

   b. Circumference of circle
   4 cm

   c.  Side length of square
   $\sqrt{72}$ cm

Calculating squares

This is a square of side 1 cm.

This is a square of side 2 cm.

It has four squares of side 1 cm in it.

Exercise 1.10

Calculate how many squares of side 1 cm there would be in squares of side:
a. 3 cm
b. 5 cm
c. 8 cm
d. 10 cm
e. 11 cm
f. 12 cm
g. 7 cm
h. 13 cm
i. 15 cm
j. 20 cm

In index notation, the square numbers are $1^2, 2^2, 3^2, 4^2$, etc. 4^2 is read as '4 squared'.

Square roots

Worked example

This square is of side 1.1 units.

Its area is 1.1×1.1 units^2.

$A = 1 \times 1 = 1$

$B = 1 \times 0.1 = 0.1$

$B = 1 \times 0.1 = 0.1$

$C = 0.1 \times 0.1 = 0.01$

Total = 1.21 units^2

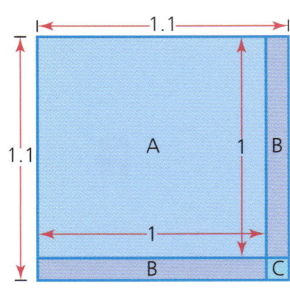

Exercise 1.11

1. Draw diagrams and use them to find the area of squares of side:
   - a 2.1 units
   - b 3.1 units
   - c 1.2 units
   - d 2.2 units
   - e 2.5 units
   - f 1.4 units

2. Use long multiplication to work out the area of squares of side:
   - a 2.4
   - b 3.3
   - c 2.8
   - d 6.2
   - e 4.6
   - f 7.3
   - g 0.3
   - h 0.8
   - i 0.1
   - j 0.9

3. Check your answers to Q.1 and 2 by using the x^2 key on a calculator.

Using a graph

Exercise 1.12

1. Copy and complete the table for the equation $y = x^2$.

x	0	1	2	3	4	5	6	7	8
y				9				49	

Plot the graph of $y = x^2$. Use your graph to find the value of the following:
   - a 2.5^2
   - b 3.5^2
   - c 4.5^2
   - d 5.5^2
   - e 7.2^2
   - f 6.4^2
   - g 0.8^2
   - h 0.2^2
   - i 5.3^2
   - j 6.3^2

2. Check your answers to Q.1 by using the x^2 key on a calculator.

Square roots

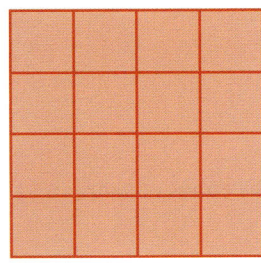

The orange square (left) contains 16 squares. It has sides of length 4 units. So the square root of 16 is 4. This can be written as $\sqrt{16} = 4$.

Note that $4 \times 4 = 16$ so 4 is the square root of 16.

However, -4×-4 is also 16 so -4 is also the square root of 16.

By convention, $\sqrt{16}$ means 'the positive square root of 16' so $\sqrt{16} = 4$ but the square root of 16 is ± 4, i.e. $+4$ or -4.

Note that -16 has no square root since any integer squared is positive.

1 NUMBER AND LANGUAGE

Exercise 1.13

1 Find the following:
  a $\sqrt{25}$ b $\sqrt{9}$ c $\sqrt{49}$ d $\sqrt{100}$
  e $\sqrt{121}$ f $\sqrt{169}$ g $\sqrt{0.01}$ h $\sqrt{0.04}$
  i $\sqrt{0.09}$ j $\sqrt{0.25}$

2 Use the $\sqrt{\ }$ key on your calculator to check your answers to Q.1.

3 Calculate the following:
  a $\sqrt{\frac{1}{9}}$ b $\sqrt{\frac{1}{16}}$ c $\sqrt{\frac{1}{25}}$ d $\sqrt{\frac{1}{49}}$
  e $\sqrt{\frac{1}{100}}$ f $\sqrt{\frac{4}{9}}$ g $\sqrt{\frac{9}{100}}$ h $\sqrt{\frac{49}{81}}$
  i $\sqrt{2\frac{7}{9}}$ j $\sqrt{6\frac{1}{4}}$

Using a graph

Exercise 1.14

1 Copy and complete the table below for the equation $y = \sqrt{x}$.

x	0	1	4	9	16	25	36	49	64	81	100
y											

Plot the graph of $y = \sqrt{x}$. Use your graph to find the approximate values of the following:
  a $\sqrt{70}$ b $\sqrt{40}$ c $\sqrt{50}$ d $\sqrt{90}$
  e $\sqrt{35}$ f $\sqrt{45}$ g $\sqrt{55}$ h $\sqrt{60}$
  i $\sqrt{2}$ j $\sqrt{3}$ k $\sqrt{20}$ l $\sqrt{30}$
  m $\sqrt{12}$ n $\sqrt{75}$ o $\sqrt{115}$

2 Check your answers to Q.1 above by using the $\sqrt{\ }$ key on a calculator.

Cubes of numbers

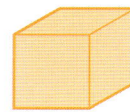

The small cube has sides of 1 unit and occupies 1 cubic unit of space.

The large cube has sides of 2 units and occupies 8 cubic units of space.

That is, $2 \times 2 \times 2$.

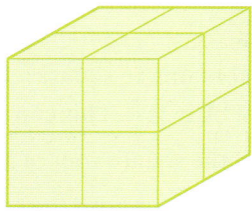

Exercise 1.15

Calculate how many cubic units would be occupied by cubes of side:
  a 3 units   b 5 units   c 10 units
  d 4 units   e 9 units   f 100 units

Further powers and roots

> **Note**
> There is more information on using scientific calculators to work with brackets, powers and fractions on pages 27–29.

In index notation, the **cube numbers** are $1^3, 2^3, 3^3, 4^3$, etc. 4^3 is read as '4 cubed'.
Some calculators have an x^3 key.

Exercise 1.16

1 Copy and complete the table below:

Number	1	2	3	4	5	6	7	8	9	10
Cube			27							

2 Use a calculator to find the following:
   a 11^3
   b 0.5^3
   c 1.5^3
   d 2.5^3
   e 20^3
   f 30^3
   g $3^3 + 2^3$
   h $(3 + 2)^3$
   i $7^3 + 3^3$
   j $(7 + 3)^3$

Cube roots

$\sqrt[3]{}$ is read as 'the cube root of …'.

$\sqrt[3]{64}$ is 4, since $4 \times 4 \times 4 = 64$.

Note that $\sqrt[3]{64}$ is not -4

since $-4 \times -4 \times -4 = -64$

but $\sqrt[3]{-64}$ is -4.

Exercise 1.17 Find the following cube roots:
   a $\sqrt[3]{8}$
   b $\sqrt[3]{125}$
   c $\sqrt[3]{27}$
   d $\sqrt[3]{0.001}$
   e $\sqrt[3]{0.027}$
   f $\sqrt[3]{216}$
   g $\sqrt[3]{1000}$
   h $\sqrt[3]{1\,000\,000}$
   i $\sqrt[3]{-8}$
   j $\sqrt[3]{-27}$
   k $\sqrt[3]{-1000}$
   l $\sqrt[3]{-1}$

Further powers and roots

We have seen that the square of a number is the same as raising that number to the power of 2. For example, the square of 5 is written as 5^2 and means 5×5. Similarly, the cube of a number is the same as raising that number to the power of 3. For example, the cube of 5 is written as 5^3 and means $5 \times 5 \times 5$.

Numbers can be raised by other powers too. Therefore, 5 raised to the power of 6 can be written as 5^6 and means $5 \times 5 \times 5 \times 5 \times 5 \times 5$.

You will find a button on your calculator to help you to do this. On most calculators, it will look like y^x.

We have also seen that the square root of a number can be written using the $\sqrt{}$ symbol. Therefore, the square root of 16 is written as $\sqrt{16}$.

11

1 NUMBER AND LANGUAGE

> **Note**
>
> Different calculators work out the power of numbers in different ways. It is therefore important that you know how your particular calculator works.

The **cube root** of a number can be written using the $\sqrt[3]{}$ symbol. Therefore, the cube root of 125 is written as $\sqrt[3]{125}$ and is 5 because $5 \times 5 \times 5 = 125$.

Numbers can be rooted by other values as well. The fourth root of a number can be written using the symbol $\sqrt[4]{}$. Therefore, the fourth root of 625 can be expressed as $\sqrt[4]{625}$.

You will find a button on your calculator to help you to calculate with roots too. On most calculators, it will look like $\sqrt[x]{y}$.

Exercise 1.18

Work out:
a 6^4
b $3^5 + 2^4$
c $(3^4)^2$
d $0.1^6 \div 0.01^4$
e $\sqrt[4]{2401}$
f $\sqrt[8]{256}$
g $\left(\sqrt[5]{243}\right)^3$
h $\left(\sqrt[9]{36}\right)^9$
i $2^7 \times \sqrt{\dfrac{1}{4}}$
j $\sqrt[6]{\dfrac{1}{64}} \times 2^7$
k $\sqrt[4]{5^4}$
l $\left(\sqrt[10]{59049}\right)^2$

Directed numbers

> **Worked example**
>
>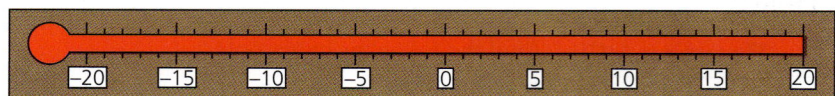
>
> The diagram shows the scale of a thermometer. The temperature at 04 00 was −3 °C. By 09 00 it had risen by 8 °C. What was the temperature at 09 00?
>
> $(-3)° + (8)° = (5)°$

Exercise 1.19

1 Find the new temperature if:
 a The temperature was −5 °C, and rises 9 °C.
 b The temperature was −12 °C, and rises 8 °C.
 c The temperature was +14 °C, and falls 8 °C.
 d The temperature was −3 °C, and falls 4 °C.
 e The temperature was −7 °C, and falls 11 °C.
 f The temperature was 2 °C, it falls 8 °C, then rises 6 °C.
 g The temperature was 5 °C, it falls 8 °C, then falls a further 6 °C.
 h The temperature was −2 °C, it falls 6 °C, then rises 10 °C.
 i The temperature was 20 °C, it falls 18 °C, then falls a further 8 °C.
 j The temperature was 5 °C below zero and falls 8 °C.

Directed numbers

2 Mark lives in Canada. Every morning before school he reads a thermometer to find the temperature in the garden. The thermometer below shows the results for 5 days in winter.

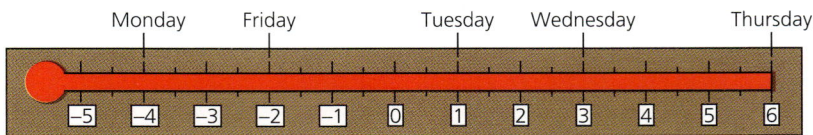

Find the change in temperature between:
a Monday and Friday
b Monday and Thursday
c Tuesday and Friday
d Thursday and Friday
e Monday and Tuesday.

Note
BCE means the years before the year 0, whilst CE means the years after 0.

3 Julius Caesar was born in 100 BCE and was 56 years old when he died. In what year did he die?

4 Marcus Flavius was born in 20 BCE and died in CE 42. How old was he when he died?

5 Rome was founded in 753 BCE. The last Roman city, Constantinople, fell in CE 1453. How long did the Roman Empire last?

6 Ms Yang's bank account shows a credit balance of $105. Describe her bank balance as a positive or negative number after each of these transactions is made in sequence:
a rent $140
b car insurance $283
c 1 week's salary $230
d food bill $72
e a deposit (money paid in to the account) of $250

Note
A credit balance means there is money in the account and it is treated as a positive value.

7 A lift in a skyscraper has stopped somewhere close to the halfway point. Call this 'floor zero'. Show on a number line the floors it stops at as it makes the following sequence of journeys:
a up 75 floors
b down 155 floors
c up 110 floors
d down 60 floors
e down 35 floors
f up 100 floors

8 A hang-glider is launched from a mountainside. It climbs 650 m and then starts its descent. It falls 1220 m before landing.
a How far below its launch point was the hang-glider when it landed?
b If the launch point was at 1650 m above sea level, at what height above sea level did it land?

9 The average noon temperature in Sydney in January is +32 °C. The average midnight temperature in Boston in January is −12 °C. What is the temperature difference between the two cities?

10 The temperature in Madrid on New Year's Day is −2 °C. The temperature in Moscow on the same day is −14 °C. What is the temperature difference between the two cities?

11 The temperature inside a freezer is −8 °C. To defrost it, the temperature is allowed to rise by 12 °C. What will the temperature be after this rise?

12 A plane flying at 8500 m drops a recording device onto the ocean floor. If the device falls a total of 10 200 m, how deep is the ocean at this point?

1 NUMBER AND LANGUAGE

13 The roof of an apartment block is 130 m above ground level. The car park beneath the apartment is 35 m below ground level. How high is the roof above the floor of the car park?

14 A submarine is at a depth of 165 m. If the ocean floor is 860 m from the surface, how far is the submarine from the ocean floor?

Student assessment 1

1 List the prime factors of the following numbers:
  a 28   **b** 38

2 Find the lowest common multiple of the following numbers:
  a 6, 10   **b** 7, 14, 28

3 The diagram shows a square with a side length of $\sqrt{6}$ cm.

Explain, giving reasons, whether the following are rational or irrational:
  a the perimeter of the square
  b the area of the square.

4 Find the value of:
  a 9^2 **b** 15^2 **c** $(0.2)^2$ **d** $(0.7)^2$

5 Draw a square of side 2.5 units. Use it to find $(2.5)^2$.

6 Calculate:
  a $(3.5)^2$ **b** $(4.1)^2$ **c** $(0.15)^2$

7 Copy and complete the table for $y = \sqrt{x}$.

x	0	1	4	9	16	25	36	49
y								

Plot the graph of $y = \sqrt{x}$. Use your graph to find:
  a $\sqrt{7}$ **b** $\sqrt{30}$ **c** $\sqrt{45}$

8 Without using a calculator, find:
  a $\sqrt{225}$ **b** $\sqrt{0.01}$ **c** $\sqrt{0.81}$
  d $\sqrt{\frac{9}{25}}$ **e** $\sqrt{5\frac{4}{9}}$ **f** $\sqrt{2\frac{23}{49}}$

9 Without using a calculator, find:
  a 4^3 **b** $(0.1)^3$ **c** $\left(\frac{2}{3}\right)^3$

10 Without using a calculator, find:
  a $\sqrt[3]{27}$ **b** $\sqrt[3]{1\,000\,000}$ **c** $\sqrt[3]{\frac{64}{125}}$

11 Using a calculator if necessary, work out:
  a $3^5 \div 3^7$
  b $5^4 \times \sqrt[4]{625}$
  c $\sqrt[7]{2187} \div 3^3$

Directed numbers

12 Write down the reciprocal of the following numbers:
  a 6   **b** $\frac{1}{3}$ **c** $\frac{2}{7}$

13 The number X can be written as the product of prime factors $2^2 \times 5^2$.
  a Calculate the value of X.
  b Find the highest common factor of X and 150.
  c Find the lowest common multiple of X and 150.

Student assessment 2

1 The table shows dates of some significance to mathematics.

Date	Event	Date	Event
2900 BCE	Great Pyramid built	CE 290	Liu Hui calculated π as 3.14
1650 BCE	Rhind Papyrus written	CE 1500	Leonardo da Vinci born
540 BCE	Pythagoras born	CE 1900	Albert Einstein born
300 BCE	Euclid born	CE 1998	Fermat's last theorem proved

  a How many years before Einstein was born was the Great Pyramid built?
  c How many years after Liu Hui's calculation of π was Fermat's last theorem proved?
  e How long before Fermat's last theorem was proved was the Rhind Papyrus written?
  b How many years before Leonardo was born was Pythagoras born?
  d How many years were there between the births of Euclid and Einstein?
  f How old was the Great Pyramid when Leonardo was born?

2 A bus route runs past Issa's house. Each stop is given the name of a street. From home to Melon Street is the positive direction.

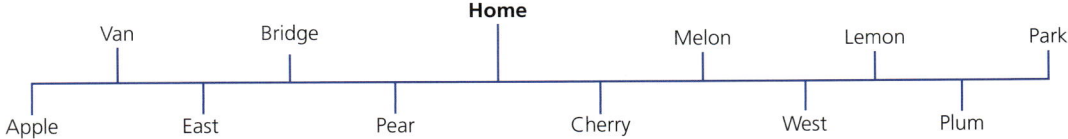

  Find where Issa is after the stages of these journeys from home:
  a $+4-3$ **b** $+2-5$ **c** $+2-7$
  d $+3-2$ **e** $-1-1$ **f** $+6-8+1$
  g $-1+3-5$ **h** $-2-2+8$ **i** $+1-3+5$
  j $-5+8-1$

3 Using the diagram from the question above and starting from home each time, find the missing stages in these journeys if they end at the stop given:
  a $+3+?$ Pear   **b** $+6+?$ Cherry   **c** $-1+?$ Van
  d $-5+?$ Lemon   **e** $+5+?$ Home   **f** $?-2$ Melon
  g $?+2$ East   **h** $?-5$ Van   **i** $?-1$ East
  j $?+4$ Pear

4 A number X is both a cube number and a square number. If X is greater than 1, what is the smallest possible value of X?

15

2 Accuracy

Approximation

In many instances exact numbers are not necessary or even desirable. In those circumstances approximations are given. The approximations can take several forms. Common types of approximation are dealt with in this chapter.

Rounding

If 28 617 people attend a gymnastics competition, this figure can be reported to various levels of accuracy.

To the nearest 10 000 this figure would be rounded up to 30 000.

To the nearest 1000 this figure would be rounded up to 29 000.

To the nearest 100 this figure would be rounded down to 28 600.

In this type of situation, it is unlikely that the exact number would be reported.

> **Note**
>
> If a number falls exactly halfway, then it is rounded up. For example, rounding 16 500 to the nearest thousand can be visualised as follows:
>
> 16 000   16 500   17 000
>
> 16 000 and 17 000 are the numbers in thousands either side of 16 500. As 16 500 falls exactly half-way, it gets rounded up to 17 000 if the answer is required to the nearest thousand.

Exercise 2.1

1. Round these numbers to the nearest 1000:
   - a 68 786
   - b 74 245
   - c 89 000
   - d 4020
   - e 99 500
   - f 999 999

2. Round these numbers to the nearest 100:
   - a 78 540
   - b 6858
   - c 14 099
   - d 8084
   - e 950
   - f 2984

3. Round these numbers to the nearest 10:
   - a 485
   - b 692
   - c 8847
   - d 83
   - e 4
   - f 997

Rounding

Decimal places

A number can also be approximated to a given number of **decimal places** (d.p.). This refers to the number of digits written after a decimal point.

→ Worked examples

1. Write 7.864 to 1 d.p.

   The answer needs to be written with one digit after the decimal point. However, to do this, the second digit after the decimal point needs to be considered. If it is 5 or more then the first digit is rounded up.
   i.e. 7.864 is written as 7.9 to 1 d.p.

2. Write 5.574 to 2 d.p.

   The answer here is to be given with two digits after the decimal point. In this case the third digit after the decimal point needs to be considered. As the third digit after the decimal point is less than 5, the second digit is not rounded up.
   i.e. 5.574 is written as 5.57 to 2 d.p.

Exercise 2.2

1. Give the following to 1 d.p.
   - a 5.58
   - b 0.73
   - c 11.86
   - d 157.39
   - e 4.04
   - f 15.045
   - g 2.95
   - h 0.98
   - i 12.049

2. Give the following to 2 d.p.
   - a 6.473
   - b 9.587
   - c 16.476
   - d 0.088
   - e 0.014
   - f 9.3048
   - g 99.996
   - h 0.0048
   - i 3.0037

Significant figures

Numbers can also be approximated to a given number of **significant figures** (s.f.). In the number 43.25, the 4 is the most significant figure as it has a value of 40. In contrast, the 5 is the least significant as it only has a value of 5 hundredths.

→ Worked examples

1. Write 43.25 to 3 s.f.

   Only the three most significant digits are written, however the fourth digit needs to be considered to see whether the third digit is to be rounded up or not.
   i.e. 43.25 is written as 43.3 to 3 s.f.

2. Write 0.0043 to 1 s.f.

   In this example only two digits have any significance, the 4 and the 3. The 4 is the most significant and therefore is the only one of the two to be written in the answer.
   i.e. 0.0043 is written as 0.004 to 1 s.f.

2 ACCURACY

Exercise 2.3

1   Write the following to the number of significant figures stated:
    a 48 599 (1 s.f.)   b 48 599 (3 s.f.)   c 6841 (1 s.f.)
    d 7538 (2 s.f.)   e 483.7 (1 s.f.)   f 2.5728 (3 s.f.)
    g 990 (1 s.f.)   h 2045 (2 s.f.)   i 14.952 (3 s.f.)

2   Write the following to the number of significant figures stated:
    a 0.085 62 (1 s.f.)   b 0.5932 (1 s.f.)   c 0.942 (2 s.f.)
    d 0.954 (1 s.f.)   e 0.954 (2 s.f.)   f 0.003 05 (1 s.f.)
    g 0.003 05 (2 s.f.)   h 0.009 73 (2 s.f.)   i 0.009 73 (1 s.f.)

Appropriate accuracy

In many instances calculations carried out using a calculator produce answers which are not whole numbers. A calculator will give the answer to as many decimal places as will fit on its screen. In most cases this degree of accuracy is neither desirable nor necessary. Unless specifically asked for, answers should not be given to more than three significant figures (3 s.f.), or two decimal places. Indeed, one decimal place is usually sufficient unless the answer is a whole number.

➡ Worked example

Calculate 4.64 ÷ 2.3, giving your answer to an appropriate degree of accuracy.

The calculator will give the answer to 4.64 ÷ 2.3 as 2.017 391 3. However, the answer given to 1 d.p. is sufficient.

Therefore 4.64 ÷ 2.3 = 2.0 (1 d.p.)

Estimating answers to calculations

Even though many calculations can be done quickly and effectively on a calculator, often an **estimate** for an answer can be a useful check. This is done by rounding each of the numbers so that the calculation becomes relatively straightforward.

➡ Worked examples

1   Estimate the answer to 57 × 246.
    Here are two possibilities:
    a   60 × 200 = 12 000
    b   50 × 250 = 12 500

In a) each number is rounded to 1 s.f. In b) each number is rounded to the nearest 50.

2   Estimate the answer to 6386 ÷ 27.
    6000 ÷ 30 = 200

3   Estimate the answer to $\sqrt[3]{120} \times 48$.
    As $\sqrt[3]{125} = 5$, $\sqrt[3]{120} \approx 5$
    Therefore $\sqrt[3]{120} \times 48 \approx 5 \times 50$
    ≈ 250

≈ is used to state that the actual answer is approximately equal to the answer shown.

Estimating answers to calculations

4 Estimate the answer to $\frac{2^5 \times \sqrt[4]{600}}{8}$.

An approximate answer can be calculated using the knowledge that $2^5 = 32$ and $\sqrt[4]{625} = 5$.

Therefore $\frac{2^5 \times \sqrt[4]{600}}{8} \approx \frac{30 \times 5}{8} \approx \frac{150}{8}$
≈ 20

Exercise 2.4

1 Without using a calculator, estimate the answers to:
  a 62×19 b 270×12 c 55×60
  d 4950×28 e 0.8×0.95 f 0.184×475

2 Without using a calculator, estimate the answers to:
  a $3946 \div 18$ b $8287 \div 42$ c $906 \div 27$
  d $5520 \div 13$ e $48 \div 0.12$ f $610 \div 0.22$

3 Without using a calculator, estimate the answers to:
  a $78.45 + 51.02$ b $168.3 - 87.09$ c 2.93×3.14
  d $84.2 \div 19.5$ e $\frac{4.3 \times 752}{15.6}$ f $\frac{(9.8)^3}{(2.2)^2}$
  g $\frac{\sqrt[3]{78} \times 6}{5^3}$ h $\frac{38 \times 6^3}{\sqrt[4]{9900}}$ i $\sqrt[4]{17} \times \sqrt[4]{15}$

4 Using estimation, identify which of the following are definitely incorrect. Explain your reasoning clearly.
  a $95 \times 212 = 20\,140$ b $44 \times 17 = 748$
  c $689 \times 413 = 28\,457$ d $142\,656 \div 8 = 17\,832$
  e $77.9 \times 22.6 = 2512.54$ f $\frac{8.42 \times 46}{0.2} = 19\,366$

5 Estimate the shaded area of the following shapes. Do *not* work out an exact answer.

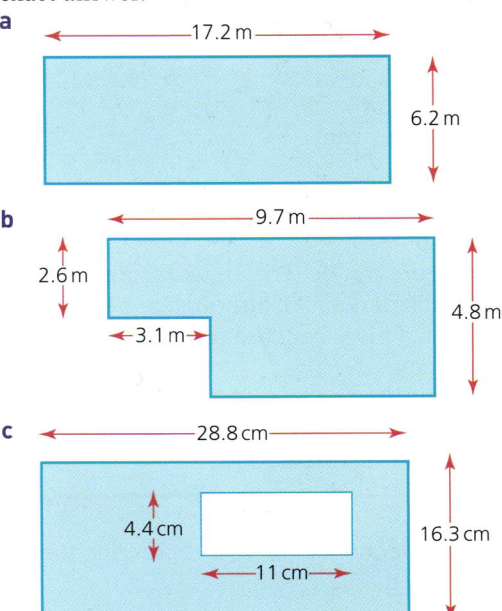

2 ACCURACY

Exercise 2.4 (cont)

6 Estimate the volume of each solid. Do *not* work out an exact answer.

a

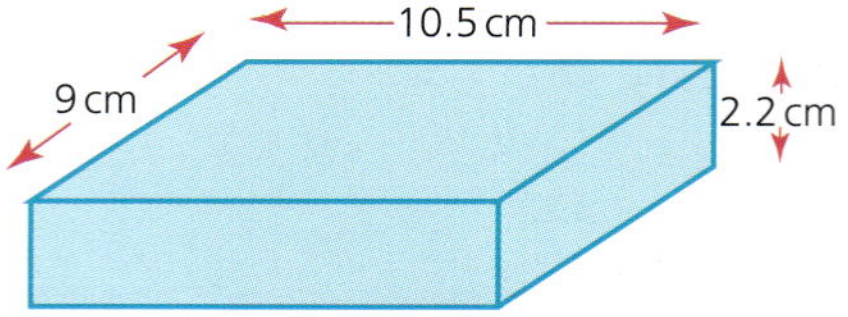

b

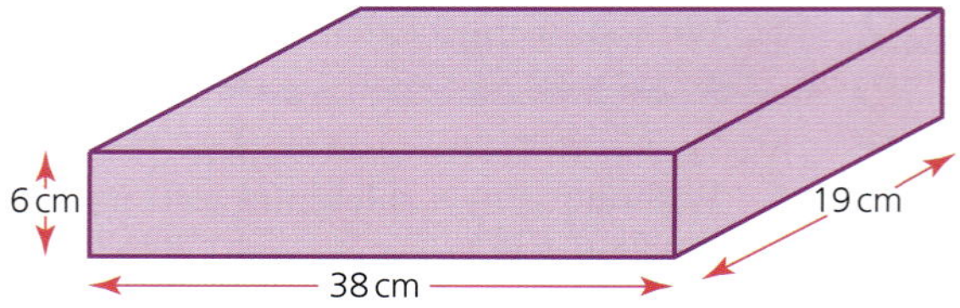

c

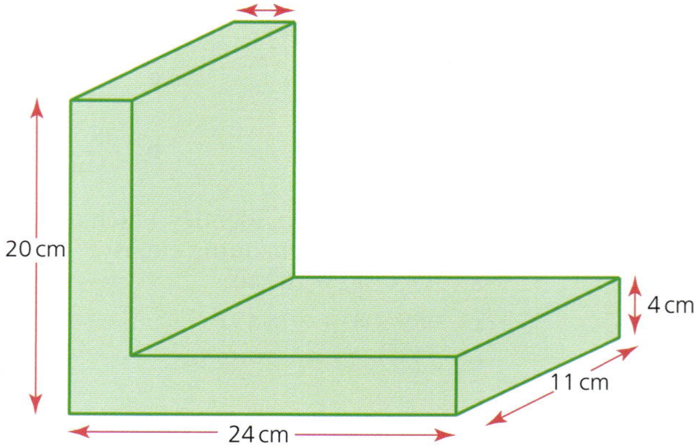

7 Calculate the following, giving your answer to an appropriate degree of accuracy:
  a 23.456×17.89
  b 0.4×12.62
  c 18×9.24
  d $76.24 \div 3.2$
  e 7.6^2
  f 16.42^3
  g $\frac{2.3 \times 3.37}{4}$
  h $\frac{8.31}{2.02}$
  i $9.2 \div 4^2$

Upper and lower bounds

Numbers can be written to different degrees of accuracy. For example, 4.5, 4.50 and 4.500, although appearing to represent the same number, do not. This is because they are written to different degrees of accuracy.

4.5 is written to one decimal place and therefore could represent any number from 4.45 up to but not including 4.55. On a number line this would be represented as:

As an inequality where *x* represents the number, 4.5 would be expressed as:

$4.45 \leq x < 4.55$

Upper and lower bounds

4.45 is known as the **lower bound** of 4.5, whilst 4.55 is known as the **upper bound**.

4.50, on the other hand, is written to two decimal places and only numbers from 4.495 up to, but not including, 4.505 would be rounded to 4.50. This therefore represents a much smaller range of numbers than those which would be rounded to 4.5. Similarly, the range of numbers being rounded to 4.500 would be even smaller.

➜ Worked example

A girl's height is given as 162 cm to the nearest centimetre.

a Work out the lower and upper bounds within which her height can lie.

Lower bound = 161.5 cm

Upper bound = 162.5 cm

b Represent this range of numbers on a number line.

161   161.5   162   162.5   163

c If the girl's height is h cm, express this range as an inequality.
$161.5 \leq h < 162.5$

Exercise 2.5

1 Each of the following numbers is expressed to the nearest whole number.
  i Give the upper and lower bounds of each.
  ii Using x as the number, express the range in which the number lies as an inequality.
  a 8   **b** 71   **c** 146
  d 200   **e** 1

2 Each of the following numbers is correct to one decimal place.
  i Give the upper and lower bounds of each.
  ii Using x as the number, express the range in which the number lies as an inequality.
  a 2.5   **b** 14.1   **c** 2.0
  d 20.0   **e** 0.5

3 Each of the following numbers is correct to two significant figures.
  i Give the upper and lower bounds of each.
  ii Using x as the number, express the range in which the number lies as an inequality.
  a 5.4   **b** 0.75   **c** 550
  d 6000   **e** 0.012   **f** 12 000

4 The mass of a sack of vegetables is given as 7.8 kg.
  a Illustrate the lower and upper bounds of the mass on a number line.
  b Using M kg for the mass, express the range of values in which M must lie as an inequality.

21

2 ACCURACY

Exercise 2.5 (cont)

5 At a school sports day, the winning time for the 100 m race was given as 12.1 s.
   a Illustrate the lower and upper bounds of the time on a number line.
   b Using T seconds for the time, express the range of values in which T must lie as an inequality.

6 The capacity of a swimming pool is given as 740 m^3, correct to two significant figures.
   a Calculate the lower and upper bounds of the pool's capacity.
   b Using x cubic metres for the capacity, express the range of values in which x must lie as an inequality.

7 Hadiza is a surveyor. She measures the dimensions of a rectangular field to the nearest 10 m. The length is recorded as 570 m and the width is recorded as 340 m.
   a Calculate the lower and upper bounds of the length.
   b Using W metres for the width, express the range of values in which W must lie as an inequality.

Student assessment 1

1 Round the following numbers to the degree of accuracy shown in brackets:
   a 2841 (nearest 100)
   b 7286 (nearest 10)
   c 40 756 (nearest 1000)
   d 951 (nearest 100)

2 Round the following numbers to the number of decimal places shown in brackets:
   a 3.84 (1 d.p.)
   b 6.792 (1 d.p.)
   c 0.8526 (2 d.p.)
   d 1.0959 (2 d.p.)
   e 9.954 (1 d.p.)
   f 0.0077 (3 d.p.)

3 Round the following numbers to the number of significant figures shown in brackets:
   a 3.84 (1 s.f.)
   b 6.792 (2 s.f.)
   c 0.7765 (1 s.f.)
   d 9.624 (1 s.f.)
   e 80.497 (2 s.f.)
   f 0.004 51 (1 s.f.)

4 A cuboid's dimensions are given as 12.32 cm by 1.8 cm by 4.16 cm. Calculate its volume, giving your answer to an appropriate degree of accuracy.

5 Estimate the answers to the following. Do *not* work out an exact answer.
   a $\dfrac{5.3 \times 11.2}{2.1}$
   b $\dfrac{(9.8)^2}{(4.7)^2}$
   c $\dfrac{18.8 \times (7.1)^2}{(3.1)^2 \times (4.9)^2}$

6 1 mile is 1760 yards. Estimate the number of yards in 19 miles.

Upper and lower bounds

Student assessment 2

1. The following numbers are expressed to the nearest whole number. Illustrate on a number line the range in which each must lie.
   a 7   b 40   c 300

2. The following numbers are expressed correct to two significant figures. Representing each number by the letter x, express the range in which each must lie using an inequality.
   a 210   b 64   c 300

3. A school measures the dimensions of its rectangular playing field to the nearest metre. The length was recorded as 350 m and the width as 200 m. Express the ranges in which the length and width lie using inequalities.

4. A boy's mass was measured to the nearest 0.1 kg. If his mass was recorded as 58.9 kg, illustrate on a number line the range within which it must lie.

5. An electronic clock is accurate to $\frac{1}{1000}$ of a second. The duration of a flash from a camera is timed at 0.004 seconds. Express the upper and lower bounds of the duration of the flash using inequalities.

6. The following numbers are rounded to the degree of accuracy shown in brackets. Express the lower and upper bounds of these numbers as an inequality.
   a $x = 4.83$ (2 d.p.)   b $y = 5.05$ (2 d.p.)   c $z = 10.0$ (1 d.p.)

7. Estimate the area of the figure:

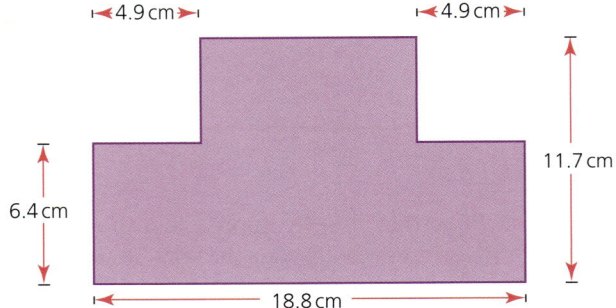

8. Estimate the answers to the following. Do *not* work out exact answers.
   a $\dfrac{3.9 \times 26.4}{4.85}$ b $\dfrac{(3.2)^3}{(5.4)^2}$ c $\dfrac{2.8 \times (7.3)^2}{(3.2)^2 \times 6.2}$

3 Calculations and order

Ordering

The following symbols have a specific meaning in mathematics:

- $=$ is equal to
- $\neq$ is not equal to
- $>$ is greater than
- $\geq$ is greater than or equal to
- $<$ is less than
- $\leq$ is less than or equal to

$x \geq 3$ means that x is greater than or equal to 3, i.e. x can be 3, 4, 4.2, 5, 5.6, etc.

$3 \leq x$ means that 3 is less than or equal to x, i.e. x can be 3, 4, 4.2, 5, 5.6, etc.

Therefore:

$5 > x$ can be rewritten as $x < 5$, i.e. x can be 4, 3.2, 3, 2.8, 2, 1, etc.

$-7 \leq x$ can be rewritten as $x \geq -7$, i.e. x can be $-7, -6, -5$, etc.

These inequalities can also be represented on a number line:

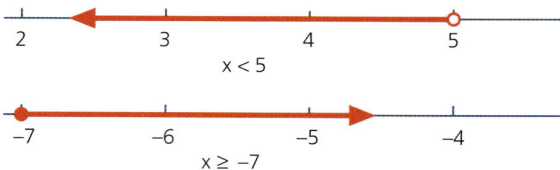

Note that ○→ implies that the number is not included in the solution whilst ●→ implies that the number is included in the solution.

→ Worked examples

1. Write $a > 3$ in words.

    a is greater than 3.

2. Write 'x is greater than or equal to 8' using appropriate symbols.

    $x \geq 8$

3. Write 'V is greater than 5, but less than or equal to 12' using the appropriate symbols.

    $5 < V \leq 12$

Ordering

Exercise 3.1

1 Write the following in words:
   a $a < 7$
   b $b > 4$
   c $c \neq 8$
   d $d \leq 3$
   e $e \geq 9$
   f $f \leq 11$

2 Rewrite the following, using the appropriate symbols:
   a a is less than 4
   b b is greater than 7
   c c is equal to or less than 9
   d d is equal to or greater than 5
   e e is not equal to 3
   f f is not more than 6
   g g is not less than 9
   h h is at least 6
   i i is not 7
   j j is not greater than 20

3 Write the following in words:
   a $5 < n < 10$
   b $6 \leq n \leq 15$
   c $3 \leq n < 9$
   d $8 < n \leq 12$

4 Write the following using the appropriate symbols:
   a p is more than 7, but less than 10
   b q is less than 12, but more than 3
   c r is at least 5, but less than 9
   d s is greater than 8, but not more than 15

➔ Worked examples

1 The maximum number of players from one football team allowed on the pitch at any one time is 11. Represent this information:
   a as an inequality

   Let the number of players be represented by the letter n. n must be less than or equal to 11. Therefore, $n \leq 11$.

   b on a number line.

2 The maximum number of players from one football team allowed on the pitch at any one time is 11. The minimum allowed is 7 players. Represent this information:
   a as an inequality

   Let the number of players be represented by the letter n. n must be greater than or equal to 7, but less than or equal to 11. Therefore $7 \leq n \leq 11$.

   b on a number line.

   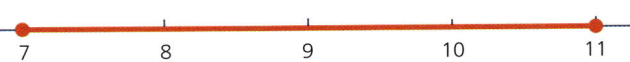

3 CALCULATIONS AND ORDER

Exercise 3.2

1 Copy each statement and insert one of the symbols =, > or < into the space to make the statement correct:
   a 7×2 ... $8 + 7$
   b 6^2 ... 9×4
   c 5×10 ... 7^2
   d 80 cm ... 1 m
   e 1000 litres ... 1 m^3
   f $48 \div 6$ ... $54 \div 9$

2 Represent each of the following inequalities on a number line, where x is a real number:
   a $x < 2$
   b $x \geqslant 3$
   c $x \leqslant -4$
   d $x \geqslant -2$
   e $2 < x < 5$
   f $-3 < x < 0$
   g $-2 \leqslant x < 2$
   h $2 \geqslant x \geqslant -1$

3 Write down the inequalities which correspond to the following number lines:

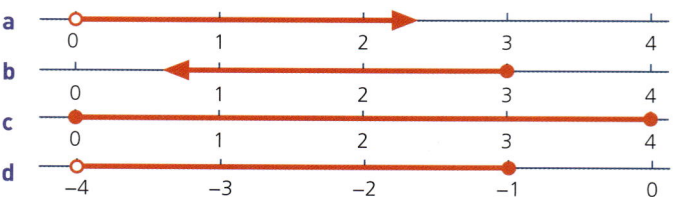

4 Write the following sentences using inequality signs:
   a The maximum capacity of an athletics stadium is 20 000 people.
   b In a class the tallest student is 180 cm and the shortest is 135 cm.
   c Five times a number plus 3 is less than 20.
   d The maximum temperature in May was 25 °C.
   e A farmer has between 350 and 400 apples on each tree in her orchard.
   f In December, temperatures in Kenya were between 11 °C and 28 °C.

Exercise 3.3

1 Write the following decimals in order of **magnitude**, starting with the largest:
   0.45   0.405   0.045   4.05   4.5

2 Write the following decimals in order of magnitude, starting with the smallest:
   6.0   0.6   0.66   0.606   0.06   6.6   6.606

3 Write the following decimals in order of magnitude, starting with the largest:
   0.906   0.96   0.096   9.06   0.609   0.690

4 Write the following fractions in order of magnitude, starting with the smallest:
   $\frac{1}{3}$ $\frac{1}{4}$ $\frac{1}{2}$ $\frac{2}{5}$ $\frac{3}{10}$ $\frac{3}{4}$

5 Write the following fractions in order of magnitude, starting with the largest:
   $\frac{1}{2}$ $\frac{1}{3}$ $\frac{6}{13}$ $\frac{4}{5}$ $\frac{7}{18}$ $\frac{2}{19}$

6 Write the following fractions in order of magnitude, starting with the smallest:
   $\frac{3}{4}$ $\frac{3}{5}$ $\frac{2}{3}$ $\frac{4}{7}$ $\frac{5}{9}$ $\frac{1}{2}$

The four basic operations

 Exercise 3.4

1. Write the lengths in order of magnitude, starting with the smallest:
 0.5 km   5000 m   15 000 cm $\frac{2}{5}$ km   750 m

2. Write the lengths in order of magnitude, starting with the smallest:
 2 m   60 cm   800 mm   180 cm   0.75 m

3. Write the masses in order of magnitude, starting with the largest:
 4 kg   3500 g $\frac{3}{4}$ kg   700 g   1 kg

4. Write the volumes in order of magnitude, starting with the smallest:
 1 litre   430 ml   800 cm^3 120 cl   150 cm^3

Use of a scientific calculator

There are many different types of calculator available today. These include basic calculators, scientific calculators and the latest graphical calculators. However, these are all useless unless you make use of their potential. The following sections are aimed at familiarising you with some of the basic operations.

The four basic operations

Worked examples

1. Using a calculator, work out the answer to:
 12.3 + 14.9 =
 [1][2][.][3][+][1][4][.][9][=] 27.2

2. Using a calculator, work out the answer to:
 16.3 × 10.8 =
 [1][6][.][3][×][1][0][.][8][=] 176.04

3. Using a calculator, work out the answer to:
 4.1 × −3.3 =
 [4][.][1][×][(−)][3][.][3][=] −13.53

 Exercise 3.5

1. Using a calculator, work out the answers to:
 a 9.7 + 15.3   b 13.6 + 9.08   c 12.9 + 4.92
 d 115.0 + 6.24   e 86.13 + 48.2   f 108.9 + 47.2

2. Using a calculator, work out the answers to:
 a 15.2 − 2.9   b 12.4 − 0.5   c 19.06 − 20.3
 d 4.32 − 4.33   e −9.1 − 21.2   f −6.3 − 2.1
 g −28 − −15   h −2.41 − −2.41

3. Using a calculator, work out the answers to:
 a 9.2 × 8.7   b 14.6 × 8.1   c 4.1 × 3.7 × 6
 d 9.3 ÷ 3.1   e 14.2 × −3   f 15.5 ÷ −5
 g −2.2 × −2.2   h −20 ÷ −4.5

27

3 CALCULATIONS AND ORDER

The order of operations

When carrying out calculations, care must be taken to ensure that they are carried out in the correct order.

Worked examples

1 Use a scientific calculator to work out the answer to:
$$2 + 3 \times 4 =$$
$\boxed{2}\ \boxed{+}\ \boxed{3}\ \boxed{\times}\ \boxed{4}\ \boxed{=}\ 14$

2 Use a scientific calculator to work out the answer to:
$$(2 + 3) \times 4 =$$
$\boxed{(}\ \boxed{2}\ \boxed{+}\ \boxed{3}\ \boxed{)}\ \boxed{\times}\ \boxed{4}\ \boxed{=}\ 20$

The reason why different answers are obtained is because, by convention, the operations have different priorities. These are:

1 brackets
2 indices
3 multiplication/division
4 addition/subtraction.

Therefore, in Worked example 1, 3×4 is evaluated first, and then the 2 is added, whilst in Worked example 2, $(2 + 3)$ is evaluated first, followed by multiplication by 4.

3 Use a scientific calculator to work out the answer to $-4 \times (8 + -3) = -20$.

The $(8 + -3)$ is evaluated first as it is in the brackets. The answer 5 is then multiplied by -4.

4 Use a scientific calculator to work out the answer to $-4 \times 8 + -3 = -35$.

The -4×8 is evaluated first as it is a multiplication. The answer -32 then has -3 subtracted from it.

Exercise 3.6

In each of the following questions, evaluate the answers:
  i in your head
  ii using a scientific calculator.

1 a $8 \times 3 + 2$ b $4 \div 2 + 8$ c $12 \times 4 - 6$
   d $4 + 6 \times 2$ e $10 - 6 \div 3$ f $6 - 3 \times 4$

2 a $7 \times 2 + 3 \times 2$ b $12 \div 3 + 6 \times 5$ c $9 + 3 \times 8 - 1$
   d $36 - 9 \div 3 - 2$ e $-14 \times 2 - 16 \div 2$ f $4 + 3 \times 7 - 6 \div 3$

3 a $(4 + 5) \times 3$ b $8 \times (12 - 4)$ c $3 \times (-8 + -3) - 3$
   d $(4 + 11) \div (7 - 2)$ e $4 \times 3 \times (7 + 5)$ f $24 \div 3 \div (10 - 5)$

The order of operations

Exercise 3.7 In each of the following questions:
  i Copy the calculation. Put in any brackets needed to make it correct.
  ii Check your answer using a scientific calculator.

1   a $6 \times 2 + 1 = 18$ b $1 + 3 \times 5 = 16$
    c $8 + 6 \div 2 = 7$ d $9 + 2 \times 4 = 44$
    e $9 \div 3 \times 4 + 1 = 13$ f $3 + 2 \times 4 - 1 = 15$

2   a $12 \div 4 - 2 + 6 = 7$ b $12 \div 4 - 2 + 6 = 12$
    c $12 \div 4 - 2 + 6 = -5$ d $12 \div 4 - 2 + 6 = 1.5$
    e $4 + 5 \times 6 - 1 = 33$ f $4 + 5 \times 6 - 1 = 29$
    g $4 + 5 \times 6 - 1 = 53$ h $4 + 5 \times 6 - 1 = 45$

It is important to use brackets when dealing with more complex calculations.

Worked examples

1 **Evaluate** the following using a scientific calculator:
$$\frac{12 + 9}{10 - 3} =$$
$$(\ 1\ 2\ +\ 9\ )\ \div\ (\ 1\ 0\ -\ 3\ )\ =\ 3$$

Your calculator may have a fraction button. It may look like this: ▬/▭

2 Evaluate the following using a scientific calculator:
$$\frac{20 + 12}{4^2} =$$
$$(\ 2\ 0\ +\ 1\ 2\ )\ \div\ 4\ x^2\ =\ 2$$

3 Evaluate the following using a scientific calculator:
$$\frac{90 + 38}{4^3} =$$
$$(\ 9\ 0\ +\ 3\ 8\ )\ \div\ 4\ x^y\ 3\ =\ 2$$

Note: Different types of calculator have different 'to the power of' buttons.

Exercise 3.8 Using a scientific calculator, evaluate:

1   a $\dfrac{9+3}{6}$ b $\dfrac{30-6}{5+3}$
    c $\dfrac{40+9}{12-5}$ d $\dfrac{15 \times 2}{7+8} + 2$
    e $\dfrac{100+21}{11} + 4 \times 3$ f $\dfrac{7 + 2 \times 4}{7-2} - 3$

2   a $\dfrac{4^2 - 6}{2+8}$ b $\dfrac{3^2 + 4^2}{5}$
    c $\dfrac{6^3 - 4^2}{4 \times 25}$ d $\dfrac{3^3 \times 4^4}{12^2} + 2$
    e $\dfrac{3+3^3}{5} + \dfrac{4^2 - 2^3}{8}$ f $\dfrac{(6+3) \times 4}{2^3} - 2 \times 3$

29

3 CALCULATIONS AND ORDER

Exercise 3.9 In each of the following questions:
  a Write the calculation represented by each problem.
  b Work out the answer to each calculation.

1 The temperature of water in a beaker is initially 48 °C. It is allowed to cool by 16 °C before being heated up again. When heated up, the temperature of the water is trebled.
What is the temperature T °C of the water once it has been heated up?

2 A submarine is initially at a depth of 400 m below the water's surface. It then dives a further distance so that it is at a depth of double what it was initially. The submarine later climbs 620 m.
Calculate the depth D m the submarine climbs to.

3 5 bags of flour are arranged in a line. The number of bags is then squared and a further 11 bags added to this amount. Finally the number of bags is divided equally between 2 chefs so that they each receive N bags of flour.
Calculate the value of N.

Student assessment 1

1 Write the following in words:
  a $p \neq 2$ b $q > 0$ c $r \leq 3$
  d $s = 2$ e $t \geq 1$ f $u < -5$

2 Rewrite the following using the appropriate symbols:
  a a is less than 2   b b is less than or equal to 4
  c c is equal to 8   d d is not greater than 0

3 Illustrate each of the following inequalities on a number line:
  a $j > 2$ b $k \leq 16$
  c $-2 \leq l \leq 5$ d $3 \leq m < 7$

4 Illustrate the information in each of the following statements on a number line:
  a A ferry can carry no more than 280 cars.
  b The minimum temperature overnight was 4 °C.

5 Write the following masses in order of magnitude, starting with the largest:
  900 g   1 kg   1800 g   1.09 kg   9 g

6 Here are five cards with numbers.

  | 0 | 1 | 2 | 5 | 6 |

  Using only four of the cards once each time, write down two numbers between 5000 and 5100.

7 Using a calculator, work out the answers to:
  a $7.1 + 8.02$ b $2.2 - 5.8$ c $-6.1 + 4$
  d $4.2 - -5.2$ e -3.6×4.1 f $-18 \div -2.5$

8 Evaluate:
   a $3 \times 9 - 7$
   b $12 + 6 \div 2$
   c $3 + 4 \div 2 \times 4$
   d $6 + 3 \times 4 - 5$
   e $(5 + 2) \div 7$
   f $14 \times 2 \div (9 - 2)$

Student assessment 2

1 Copy the following. Insert one of the symbols =, > or < into the space to make the statements correct:
   a $4 \times 2 \ldots 2^3$
   b $6^2 \ldots 2^6$
   c 850 ml ... 0.5 litre
   d Days in May ... 30 days

2 Illustrate the following information on a number line:
   a The temperature during the day reached a maximum of 35 °C.
   b There were 20 to 25 pupils in a class.
   c The world record for the 100 m sprint is under 10 seconds.
   d Doubling a number and subtracting 4 gives an answer greater than 16.

3 Write the information on the following number lines as inequalities:

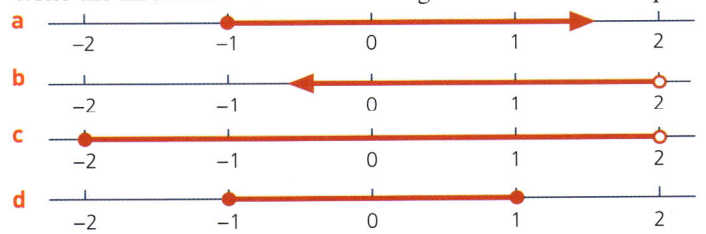

4 Illustrate each of the following inequalities on a number line:
   a $x \geqslant 3$
   b $x < 4$
   c $0 < x < 4$
   d $-3 \leqslant x < 1$

5 Write the fractions in order of magnitude, starting with the smallest:
   $$\frac{4}{7} \quad \frac{3}{14} \quad \frac{9}{10} \quad \frac{1}{2} \quad \frac{2}{5}$$

6 Copy the following, if necessary putting in brackets to make each statement correct:
   a $7 - 5 \times 3 = 6$
   b $16 + 4 \times 2 + 4 = 40$
   c $4 + 5 \times 6 - 1 = 45$
   d $1 + 5 \times 6 - 6 = 30$

7 Using a calculator, evaluate:
   a $\dfrac{3^3 - 4^2}{2}$
   b $\dfrac{(15 - 3) \div 3}{2} + 7$

8 Calculate $\dfrac{14.6 - 3.9}{-1.1 + \sqrt[3]{27.3}}$

Give your answer correct to two decimal places.

4 Integers, fractions, decimals and percentages

Fractions

A single unit can be broken into equal parts called **fractions**, e.g. $\frac{1}{2}, \frac{1}{3}, \frac{1}{6}$. If, for example, the unit is broken into ten equal parts and three parts are then taken, the fraction is written as $\frac{3}{10}$. That is, three parts out of ten parts.

In the fraction $\frac{3}{10}$:

- The three is called the **numerator**.
- The ten is called the **denominator**.
- A **proper fraction** has its numerator less than its denominator, e.g. $\frac{3}{4}$.
- An **improper fraction** has its numerator more than its denominator, e.g. $\frac{9}{2}$.
- A **mixed number** is made up of a whole number and a proper fraction, e.g. $4\frac{1}{5}$.

Exercise 4.1

1   a   Write two proper fractions with a numerator of 5.
    b   Write two improper fractions with a denominator of 7.

2   Separate the following into three sets: 'proper fractions', 'improper fractions' and 'mixed numbers'.

   a $\frac{2}{3}$ b $\frac{15}{22}$ c $\frac{4}{3}$ d $\frac{5}{2}$
   e $1\frac{1}{2}$ f $2\frac{3}{4}$ g $\frac{7}{4}$ h $\frac{7}{11}$
   i $7\frac{1}{4}$ j $\frac{5}{6}$ k $\frac{6}{5}$ l $1\frac{1}{5}$
   m $\frac{1}{10}$ n $2\frac{7}{8}$ o $\frac{5}{3}$

A fraction of an amount

➡ Worked examples

1   Find $\frac{1}{5}$ of 35.

    This means 'divide 35 into five equal parts'.

    $\frac{1}{5}$ of 35 is 7.

2   Find $\frac{3}{5}$ of 35.

    Since $\frac{1}{5}$ of 35 is 7, $\frac{3}{5}$ of 35 is 7×3.

    That is, 21.

Fractions

Exercise 4.2

1 Evaluate:

a $\frac{1}{5}$ of 40   b $\frac{3}{5}$ of 40   c $\frac{1}{9}$ of 36   d $\frac{5}{9}$ of 36

e $\frac{1}{8}$ of 72   f $\frac{7}{8}$ of 72   g $\frac{1}{12}$ of 60   h $\frac{5}{12}$ of 60

i $\frac{1}{4}$ of 8   j $\frac{3}{4}$ of 8

2 Evaluate:

a $\frac{3}{4}$ of 12   b $\frac{4}{5}$ of 20   c $\frac{4}{9}$ of 45   d $\frac{5}{8}$ of 64

e $\frac{3}{11}$ of 66   f $\frac{9}{10}$ of 80   g $\frac{5}{7}$ of 42   h $\frac{8}{9}$ of 54

i $\frac{7}{8}$ of 240   j $\frac{4}{5}$ of 65

Changing a mixed number to an improper fraction

> **Worked examples**
>
> 1 Change $2\frac{3}{4}$ to an improper fraction.
>
> $1 = \frac{4}{4}$
>
> $2 = \frac{8}{4}$
>
> $2\frac{3}{4} = \frac{8}{4} + \frac{3}{4}$
>
> $= \frac{11}{4}$
>
> 2 Change $3\frac{5}{8}$ to an improper fraction.
>
> $3\frac{5}{8} = \frac{24}{8} + \frac{5}{8}$
>
> $= \frac{24 + 5}{8}$
>
> $= \frac{29}{8}$

Exercise 4.3

Change the following mixed numbers to improper fractions:

a $4\frac{2}{3}$ b $3\frac{3}{5}$ c $5\frac{7}{8}$ d $2\frac{5}{6}$

e $8\frac{1}{2}$ f $9\frac{5}{7}$ g $6\frac{4}{9}$ h $4\frac{3}{5}$

i $5\frac{4}{11}$ j $7\frac{6}{7}$ k $4\frac{3}{10}$ l $11\frac{3}{13}$

Changing an improper fraction to a mixed number

> **Worked example**
>
> Change $\frac{27}{4}$ to a mixed number.
>
> $\frac{27}{4} = \frac{24 + 3}{4}$
>
> $= \frac{24}{4} + \frac{3}{4}$
>
> $= 6\frac{3}{4}$

24 is the largest multiple of 4 less than 27

4 INTEGERS, FRACTIONS, DECIMALS AND PERCENTAGES

Exercise 4.4 Change the following improper fractions to mixed numbers:
- a $\frac{29}{4}$
- b $\frac{33}{5}$
- c $\frac{41}{6}$
- d $\frac{53}{8}$
- e $\frac{49}{9}$
- f $\frac{17}{12}$
- g $\frac{66}{7}$
- h $\frac{33}{10}$
- i $\frac{19}{2}$
- j $\frac{73}{12}$

Decimals

H	T	U	.	$\frac{1}{10}$	$\frac{1}{100}$	$\frac{1}{1000}$
		3	.	2	7	
		0	.	0	3	8

3.27 is 3 units, 2 tenths and 7 hundredths

i.e. $3.27 = 3 + \frac{2}{10} + \frac{7}{100}$

0.038 is 3 hundredths and 8 thousandths

i.e. $0.038 = \frac{3}{100} + \frac{8}{1000}$

Note that 2 tenths and 7 hundredths is equivalent to 27 hundredths

i.e. $\frac{2}{10} + \frac{7}{100} = \frac{27}{100}$

and that 3 hundredths and 8 thousandths is equivalent to 38 thousandths

i.e. $\frac{3}{100} + \frac{8}{1000} = \frac{38}{1000}$

A **decimal fraction** is a fraction between 0 and 1 in which the denominator is a power of 10 and the numerator is an integer. $\frac{3}{10}, \frac{23}{100}, \frac{17}{1000}$ are all examples of decimal fractions.

- $\frac{1}{20}$ is not a decimal fraction because the denominator is not a power of 10.
- $\frac{11}{10}$ is not a decimal fraction because its value is greater than 1.

Exercise 4.5

1 Make a table similar to the one you have just seen. List the digits in the following numbers in their correct position:
- a 6.023
- b 5.94
- c 18.3
- d 0.071
- e 2.001
- f 3.56

2 Write these fractions as decimals:
- a $4\frac{5}{10}$
- b $6\frac{3}{10}$
- c $17\frac{8}{10}$
- d $3\frac{7}{100}$
- e $9\frac{27}{100}$
- f $11\frac{36}{100}$
- g $4\frac{6}{1000}$
- h $5\frac{27}{1000}$
- i $4\frac{356}{1000}$
- j $9\frac{204}{1000}$

3 Evaluate the following without using a calculator:
- **a** 2.7 + 0.35 + 16.09
- **b** 1.44 + 0.072 + 82.3
- **c** 23.8 − 17.2
- **d** 16.9 − 5.74
- **e** 121.3 − 85.49
- **f** 6.03 + 0.5 − 1.21
- **g** 72.5 − 9.08 + 3.72
- **h** 100 − 32.74 − 61.2
- **i** 16.0 − 9.24 − 5.36
- **j** 1.1 − 0.92 − 0.005

Percentages

A fraction whose denominator is 100 can be expressed as a percentage.

$\frac{29}{100}$ can be written as 29% $\frac{45}{100}$ can be written as 45%

Exercise 4.6

Write the fractions as percentages:
- **a** $\frac{39}{100}$
- **b** $\frac{42}{100}$
- **c** $\frac{63}{100}$
- **d** $\frac{5}{100}$

Changing a fraction to a percentage

By using equivalent fractions to change the denominator to 100, other fractions can be written as percentages.

Worked example

Change $\frac{3}{5}$ to a percentage.

$\frac{3}{5} = \frac{3}{5} \times \frac{20}{20} = \frac{60}{100}$

$\frac{60}{100}$ can be written as 60%

Exercise 4.7

1 Express each of the following as a fraction with denominator 100, then write them as percentages:
- **a** $\frac{29}{50}$
- **b** $\frac{17}{25}$
- **c** $\frac{11}{20}$
- **d** $\frac{3}{10}$
- **e** $\frac{23}{25}$
- **f** $\frac{19}{50}$
- **g** $\frac{3}{4}$
- **h** $\frac{2}{5}$

2 Copy and complete the table of equivalents:

Fraction	Decimal	Percentage
$\frac{1}{10}$		
	0.2	
		30%
$\frac{4}{10}$		
	0.5	
		60%
	0.7	
$\frac{4}{5}$		
	0.9	
$\frac{1}{4}$		
		75%

4 INTEGERS, FRACTIONS, DECIMALS AND PERCENTAGES

Exercise 4.7 (cont)

3 Arrange these numbers in order of magnitude, starting with the largest.

$\frac{3}{8}$, 0.614, 4%, 61%, $\frac{2}{9}$, 0.4

> **Note**
> Addition, subtraction, multiplication and division are mathematical operations.

The four rules

Calculations with whole numbers

Long multiplication

When carrying out long multiplication, it is important to remember place value.

> **Worked example**

a $184 \times 37 =$

```
      1 8 4
    ×   3 7
    ───────
    1 2 8 8   (184 × 7)
    5 5 2 0   (184 × 30)
    ───────
    6 8 0 8   (184 × 37)
```

b 184×3.7
By comparing 184×3.7 with 184×37, we can see that 3.7 is ten times smaller than 37, therefore the answer to 184×3.7 will be ten times smaller than the answer to 184×37 i.e. 680.8

c 1.84×3.7
By comparing 1.84×3.7 with 184×37, we can see that 1.84 is one hundred times smaller than 184 and 3.7 is ten time smaller than 37. Therefore the answer to 1.84×3.7 will be 1000 times smaller than the answer to 184×37 i.e. 6.808

Short division

> **Worked example**

$453 \div 6 =$

```
       7 5 r3
    6)4 5 ³3
```

It is usual, however, to give the final answer in decimal form rather than with a remainder. The division should therefore be continued:

$453 \div 6$

```
         7 5 . 5
    6)4 5 ³3 . ³0
```

The four rules

Long division

→ Worked example

Calculate 7184 ÷ 23 to one decimal place (1 d.p.).

```
        3 1 2 . 3 4
    23 )7 1 8 4 . 0 0
        6 9
        ───
          2 8
          2 3
          ───
            5 4
            4 6
            ───
              8 0
              6 9
              ───
              1 1 0
                9 2
              ─────
                1 8
```

Note how the question asks for the answer to 1 d.p. but the calculation is continued until the second d.p. This is to see whether the answer needs to be rounded up.

Therefore 7184 ÷ 23 = 312.3 to 1 d.p.

Mixed operations

The order of operations was also covered in Chapter 3.

When a calculation involves a mixture of operations, the order of the operations is important. Multiplications and divisions are done first, whilst additions and subtractions are done afterwards. To override this, brackets need to be used.

→ Worked examples

1 $3 + 7 \times 2 - 4$
   $= 3 + 14 - 4$
   $= 13$

2 $(3 + 7) \times 2 - 4$
   $= 10 \times 2 - 4$
   $= 20 - 4$
   $= 16$

3 $3 + 7 \times (2 - 4)$
   $= 3 + 7 \times (-2)$
   $= 3 - 14$
   $= -11$

4 $(3 + 7) \times (2 - 4)$
   $= 10 \times (-2)$
   $= -20$

4 INTEGERS, FRACTIONS, DECIMALS AND PERCENTAGES

Exercise 4.8

1. Evaluate the answer to:
   a $3 + 5 \times 2 - 4$
   b $6 + 4 \times 7 - 12$
   c $3 \times 2 + 4 \times 6$
   d $4 \times 5 - 3 \times 6$
   e $8 \div 2 + 18 \div 6$
   f $12 \div 8 + 6 \div 4$

2. Copy these equations and put brackets in the correct places to make them correct:
   a $6 \times 4 + 6 \div 3 = 20$
   b $6 \times 4 + 6 \div 3 = 36$
   c $8 + 2 \times 4 - 2 = 12$
   d $8 + 2 \times 4 - 2 = 20$
   e $9 - 3 \times 7 + 2 = 44$
   f $9 - 3 \times 7 + 2 = 54$

3. Work out the solutions to these multiplications:
   a 63×24
   b 531×64
   c 785×38
   d 164×253
   e 144×144
   f 170×240

4. Work out the remainders in these divisions:
   a $33 \div 7$
   b $68 \div 5$
   c $72 \div 7$
   d $430 \div 9$
   e $156 \div 5$
   f $687 \div 10$

5. a The sum of two numbers is 16, their product is 63. What are the two numbers?
   b When a number is divided by 7 the result is 14 remainder 2. What is the number?
   c The difference between two numbers is 5, their product is 176. What are the numbers?
   d How many nines can be added to 40 before the total exceeds 100?
   e A length of rail track is 9 m long. How many complete lengths will be needed to lay 1 km of track?
   f How many 35 cent stamps can be bought for 10 dollars?

6. Work out the following long divisions. Round your answers to 1 d.p. where appropriate:
   a $7892 \div 7$
   b $45\,623 \div 6$
   c $9452 \div 8$
   d $4564 \div 4$
   e $7892 \div 15$
   f $79\,876 \div 24$

Calculations with fractions

Equivalent fractions

$\frac{1}{2}$ $\frac{2}{4}$ $\frac{4}{8}$

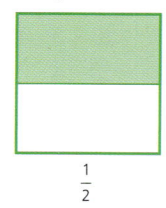

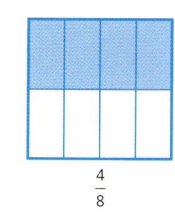

The diagrams show that $\frac{1}{2}, \frac{2}{4}$ and $\frac{4}{8}$ are **equivalent fractions**. Similarly, $\frac{1}{3}, \frac{2}{6}, \frac{3}{9}$ and $\frac{4}{12}$ are equivalent, as are $\frac{1}{5}, \frac{10}{50}$ and $\frac{20}{100}$. Equivalent fractions are mathematically the same as each other. In the diagrams above, $\frac{1}{2}$ is mathematically the same as $\frac{4}{8}$. However, $\frac{1}{2}$ is a simplified form of $\frac{4}{8}$.

Calculations with fractions

When carrying out calculations involving fractions it is usual to give your answer in its **simplest form**. Another way of saying 'simplest form' is '**lowest terms**'.

> ## Worked examples

1. Write $\frac{4}{22}$ in its simplest form.
   Divide both the numerator and the denominator by their highest common factor.
   The highest common factor of both 4 and 22 is 2.
   Dividing both 4 and 22 by 2 gives $\frac{2}{11}$.
   Therefore $\frac{2}{11}$ is $\frac{4}{22}$ written in its simplest form.

2. Write $\frac{12}{40}$ in its lowest terms.
   Divide both the numerator and the denominator by their highest common factor.
   The highest common factor of both 12 and 40 is 4.
   Dividing both 12 and 40 by 4 gives $\frac{3}{10}$.
   Therefore $\frac{3}{10}$ is $\frac{12}{40}$ written in its lowest terms.

Writing a fraction in its 'simplest form' or in its 'lowest terms' means the same thing.

Exercise 4.9

1. Copy the following sets of equivalent fractions and fill in the blanks:

   a $\frac{2}{5} = \frac{4}{\square} = \frac{\square}{20} = \frac{\square}{50} = \frac{16}{\square}$

   b $\frac{3}{8} = \frac{6}{\square} = \frac{\square}{24} = \frac{15}{\square} = \frac{\square}{72}$

   c $\frac{\square}{7} = \frac{8}{14} = \frac{12}{\square} = \frac{\square}{56} = \frac{36}{\square}$

   d $\frac{5}{\square} = \frac{\square}{27} = \frac{20}{36} = \frac{\square}{90} = \frac{55}{\square}$

2. Express the fractions in their lowest terms:

   a $\frac{5}{10}$ b $\frac{7}{21}$ c $\frac{8}{12}$

   d $\frac{16}{36}$ e $\frac{75}{100}$ f $\frac{81}{90}$

3. Write these improper fractions as mixed numbers, e.g. $\frac{15}{4} = 3\frac{3}{4}$

   a $\frac{17}{4}$ b $\frac{23}{5}$ c $\frac{8}{3}$

   d $\frac{19}{3}$ e $\frac{13}{3}$ f $\frac{43}{12}$

4. Write these mixed numbers as improper fractions, e.g. $3\frac{4}{5} = \frac{19}{5}$

   a $6\frac{1}{2}$ b $7\frac{1}{4}$ c $3\frac{3}{8}$

   d $11\frac{1}{9}$ e $6\frac{4}{5}$ f $8\frac{9}{11}$

Addition and subtraction of fractions

For fractions to be either added or subtracted, the denominators need to be the same.

4 INTEGERS, FRACTIONS, DECIMALS AND PERCENTAGES

> **Worked examples**
>
> 1 $\frac{3}{11} + \frac{5}{11} = \frac{8}{11}$
>
> 2 $\frac{7}{8} + \frac{5}{8} = \frac{12}{8} = 1\frac{1}{2}$
>
> 3 $\frac{1}{2} + \frac{1}{3} = \frac{3}{6} + \frac{2}{6} = \frac{5}{6}$
>
> 4 $\frac{4}{5} - \frac{1}{3} = \frac{12}{15} - \frac{5}{15} = \frac{7}{15}$

When dealing with calculations involving mixed numbers, it is sometimes easier to change them to improper fractions first.

> **Worked examples**
>
> 1 $5\frac{3}{4} - 2\frac{5}{8}$
> $= \frac{23}{4} - \frac{21}{8}$
> $= \frac{46}{8} - \frac{21}{8}$
> $= \frac{25}{8} = 3\frac{1}{8}$
>
> 2 $1\frac{4}{7} + 3\frac{3}{4}$
> $= \frac{11}{7} + \frac{15}{4}$
> $= \frac{44}{28} + \frac{105}{28}$
> $= \frac{149}{28} = 5\frac{9}{28}$

Exercise 4.10 Evaluate each of the following and write the answer as a fraction in its simplest form:

1 a $\frac{3}{5} + \frac{4}{5}$ b $\frac{3}{11} + \frac{7}{11}$ c $\frac{2}{3} + \frac{1}{4}$

   d $\frac{3}{5} + \frac{4}{9}$ e $\frac{8}{13} + \frac{2}{5}$ f $\frac{1}{2} + \frac{2}{3} + \frac{3}{4}$

2 a $\frac{1}{8} + \frac{3}{8} + \frac{5}{8}$ b $\frac{3}{7} + \frac{5}{7} + \frac{4}{7}$ c $\frac{1}{3} + \frac{1}{2} + \frac{1}{4}$

   d $\frac{1}{5} + \frac{1}{3} + \frac{1}{4}$ e $\frac{3}{8} + \frac{3}{5} + \frac{3}{4}$ f $\frac{3}{13} + \frac{1}{4} + \frac{1}{2}$

3 a $\frac{3}{7} - \frac{2}{7}$ b $\frac{4}{5} - \frac{7}{10}$ c $\frac{8}{9} - \frac{1}{3}$

   d $\frac{7}{12} - \frac{1}{2}$ e $\frac{5}{8} - \frac{2}{5}$ f $\frac{3}{4} - \frac{2}{5} + \frac{7}{10}$

4 a $\frac{3}{4} + \frac{1}{5} - \frac{2}{3}$ b $\frac{3}{8} + \frac{7}{11} - \frac{1}{2}$ c $\frac{4}{5} - \frac{3}{10} + \frac{7}{20}$

   d $\frac{9}{13} + \frac{1}{3} - \frac{4}{5}$ e $\frac{9}{10} - \frac{1}{5} - \frac{1}{4}$ f $\frac{8}{9} - \frac{1}{3} - \frac{1}{2}$

5 a $2\frac{1}{2} + 3\frac{3}{4}$ b $3\frac{3}{5} + 1\frac{7}{10}$ c $6\frac{1}{2} - 3\frac{2}{5}$

   d $8\frac{5}{8} - 2\frac{1}{2}$ e $5\frac{7}{8} - 4\frac{3}{4}$ f $3\frac{1}{4} - 2\frac{5}{9}$

6 a $2\frac{1}{2} + 1\frac{1}{4} + 1\frac{3}{8}$ b $2\frac{4}{5} + 3\frac{1}{8} + 1\frac{3}{10}$ c $4\frac{1}{2} - 1\frac{1}{4} - 3\frac{5}{8}$

   d $6\frac{1}{2} - 2\frac{3}{4} - 3\frac{2}{5}$ e $2\frac{4}{7} - 3\frac{1}{4} - 1\frac{3}{5}$ f $4\frac{7}{20} - 5\frac{1}{5} + 2\frac{2}{5}$

Calculations with fractions

Multiplication and division of fractions

→ Worked examples

1. $\frac{3}{4} \times \frac{2}{3}$

   $= \frac{6}{12}$

   $= \frac{1}{2}$

2. $3\frac{1}{2} \times 4\frac{4}{7}$

   $= \frac{7}{2} \times \frac{32}{7}$

   $= \frac{224}{14}$

   $= 16$

The reciprocal of a number is obtained when 1 is divided by that number. The reciprocal of 5 is $\frac{1}{5}$, the reciprocal of $\frac{2}{5}$ is $\frac{1}{\frac{2}{5}} = \frac{5}{2}$, etc.

Dividing fractions is the same as multiplying by the reciprocal.

→ Worked examples

1. $\frac{3}{8} \div \frac{3}{4}$

   $= \frac{3}{8} \times \frac{4}{3}$

   $= \frac{12}{24}$

   $= \frac{1}{2}$

2. $5\frac{1}{2} \div 3\frac{2}{3}$

   $= \frac{11}{2} \div \frac{11}{3}$

   $= \frac{11}{2} \times \frac{3}{11}$

   $= \frac{3}{2}$

Exercise 4.11

1. Write the reciprocal of:
   - a $\frac{3}{4}$
   - b $\frac{5}{9}$
   - c 7
   - d $\frac{1}{9}$
   - e $2\frac{3}{4}$
   - f $4\frac{5}{8}$

2. Write the reciprocal of:
   - a $\frac{1}{8}$
   - b $\frac{7}{12}$
   - c $\frac{3}{5}$
   - d $1\frac{1}{2}$
   - e $3\frac{3}{8}$
   - f 6

3. Evaluate:
   - a $\frac{3}{8} \times \frac{4}{9}$
   - b $\frac{2}{3} \times \frac{9}{10}$
   - c $\frac{5}{7} \times \frac{4}{15}$
   - d $\frac{3}{4}$ of $\frac{8}{9}$
   - e $\frac{5}{6}$ of $\frac{3}{10}$
   - f $\frac{7}{8}$ of $\frac{2}{5}$

4. Evaluate:
   - a $\frac{5}{8} \div \frac{3}{4}$
   - b $\frac{5}{6} \div \frac{1}{3}$
   - c $\frac{4}{5} \div \frac{7}{10}$
   - d $1\frac{5}{8} \div \frac{2}{5}$
   - e $\frac{3}{7} \div 2\frac{1}{7}$
   - f $1\frac{1}{4} \div 1\frac{7}{8}$

4 INTEGERS, FRACTIONS, DECIMALS AND PERCENTAGES

Exercise 4.11 (cont)

5 Evaluate:
   a $\frac{3}{4} \times \frac{4}{5}$
   b $\frac{7}{8} \times \frac{2}{3}$
   c $\frac{3}{4} \times \frac{4}{7} \times \frac{3}{10}$
   d $\frac{4}{5} \div \frac{2}{3} \times \frac{7}{10}$
   e $\frac{1}{2}$ of $\frac{3}{4}$
   f $4\frac{1}{5} \div 3\frac{1}{9}$

6 Evaluate:
   a $\left(\frac{3}{8} \times \frac{4}{5}\right) + \left(\frac{1}{2} \text{ of } \frac{3}{5}\right)$
   b $\left(1\frac{1}{2} \times 3\frac{3}{4}\right) - \left(2\frac{3}{5} \div 1\frac{1}{2}\right)$
   c $\left(\frac{3}{5} \text{ of } \frac{4}{9}\right) + \left(\frac{4}{9} \text{ of } \frac{3}{5}\right)$
   d $\left(1\frac{1}{3} \times 2\frac{5}{8}\right)^2$

7 Using the correct order of operations, evaluate the following:
   a $\frac{1}{4} + \frac{2}{7} \times \frac{3}{4}$
   b $\frac{1}{2} + \frac{3}{8} \div \frac{1}{4} - 2\frac{1}{2}$
   c $\left(\frac{1}{6}\right)^2 - \frac{1}{8} \times \frac{5}{9}$
   d $\left(5\frac{2}{3} - \frac{14}{3}\right)^2 \div \frac{2}{7} + 3\frac{1}{2}$

Changing a fraction to a decimal

To change a fraction to a decimal, divide the numerator by the denominator.

→ Worked examples

1 Change $\frac{5}{8}$ to a decimal.

   $0.6\ 2\ 5$
   $8\overline{|5.0^20^40}$

2 Change $2\frac{3}{5}$ to a decimal.

   This can be represented as $2 + \frac{3}{5}$

   0.6
   $5\overline{|3.0}$

   Therefore $2\frac{3}{5} = 2 + 0.6 = 2.6$

Exercise 4.12

1 Change the fractions to decimals:
   a $\frac{3}{4}$
   b $\frac{4}{5}$
   c $\frac{9}{20}$
   d $\frac{17}{50}$
   e $\frac{1}{3}$
   f $\frac{3}{8}$
   g $\frac{7}{16}$
   h $\frac{2}{9}$

2 Change the mixed numbers to decimals:
   a $2\frac{3}{4}$
   b $3\frac{3}{5}$
   c $4\frac{7}{20}$
   d $6\frac{11}{50}$
   e $5\frac{2}{3}$
   f $6\frac{7}{8}$
   g $5\frac{9}{16}$
   h $4\frac{2}{8}$

Changing a decimal to a fraction

Changing a decimal to a fraction is done by knowing the 'value' of each of the digits in any decimal.

Calculations with fractions

> **Worked examples**

1 Change 0.45 from a decimal to a fraction.

   units . tenths hundredths
   0   .   4   5

   0.45 is therefore equivalent to 4 tenths and 5 hundredths, which in turn is the same as 45 hundredths.

   Therefore $0.45 = \frac{45}{100} = \frac{9}{20}$

2 Change 2.325 from a decimal to a fraction.

   units . tenths hundredths thousandths
   2   .   3   2   5

   Therefore $2.325 = 2\frac{325}{1000} = 2\frac{13}{40}$

Exercise 4.13

1 Change the decimals to fractions:
   a 0.5   b 0.7   c 0.6
   d 0.75   e 0.825   f 0.05
   g 0.050   h 0.402   i 0.0002

2 Change the decimals to mixed numbers:
   a 2.4   b 6.5   c 8.2
   d 3.75   e 10.55   f 9.204
   g 15.455   h 30.001   i 1.0205

Student assessment 1

1 Copy the numbers. Circle improper fractions and underline mixed numbers:
   a $\frac{3}{11}$ b $5\frac{3}{4}$ c $\frac{27}{8}$ d $\frac{3}{7}$

2 Evaluate:
   a $\frac{1}{3}$ of 63   b $\frac{3}{8}$ of 72   c $\frac{2}{5}$ of 55   d $\frac{3}{13}$ of 169

3 Change the mixed numbers to improper fractions:
   a $2\frac{3}{5}$ b $3\frac{4}{9}$ c $5\frac{5}{8}$

4 Change the improper fractions to mixed numbers:
   a $\frac{33}{5}$ b $\frac{47}{9}$ c $\frac{67}{11}$

5 Copy the set of equivalent fractions and fill in the missing numerators:
   $\frac{2}{3} = \frac{}{6} = \frac{}{12} = \frac{}{18} = \frac{}{27} = \frac{}{30}$

6 Write the fractions as decimals:
   a $\frac{35}{100}$ b $\frac{275}{1000}$ c $\frac{675}{100}$ d $\frac{35}{1000}$

4 INTEGERS, FRACTIONS, DECIMALS AND PERCENTAGES

7 Write the following as percentages:

    a $\frac{3}{5}$ **b** $\frac{49}{100}$ **c** $\frac{1}{4}$ **d** $\frac{9}{10}$

    e $1\frac{1}{2}$ **f** $3\frac{27}{100}$ **g** $\frac{5}{100}$ **h** $\frac{7}{20}$

    i 0.77   **j** 0.03   **k** 2.9   **l** 4

8 A hot water tank is filled with 90 litres of water. Stefan uses $\frac{1}{6}$ of the water for a shower. How much water is left in the hot water tank after Stefan's shower?

Student assessment 2

1 Evaluate:
    a $6 \times 4 - 3 \times 8$ **b** $15 \div 3 + 2 \times 7$

2 The product of two numbers is 72, and their sum is 18. What are the two numbers?

3 How many days are there in 42 weeks?

4 Work out 368×49.

5 Work out $7835 \div 23$ giving your answer to 1 d.p.

6 Copy these equivalent fractions and fill in the blanks:
$\frac{24}{36} = \frac{\ }{12} = \frac{4}{30} = \frac{60}{\ }$

7 Evaluate:
    a $2\frac{1}{2} - \frac{4}{5}$ **b** $3\frac{1}{2} \times \frac{4}{7}$

8 Change the fractions to decimals:
    a $\frac{7}{8}$ **b** $1\frac{2}{5}$

9 Change the decimals to fractions. Give each fraction in its simplest form.
    a 6.5   **b** 0.04   **c** 3.65   **d** 3.008

10 Write the reciprocals of the following numbers:
    a $\frac{5}{9}$ **b** $3\frac{2}{5}$ **c** 0.1

5 Further percentages

You should already be familiar with the percentage equivalents of simple fractions and decimals as outlined in the table:

Fraction	Decimal	Percentage
$\frac{1}{2}$	0.5	50%
$\frac{1}{4}$	0.25	25%
$\frac{3}{4}$	0.75	75%
$\frac{1}{8}$	0.125	12.5%
$\frac{3}{8}$	0.375	37.5%
$\frac{5}{8}$	0.625	62.5%
$\frac{7}{8}$	0.875	87.5%
$\frac{1}{10}$	0.1	10%
$\frac{2}{10}$ or $\frac{1}{5}$	0.2	20%
$\frac{3}{10}$	0.3	30%
$\frac{4}{10}$ or $\frac{2}{5}$	0.4	40%
$\frac{6}{10}$ or $\frac{3}{5}$	0.6	60%
$\frac{7}{10}$	0.7	70%
$\frac{8}{10}$ or $\frac{4}{5}$	0.8	80%
$\frac{9}{10}$	0.9	90%

Simple percentages

➔ Worked examples

1 There are 100 sheep in a field. 88 of the sheep are ewes.
   a What percentage of the sheep are ewes?
      88 out of 100 are ewes = 88%

5 FURTHER PERCENTAGES

    b What percentage are not ewes?
       12 out of 100 are not ewes = 12%

2 A gymnast received marks from five judges. Each mark was out of 10.

The marks were: 8.0, 8.2, 7.9, 8.3 and 7.6.

Express these marks as percentages.

$\frac{8.0}{10} = \frac{80}{100} = 80\%$ $\frac{8.2}{10} = \frac{82}{100} = 82\%$ $\frac{7.9}{10} = \frac{79}{100} = 79\%$

$\frac{8.3}{10} = \frac{83}{100} = 83\%$ $\frac{7.6}{10} = \frac{76}{100} = 76\%$

3 Convert the percentages into fractions and decimals:

  a 27%   **b** 5%

    $\frac{27}{100} = 0.27$ $\frac{5}{100} = \frac{1}{20} = 0.05$

Exercise 5.1

1 In a survey of 100 cars, 47 were white, 23 were blue and 30 were red. Express each of these numbers as a percentage of the total.

2 $\frac{7}{10}$ of the surface of the Earth is water. Express this as a percentage.

3 There are 200 birds in a flock. 120 of them are female. What percentage of the flock are:
  a female   **b** male?

4 Write these percentages as fractions of 100:
  a 73%   **b** 28%   **c** 10%   **d** 25%

5 Write these fractions as percentages:
  a $\frac{27}{100}$ **b** $\frac{3}{10}$ **c** $\frac{7}{50}$ **d** $\frac{1}{4}$

6 Convert the percentages to decimals:
  a 39%   **b** 47%   **c** 83%
  d 7%   **e** 2%   **f** 20%

7 Convert the decimals to percentages:
  a 0.31   **b** 0.67   **c** 0.09
  d 0.05   **e** 0.2   **f** 0.75

Calculating a percentage of a quantity

Worked examples

1 Find 25% of 300 m.
25% can be written as 0.25
0.25 × 300 m = 75 m

2 Find 35% of 280 m.
35% can be written as 0.35
0.35 × 280 m = 98 m

Expressing one quantity as a percentage of another

Exercise 5.2

1. Write the percentage equivalent of these fractions:
   a. $\frac{1}{4}$
   b. $\frac{2}{3}$
   c. $\frac{5}{8}$
   d. $1\frac{4}{5}$
   e. $4\frac{9}{10}$
   f. $3\frac{7}{8}$

2. Write the decimal equivalent of the following:
   a. $\frac{3}{4}$
   b. 80%
   c. $\frac{1}{5}$
   d. 7%
   e. $1\frac{7}{8}$
   f. $\frac{1}{6}$

3. Evaluate:
   a. 25% of 80
   b. 80% of 125
   c. 62.5% of 80
   d. 30% of 120
   e. 90% of 5
   f. 25% of 30

4. Evaluate:
   a. 17% of 50
   b. 50% of 17
   c. 65% of 80
   d. 80% of 65
   e. 7% of 250
   f. 250% of 7

5. In a class of 30 students, 20% travel to school by car, 10% walk and 70% travel by bus. Calculate the numbers of students who travel to school by:
   a. car
   b. walking
   c. bus.

6. A survey conducted among 120 students looked at which type of fruit they preferred. 55% said they preferred apple, 20% said they preferred mango, 15% preferred pineapple and 10% grapes. Calculate the number of children in each category.

7. A survey was carried out in a school to see what nationality its students were. Of the 220 students in the school, 65% were Australian, 20% were Pakistani, 5% were Greek and 10% belonged to other nationalities. Calculate the number of students of each nationality and how many belong to other nationalities.

8. A shopkeeper keeps a record of the numbers of items she sells in one day. Of the 150 items she sold, 46% were newspapers, 24% were pens, 12% were books, while the remaining 18% were other items. Calculate the number of newspapers, pens and books she sold and how many belong to the other items category.

Expressing one quantity as a percentage of another

To express one quantity as a percentage of another, write the first quantity as a fraction of the second and then multiply by 100.

Worked example

In an examination, a girl obtains 69 marks out of 75. Express this result as a percentage.

$\frac{69}{75} \times 100 = 92\%$

5 FURTHER PERCENTAGES

Exercise 5.3

1 For each of the following, express the first quantity as a percentage of the second.
   a 24 out of 50   b 46 out of 125
   c 7 out of 20   d 45 out of 90
   e 9 out of 20   f 16 out of 40
   g 13 out of 39   h 20 out of 35

2 A hockey team plays 42 matches. It wins 21, draws 14 and loses the rest. Express each of these results as a percentage of the total number of games played.

3 Four candidates stood in an election:

   A received 24 500 votes.   B received 18 200 votes.
   C received 16 300 votes.   D received 12 000 votes.

   Express each of these as a percentage of the total votes cast.

4 A car manufacturer produces 155 000 cars a year. The cars are available in six different colours. The numbers sold of each colour were:

   Red   55 000   Silver   10 200
   Blue   48 000   Green   9300
   White   27 500   Black   5000

   Express each of these as a percentage of the total number of cars produced. Give your answers to 1 d.p.

Percentage increases and decreases

> **Worked examples**

1 A doctor has a salary of $18 000 per month. If her salary increases by 8%, calculate:
   a the amount extra she receives per month
      Increase = 8% of $18 000 = 0.08 × $18 000 = $1440
   b her new monthly salary.
      New salary = old salary + increase = $18 000 + $1440 per month
                 = $19 440 per month

2 A garage increases the price of a truck by 12%. If the original price was $14 500, calculate its new price.
   The original price represents 100%, therefore the increase can be represented as 112%.
   New price = 112% of $14 500
             = 1.12 × $14 500
             = $16 240

3 A shop is having a sale. It sells a set of tools costing $130 at a 15% discount. Calculate the sale price of the tools.

   The old price represents 100%, therefore the new price can be represented as (100 − 15)% = 85%.

   $$85\% \text{ of } \$130 = 0.85 \times \$130$$
   $$= \$110.50$$

Percentage increases and decreases

Exercise 5.4

1. Increase the following by the given percentage:
   a 150 by 25%   b 230 by 40%   c 7000 by 2%
   d 70 by 250%   e 80 by 12.5%   f 75 by 62%

2. Decrease the following by the given percentage:
   a 120 by 25%   b 40 by 5%   c 90 by 90%
   d 1000 by 10%   e 80 by 37.5%   f 75 by 42%

3. In the following questions the first number is increased to become the second number. Calculate the percentage increase in each case.
   a 50 → 60   b 75 → 135   c 40 → 84
   d 30 → 31.5   e 18 → 33.3   f 4 → 13

4. In the following questions the first number is decreased to become the second number. Calculate the percentage decrease in each case.
   a 50 → 25   b 80 → 56   c 150 → 142.5
   d 3 → 0   e 550 → 352   f 20 → 19

5. A farmer increases the yield on his farm by 15%. If his previous yield was 6500 tonnes, what is his present yield?

6. The cost of a computer in a computer store is discounted by 12.5% in a sale. If the computer was priced at $7800, what is its price in the sale?

7. A winter coat is priced at $100. In the sale its price is discounted by 25%.
   a Calculate the sale price of the coat.
   b After the sale its price is increased by 25% again. Calculate the coat's price after the sale.

8. A farmer takes 250 chickens to be sold at a market. In the first hour she sells 8% of her chickens. In the second hour she sells 10% of those that were left.
   a How many chickens has she sold in total?
   b What percentage of the original number did she manage to sell in the two hours?

9. The number of fish on a fish farm increases by approximately 10% each month. If there were originally 350 fish, calculate to the nearest 100 how many fish there would be after 12 months.

Student assessment 1

1. Copy the table and fill in the missing values:

Fraction	Decimal	Percentage
$\frac{3}{4}$		
	0.8	
$\frac{5}{8}$		
	1.5	

2. Find 40% of 1600 m.

3. A shop increases the price of a television set by 8%. If the original price was $320, what is the new price?

4. A car loses 55% of its value after four years. If it cost $22 500 when new, what is its value after the four years?

5. Express the first quantity as a percentage of the second.
   a 40 cm, 2 m   b 25 mins, 1 hour
   c 450 g, 2 kg   d 3 m, 3.5 m
   e 70 kg, 1 tonne   f 75 cl, 2.5 litres

5 FURTHER PERCENTAGES

6 A house is bought for $75 000, then resold for $87 000. Calculate the percentage profit.

7 A pair of shoes is priced at $45. During a sale the price is reduced by 20%.
   a Calculate the sale price of the shoes.
   b What is the percentage increase in the price if after the sale it is once again restored to $45?

8 The population of a town increases by 5% each year. If in 2023 the population was 86 000, in which year is the population expected to exceed 100 000 for the first time?

Student assessment 2

1 Copy the table and fill in the missing values:

Fraction	Decimal	Percentage
	0.25	
$\frac{3}{5}$		
		$62\frac{1}{2}\%$
$2\frac{1}{4}$		

2 Find 30% of 2500 m.

3 In a sale, a shop reduces its prices by 12.5%. What is the sale price of a desk previously costing $2400?

4 In the last six years the value of a house has increased by 35%. If it cost $72 000 six years ago, what is its value now?

5 Express the first quantity as a percentage of the second.
   a 35 mins, 2 hours
   b 650 g, 3 kg
   c 5 m, 4 m
   d 15 s, 3 mins
   e 600 kg, 3 tonnes
   f 35 cl, 3.5 litres

6 Shares in a company are bought for $600. After a year, the same shares are sold for $550. Calculate the percentage depreciation.

7 In a sale, the price of a jacket originally costing $850 is reduced by $200. Any item not sold by the last day of the sale is reduced by a further 50%. If the jacket is sold on the last day of the sale:
   a calculate the price it is finally sold for
   b calculate the overall percentage reduction in price.

8 Each day the population of a type of insect increases by approximately 10%. How many days will it take for the population to double?

6 Ratio and proportion

Direct proportion

Workers in a pottery factory are paid according to how many plates they produce. The wage paid to them is said to be in **direct proportion** to the number of plates made. As the number of plates made increases, so does their wage. Other workers are paid for the number of hours worked. For them, the wage paid is in direct proportion to the number of hours worked.

There are two main methods for solving problems involving direct proportion: the **ratio method** and the **unitary method**.

➡ Worked example

A bottling machine fills 500 bottles in 15 minutes. How many bottles will it fill in $1\frac{1}{2}$ hours?

Note: The time units must be the same, so for either method the $1\frac{1}{2}$ hours must be changed to 90 minutes.

The ratio method

Let x be the number of bottles filled. Then:

$$\frac{x}{90} = \frac{500}{15}$$

so $x = \frac{500 \times 90}{15} = 3000$

3000 bottles are filled in $1\frac{1}{2}$ hours.

The unitary method

In 15 minutes, 500 bottles are filled.

Therefore in 1 minute, $\frac{500}{15}$ bottles are filled.

So in 90 minutes, $90 \times \frac{500}{15}$ bottles are filled.

In $1\frac{1}{2}$ hours, 3000 bottles are filled.

6 RATIO AND PROPORTION

Exercise 6.1

Use either the ratio method or the unitary method to solve these problems.

1. A machine prints 4 books in 10 minutes. How many will it print in 2 hours?

2. A gardener plants 5 apple trees in 25 minutes. If he continues to work at a constant rate, how long will it take him to plant 200 trees?

3. A television set uses 3 units of electricity in 2 hours. How many units will it use in 7 hours? Give your answer to the nearest unit.

4. A bricklayer lays 1500 bricks in an 8-hour day. Assuming she continues to work at the same rate, calculate:
   a how many bricks she would expect to lay in a 5-day week
   b how long to the nearest hour it would take her to lay 10 000 bricks.

5. A machine used to paint white lines on a road uses 250 litres of paint for each 8 km of road marked. Calculate:
   a how many litres of paint would be needed for 200 km of road
   b what length of road could be marked with 4000 litres of paint.

6. An aircraft is cruising at 720 km/h and covers 1000 km. How far would it travel in the same period of time if the speed increased to 800 km/h?

7. A production line travelling at 2 m/s labels 150 tins. In the same period of time, how many will it label at:
   a 6 m/s   b 1 m/s   c 1.6 m/s?

Exercise 6.2

Use either the ratio method or the unitary method to solve these problems.

1. A production line produces 8 cars in 3 hours. Calculate:
   a how many it will produce in 48 hours
   b how long it will take to produce 1000 cars.

2. A machine produces 6 golf balls in 15 seconds. Calculate how many are produced in:
   a 5 minutes   b 1 hour   c 1 day.

3. A smartphone uses 0.75 units of electricity in 90 minutes. Calculate:
   a how many units it will use in 8 hours
   b how long it will operate for 15 units of electricity.

4. A combine harvester takes 2 hours to harvest a 3 hectare field. If it works at a constant rate, calculate:
   a how many hectares it will harvest in 15 hours
   b how long it will take to harvest a 54 hectare field.

5. A road-surfacing machine can re-surface 8 m of road in 40 seconds. Calculate how long it will take to re-surface 18 km of road, at the same rate.

6. A sailing yacht is travelling at 1.5 km/h and covers 12 km. If its speed increased to 2.5 km/h, how far would it travel in the same period of time?

7. A plate-making machine produces 36 plates in 8 minutes.
   a How many plates are produced in 1 hour?
   b How long would it take to produce 2880 plates?

If the information is given in the form of a ratio, the method of solution is the same.

Direct proportion

→ Worked example

Tin and copper are mixed in the ratio 8 : 3. How much tin is needed to mix with 36 g of copper?

The ratio method

Let x grams be the mass of tin needed.

$$\frac{x}{36} = \frac{8}{3}$$

Therefore $x = \frac{8 \times 36}{3} = 96$

So 96 g of tin is needed.

The unitary method

3 g of copper mixes with 8 g of tin.

1 g of copper mixes with $\frac{8}{3}$ g of tin.

So 36 g of copper mixes with $36 \times \frac{8}{3}$ g of tin.

Therefore 36 g of copper mixes with 96 g of tin.

Exercise 6.3

1. Sand and gravel are mixed in the ratio 5 : 3 to form ballast.
   a. How much gravel is mixed with 750 kg of sand?
   b. How much sand is mixed with 750 kg of gravel?

2. A recipe uses 150 g butter, 500 g flour, 50 g sugar and 100 g currants to make 18 cakes.
   a. Write the ratio of the amount of butter : flour : sugar : currants in its simplest form.
   b. How much of each ingredient will be needed to make 72 cakes?
   c. How many whole cakes could be made with 1 kg of butter?

3. A paint mix uses red and white paint in a ratio of 1 : 12.
   a. How much white paint will be needed to mix with 1.4 litres of red paint?
   b. If a total of 15.5 litres of paint is mixed, calculate the amount of white paint and the amount of red paint used. Give your answers to the nearest 0.1 litre.

4. A tulip farmer sells sacks of mixed bulbs to local people. The bulbs develop into two different colours of tulips, red and yellow. The colours are packaged in a ratio of 8 : 5 respectively.
   a. If a sack contains 200 red bulbs, calculate the number of yellow bulbs.
   b. If a sack contains 351 bulbs in total, how many of each colour would you expect to find?
   c. One sack is packaged with a bulb mixture in the ratio of 7 : 5 by mistake. If the sack contains 624 bulbs, how many more yellow bulbs would you expect to have compared with a normal sack of 624 bulbs?

5. A pure fruit juice is made by mixing the juices of oranges and mangoes in the ratio of 9 : 2.
   a. If 189 litres of orange juice are used, calculate the number of litres of mango juice needed.
   b. If 605 litres of the juice are made, calculate the number of litres of orange juice and mango juice used.

6 RATIO AND PROPORTION

Divide a quantity in a given ratio

Worked examples

1. Divide 20 m in the ratio 3 : 2.

   #### The ratio method
   3 : 2 gives 5 parts.
   $\frac{3}{5} \times 20\,\text{m} = 12\,\text{m}$
   $\frac{2}{5} \times 20\,\text{m} = 8\,\text{m}$
   20 m divided in the ratio 3 : 2 is 12 m : 8 m.

   #### The unitary method
   3 : 2 gives 5 parts.
   5 parts is equivalent to 20 m.
   1 part is equivalent to $\frac{20}{5}$ m.
   Therefore 3 parts is $3 \times \frac{20}{5}$ m; i.e. 12 m.
   Therefore 2 parts is $2 \times \frac{20}{5}$ m; i.e. 8 m.

2. A factory produces cars in red, blue, white and green in the ratio 7 : 5 : 3 : 1. Out of a production of 48 000 cars, how many are white?
   7 + 5 + 3 + 1 gives a total of 16 parts.
   Therefore the total number of white cars is
   $\frac{3}{16} \times 48\,000 = 9000$.

Exercise 6.4

1. Divide 150 in the ratio 2 : 3.
2. Divide 72 in the ratio 2 : 3 : 4.
3. Divide 5 kg in the ratio 13 : 7.
4. Divide 45 minutes in the ratio 2 : 3.
5. Divide 1 hour in the ratio 1 : 5.
6. $\frac{7}{8}$ of a can of drink is water, the rest is syrup. What is the ratio of water to syrup?
7. $\frac{5}{9}$ of a litre carton of orange is pure orange juice, the rest is water. How many millilitres of each are in the carton?
8. 55% of students in a school are boys.
   a. What is the ratio of boys to girls?
   b. How many boys and how many girls are there if the school has 800 students?
9. A piece of wood is cut in the ratio 2 : 3. What fraction of the length is the longer piece?
10. If the original piece of wood in Q.9 is 80 cm long, how long is the shorter piece?

Inverse proportion

11 A gas pipe is 7 km long. A valve is positioned in such a way that it divides the length of the pipe in the ratio 4 : 3. Calculate the distance of the valve from each end of the pipe.

12 The sizes of the angles of a quadrilateral are in the ratio 1 : 2 : 3 : 3. Calculate the size of each angle.

13 The angles of a triangle are in the ratio 3 : 5 : 4. Calculate the size of each angle.

14 A millionaire leaves 1.4 million dollars in her will to be shared between her three children in the ratio of their ages. If they are 24, 28 and 32 years old, calculate to the nearest dollar the amount they will each receive.

15 A small company makes a profit of $8000. This is divided between the directors in the ratio of their initial investments. If Alex put $20 000 into the firm, Maria $35 000 and Ahmet $25 000, calculate the amount of the profit they will each receive.

> **Note**
> A calculator can be used for questions 14 and 15.

Inverse proportion

Sometimes an increase in one quantity causes a decrease in another quantity. For example, if fruit is to be picked by hand, the more people there are picking the fruit, the less time it will take. The time taken is said to be **inversely proportional** to the number of people picking the fruit.

Worked examples

1 If 8 people can pick the apples from the trees in 6 days, how long will it take 12 people?

8 people take 6 days.

1 person will take 6 × 8 days.

Therefore 12 people will take $\frac{6 \times 8}{12}$ days, i.e. 4 days.

2 A cyclist averages a speed of 27 km/h for 4 hours. At what average speed would she need to cycle to cover the same distance in 3 hours?

Completing it in 1 hour would require cycling at 27 × 4 km/h.

Completing it in 3 hours requires cycling at $\frac{27 \times 4}{3}$ km/h; i.e. 36 km/h.

Exercise 6.5

1 A teacher shares sweets among 8 students so that they get 6 each. How many sweets would they each have got if there had been 12 students?

2 The table represents the relationship between the speed and the time taken for a train to travel between two stations.

Speed (km/h)	60			120	90	50	10
Time (h)		2	3	4			

Copy and complete the table.

6 RATIO AND PROPORTION

Exercise 6.5 (cont)

3 Six people can dig a trench in 8 hours.
   a How long would it take:
      i 4 people   ii 12 people   iii 1 person?
   b How many people would it take to dig the trench in:
      i 3 hours   ii 16 hours   iii 1 hour?

4 Chairs in a hall are arranged in 35 rows of 18.
   a How many rows would there be with 21 chairs to a row?
   b How many chairs would each row have if there were 15 rows?

5 A train travelling at 100 km/h takes 4 hours for a journey. How long would it take a train travelling at 60 km/h?

6 A worker in a sugar factory packs 24 cardboard boxes with 15 bags of sugar in each. If he had boxes which held 18 bags of sugar each, how many fewer boxes would be needed?

7 A swimming pool is filled in 30 hours by 2 identical pumps. How much quicker would it be filled if 5 similar pumps were used instead?

Compound measures

A **compound measure** is one made up of two or more other measures. The most common ones are speed, density and population density.
Speed is a compound measure as it is measured using distance and time.

$$\text{Speed} = \frac{\text{distance}}{\text{time}}$$

Units of speed include metres per second (m/s) or kilometres per hour (km/h).

The relationship between speed, distance and time is often presented as:

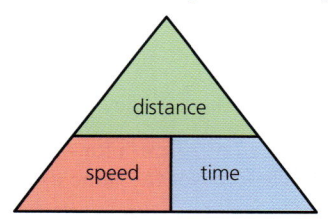

$$\text{Speed} = \frac{\text{distance}}{\text{time}}$$

$$\text{Distance} = \text{speed} \times \text{time}$$

$$\text{Time} = \frac{\text{distance}}{\text{speed}}$$

Similarly, **average speed** $= \frac{\text{total distance}}{\text{total time}}$

Density, which is a measure of the mass of a substance per unit of its volume, is calculated using the formula:

$$\text{Density} = \frac{\text{mass}}{\text{volume}}$$

Units of density include kilograms per cubic metre (kg/m^3) or grams per millilitre (g/ml).

Compound measures

The relationship between density, mass and volume, like speed, can also be presented in a helpful diagram as shown:

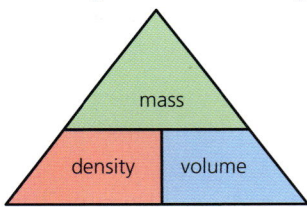

$$\text{Density} = \frac{\text{mass}}{\text{volume}}$$

$$\text{Mass} = \text{density} \times \text{volume}$$

$$\text{Volume} = \frac{\text{mass}}{\text{density}}$$

Population density is also a compound measure as it is a measure of a population per unit of area.

$$\text{Population density} = \frac{\text{population}}{\text{area}}$$

An example of its units is the number of people per square kilometre (people/km^2). Again, the relationship between population density, population and area can be represented in a triangular diagram:

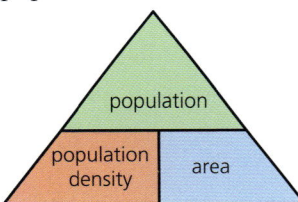

$$\text{Population density} = \frac{\text{population}}{\text{area}}$$

$$\text{Population} = \text{population density} \times \text{area}$$

$$\text{Area} = \frac{\text{population}}{\text{population density}}$$

➡ Worked examples

1. A train travels a total distance of 140 km in $1\frac{1}{2}$ hours.

   a. Calculate the average speed of the train during the journey.

   $$\text{Average speed} = \frac{\text{total distance}}{\text{total time}}$$
   $$= \frac{140}{1\frac{1}{2}}$$
   $$= 93\frac{1}{3} \text{ km/h}$$

   b. During the journey, the train spent 15 minutes stopped at stations. Calculate the average speed of the train while it was moving.

   Notice that the original time was given in hours, while the time spent stopped at stations was given in minutes. To proceed with the calculation, the units have to be consistent, i.e. either both in hours or both in minutes.

   The time spent travelling is $1\frac{1}{2} - \frac{1}{4} = 1\frac{1}{4}$ hours

   Therefore average speed $= \frac{140}{1\frac{1}{4}}$

   $= 112 \text{ km/h}$

6 RATIO AND PROPORTION

    c If the average speed was 120 km/h, calculate how long the journey took.

$$\text{Total time} = \frac{\text{total distance}}{\text{average speed}}$$
$$= \frac{140}{120} = 1.1\dot{6} \text{ hours}$$

Note: It may be necessary to convert a decimal answer to hours and minutes. To convert a decimal time to minutes, multiply by 60.

$$0.1\dot{6} \times 60 = 10$$

Therefore total time is 1 hr 10 mins or 70 mins.

2 A village has a population of 540. Its total area is 8 km².
    a Calculate the population density of the village.

$$\text{Population density} = \frac{\text{population}}{\text{area}}$$
$$= \frac{540}{8} = 67.5 \text{ people/km}^2$$

    b A building company wants to build some new houses in the existing area of the village. It is decided that the maximum population density of the village should not be greater than 110 people/km². Calculate the extra number of people the village can have.

Population = population density × area
$$= 110 \times 8$$
$$= 880 \text{ people}$$

Therefore the maximum number of extra people that will need housing is 880 − 540 = 340.

Exercise 6.6

1 Aluminium has a density of 2900 kg/m³. A construction company needs 4 cubic metres of aluminium. Calculate the mass of the aluminium needed.

2 A marathon race is 42 195 m in length. The world record in 2022 was 2 hours, 1 minute and 39 seconds held by Eliud Kipchoge of Kenya.
    a How many seconds in total did Eliud take to complete the race?
    b Calculate his average speed in m/s for the race, giving your answer to 2 decimal places.
    c What average speed would the runner need to maintain to complete the marathon in under 2 hours?

3 The approximate densities of four metals in g/cm³ are given below:

Aluminium	2.9 g/cm³	Copper	9.3 g/cm³
Brass	8.8 g/cm³	Steel	8.2 g/cm³

A cube of an unknown metal has side lengths of 5 cm. The mass of the cube is 1.1 kg.
    a By calculating the cube's density, work out which metal the cube is likely to be made from.
    b Another cube made of steel has a mass of 4.0 kg. Calculate the length of each of the sides of the steel cube, giving your answer to 3 s.f.

Compound measures

4   Singapore is the country with the highest population density in the world. Its population is 5 954 000 and it has a total area of 719 km².
    a   Calculate Singapore's population density.
    China is the country with the largest population.
    b   Explain why China has not got the world's highest population density.
    c   Find the area and population of your own country. Calculate your country's population density.

5   Kwabena has a rectangular field measuring 600 m × 800 m. He uses the field for grazing his sheep.
    a   Calculate the area of the field in km².
    b   40 sheep graze in the field. Calculate the population density of sheep in the field, giving your answer in sheep/km².
    c   Guidelines for keeping sheep state that the maximum population density for grazing sheep is 180/km². Calculate the number of sheep Kwabena is allowed to graze in his field.

6   The formula linking pressure (P N/m²), force (F N) and surface area (A m²) is given as $P = \frac{F}{A}$. A square-based box exerts a force of 160 N on a floor. If the pressure on the floor is 1000 N/m², calculate the length, in cm, of each side of the base of the box.

Student assessment 1

1   A boat travels at an average speed of 15 km/h for 1 hour.
    a   Calculate the distance it travels in one hour.
    b   At what average speed will the boat have to travel to cover the same distance in $2\frac{1}{2}$ hours?

2   A piece of wood is cut in the ratio 12 : 28.
    a   Write the ratio in its simplest form.
    b   What fraction of the whole is the longer piece?
    c   If the wood is 1.5 m long, how long is the shorter piece?

3   A recipe for two people requires $\frac{1}{4}$ kg of rice to 150 g of meat.
    a   How much meat would be needed for five people?
    b   How much rice would there be in 1 kg of the final dish?

4   The scale of a map is 1 : 10 000.
    a   Two rivers are 4.5 cm apart on the map. How far apart are they in real life? Give your answer in metres.
    b   Two towns are 8 km apart in real life. How far apart are they on the map? Give your answer in centimetres.

5   A model train is a $\frac{1}{25}$ scale model.
    a   Express this as a ratio.
    b   If the length of the model engine is 7 cm, what is its true length?

6 RATIO AND PROPORTION

The angles of a quadrilateral add up to 360°.

The interior angles of a pentagon add up to 540°.

6 Divide 3 tonnes in the ratio 2 : 5 : 13.

7 The ratio of the angles of a quadrilateral is 2 : 3 : 3 : 4. Calculate the size of each of the angles.

8 The ratio of the interior angles of a pentagon is 2 : 3 : 4 : 4 : 5. Calculate the size of the largest angle.

9 A large swimming pool takes 36 hours to fill using 3 identical pumps.
   a How long would it take to fill using 8 identical pumps?
   b If the pool needs to be filled in 9 hours, how many of these pumps will be needed?

10 The first triangle is an enlargement of the second. Calculate the size of the missing sides and angles.

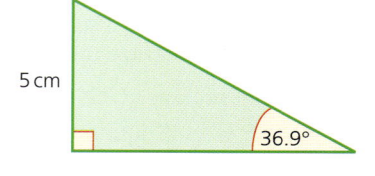

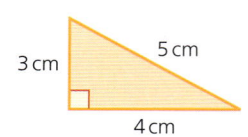

5 cm, 36.9°

3 cm, 5 cm, 4 cm

11 A boat travels at an average speed of 15 km/h for 1 hour.
   a Calculate the distance it travels in one hour.
   b At what average speed will the boat have to travel to cover the same distance in $2\frac{1}{2}$ hours?

12 A tap issuing water at a rate of 1.2 litres per minute fills a container in 4 minutes.
   a How long would it take to fill the same container if the rate was decreased to 1 litre per minute? Give your answer in minutes and seconds.
   b If the container is to be filled in 3 minutes, calculate the rate at which the water should flow.

13 The population density of a small village increases over time from 18 people/km^2 to 26.5 people/km^2. If the area of the village remains unchanged at 14 km^2 during that time, calculate the increase in the number of people in the village.

14 A small car's petrol tank can hold 22 litres of petrol. It can travel on average 530 km on a full tank. A large car's petrol tank can hold 47 litres of petrol. It can travel on average 972 km on a full tank.
   a On average how many kilometres can the small car travel on 1 litre of petrol?
   b Which car has the most efficient fuel consumption? Show your working.

7 Indices and standard form

Indices

The index refers to the **power** to which a number is raised. In the example 5^3, the number 5 is raised to the power 3. The 3 is known as the **index**.

Indices is the plural of index.

Worked examples

1. $5^3 = 5 \times 5 \times 5 = 125$
2. $7^4 = 7 \times 7 \times 7 \times 7 = 2401$
3. $3^1 = 3$

Exercise 7.1

1. Using indices, simplify these expressions:
   a. $3 \times 3 \times 3$
   b. $2 \times 2 \times 2 \times 2 \times 2$
   c. 4×4
   d. $6 \times 6 \times 6 \times 6$
   e. $8 \times 8 \times 8 \times 8 \times 8 \times 8$
   f. 5

2. Simplify the following using indices:
   a. $2 \times 2 \times 2 \times 3 \times 3$
   b. $4 \times 4 \times 4 \times 4 \times 4 \times 5 \times 5$
   c. $3 \times 3 \times 4 \times 4 \times 4 \times 5 \times 5$
   d. $2 \times 7 \times 7 \times 7 \times 7$
   e. $1 \times 1 \times 6 \times 6$
   f. $3 \times 3 \times 3 \times 4 \times 4 \times 6 \times 6 \times 6 \times 6 \times 6$

3. Write out the following in full:
   a. 4^2
   b. 5^7
   c. 3^5
   d. $4^3 \times 6^3$
   e. $7^2 \times 2^7$
   f. $3^2 \times 4^3 \times 2^4$

4. Without a calculator work out the value of:
   a. 2^5
   b. 3^4
   c. 8^2
   d. 6^3
   e. 10^6
   f. 4^4
   g. $2^3 \times 3^2$
   h. $10^3 \times 5^3$

Laws of indices

When working with numbers involving indices there are three basic laws which can be applied. These are:

1. $a^m \times a^n = a^{m+n}$ e.g. $2^3 \times 2^4 = 2^{3+4} = 2^7$
2. $a^m \div a^n = a^{m-n}$ e.g. $5^6 \div 5^4 = 5^{6-4} = 5^2$
3. $(a^m)^n = a^{mn}$ e.g. $(4^5)^3 = 4^{5 \times 3} = 4^{15}$

7 INDICES AND STANDARD FORM

Positive indices

Worked examples

1. Simplify $4^3 \times 4^2$.

   $4^3 \times 4^2 = 4^{(3+2)}$

   $= 4^5$

2. Simplify $2^5 \div 2^3$.

   $2^5 \div 2^3 = 2^{(5-3)}$

   $= 2^2$

3. Evaluate $3^3 \times 3^4$.

   $3^3 \times 3^4 = 3^{(3+4)}$

   $= 3^7$

   $= 2187$

4. Evaluate $(4^2)^3$.

   $(4^2)^3 = 4^{(2 \times 3)}$

   $= 4^6$

   $= 4096$

Exercise 7.2

1. Simplify the following using indices:
   - a $3^2 \times 3^4$
   - b $8^5 \times 8^2$
   - c $5^2 \times 5^4 \times 5^3$
   - d $4^3 \times 4^5 \times 4^2$
   - e $2^1 \times 2^3$
   - f $6^2 \times 3^2 \times 3^3 \times 6^4$
   - g $4^5 \times 4^3 \times 5^5 \times 5^4 \times 6^2$
   - h $2^4 \times 5^7 \times 5^3 \times 6^2 \times 6^6$

2. Simplify:
   - a $4^6 \div 4^2$
   - b $5^7 \div 5^4$
   - c $2^5 \div 2^4$
   - d $6^5 \div 6^2$
   - e $\frac{6^5}{6^2}$
   - f $\frac{8^6}{8^5}$
   - g $\frac{4^8}{4^5}$
   - h $\frac{3^9}{3^2}$

3. Simplify:
   - a $(5^2)^2$
   - b $(4^3)^4$
   - c $(10^2)^5$
   - d $(3^3)^5$
   - e $(6^2)^4$
   - f $(8^2)^3$

4. Simplify:
   - a $\frac{2^2 \times 2^4}{2^3}$
   - b $\frac{3^4 \times 3^2}{3^5}$
   - c $\frac{5^6 \times 5^7}{5^2 \times 5^8}$
   - d $\frac{(4^2)^5 \times 4^2}{4^7}$
   - e $\frac{4^4 \times 2^5 \times 4^2}{4^3 \times 2^3}$
   - f $\frac{6^3 \times 6^3 \times 8^5 \times 8^6}{8^6 \times 6^2}$
   - g $\frac{(5^2)^2 \times (4^4)^3}{5^8 \times 4^9}$
   - h $\frac{(6^3)^4 \times 6^3 \times 4^9}{6^8 \times (4^2)^4}$

The zero index

The zero index indicates that a number is raised to the power 0.
A number raised to the power 0 is equal to 1. This can be explained by applying the laws of indices.

$$a^m \div a^n = a^{m-n} \text{ therefore } \frac{a^m}{a^m} = a^{m-m}$$

$$= a^0$$

However, $\frac{a^m}{a^m} = 1$

therefore $a^0 = 1$

Exercise 7.3 Without using a calculator, evaluate:
a $2^3 \times 2^0$
b $5^2 \div 6^0$
c $5^2 \times 5^{-2}$
d $6^3 \times 6^{-3}$
e $(4^0)^2$
f $4^0 \div 2^2$

Negative indices

A negative index indicates that a number is being raised to a negative power, e.g. 4^{-3}.

Another law of indices states that $a^{-m} = \frac{1}{a^m}$. This can be proved as follows:

$a^{-m} = a^{0-m}$

$= \frac{a^0}{a^m}$ (from the second law of indices)

$= \frac{1}{a^m}$

therefore $a^{-m} = \frac{1}{a^m}$

Exercise 7.4 Without using a calculator, evaluate:

1 a 4^{-1}
   b 3^{-2}
   c 6×10^{-2}
   d 5×10^{-3}
   e 100×10^{-2}
   f 10^{-3}

2 a 9×3^{-2}
   b 16×2^{-3}
   c 64×2^{-4}
   d 4×2^{-3}
   e 36×6^{-3}
   f 100×10^{-1}

3 a $\frac{3}{2^{-2}}$
   b $\frac{4}{2^{-3}}$
   c $\frac{9}{5^{-2}}$
   d $\frac{5}{4^{-2}}$
   e $\frac{7^{-3}}{7^{-4}}$
   f $\frac{8^{-6}}{8^{-8}}$

Standard form

Standard form is also known as standard index form or sometimes as scientific notation. It involves writing large numbers or very small numbers in terms of powers of 10.

Positive indices and large numbers

$100 = 1 \times 10^2$

$1000 = 1 \times 10^3$

$10\,000 = 1 \times 10^4$

$3000 = 3 \times 10^3$

7 INDICES AND STANDARD FORM

For a number to be in standard form it must take the form $A \times 10^n$ where the index n is a positive or negative integer and A must lie in the range $1 \leqslant A < 10$.

e.g. 3100 can be written in many different ways:

$3.1 \times 10^3 \quad 31 \times 10^2 \quad 0.31 \times 10^4$ etc.

However, only 3.1×10^3 satisfies the above conditions and therefore is the only one which is written in standard form.

→ Worked examples

1 Write 72 000 in standard form.

   7.2×10^4

2 Write 4×10^4 as an ordinary number.

   $4 \times 10^4 = 4 \times 10000$
   $= 40000$

3 Multiply 600×4000 and write your answer in standard form.

   600×4000
   $= 2400000$
   $= 2.4 \times 10^6$

Note

Your scientific calculator will have a button for standard form. Make sure you know where it is and how to use it correctly.

Exercise 7.5

1 Work out the value of n in the following:
   a $79000 = 7.9 \times 10^n$
   b $53000 = 5.3 \times 10^n$
   c $4160000 = 4.16 \times 10^n$
   d 8 million $= 8 \times 10^n$
   e 247 million $= 2.47 \times 10^n$
   f $24000000 = 2.4 \times 10^n$

2 Write the following numbers in standard form:
   a 65 000
   b 41 000
   c 723 000
   d 18 million
   e 950 000
   f 760 million
   g 720 000
   h $\frac{1}{4}$ million

3 Write the numbers below which are written in standard form:
   a 26.3×10^5
   b 2.6×10^7
   c 0.5×10^3
   d 8×10^8
   e 0.85×10^9
   f 8.3×10^{10}
   g 1.8×10^7
   h 18×10^5
   i 3.6×10^6
   j 6.0×10^1

4 Write the following as ordinary numbers:
   a 3.8×10^3
   b 4.25×10^6
   c 9.003×10^7
   d 1.01×10^5

5 Multiply the following and write your answers in standard form:
   a 400×2000
   b 6000×5000
   c 75000×200
   d 33000×6000
   e 8 million $\times 250$
   f 95000×3000
   g 7.5 million $\times 2$
   h 8.2 million $\times 50$
   i $300 \times 200 \times 400$
   j $(7000)^2$

6 Which of the following are not in standard form?
   a 6.2×10^5
   b 7.834×10^{16}
   c 8.0×10^5
   d 0.46×10^7
   e 82.3×10^6
   f 6.75×10^1

Multiplying and dividing numbers in standard form

7 Write the following numbers in standard form:
   a 600 000   b 48 000 000   c 784 000 000 000
   d 534 000   e 7 million   f 8.5 million

8 Write the following in standard form:
   a 68×10^5 b 720×10^6 c 8×10^5
   d 0.75×10^8 e 0.4×10^{10} f 50×10^6

9 Multiply the following and write your answers in standard form:
   a 200×3000 b 6000×4000
   c 7 million $\times$ 20   d $500 \times$ 6 million
   e 3 million $\times$ 4 million   f 4500×4000

10 Light from the Sun takes approximately 8 minutes to reach Earth. If light travels at a speed of 3×10^8 m/s, calculate to three significant figures (s.f.) the distance from the Sun to the Earth.

Multiplying and dividing numbers in standard form

When you multiply or divide numbers in standard form, you work with the numbers and the powers of 10 separately. You use the laws of indices when working with the powers of 10.

Worked examples

1 Multiply the following and write your answer in standard form:

$(2.4 \times 10^4) \times (5 \times 10^7)$

$= 12 \times 10^{11}$

$= 1.2 \times 10^{12}$ when written in standard form.

2 Divide the following and write your answer in standard form:

$(6.4 \times 10^7) \div (1.6 \times 10^3)$

$= 4 \times 10^4$

Exercise 7.6

1 Multiply the following and write your answers in standard form:
   a $(4 \times 10^3) \times (2 \times 10^5)$ b $(2.5 \times 10^4) \times (3 \times 10^4)$
   c $(1.8 \times 10^7) \times (5 \times 10^6)$ d $(2.1 \times 10^4) \times (4 \times 10^7)$
   e $(3.5 \times 10^4) \times (4 \times 10^7)$ f $(4.2 \times 10^5) \times (3 \times 10^4)$
   g $(2 \times 10^4)^2$ h $(4 \times 10^8)^2$

2 Find the value of the following and write your answers in standard form:
   a $(8 \times 10^6) \div (2 \times 10^3)$ b $(8.8 \times 10^9) \div (2.2 \times 10^3)$
   c $(7.6 \times 10^8) \div (4 \times 10^7)$ d $(6.5 \times 10^{14}) \div (1.3 \times 10^7)$
   e $(5.2 \times 10^6) \div (1.3 \times 10^6)$ f $(3.8 \times 10^{11}) \div (1.9 \times 10^3)$

3 Find the value of the following and write your answers in standard form:
   a $(3 \times 10^4) \times (6 \times 10^5) \div (9 \times 10^5)$ b $(6.5 \times 10^8) \div (1.3 \times 10^4) \times (5 \times 10^3)$
   c $(18 \times 10^3) \div 900 \times 250$ d $27\,000 \div 3000 \times 8000$
   e $4000 \times 8000 \div 640$ f $2500 \times 2500 \div 1250$

65

7 INDICES AND STANDARD FORM

Exercise 7.6 (cont)

4 Find the value of the following and write your answers in standard form:
   a $(4.4 \times 10^3) \times (2 \times 10^5)$
   b $(6.8 \times 10^7) \times (3 \times 10^3)$
   c $(4 \times 10^5) \times (8.3 \times 10^5)$
   d $(5 \times 10^9) \times (8.4 \times 10^{12})$
   e $(8.5 \times 10^6) \times (6 \times 10^{15})$
   f $(5.0 \times 10^{12})^2$

5 Find the value of the following and write your answers in standard form:
   a $(3.8 \times 10^8) \div (1.9 \times 10^6)$
   b $(6.75 \times 10^9) \div (2.25 \times 10^4)$
   c $(9.6 \times 10^{11}) \div (2.4 \times 10^5)$
   d $(1.8 \times 10^{12}) \div (9.0 \times 10^7)$
   e $(2.3 \times 10^{11}) \div (9.2 \times 10^4)$
   f $(2.4 \times 10^8) \div (6.0 \times 10^3)$

Adding and subtracting numbers in standard form

You can only add and subtract numbers in standard form if the indices are the same. If the indices are different, you can change one of the numbers so that it has the same index as the other. It will not then be in standard form and you may need to change your answer back to standard form after doing the calculation.

➡ Worked examples

1 Add the following and write your answer in standard form:

   $(3.8 \times 10^6) + (8.7 \times 10^4)$

   Changing the indices to the same value gives the sum:

   $(380 \times 10^4) + (8.7 \times 10^4)$

   $= 388.7 \times 10^4$

   $= 3.887 \times 10^6$ when written in standard form.

2 Subtract the following and write your answer in standard form:

   $(6.5 \times 10^7) - (9.2 \times 10^5)$

   Changing the indices to the same value gives the sum:

   $(650 \times 10^5) - (9.2 \times 10^5)$

   $= 640.8 \times 10^5$

   $= 6.408 \times 10^7$ when written in standard form.

Exercise 7.7

Find the value of the following and write your answers in standard form:
a $(3.8 \times 10^5) + (4.6 \times 10^4)$
b $(7.9 \times 10^7) + (5.8 \times 10^8)$
c $(6.3 \times 10^7) + (8.8 \times 10^5)$
d $(3.15 \times 10^9) + (7.0 \times 10^6)$
e $(5.3 \times 10^8) - (8.0 \times 10^7)$
f $(6.5 \times 10^7) - (4.9 \times 10^6)$
g $(8.93 \times 10^{10}) - (7.8 \times 10^9)$
h $(4.07 \times 10^7) - (5.1 \times 10^6)$

Negative indices and small numbers

A negative index is used when writing a number between 0 and 1 in standard form.

e.g.
$100 = 1 \times 10^2$
$10 = 1 \times 10^1$
$1 = 1 \times 10^0$
$0.1 = 1 \times 10^{-1}$
$0.01 = 1 \times 10^{-2}$
$0.001 = 1 \times 10^{-3}$
$0.0001 = 1 \times 10^{-4}$

Note that A must still lie within the range $1 \leq A < 10$.

Worked examples

1 Write 0.0032 in standard form.

3.2×10^{-3}

2 Write 1.8×10^{-4} as an ordinary number.

$1.8 \times 10^{-4} = 1.8 \div 10^4$
$= 1.8 \div 10\,000$
$= 0.00018$

3 Write the following numbers in order of magnitude, starting with the largest:

3.6×10^{-3} 5.2×10^{-5} 1×10^{-2} 8.35×10^{-2} 6.08×10^{-8}

8.35×10^{-2} 1×10^{-2} 3.6×10^{-3} 5.2×10^{-5} 6.08×10^{-8}

Exercise 7.8

1 Copy and complete the following so that the answers are correct (the first question is done for you):
  a $0.0048 = 4.8 \times 10^{-3}$
  b $0.0079 = 7.9 \times ...$
  c $0.00081 = 8.1 \times ...$
  d $0.000009 = 9 \times ...$
  e $0.00000045 = 4.5 \times ...$
  f $0.00000000324 = 3.24 \times ...$
  g $0.00000842 = 8.42 \times ...$
  h $0.000000000403 = 4.03 \times ...$

2 Write these numbers in standard form:
  a 0.0006
  b 0.000053
  c 0.000864
  d 0.000000088
  e 0.0000007
  f 0.0004145

3 Write the following as ordinary numbers:
  a 8×10^{-3}
  b 4.2×10^{-4}
  c 9.03×10^{-2}
  d 1.01×10^{-5}

4 Write the following numbers in standard form:
  a 68×10^{-5}
  b 750×10^{-9}
  c 42×10^{-11}
  d 0.08×10^{-7}
  e 0.057×10^{-9}
  f 0.4×10^{-10}

7 INDICES AND STANDARD FORM

Exercise 7.8 (cont)

5 Deduce the value of n in each of the following:
   a $0.00025 = 2.5 \times 10^n$ **b** $0.00357 = 3.57 \times 10^n$
   c $0.00000006 = 6 \times 10^n$ **d** $0.004^2 = 1.6 \times 10^n$
   e $0.00065^2 = 4.225 \times 10^n$ **f** $0.0002^n = 8 \times 10^{-12}$

6 Write these numbers in order of magnitude, starting with the largest:
   3.2×10^{-4} 6.8×10^5 5.57×10^{-9} 6.2×10^3
   5.8×10^{-7} 6.741×10^{-4} 8.414×10^2

Student assessment 1

1 Simplify the following using indices:
   a $2 \times 2 \times 2 \times 5 \times 5$ **b** $2 \times 2 \times 3 \times 3 \times 3 \times 3 \times 3$

2 Write out in full:
   a 4^3 **b** 6^4

3 Work out the value of the following without using a calculator:
   a $2^3 \times 10^2$ **b** $1^4 \times 3^3$

4 Simplify the following using indices:
   a $3^4 \times 3^3$ **b** $6^3 \times 6^2 \times 3^4 \times 3^5$
   c $\dfrac{4^5}{2^3}$ **d** $\dfrac{(6^2)^3}{6^5}$
   e $\dfrac{3^5 \times 4^2}{3^3 \times 4^0}$ **f** $\dfrac{4^{-2} \times 2^6}{2^2}$

5 Without using a calculator, evaluate:
   a $2^4 \times 2^{-2}$ **b** $\dfrac{3^5}{3^3}$
   c $\dfrac{5^{-5}}{5^{-6}}$ **d** $\dfrac{2^5 \times 4^{-3}}{2^{-1}}$

Student assessment 2

1 Simplify the following using indices:
   a $3 \times 2 \times 2 \times 3 \times 27$ **b** $2 \times 2 \times 4 \times 4 \times 4 \times 2 \times 32$

2 Write out in full:
   a 6^5 **b** 2^{-5}

3 Work out the value of the following without using a calculator:
   a $3^3 \times 10^3$ **b** $1^{-4} \times 5^3$

4 Simplify the following using indices:
   a $2^4 \times 2^3$ **b** $7^5 \times 7^2 \times 3^4 \times 3^8$ **c** $\dfrac{4^8}{2^{10}}$
   d $\dfrac{(3^3)^4}{27^3}$ **e** $\dfrac{7^6 \times 4^2}{4^3 \times 7^6}$ **f** $\dfrac{8^{-2} \times 2^6}{2^{-2}}$

5 Without using a calculator, evaluate:
   a $5^2 \times 5^{-1}$ **b** $\dfrac{4^5}{4^3}$ **c** $\dfrac{7^{-5}}{7^{-7}}$ **d** $\dfrac{3^{-5} \times 4^2}{3^{-6}}$

Student assessment 3

1. Write the following numbers in standard form:
   a. 6 million
   b. 0.0045
   c. 3 800 000 000
   d. 0.000 000 361
   e. 460 million
   f. 3

2. Write the following as ordinary numbers:
   a. 8.112×10^6
   b. 3.05×10^{-4}

3. Write the following numbers in order of magnitude, starting with the largest:
   3.6×10^2 2.1×10^{-3} 9×10^1 4.05×10^8 1.5×10^{-2} 7.2×10^{-3}

4. Write the following numbers:
   a. in standard form
   b. in order of magnitude, starting with the smallest.

   15 million   430 000   0.000 435   4.8   0.0085

5. Work out the value of n in each of the following:
   a. $4750 = 4.75 \times 10^n$
   b. $6 440 000 000 = 6.44 \times 10^n$
   c. $0.0040 = 4.0 \times 10^n$
   d. $1000^2 = 1 \times 10^n$
   e. $0.9^3 = 7.29 \times 10^n$
   f. $800^3 = 5.12 \times 10^n$

6. Write the answers to the following calculations in standard form:
   a. $50 000 \times 2400$
   b. $(3.7 \times 10^6) \times (4.0 \times 10^4)$
   c. $(5.8 \times 10^7) + (9.3 \times 10^6)$
   d. $(4.7 \times 10^6) - (8.2 \times 10^5)$

7. The speed of light is 3×10^8 m/s. Jupiter is 778 million km from the Sun. Calculate the number of minutes it takes for sunlight to reach Jupiter.

8. A star is 300 light years away from Earth. The speed of light is 3×10^5 km/s. Calculate the distance from the star to Earth. Give your answer in kilometres and written in standard form.

8 Money and finance

Currency conversion

In 2022, 1 euro could be exchanged for 1.50 Australian dollars (A$).

The **conversion graph** from euros to dollars and from dollars to euros is:

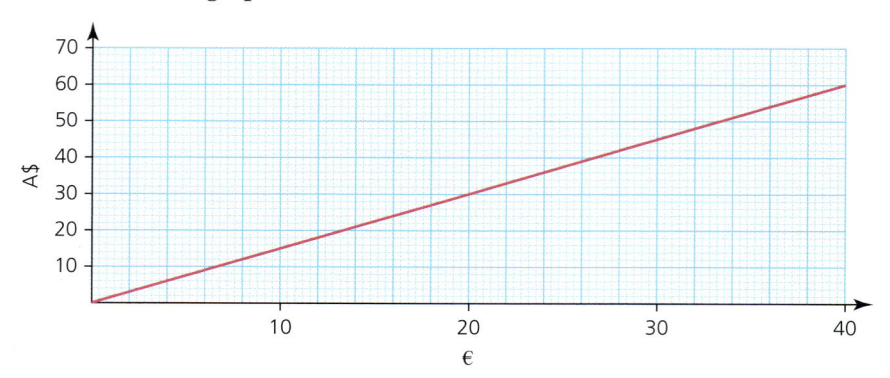

Exercise 8.1

1 Use the conversion graph to convert the following to Australian dollars:
   a €20
   b €30
   c €5
   d €25
   e €35
   f €15

2 Use the conversion graph to convert the following to euros:
   a A$20
   b A$30
   c A$40
   d A$35
   e A$25
   f A$48

3 1 euro can be exchanged for 75 Indian rupees. Draw a conversion graph. Use an appropriate scale with the horizontal scale up to €100. Use your graph to convert the following to rupees:
   a €10
   b €40
   c €50
   d €90
   e €25
   f €1000

4 Use your graph from Q.3 to convert the following to euros:
   a 140 rupees
   b 770 rupees
   c 630 rupees
   d 490 rupees
   e 5600 rupees
   f 2730 rupees

The table shows the exchange rate for €1 into various currencies. If necessary, draw conversion graphs for the exchange rates shown to answer Q.5–9.

Zimbabwe	412.8 Zimbabwe dollars
South Africa	15 rand
Turkey	4.0 Turkish lira
Japan	130 yen
Kuwait	0.35 dinar
United States of America	1.15 dollars

Personal and household finance

5 How many Zimbabwe dollars would you receive for the following?
  a €20   b €50   c €75
  d €30   e €25

6 How many euros would you receive for the following numbers of South African rand?
  a 225 rand   b 420 rand
  c 1132.50 rand   d 105 rand

7 In the Grand Bazaar in Istanbul, a visitor sees three carpets priced at 1200 Turkish lira, 400 Turkish lira and 880 Turkish lira. Draw and use a conversion graph to find the prices in euros.

8 €1 can be exchanged for US$1.15.
€1 can also be exchanged for 130 yen.
Draw a conversion graph for US dollars to Japanese yen, and answer the questions below.
  a How many yen would you receive for:
    i $300   ii $750   iii $1000?
  b How many US dollars would you receive for:
    i 5000 yen   ii 8500 yen   iii 100 yen?

9 Use the currency table (on page 70) to draw a conversion graph for Kuwaiti dinars to South African rand. Use the graph to find the number of rand you would receive for:
  a 35 dinars   b 140 dinars
  c 41.30 dinars   d 297.50 dinars

Personal and household finance

Net pay is what is left after deductions such as tax, insurance and pension contributions are taken from **gross earnings**. That is,

  Net pay = Gross pay − Deductions

A **bonus** is an extra payment sometimes added to an employee's **basic pay**.

In many companies, there is a fixed number of hours that an employee is expected to work. Any work done in excess of this **basic week** is paid at a higher rate, referred to as **overtime**. Overtime may be 1.5 times basic pay, called **time and a half**, or twice basic pay, called **double time**.

Exercise 8.2

1 Copy the table and find the net pay for each employee:

	Gross pay ($)	Deductions ($)	Net pay ($)
a A Ahmet	162.00	23.50	
b B Martinez	205.50	41.36	
c C Stein	188.25	33.43	
d D Wong	225.18	60.12	

8 MONEY AND FINANCE

Exercise 8.2 (cont)

2 Copy and complete the table for each employee:

	Basic pay ($)	Overtime ($)	Bonus ($)	Gross pay ($)
a P Small	144	62	23	
b B Smith	152		31	208
c A Chang		38	12	173
d U Zafer	115	43		213
e M Said	128	36	18	

3 Copy and complete the table for each employee:

	Gross pay ($)	Tax ($)	Pension ($)	Net pay ($)
a A Hafar	203	54	18	
b K Zyeb		65	23	218
c H Such	345		41	232
d K Donald	185	23		147

4 Copy and complete the table to find the basic pay in each case:

	No. of hours worked	Basic rate per hour ($)	Basic pay ($)
a	40	3.15	
b	44	4.88	
c	38	5.02	
d	35	8.30	
e	48	7.25	

5 Copy and complete the table, which shows basic pay and overtime at time and a half:

	Basic hours worked	Rate per hour ($)	Basic pay ($)	Overtime hours worked	Overtime pay ($)	Total gross pay ($)
a	40	3.60		8		
b	35		203.00	4		
c	38	4.15		6		
d		6.10	256.20	5		
e	44	5.25		4		
f		4.87	180.19	3		
g	36	6.68		6		
h	45	7.10	319.50	7		

6 In Q.5, deductions amount to 32% of the total gross pay. Calculate the net pay for each employee.

Personal and household finance

Piece work is a method of payment where an employee is paid for the number of articles made, not for time taken.

Exercise 8.3

1 Four people help to pick grapes in a vineyard. They are paid $5.50 for each basket of grapes. Copy and complete the table:

	Mon	Tue	Wed	Thur	Fri	Total	Gross pay
Joe	4	5	7	6	6		
Kirra	3	4	4	5	5		
Delores	5	6	6	5	6		
Zaffar	3	4	6	6	6		

2 Five people work in a pottery factory making plates. They are paid $5 for every 12 plates made. Copy and complete the table, which shows the number of plates that each person produces:

	Mon	Tue	Wed	Thur	Fri	Total	Gross pay
Maria	240	360	288	192	180		
Chul	168	192	312	180	168		
Yao	288	156	192	204	180		
Bianca	228	144	108	180	120		
Erik	192	204	156	228	144		

3 A group of five people work at home making clothes. The patterns and material are provided by the company, and for each article produced they are paid:

Jacket $25   Shirt $13   Trousers $11   Dress $12

The five people make the numbers of articles of clothing shown in the table below.

a Find each person's gross pay.
b If the deductions amount to 15% of gross earnings, calculate each person's net pay.

	Jackets	Shirts	Trousers	Dresses
Neo	3	12	7	0
Jing	8	5	2	9
Luis	0	14	12	2
Mpho	6	8	3	12
Saki	4	9	16	5

8 MONEY AND FINANCE

Exercise 8.3 (cont)

4 A school organises a sponsored walk. The table shows how far students walked, the amount they were sponsored per mile, and the total each student raised.

   a Copy and complete the table.

Distance walked (km)	Amount per km ($)	Total raised ($)
10	0.80	
	0.65	9.10
18	0.38	
	0.72	7.31
12		7.92
	1.20	15.60
15	1	
	0.88	15.84
18		10.44
17		16.15

   b How much was raised in total?
   c This total was divided between three children's charities in the ratio of 2 : 3 : 5. How much did each charity receive?

Simple interest

Interest can be defined as money added by a bank to sums deposited by customers. The money deposited is called the **principal**. The **percentage interest** is the given rate and the money is left for a fixed period of time.

A formula can be obtained for **simple interest**:

$$SI = \frac{Ptr}{100}$$

where SI = simple interest, i.e. the interest paid
P = the principal
t = time in years
r = rate per cent

➡ Worked example

Find the simple interest earned on $250 deposited for 6 years at 8% each year.

$$SI = \frac{Ptr}{100}$$

$$SI = \frac{250 \times 6 \times 8}{100}$$

$$SI = 120$$

So the interest paid is $120.

Simple interest

Exercise 8.4 All rates of interest given here are annual rates. Find the simple interest paid in the following cases:
  a Principal $300   rate 6%   time 4 years
  b Principal $750   rate 8%   time 7 years
  c Principal $425   rate 6%   time 4 years
  d Principal $2800   rate 4.5%   time 2 years
  e Principal $6500   rate 6.25%   time 8 years
  f Principal $880   rate 6%   time 7 years

Worked example

How long will it take for a sum of $250, invested at 8%, to earn interest of $80?

$$SI = \frac{Ptr}{100}$$

$$80 = \frac{250 \times t \times 8}{100}$$

$$80 = 20t$$

$$4 = t$$

It will take 4 years.

Exercise 8.5 Calculate how long it will take for the following amounts of interest to be earned at the given rate.
  a $P = \$500$ $r = 6\%$ $SI = \$150$
  b $P = \$4800$ $r = 4\%$ $SI = \$96$
  c $P = \$4000$ $r = 7.5\%$ $SI = \$1500$
  d $P = \$2800$ $r = 8.5\%$ $SI = \$1904$
  e $P = \$900$ $r = 4.5\%$ $SI = \$243$
  f $P = \$400$ $r = 9\%$ $SI = \$252$

Worked example

What rate per year must be paid for a principal of $750 to earn interest of $180 in 4 years?

$$SI = \frac{Ptr}{100}$$

$$180 = \frac{750 \times 4 \times r}{100}$$

$$180 = 30r$$

$$6 = r$$

The rate must be 6% per year.

8 MONEY AND FINANCE

Exercise 8.6 Calculate the rate of interest per year which will earn the given amount of interest:
  a Principal $400   time 4 years   interest $112
  b Principal $800   time 7 years   interest $224
  c Principal $2000   time 3 years   interest $210
  d Principal $1500   time 6 years   interest $675
  e Principal $850   time 5 years   interest $340
  f Principal $1250   time 2 years   interest $275

➡ Worked example

Find the principal which will earn interest of $120 in 6 years at 4%.

$$SI = \frac{Ptr}{100}$$
$$120 = \frac{P \times 6 \times 4}{100}$$
$$120 = \frac{24P}{100}$$
$$12\,000 = 24P$$
$$500 = P$$

So the principal is $500.

Exercise 8.7

1 Calculate the principal which will earn the interest below in the given number of years at the given rate:
  a $SI = \$80$ time = 4 years   rate = 5%
  b $SI = \$36$ time = 3 years   rate = 6%
  c $SI = \$340$ time = 5 years   rate = 8%
  d $SI = \$540$ time = 6 years   rate = 7.5%
  e $SI = \$540$ time = 3 years   rate = 4.5%
  f $SI = \$348$ time = 4 years   rate = 7.25%

2 What rate of interest is paid on a deposit of $2000 which earns $400 interest in 5 years?

3 How long will it take a principal of $350 to earn $56 interest at 8% per year?

4 A principal of $480 earns $108 interest in 5 years. What rate of interest was being paid?

5 A principal of $750 becomes a total of $1320 in 8 years. What rate of interest was being paid?

6 $1500 is invested for 6 years at 3.5% per year. What is the interest earned?

7 $500 is invested for 11 years and becomes $830 in total. What rate of interest was being paid?

Compound interest

Compound interest means that interest is paid not only on the principal amount, but also on the interest itself: it is compounded

Compound interest

(or added to). This sounds complicated but the example below will make it clearer.

A builder is going to build six houses on a plot of land. He borrows $500 000 at 10% compound interest per annum and will pay the loan off in full after three years.

10% of $500 000 is $50 000, therefore at the end of the first year he will owe a total of $550 000 as shown:

An increase of 10% is the same as multiplying by 1.10.

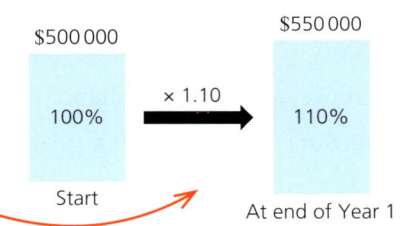

$500 000 — 100% — × 1.10 → $550 000 — 110%
Start — At end of Year 1

For the second year, the amount he owes increases again by 10%, but this is calculated by adding 10% to the amount he owed at the end of the first year, i.e. 10% of $550 000. This can be represented using this diagram:

Once again, an increase of 10% is the same as multiplying by 1.10.

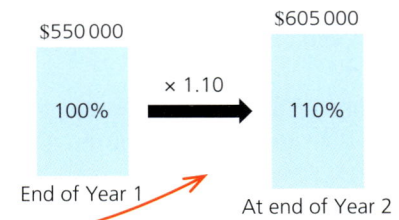

$550 000 — 100% — × 1.10 → $605 000 — 110%
End of Year 1 — At end of Year 2

For the third year, the amount he owes increases again by 10%. This is calculated by adding 10% to the amount he owed at the end of the second year, i.e. 10% of $605 000 as shown:

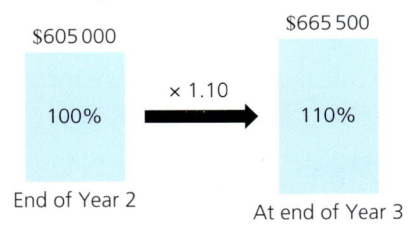

$605 000 — 100% — × 1.10 → $665 500 — 110%
End of Year 2 — At end of Year 3

Therefore, the compound interest he has to pay at the end of three years is $665 500 − $500 000 = $165 500.

By looking at the diagrams above it can be seen that the principal amount has in effect been multiplied by 1.10 three times (this is the same as multiplying by 1.10^3), i.e. $500 000 × 1.10^3 = $665 500.

77

8 MONEY AND FINANCE

You should learn this formula and know how to use it. →

There is a formula for calculating the compound interest. It is written as:

$$I = P\left(1 + \frac{r}{100}\right)^n - P$$

Where I = compound interest

P = the principal (amount originally borrowed)

r = interest rate

n = number of years.

For the example above, $P = 500\,000$ dollars, $r = 10\%$ and $n = 3$.

Therefore $I = 500\,000\left(1 + \frac{10}{100}\right)^3 - 500\,000 = 165\,000$ dollars.

Exercise 8.8

Using the formula for compound interest or otherwise, calculate the following:

1. A shipping company borrows $70 million at 5% compound interest to build a new cruise ship. If it repays the debt after 3 years, how much interest will the company pay?

2. Juan borrows $100 000 to improve her house. She borrows the money at 15% interest and repays it in full after 3 years. What interest will she pay?

3. Jivan owes $5000 on his credit cards. He pays compound interest of 20% per year. If Jivan lets the debt grow, how much will he owe in 4 years?

4. A school increases its intake by 10% each year. If it starts with 1000 students, how many will it have at the beginning of the fourth year of expansion?

5. 8 million tonnes of fish were caught in the North Sea in 2022. If the catch is reduced by 20% each year for 4 years, what amount can be caught at the end of this time?

It is possible to calculate the time taken for a debt to grow using compound interest.

➡ Worked example

How many years will it take for a debt, D, to double at 27% compound interest?

After 1 year the debt will be $D \times (1 + 27\%)$ or $1.27D$.

After 2 years the debt will be $D \times (1.27 \times 1.27)$ or $1.61D$.

After 3 years the debt will be $D \times (1.27 \times 1.27 \times 1.27)$ or $2.05D$.

So the debt will have doubled after 3 years.

Note that the amount of the debt does not affect this calculation. Note also that if the debt were reducing it would take the same number of years to halve.

Exercise 8.9

1. How many years would it take a debt to double at a compound interest rate of 42%?
2. How many years would it take a debt to double at a compound interest rate of 15%?
3. A car loses value at 27% compound interest each year. How many years will it take to halve in value?
4. The value of a house increases by 20% compound interest each year. How many years before it doubles in value?
5. A boat loses value at a rate of 15% compound interest per year. How many years before its value has halved?

Profit and loss

Foodstuffs and manufactured goods are produced at a cost, known as the **cost price**, and sold at the **selling price**. If the selling price is greater than the cost price, a **profit** is made.

> ### Worked example
>
> A market trader buys oranges in boxes of 144 for $14.40 per box. She buys 3 boxes and sells all the oranges for 12c each. What is her profit or loss?
>
> Cost price: 3 × $14.40 = $43.20
>
> Selling price: 3 × 144 × 12c = $51.84
>
> In this case she makes a profit of $51.84 – $43.20.
>
> Her profit is $8.64.
>
> A second way of solving this problem would be:
>
> $14.40 for a box of 144 oranges is 10c each.
>
> So cost price of each orange is 10c, and selling price of each orange is 12c.
>
> The profit is 2c per orange.
>
> So 3 boxes would give a profit of 3 × 144 × 2c.
>
> That is, $8.64.

Exercise 8.10

1. A market trader buys peaches in boxes of 120. He buys 4 boxes at a cost price of $13.20 per box. He sells 425 peaches at 12c each – the rest are ruined. How much profit or loss does he make?
2. A shopkeeper buys 72 bars of chocolate for $5.76. What is his profit if he sells them for 12c each?
3. A holiday company charters an aircraft to fly to Malta at a cost of $22 000. It then sells 195 seats at $185 each. Calculate the profit made per seat if the plane has 200 seats.

8 MONEY AND FINANCE

Exercise 8.10 (cont)

4 A car is priced at $7200. The car dealer allows a customer to pay a one-third deposit and 12 payments of $420 per month. How much extra does it cost the customer?

5 At an auction, a company sells 150 television sets for an average of $65 each. The production cost was $10 000. How much loss did the company make?

6 An electronics shop sells tools and electrical goods. Find the profit or loss if they sells each of the following:
   a 15 torches: cost price $2 each, selling price $2.30 each
   b 60 plugs: cost price $10 for 12, selling price $1.10 each
   c 200 DVDs: cost price $9 for 10, selling price $1.30 each
   d 5 MP3 players: cost price $82, selling price $19 each
   e 96 batteries costing $1 for 6, selling price 59c for 3
   f 3 clock radios costing $65, sold for $14 each

Percentage profit and loss

Most profits or losses are expressed as a percentage.

$$\text{Percentage profit or loss} = \frac{\text{profit or loss}}{\text{cost price}} \times 100$$

Worked example

A woman buys a car for $7500 and sells it two years later for $4500. Calculate her loss over two years as a percentage of the cost price.

Cost price = $7500   Selling price = $4500   Loss = $3000

Percentage loss = $\frac{3000}{7500} \times 100 = 40$

Her loss is 40%.

When something becomes worth less over a period of time, it is said to **depreciate**.

Exercise 8.11

1 Find the depreciation of each car as a percentage of the cost price. (C.P. = Cost price, S.P. = Selling price.)
   a Car A   C.P. $4500   S.P. $4005
   b Car B   C.P. $9200   S.P. $6900
   c Car C   C.P. $11 000 S.P. $5500
   d Car D   C.P. $4350   S.P. $3480
   e Car E   C.P. $6850   S.P. $4795
   f Car F   C.P. $7800   S.P. $2600

2 A company manufactures electrical items for the kitchen. Find the percentage profit on each appliance:
   a Cooker   C.P. $240   S.P. $300
   b Fridge   C.P. $50   S.P. $65
   c Freezer   C.P. $80   S.P. $96
   d Microwave   C.P. $120   S.P. $180
   e Washing machine C.P. $260   S.P. $340
   f Dryer   C.P. $70   S.P. $91

3 A developer builds a number of different kinds of house on a village site. Given the cost prices and the selling prices in the table, which type of house gives the developer the largest percentage profit?

	Cost price ($)	Selling price ($)
Type A	40 000	52 000
Type B	65 000	75 000
Type C	81 000	108 000
Type D	110 000	144 000
Type E	132 000	196 000

4 Students in a school organise a disco. The disco company charges $350 for hire. The students sell 280 tickets at $2.25. What is the percentage profit?

5 A shop sells second-hand boats. Calculate the percentage profit on each of the following:

	Cost price ($)	Selling price ($)
Mirror	400	520
Wayfarer	1100	1540
Laser	900	1305
Fireball	1250	1720

Student assessment 1

1 1 Australian dollar can be exchanged for €0.80. Draw a conversion graph to find the number of Australian dollars you would get for:
   a €50   b €80   c €70

2 Use your graph from Q.1 to find the number of euros you would receive for:
   a A$54   b A$81   c A$320

The currency conversion table shows the amounts of foreign currency received for €1. Draw appropriate conversion graphs to answer Q.3–5.

Nigeria	203 nairas
Malaysia	3.9 ringgits
Jordan	0.9 dinars

3 Convert the following numbers of Malaysian ringgits into Jordanian dinars:
   a 100 ringgits   b 1200 ringgits   c 150 ringgits

4 Convert the following numbers of Jordanian dinars into Nigerian nairas:
   a 1 dinar   b 6 dinars   c 4 dinars

5 Convert the following numbers of Nigerian nairas into Malaysian ringgits:
   a 1000 nairas   b 5000 nairas   c 7500 nairas

8 MONEY AND FINANCE

Student assessment 2

1. A man worked 3 hours a day Monday to Friday for $3.75 per hour. What was his 4-weekly gross payment?

2. A woman works at home making curtains. In 1 week she makes 4 pairs of long curtains and 13 pairs of short curtains. What is her gross pay if she receives $2.10 for each long curtain, and $1.85 for each short curtain?

3. Calculate the missing numbers from the simple interest table:

Principal ($)	Rate (%)	Time (years)	Interest ($)
200	9	3	a
350	7	b	98
520	c	5	169
d	3.75	6	189

4. A car cost $7200 new and sold for $5400 after 2 years. What was the percentage average annual depreciation?

5. A farmer sold 8 sheep at market at an average sale price of $48 each. If his total costs for rearing all the animals were $432, what was his percentage loss on each animal?

Student assessment 3

1. A girl works in a shop on Saturdays for 8.5 hours. She is paid $3.60 per hour. What is her gross pay for 4 weeks' work?

2. Razik makes cups and saucers in a factory. He is paid $1.44 per batch of cups and $1.20 per batch of saucers. What is Razik's gross pay if he makes 9 batches of cups and 11 batches of saucers in 1 day?

3. Calculate the missing numbers from the simple interest table:

Principal ($)	Rate (%)	Time (years)	Interest ($)
300	6	4	a
250	b	3	60
480	5	c	96
650	d	8	390
e	3.75	4	187.50

4. A house was bought for $48 000 12 years ago. It is now valued at $120 000. What is the average annual increase in the value of the house?

5. An electrician bought 5 broken washing machines for $550. She repaired them and sold them for $143 each. What was her percentage profit?

6 Two sisters, Meera and Jacinda, sell their house at a profit of $26 000.
Meera receives 18% of the profit, whilst Jacinda receives $6200 of the profit.
The rest is deposited in a savings account offering a compound interest rate of 3.2% per year.
   a How much does Meera receive?
   b Assuming no money is withdrawn from the savings account, calculate the amount saved after 6 years.

9 Time

Times may be given in terms of the 12-hour clock. We tend to say, 'I get up at seven o'clock in the morning, play football at half past two in the afternoon, and go to bed before eleven o'clock'.

These times can be written as 7 a.m., 2.30 p.m. and 11 p.m.

In order to save confusion, most timetables are written using the 24-hour clock.
- 7 a.m. is written as 07 00
- 2.30 p.m. is written as 14 30
- 11 p.m. is written as 23 00

To change p.m. times to 24-hour clock times, add 12 hours. To change 24-hour clock times later than 12.00 noon to 12-hour clock times, subtract 12 hours.

Exercise 9.1

1 These clocks show times in the morning. Write down the times using both the 12-hour and the 24-hour clock.
   a   b

2 These clocks show times in the afternoon. Write down the times using both the 12-hour and the 24-hour clock.
   a   b

3 Change these times into the 24-hour clock:
   a 2.30 p.m.   b 9 p.m.   c 8.45 a.m.   d 6 a.m.
   e midday   f 10.55 p.m.   g 7.30 a.m.   h 7.30 p.m.
   i 1 a.m.   j midnight

4 Change these times into the 24-hour clock:
   a A quarter past seven in the morning
   b Eight o'clock at night
   c Ten past nine in the morning
   d A quarter to nine in the morning
   e A quarter to three in the afternoon
   f Twenty to eight in the evening

Time

5 These times are written for the 24-hour clock. Rewrite them using a.m. or p.m.
  a 0720   **b** 0900   **c** 1430   **d** 1825
  e 2340   **f** 0115   **g** 0005   **h** 1135
  i 1750   **j** 2359   **k** 0410   **l** 0545

6 A journey to work takes a woman three-quarters of an hour. If she catches the bus at the following times, when does she arrive?
  a 0720   **b** 0755   **c** 0820   **d** 0845

7 The journey home for the same woman takes 55 minutes. If she catches the bus at these times, when does she arrive?
  a 1725   **b** 1750   **c** 1805   **d** 1820

8 A boy cycles to school each day. His journey takes 70 minutes. When will he arrive if he leaves home at:
  a 0715   **b** 0825   **c** 0840   **d** 0855?

9 The train into the city from a village takes 1 hour and 40 minutes. Copy and complete the train timetable.

Depart	0615		0925		1318		1854	
Arrive		0810		1200		1628		2105

10 The same journey by bus takes 2 hours and 5 minutes. Copy and complete the bus timetable.

Depart	0600		0855		1348		2125	
Arrive		0850		1114		1622		0010

11 A coach runs from Cambridge to the airports at Stansted, Gatwick and Heathrow. The time taken for the journey remains constant. Copy and complete the timetables for the outward and return journeys.

Cambridge	0400	0835	1250	1945	2110
Stansted	0515				
Gatwick	0650				
Heathrow	0735				

Heathrow	0625	0940	1435	1810	2215
Gatwick	0812				
Stansted	1003				
Cambridge	1100				

9 TIME

12 The flight time from Singapore to Johannesburg is 10 hours and 40 minutes. Copy and complete the timetable.

	Singapore	Jo'burg	Singapore	Jo'burg
Sunday	0615		1420	
Monday		1845		0525
Tuesday	0720		1513	
Wednesday		1912		0730
Thursday	0610		1627	
Friday		1725		0815
Saturday	0955		1850	

13 The flight time from Melbourne to Abu Dhabi is 14 hours and 25 minutes. Copy and complete the timetable.

	London	Kuala Lumpur	London	Kuala Lumpur	London	Kuala Lumpur
Sunday	0828		1400		1830	
Monday		2200		0315		0950
Tuesday	0915		1525		1755	
Wednesday		2135		0400		0822
Thursday	0700		1345		1840	
Friday		0010		0445		0738
Saturday	1012		1420		1908	

Average speed

➔ Worked example

A train covers the 480 km journey from Paris to Lyon at an average speed of 100 km/h. If the train leaves Paris at 0835, when does it arrive in Lyon?

Time taken = $\frac{\text{distance}}{\text{speed}}$

Paris to Lyon: $\frac{480}{100}$ hours, i.e. 4.8 hours.

4.8 hours is 4 hours and (0.8 × 60 minutes), i.e. 4 hours and 48 minutes.

Departure 0835; arrival 0835 + 0448

Arrival time is 1323.

Note that 4.80 hrs does not represent 4 hrs and 80 minutes. This is because time is not a decimal system which has 10 as its base number. Time is a **sexagesimal** number system with 60 as its base number. That is, there are 60 minutes in an hour and 60 seconds in a minute.

Average speed

As shown above, converting 0.8 hrs into minutes can be done by multiplying by 60.

0.8 hrs is equivalent to 0.8 × 60 = 48 minutes.

Your scientific calculator will have a sexagesimal button and it will look similar to:

To convert 4.80 hrs to hours, minutes and seconds, enter the number into your calculator followed by the button above. The calculator will show an answer of 4° 48′ 0″ which implies 4 hrs, 48 mins and 0 secs.

Exercise 9.2

1 Using your calculator, convert the following times written as decimals into hours, minutes and seconds.
   a 0.25 hrs
   b 3.765 hrs
   c 0.22 hrs

2 A train leaves a station at 06 24. The journey has four stops. Calculate the time the train arrives at each stop if the time taken from one stop to the next is as follows:
   – Start to stop 1 takes 0.35 hrs.
   – Stop 1 to stop 2 takes 1.30 hrs.
   – Stop 2 to stop 3 takes 1.65 hrs.
   – Stop 3 to final stop takes 2.91 hrs.

3 Find the time in hours and minutes for the following journeys of the given distance at the average speed stated:
   a 240 km at 60 km/h
   b 340 km at 40 km/h
   c 270 km at 80 km/h
   d 100 km at 60 km/h
   e 70 km at 30 km/h
   f 560 km at 90 km/h
   g 230 km at 100 km/h
   h 70 km at 50 km/h
   i 4500 km at 750 km/h
   j 6000 km at 800 km/h

4 Grand Prix racing cars cover a 120 km race at the following average speeds. How long do the first five cars take to complete the race? Give your answer in minutes and seconds.
   First 240 km/h   Second 220 km/h   Third 210 km/h
   Fourth 205 km/h   Fifth 200 km/h

5 A train covers the 1500 km distance from Amsterdam to Barcelona at an average speed of 100 km/h. If the train leaves Amsterdam at 09 30, when does it arrive in Barcelona?

6 A plane takes off at 16 25 for the 3200 km journey from Moscow to Athens. If the plane flies at an average speed of 600 km/h, when will it land in Athens?

7 A plane leaves Lisbon for Montreal, covering a distance of 5200 km, at 09 45. The plane travels at an average speed of 800 km/h. If Montreal time is 5 hours behind Lisbon time, what is the time in Montreal when the aircraft lands?

9 TIME

Student assessment 1

1. The clock shows a time in the afternoon. Write down the time using:
   a. the 12-hour clock
   b. the 24-hour clock.

2. Change these times into the 24-hour clock:
   a. 4.35 a.m.
   b. 6.30 p.m.
   c. a quarter to eight in the morning
   d. half past seven in the evening

3. These times are written using the 24 hour clock. Rewrite them using a.m. or p.m.
   a. 08 45
   b. 18 35
   c. 21 12
   d. 00 15

4. A journey to school takes Monica 0.4 hours. What time does she arrive if she leaves home at the following times?
   a. 07 45
   b. 08 15
   c. 08 38

5. A bus service visits the towns on this timetable. Copy the timetable and fill in the missing times, given that the journey from:
   - Alphaville to Betatown takes 37 minutes
   - Betatown to Gammatown takes 18 minutes
   - Gammatown to Deltaville takes 42 minutes.

Alphaville	07 50		
Betatown		11 38	
Gammatown			16 48
Deltaville			

6. Find the times for the following journeys of given distance at the average speed stated. Give your answers in hours and minutes.
   a. 250 km at 50 km/h
   c. 80 km at 60 km/h
   e. 70 km at 30 km/h
   b. 375 km at 100 km/h
   d. 200 km at 120 km/h
   f. 300 km at 80 km/h

Student assessment 2

1. The clock shows a time in the morning. Write down the time using:
   a. the 12-hour clock
   b. the 24-hour clock.

2. Change these times to the 24-hour clock:
   a. 5.20 a.m.
   b. 8.15 p.m.
   c. ten to nine in the morning
   d. half past eleven at night

3. These times are written using the 24-hour clock. Rewrite them using a.m. or p.m.
   a. 07 15
   b. 16 43
   c. 19 30
   d. 00 35

4. A journey to school takes a boy 22 minutes. When does he arrive if he leaves home at the following times?
   a. 07 48
   b. 08 17
   c. 08 38

5. A train stops at the following stations. Copy the timetable and fill in the times, given that the journey from:
   - Apple to Peach is 1 hr 38 minutes
   - Peach to Pear is 2 hrs 4 minutes
   - Pear to Plum is 1 hr 53 minutes.

Apple	10 14		
Peach		17 20	
Pear			23 15
Plum			

6. Find the time for the following journeys of given distance at the average speed stated. Give your answers in hours and minutes.
   a. 350 km at 70 km/h
   b. 425 km at 100 km/h
   c. 160 km at 60 km/h
   d. 450 km at 120 km/h
   e. 600 km at 160 km/h

7. A plane flies from the UK to Singapore.
   - It takes off from London at 09 20 on Monday morning.
   - The flight lasts 13 hrs and 10 minutes.
   - Singapore time is 7 hrs ahead of UK time.

   What time and day does the plane land in Singapore? Give your answer in Singapore local time.

10 Set notation and Venn diagrams

Sets

A **set** is a well-defined group of objects or symbols. The objects or symbols are called the **elements** of the set.

Worked examples

1. A particular set consists of the following elements:

   {South Africa, Namibia, Egypt, Angola, ...}

   a Describe the set.

   The elements of the set are countries of Africa.

   b Add another two elements to the set.

   e.g. Zimbabwe, Ghana

   c Is the set finite or infinite?

   Finite. There is a finite number of countries in Africa.

2. Consider the set $A = \{x: x \text{ is a natural number}\}$.

   a Describe the set.

   The elements of the set are the natural numbers.

   b Write down two elements of the set.

   e.g. 3 and 15

Exercise 10.1

1. In the following questions:
   i describe the set in words
   ii write down another two elements of the set.
      a {Asia, Africa, Europe, ...}
      b {2, 4, 6, 8, ...}
      c {Sunday, Monday, Tuesday, ...}
      d {January, March, July, ...}
      e {1, 3, 6, 10, ...}
      f {Mehmet, Michael, Mustapha, Matthew, ...}
      g {11, 13, 17, 19, ...}
      h {a, e, i, ...}
      i {Earth, Mars, Venus, ...}

2. The number of elements in a set A is written as n(A).
   Give the value of n(A) for the finite sets in Q.1a–i above.

Universal set

The **universal set** ($\mathscr{E}$) for any particular problem is the set which contains all the possible elements for that problem.

10 SET NOTATION AND VENN DIAGRAMS

The **complement** of a set A is the set of elements which are in $\mathscr{E}$ but not in A. The complement of A is identified as A'.

→ Worked examples

1. If $\mathscr{E} = \{$integers from 1 to 10$\}$, state the numbers which form part of $\mathscr{E}$.
   Therefore $\mathscr{E} = \{1, 2, 3, 4, 5, 6, 7, 8, 9, 10\}$.

2. If $\mathscr{E} = \{$all 3D shapes$\}$ state three elements of $\mathscr{E}$.
   e.g. sphere, cube, cylinder

3. If $\mathscr{E} = \{1, 2, 3, 4, 5, 6, 7, 8, 9, 10\}$ and $A = \{1, 2, 3, 4, 5\}$ what set is represented by A'?
   A' consists of those elements in $\mathscr{E}$ which are not in A.
   Therefore $A' = \{6, 7, 8, 9, 10\}$.

4. If $\mathscr{E} = \{$all 3D shapes$\}$ and $P = \{$**prisms**$\}$ what set is represented by P'?
   $P' = \{$all 3D shapes except prisms$\}$.

Set notation and Venn diagrams

Venn diagrams are the principal way of showing sets diagrammatically. The method consists primarily of entering the elements of a set into a circle or circles. Some examples of the uses of Venn diagrams are shown.

$A = \{2, 4, 6, 8, 10\}$ can be represented as:

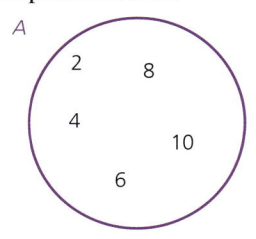

Elements which are in more than one set can also be represented using a Venn diagram.

$P = \{3, 6, 9, 12, 15, 18\}$ and $Q = \{2, 4, 6, 8, 10, 12\}$ can be represented as:

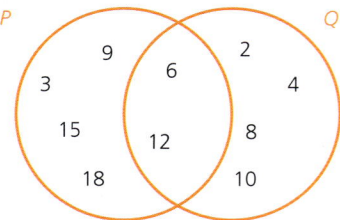

In the previous diagram, it can be seen that those elements which belong to both sets are placed in the region of overlap of the two circles.

When two sets P and Q overlap, as they do above, the notation $P \cap Q$ is used to denote the set of elements in the **intersection**, i.e. $P \cap Q = \{6, 12\}$.

Set notation and Venn diagrams

Note that 6 belongs to the intersection of $P \cap Q$; 8 does not belong to the intersection of $P \cap Q$.

$J = \{10, 20, 30, 40, 50, 60, 70, 80, 90, 100\}$ and $K = \{60, 70, 80\}$.

As all the elements of K belong to J as well, this can be shown as:

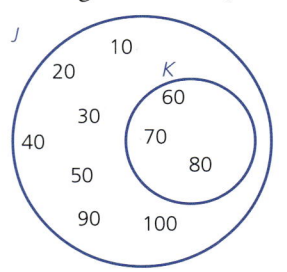

$X = \{1, 3, 6, 7, 14\}$ and $Y = \{3, 9, 13, 14, 18\}$ are represented as:

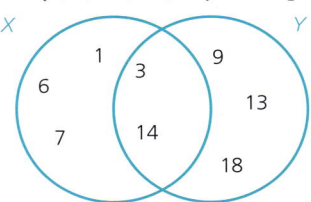

The **union** of two sets is everything which belongs to either or both sets and is represented by the symbol $\cup$.

Therefore, in the previous example, $X \cup Y = \{1, 3, 6, 7, 9, 13, 14, 18\}$.

Exercise 10.2

1 Using the Venn diagram, indicate whether the following statements are true or false.

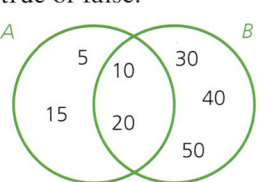

   a 5 is an element of A.
   b 20 is an element of B.
   c 20 is not an element of A.
   d 50 is an element of A.
   e 50 is not an element of B.
   f $A \cap B = \{10, 20\}$.

2 Complete the statement $A \cap B = \{...\}$ for each of the Venn diagrams below.

   a 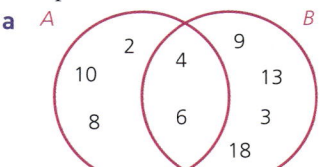
   b 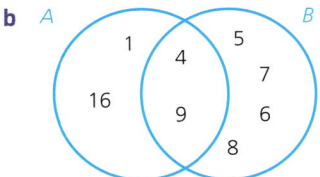
   c

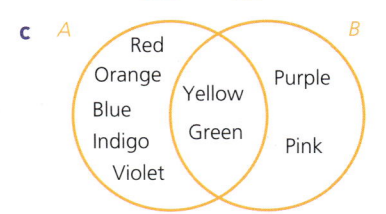

10 SET NOTATION AND VENN DIAGRAMS

Exercise 10.2 (cont)

3 Complete the statement $A \cup B = \{...\}$ for each of the Venn diagrams in question 2.

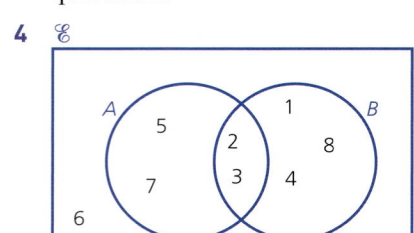

4

Copy and complete the following statements:
a $\mathscr{E} = \{...\}$
b $A \cap B = \{...\}$
c $A \cup B = \{...\}$
d $A' = \{...\}$
e $B' = \{...\}$

Exercise 10.3

1 $A = \{$Egypt, Libya, Morocco, Chad$\}$
$B = \{$Iran, Iraq, Turkey, Egypt$\}$
a Draw a Venn diagram to illustrate the above information.
b Copy and complete the following statements:
   i $A \cap B = \{...\}$ ii $A \cup B = \{...\}$

2 $P = \{2, 3, 5, 7, 11, 13, 17\}$
$Q = \{11, 13, 15, 17, 19\}$
a Draw a Venn diagram to illustrate the above information.
b Copy and complete the following statements:
   i $P \cap Q = \{...\}$ ii $P \cup Q = \{...\}$

3 $B = \{2, 4, 6, 8, 10\}$
$A \cup B = \{1, 2, 3, 4, 6, 8, 10\}$
$A \cap B = \{2, 4\}$
Represent the above information on a Venn diagram.

4 $X = \{a, c, d, e, f, g, l\}$
$Y = \{b, c, d, e, h, i, k, l, m\}$
$Z = \{c, f, i, j, m\}$
Represent the above information on a Venn diagram.

5 $P = \{1, 4, 7, 9, 11, 15\}$
$Q = \{5, 10, 15\}$
$R = \{1, 4, 9\}$
Represent the above information on a Venn diagram.

Problem-solving involving sets

> ## Worked example

In a class of 31 students, some study Physics and some study Chemistry. If 22 study Physics, 20 study Chemistry and 5 study neither, calculate the number of students who take both subjects.

The information can be entered in a Venn diagram in stages.

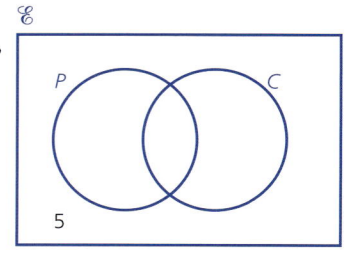

Problem-solving involving sets

The students taking neither Physics nor Chemistry can be put in first (as shown bottom left). This leaves 26 students to be entered into the set circles.

If x students take both subjects then:

$n(P) = 22 - x + x$
$n(C) = 20 - x + x$
$P \cup C = 31 - 5 = 26$

Therefore $22 - x + x + 20 - x = 26$
$\qquad\qquad\quad 42 - x = 26$
$\qquad\qquad\qquad\quad x = 16$

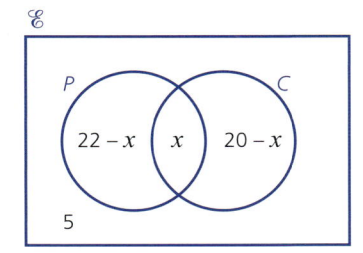

Substituting the value of x into the Venn diagram gives:

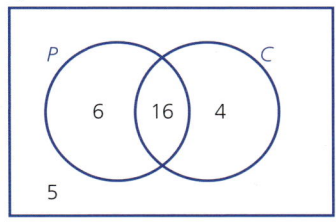

Therefore the number of students taking both Physics and Chemistry is 16.

Exercise 10.4

Note
A diagram may help you answer these questions.

1 In a class of 35 students, 19 take Spanish, 18 take French and 3 take neither. Calculate how many take:
   a both French and Spanish
   b just Spanish
   c just French.

2 In a year group of 108 students, 60 liked football, 53 liked tennis and 10 liked neither. Calculate the number of students who liked football but not tennis.

3 In a year group of 113 students, 60 liked hockey, 45 liked rugby and 18 liked neither. Calculate the number of students who:
   a liked both hockey and rugby
   b liked only hockey.

Student assessment 1

1 Describe the following sets in words:
   a {2, 4, 6, 8}
   b {2, 4, 6, 8, ...}
   c {1, 4, 9, 16, 25, ...}
   d {Arctic, Atlantic, Indian, Pacific}

2 Calculate the value of $n(A)$ for each of the sets shown below:
   a $A = \{$days of the week$\}$
   b $A = \{$prime numbers between 50 and 60$\}$
   c $A = \{x : x$ is an integer and $5 \leqslant x \leqslant 10\}$
   d $A = \{$days in a leap year$\}$

10 SET NOTATION AND VENN DIAGRAMS

3 Copy out the Venn diagram twice.
    a On one copy, shade and label the region which represents $A \cap B$.
    b On the other copy, shade and label the region which represents $A \cup B$.

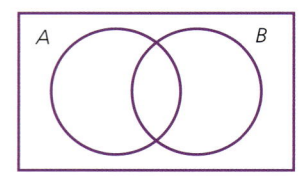

4 J = {London, Paris, Rome, Washington, Canberra, Ankara, Cairo}
    K = {Cairo, Nairobi, Pretoria, Ankara}
    a Draw a Venn diagram to represent the above information.
    b Copy and complete the statement $J \cap K = \{...\}$.

5 $\mathscr{E}$ = {natural numbers}, M = {even numbers} and N = {multiples of 5}.
    a Draw a Venn diagram and place the numbers 1, 2, 3, 4, 5, 6, 7, 8, 9, 10 in the appropriate places in it.
    b If $X = M \cap N$, describe set X in words.

6 A group of 40 people were asked whether they like cricket (C) and football (F). The number liking both cricket and football was three times the number liking only cricket. Adding three to the number liking only cricket and doubling the answer equals the number of people liking only football. Four people said they did not like sport at all.
    a Draw a Venn diagram to represent this information.
    b Calculate n($C \cap F$).

7 If $\mathscr{E}$ = {m, a, t, h, s} and A = {a, s}, what set is represented by A'?

Mathematical investigations and ICT 1

Investigations are an important part of mathematical learning. All mathematical discoveries stem from an idea that a mathematician has and then investigates.

Sometimes when faced with a mathematical investigation, it can seem difficult to know how to start. The structure and example below may help you.

1. Read the question carefully and start with simple cases.
2. Draw simple diagrams to help.
3. Put the results from simple cases in a table.
4. Look for a pattern in your results.
5. Try to find a general rule in words.
6. Express your rule algebraically.
7. Test the rule for a new example.
8. Check that the original question has been answered.

→ Worked example

A mystic rose is created by placing a number of points evenly spaced on the circumference of a circle. Straight lines are then drawn from each point to every other point. The diagram shows a mystic rose with 20 points.

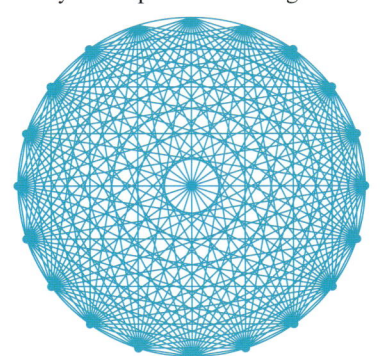

a How many straight lines are there?

b How many straight lines would there be on a mystic rose with 100 points?

MATHEMATICAL INVESTIGATIONS AND ICT 1

To answer these questions, you are not expected to draw either of the shapes and count the number of lines.

1/2 Try simple cases:

By drawing some simple cases and counting the lines, some results can be found:

Mystic rose with 2 points

Number of lines = 1

Mystic rose with 3 points

Number of lines = 3

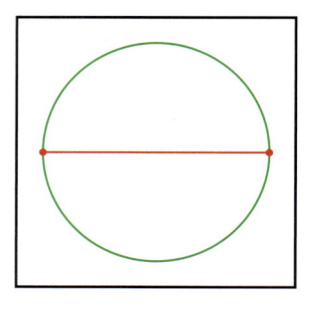

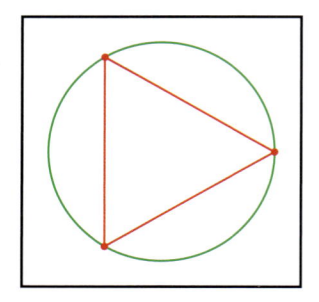

Mystic rose with 4 points

Number of lines = 6

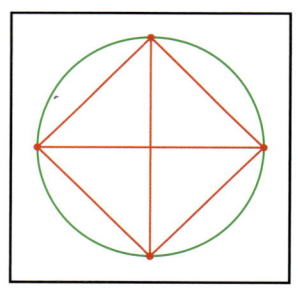

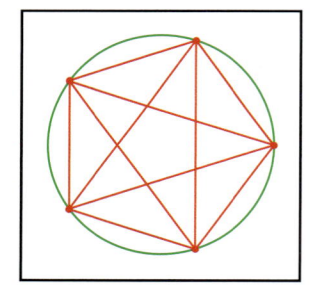

Mystic rose with 5 points

Number of lines = 10

3 Enter the results in an ordered table:

Number of points	2	3	4	5
Number of lines	1	3	6	10

4/5 Look for a pattern in the results:

There are two patterns.

The first pattern shows how the values change.

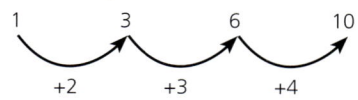

1   3   6   10
 +2   +3   +4

It can be seen that the difference between successive terms is increasing by one each time.

Mathematical investigations and ICT 1

The problem with this pattern is that to find the 20th or 100th term, it would be necessary to continue this pattern and find all the terms leading up to the 20th or 100th term.

The second pattern is the relationship between the number of points and the number of lines.

Number of points	2	3	4	5
Number of lines	1	3	6	10

It is important to find a relationship that works for all values; e.g. subtracting one from the number of points gives the number of lines in the first example only, so is not useful. However, halving the number of points and multiplying this by one less than the number of points works each time, i.e. number of lines = (half the number of points) × (one less than the number of points).

6 Express the rule algebraically:

The rule expressed in words above can be written more elegantly using algebra. Let the number of lines be l and the number of points be p.

$l = \frac{1}{2}p(p-1)$

Note: Any letters can be used to represent the number of lines and the number of points, not just l and p.

7 Test the rule:

The rule was derived from the original results. It can be tested by generating a further result.

If the number of points $p = 6$, then the number of lines l is:

$l = \frac{1}{2} \times 6(6-1)$
$= 3 \times 5$
$= 15$

From the diagram to the left, the number of lines can also be counted as 15.

8 Check that the original questions have been answered:

Using the formula, the number of lines in a mystic rose with 20 points is:

$l = \frac{1}{2} \times 20(20-1)$
$= 10 \times 19$
$= 190$

The number of lines in a mystic rose with 100 points is:

$l = \frac{1}{2} \times 100(100-1)$
$= 50 \times 99$
$= 4950$

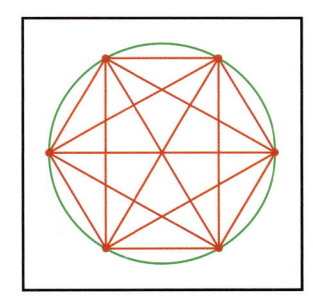

MATHEMATICAL INVESTIGATIONS AND ICT 1

Primes and squares

13, 41 and 73 are prime numbers.
Two different square numbers can be added together to make these prime numbers, e.g. $3^2 + 8^2 = 73$.

1. Find the two square numbers that can be added to make 13 and 41.
2. List the prime numbers less than 100.
3. Which of the prime numbers less than 100 can be shown to be the sum of two different square numbers?
4. Is there a rule to the numbers in Q.3?
5. Your rule is a predictive rule not a formula. Discuss the difference.

Football leagues

There are 18 teams in a football league.

1. If each team plays the other teams twice, once at home and once away, then how many matches are played in a season?
2. If there are t teams in a league, how many matches are played in a season?

ICT activity 1

The step patterns follow a rule.

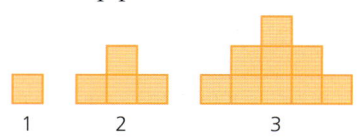

1. On squared paper, draw the next two patterns in this sequence.
2. Count the number of squares used in each of the first five patterns. Enter the results into a spreadsheet, similar to the one shown.

	A	B
1	Pattern	Number of squares
2	1	
3	2	
4	3	
5	4	
6	5	
7	10	
8	20	
9	50	

3 The number of squares needed for each pattern follows a rule. Describe the rule.
4 By writing a formula in cell B7 and copying it down to B9, use the spreadsheet to generate the results for the 10th, 20th and 50th patterns.
5 Repeat Q.1–4 for the following patterns:

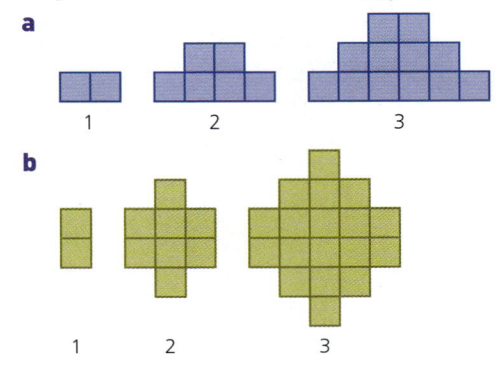

a

1   2   3

b

1   2   3

ICT activity 2

In this activity, you will be using both the internet and a spreadsheet in order to produce currency conversions.

1 Log on to the internet and search for a website that shows the exchange rates between different currencies.
2 Compare your own currency with another currency of your choice. Write down the exchange rate, e.g. $1 = €1.29.
3 Use a spreadsheet to construct a currency converter. Like this:

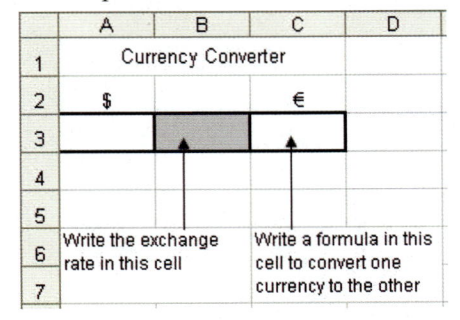

	A	B	C	D
1		Currency Converter		
2		$		€
3				
4				
5				
6		Write the exchange rate in this cell	Write a formula in this cell to convert one currency to the other	
7				

4 By entering different amounts of your own currency, use the currency converter to calculate the correct conversion. Record your answers in a table.
5 Repeat Q.1–4 for five different currencies of your choice.

TOPIC 2

Algebra and graphs

Contents

Chapter 11   Algebraic representation and manipulation (C2.1, C2.2, C2.5)
Chapter 12   Algebraic indices (C2.4)
Chapter 13   Equations (C2.5)
Chapter 14   Sequences (C2.7)
Chapter 15   Graphs in practical situations (C2.9)
Chapter 16   Graphs of functions (C2.10, C2.11)

Learning objectives

C2.1
1. Know that letters can be used to represent generalised numbers.
2. Substitute numbers into expressions and formulas.

C2.2
1. Simplify expressions by collecting like terms.
2. Expand products of algebraic expressions.
3. Factorise by extracting common factors.

C2.4
1. Understand and use indices (positive, zero and negative).
2. Understand and use the rules of indices.

C2.5
1. Construct expressions, equations and formulas.
2. Solve linear equations in one unknown.
3. Solve simultaneous linear equations in two unknowns.
4. Change the subject of simple formulas.

C2.6
Represent and interpret inequalities, including on a number line.

C2.7
1. Continue a given number sequence or pattern.
2. Recognise patterns in sequences, including the term-to-term rule, and relationships between different sequences.

3. Find and use the nth term of the following sequences:
   a linear
   b simple quadratic
   c simple cubic.

C2.9
1. Use and interpret graphs in practical situations including travel graphs and conversion graphs.
2. Draw graphs from given data.

C2.10
1. Construct tables of values, and draw, recognise and interpret graphs for functions of the form
   - $ax + b$
   - $\pm x^2 + ax + b$
   - $\frac{a}{x}$ $(x \neq 0)$

   where a and b are integer constants.
2. Solve associated equations graphically, including finding and interpreting roots by graphical methods.

C2.11
Recognise, sketch and interpret graphs of the following functions:
a linear
b quadratic.

The development of algebra

The roots of algebra can be traced to the ancient Babylonians, who used formulae for solving problems. However, the word *algebra* comes from the Arabic language. Muhammad ibn Musa al-Khwarizmi (790–850) wrote *Kitab al-Jabr (The Compendious Book on Calculation by Completion and Balancing)*, which established algebra as a mathematical subject. He is known as the father of algebra.

Persian mathematician Omar Khayyam (1048–1131), who studied in Bukhara (now in Uzbekistan), discovered algebraic geometry and found the general solution of a cubic equation.

In 1545, Italian mathematician Girolamo Cardano published *Ars Magna (The Great Art)*, a 40-chapter book in which he gave, for the first time, a method for solving a quartic equation.

Still alive today is the Indian mathematician Raman Parimala (born in 1948). Her work is famous in the fields of algebra and its connections with algebraic geometry and number theory.

al-Khwarizmi (790–850)

11 Algebraic representation and manipulation

Algebra is a mathematical language and is at the heart of mathematics. As well as numbers, letters are also used. The letters are used to represent unknown quantities or a variety of possible different values.

Using algebra may at first seem complicated, but as with any language, the more you use it and the more you understand its rules, the easier it becomes.

This topic deals with those rules.

Expanding brackets

When removing brackets, every term inside the bracket must be multiplied by whatever is outside the bracket.

> **Worked example**
>
> Expand:
>
> a $3(x + 4)$
>
> $3x + 12$
>
> b $5x(2y + 3)$
>
> $10xy + 15x$
>
> c $2a(3a + 2b - 3c)$
>
> $6a^2 + 4ab - 6ac$
>
> d $-4p(2p - q + r^2)$
>
> $-8p^2 + 4pq - 4pr^2$

Exercise 11.1

Expand:

1. a $2(a + 3)$
   b $4(b + 7)$
   c $5(2c + 8)$
   d $7(3d + 9)$
   e $9(8e - 7)$
   f $6(4f - 3)$

2. a $3a(a + 2b)$
   b $4b(2a + 3b)$
   c $2c(a + b + c)$
   d $3d(2b + 3c + 4d)$
   e $e(3c - 3d - e)$
   f $f(3d - e - 2f)$

3. a $2(2a^2 + 3b^2)$
   b $4(3a^2 + 4b^2)$
   c $-3(2c + 3d)$
   d $-(2c + 3d)$
   e $-4(c^2 - 2d^2 + 3e^2)$
   f $-5(2e - 3f^2)$

4. a $2a(a + b)$
   b $3b(a - b)$
   c $4c(b^2 - c^2)$
   d $3d^2(a^2 - 2b^2 + c^2)$
   e $-3e^2(4d - e)$
   f $-2f(2d - 3e^2 - 2f)$

Expanding brackets

Exercise 11.2

Expand:

1.
   a. $4(x - 3)$
   b. $5(2p - 4)$
   c. $-6(7x - 4y)$
   d. $3(2a - 3b - 4c)$
   e. $-7(2m - 3n)$
   f. $-2(8x - 3y)$

2.
   a. $3x(x - 3y)$
   b. $a(a + b + c)$
   c. $4m(2m - n)$
   d. $-5a(3a - 4b)$
   e. $-4x(-x + y)$
   f. $-8p(-3p + q)$

3.
   a. $-(2x^2 - 3y^2)$
   b. $-(-a + b)$
   c. $-(-7p + 2q)$
   d. $\frac{1}{2}(6x - 8y + 4z)$
   e. $\frac{3}{4}(4x - 2y)$
   f. $\frac{1}{5}x(10x - 15y)$

4.
   a. $3r(4r^2 - 5s + 2t)$
   b. $a^2(a + b + c)$
   c. $3a^2(2a - 3b)$
   d. $pq(p + q - pq)$
   e. $m^2(m - n + nm)$
   f. $a^3(a^3 + a^2b)$

Exercise 11.3

Expand and simplify:

1.
   a. $2a + 2(3a + 2)$
   b. $4(3b - 2) - 5b$
   c. $6(2c - 1) - 7c$
   d. $-4(d + 2) + 5d$
   e. $-3e + (e - 1)$
   f. $5f - (2f - 7)$

2.
   a. $2(a + 1) + 3(b + 2)$
   b. $4(a + 5) - 3(2b + 6)$
   c. $3(c - 1) + 2(c - 2)$
   d. $4(d - 1) - 3(d - 2)$
   e. $-2(e - 3) - (e - 1)$
   f. $2(3f - 3) + 4(1 - 2f)$

3.
   a. $2a(a + 3) + 2b(b - 1)$
   b. $3a(a - 4) - 2b(b - 3)$
   c. $2a(a + b + c) - 2b(a + b - c)$
   d. $a^2(c^2 + d^2) - c^2(a^2 + d^2)$
   e. $a(b + c) - b(a - c)$
   f. $a(2d + 3e) - 2e(a - c)$

Exercise 11.4

Expand and simplify:

1.
   a. $3a - 2(2a + 4)$
   b. $8x - 4(x + 5)$
   c. $3(p - 4) - 4$
   d. $7(3m - 2n) + 8n$
   e. $6x - 3(2x - 1)$
   f. $5p - 3p(p + 2)$

2.
   a. $7m(m + 4) + m^2 + 2$
   b. $3(x - 4) + 2(4 - x)$
   c. $6(p + 3) - 4(p - 1)$
   d. $5(m - 8) - 4(m - 7)$
   e. $3a(a + 2) - 2(a^2 - 1)$
   f. $7a(b - 2c) - c(2a - 3)$

3.
   a. $\frac{1}{2}(6x + 4) + \frac{1}{3}(3x + 6)$
   b. $\frac{1}{4}(2x + 6y) + \frac{3}{4}(6x - 4y)$
   c. $\frac{1}{8}(6x - 12y) + \frac{1}{2}(3x - 2y)$
   d. $\frac{1}{5}(15x + 10y) + \frac{3}{10}(5x - 5y)$
   e. $\frac{2}{3}(6x - 9y) + \frac{1}{3}(9x + 6y)$
   f. $\frac{x}{7}(14x - 21y) - \frac{x}{2}(4x - 6y)$

11 ALGEBRAIC REPRESENTATION AND MANIPULATION

Expanding a pair of brackets

When multiplying together expressions in brackets, it is necessary to multiply all the terms in one bracket by all the terms in the other bracket.

➡ Worked example

Expand:

a $(x+3)(x+5)$

	x	$+3$
x	x^2	$3x$
$+5$	$5x$	15

$= x^2 + 3x + 5x + 15$
$= x^2 + 8x + 15$

As the 3x and 5x are 'like terms' they can be combined to produce 8x. This simplifies the final answer.

b $(2x-3)(3x-6)$

	$2x$	-3
$3x$	$6x^2$	$-9x$
-6	$-12x$	18

$= 6x^2 - 9x - 12x + 18$
$= 6x^2 - 21x + 18$

As the -9x and -12x are 'like terms' they can be combined to produce -21x. This simplifies the final answer.

Exercise 11.5

Expand and simplify:

1. **a** $(x+2)(x+3)$ **b** $(x+3)(x+4)$ **c** $(x+5)(x+2)$
   d $(x+6)(x+1)$ **e** $(x-2)(x+3)$ **f** $(x+8)(x-3)$

2. **a** $(x-4)(x+6)$ **b** $(x-7)(x+4)$ **c** $(x+5)(x-7)$
   d $(x+3)(x-5)$ **e** $(x+1)(x-3)$ **f** $(x-7)(x+9)$

3. **a** $(x-2)(x-3)$ **b** $(x-5)(x-2)$ **c** $(x-4)(x-8)$
   d $(x+3)(x+3)$ **e** $(x-3)(x-3)$ **f** $(x-7)(x-5)$

4. **a** $(x+3)(x-3)$ **b** $(x+7)(x-7)$ **c** $(x-8)(x+8)$
   d $(x+y)(x-y)$ **e** $(a+b)(a-b)$ **f** $(p-q)(p+q)$

5. **a** $(2x+1)(x+3)$ **b** $(3x-2)(2x+5)$ **c** $(4-3x)(x+2)$
   d $(7-5y)^2$ **e** $(3+2x)(3-2x)$ **f** $(3+4x)(3-4x)$

Factorising

When factorising, the largest possible factor is removed from each of the terms and placed outside the brackets.

➡ Worked example

Factorise the following expressions:

a $10x + 15$
   $5(2x + 3)$

b $8p - 6q + 10r$
   $2(4p - 3q + 5r)$

c $-2q - 6p + 12$
   $2(-q - 3p + 6)$

d $2a^2 + 3ab - 5ac$
   $a(2a + 3b - 5c)$

104

Substitution

e $6ax - 12ay - 18a^2$	f $3b + 9ba - 6bd$
$6a(x - 2y - 3a)$	$3b(1 + 3a - 2d)$

Exercise 11.6 Factorise:

1. a $4x - 6$
   b $18 - 12p$
   c $6y - 3$
   d $4a + 6b$
   e $3p - 3q$
   f $8m + 12n + 16r$

2. a $3ab + 4ac - 5ad$
   b $8pq + 6pr - 4ps$
   c $a^2 - ab$
   d $4x^2 - 6xy$
   e $abc + abd + fab$
   f $3m^2 + 9m$

3. a $3pqr - 9pqs$
   b $5m^2 - 10mn$
   c $8x^2y - 4xy^2$
   d $2a^2b^2 - 3b^2c^2$
   e $12p - 36$
   f $42x - 54$

4. a $18 + 12y$
   b $14a - 21b$
   c $11x + 11xy$
   d $4s - 16t + 20r$
   e $5pq - 10qr + 15qs$
   f $4xy + 8y^2$

5. a $m^2 + mn$
   b $3p^2 - 6pq$
   c $pqr + qrs$
   d $ab + a^2b + ab^2$
   e $3p^3 - 4p^4$
   f $7b^3c + b^2c^2$

6. a $m^3 - m^2n + mn^2$
   b $4r^3 - 6r^2 + 8r^2s$
   c $56x^2y - 28xy^2$
   d $72m^2n + 36mn^2 - 18m^2n^2$

7. a $3a^2 - 2ab + 4ac$
   b $2ab - 3b^2 + 4bc$
   c $2a^2c - 4b^2c + 6bc^2$
   d $39cd^2 + 52c^2d$

8. a $12ac - 8ac^2 + 4a^2c$
   b $34a^2b - 51ab^2$
   c $33ac^2 + 121c^3 - 11b^2c^2$
   d $38c^3d^2 - 57c^2d^3 + 95c^2d^2$

Substitution

> **Worked example**

Evaluate these expressions if $a = 3$, $b = 4$, $c = -5$:

a $2a + 3b - c$
   $2 \times 3 + 3 \times 4 - (-5)$
   $= 6 + 12 + 5$
   $= 23$

b $3a - 4b + 2c$
   $3 \times 3 - 4 \times 4 + 2 \times (-5)$
   $= 9 - 16 - 10$
   $= -17$

c $-2a + 2b - 3c$
   $-2 \times 3 + 2 \times 4 - 3 \times (-5)$
   $= -6 + 8 + 15$
   $= 17$

d $a^2 + b^2 + c^2$
   $3^2 + 4^2 + (-5)^2$
   $= 9 + 16 + 25$
   $= 50$

105

11 ALGEBRAIC REPRESENTATION AND MANIPULATION

e $\quad 3a(2b - 3c)$
$\quad 3 \times 3 \times (2 \times 4 - 3 \times (-5))$
$\quad = 9 \times (8 + 15)$
$\quad = 9 \times 23$
$\quad = 207$

f $\quad -2c(-a + 2b)$
$\quad -2 \times (-5) \times (-3 + 2 \times 4)$
$\quad = 10 \times (-3 + 8)$
$\quad = 10 \times 5$
$\quad = 50$

Exercise 11.7

Evaluate the following expressions if $a = 2$, $b = 3$ and $c = 5$:

1.   a $\quad 3a + 2b$ b $\quad 4a - 3b$
    c $\quad a - b - c$ d $\quad 3a - 2b + c$

2.   a $\quad -b(a + b)$ b $\quad -2c(a - b)$
    c $\quad -3a(a - 3c)$ d $\quad -4b(b - c)$

3.   a $\quad a^2 + b^2$ b $\quad b^2 + c^2$
    c $\quad 2a^2 - 3b^2$ d $\quad 3c^2 - 2b^2$

4.   a $\quad -a^2$ b $\quad (-a)^2$
    c $\quad -b^3$ d $\quad (-b)^3$

5.   a $\quad -c^3$ b $\quad (-c)^3$
    c $\quad (-ac)^2$ d $\quad -(ac)^2$

Exercise 11.8

Evaluate the following expressions if $p = 4$, $q = -2$, $r = 3$ and $s = -5$:

1.   a $\quad 2p + 4q$ b $\quad 5r - 3s$
    c $\quad 3q - 4s$ d $\quad 6p - 8q + 4s$
    e $\quad 3r - 3p + 5q$ f $\quad -p - q + r + s$

2.   a $\quad 2p - 3q - 4r + s$ b $\quad 3s - 4p + r + q$
    c $\quad p^2 + q^2$ d $\quad r^2 - s^2$
    e $\quad p(q - r + s)$ f $\quad r(2p - 3q)$

3.   a $\quad 2s(3p - 2q)$ b $\quad pq + rs$
    c $\quad 2pr - 3rq$ d $\quad q^3 - r^2$
    e $\quad s^3 - p^3$ f $\quad r^4 - q^5$

4.   a $\quad -2pqr$ b $\quad -2p(q + r)$
    c $\quad -2rq + r$ d $\quad (p + q)(r - s)$
    e $\quad (p + s)(r - q)$ f $\quad (r + q)(p - s)$

5.   a $\quad (2p + 3q)(p - q)$ b $\quad (q + r)(q - r)$
    c $\quad q^2 - r^2$ d $\quad p^2 - r^2$
    e $\quad (p + r)(p - r)$ f $\quad (-s + p)q^2$

Rearrangement of formulae

In the formula $a = 2b + c$, a is the **subject**. In order to make either b or c the subject, the formula has to be rearranged.

> **Worked example**
>
> Rearrange the following formulae to make the red letter the subject:
>
> a $\quad a = 2b + c$
> $\quad\quad a - 2b = c$
> $\quad\quad\quad c = a - 2b$
>
> b $\quad 2r + p = q$
> $\quad\quad p = q - 2r$
>
> c $\quad ab = cd$
> $\quad\quad \frac{ab}{d} = c$
> $\quad\quad\quad c = \frac{ab}{d}$
>
> d $\quad \frac{a}{b} = \frac{c}{d}$
> $\quad\quad ad = cb$
> $\quad\quad\quad d = \frac{cb}{a}$

Exercise 11.9

In the following questions, make the letter in red the subject of the formula:

1. a $\quad a + b = c$ b $\quad b + 2c = d$
   c $\quad 2b + c = 4a$ d $\quad 3d + b = 2a$

2. a $\quad ab = c$ b $\quad ac = bd$
   c $\quad ab = c + 3$ d $\quad ac = b - 4$

3. a $\quad m + n = r$ b $\quad m + n = p$
   c $\quad 2m + n = 3p$ d $\quad 3x = 2p + q$
   e $\quad ab = cd$ f $\quad ab = cd$

4. a $\quad 3xy = 4m$ b $\quad 7pq = 5r$
   c $\quad 3x = c$ d $\quad 3x + 7 = y$
   e $\quad 5y - 9 = 3r$ f $\quad 5y - 9 = 3x$

5. a $\quad 6b = 2a - 5$ b $\quad 6b = 2a - 5$
   c $\quad 3x - 7y = 4z$ d $\quad 3x - 7y = 4z$
   e $\quad 3x - 7y = 4z$ f $\quad 2pr - q = 8$

6. a $\quad \frac{p}{4} = r$ b $\quad \frac{4}{p} = 3r$
   c $\quad \frac{1}{5}n = 2p$ d $\quad \frac{1}{5}n = 2p$
   e $\quad p(q + r) = 2t$ f $\quad p(q + r) = 2t$

7. a $\quad 3m - n = rt(p + q)$ b $\quad 3m - n = rt(p + q)$
   c $\quad 3m - n = rt(p + q)$ d $\quad 3m - n = rt(p + q)$
   e $\quad 3m - n = rt(p + q)$ f $\quad 3m - n = rt(p + q)$

8. a $\quad \frac{ab}{c} = de$ b $\quad \frac{ab}{c} = de$
   c $\quad \frac{ab}{c} = de$ d $\quad \frac{a+b}{c} = d$
   e $\quad \frac{a}{c} + b = d$ f $\quad \frac{a}{c} + b = d$

11 ALGEBRAIC REPRESENTATION AND MANIPULATION

Student assessment 1

1. Expand:
   a. $4(a + 2)$
   b. $5(2b - 3)$
   c. $2c(c + 2d)$
   d. $3d(2c - 4d)$
   e. $-5(3e - f)$
   f. $-(-f + 2g)$

2. Expand and simplify where possible:
   a. $2a + 5(a + 2)$
   b. $3(2b - 3) - b$
   c. $-4c - (4 - 2c)$
   d. $3(d + 2) - 2(d + 4)$
   e. $-e(2e + 3) + 3(2 + e^2)$
   f. $f(d - e - f) - e(e + f)$
   g. $(x - 7)(x + 8)$
   h. $(3x + 1)(x + 2)$
   i. $(4x - 3)(-x + 2)$

3. Factorise:
   a. $7a + 14$
   b. $26b^2 + 39b$
   c. $3cf - 6df + 9gf$
   d. $5d^2 - 10d^3$

4. If $a = 2$, $b = 3$ and $c = 5$, evaluate the following:
   a. $a - b - c$
   b. $2b - c$
   c. $a^2 - b^2 + c^2$
   d. $(a + c)^2$

5. Rearrange the formulae to make the **green** letter the subject:
   a. $a - b = c$
   b. $2c = b - 3d$
   c. $ad = bc$
   d. $e = 5d - 3c$
   e. $4a = e(f + g)$
   f. $4a = e(f + g)$

Student assessment 2

1. Expand and simplify where possible:
   a. $3(2x - 3y + 5z)$
   b. $4p(2m - 7)$
   c. $-4m(2mn - n^2)$
   d. $4p^2(5pq - 2q^2 - 2p)$
   e. $4x - 2(3x + 1)$
   f. $4x(3x - 2) + 2(5x^2 - 3x)$
   g. $\frac{1}{5}(15x - 10) - \frac{1}{2}(9x - 12)$
   h. $\frac{1}{2}(4x - 6) + \frac{x}{4}(2x + 8)$
   i. $(10 - x)(10 + x)$
   j. $(c - d)(c + d)$
   k. $(3x - 5)^2$
   l. $(-2x + 1)(\frac{1}{2}x + 2)$

2. Factorise:
   a. $16p - 8q$
   b. $p^2 - 6pq$
   c. $5p^2q - 10pq^2$
   d. $9pq - 6p^2q + 12q^2p$

3. If $a = 4$, $b = 3$ and $c = -2$, evaluate the following:
   a. $3a - 2b + 3c$
   b. $5a - 3b^2$
   c. $a^2 + b^2 + c^2$
   d. $(a + b)(a - b)$
   e. $a^2 - b^2$
   f. $b^3 - c^3$

4. Rearrange the formulae to make the **green** letter the subject:
   a. $p = 4m + n$
   b. $4x - 3y = 5z$
   c. $2x = \frac{3y}{5p}$
   d. $m(x + y) = 3w$
   e. $\frac{pq}{4r} = \frac{mn}{t}$
   f. $\frac{p + q}{r} = m - n$

108

12 Algebraic indices

In Chapter 7 you saw how numbers can be expressed using indices. For example, $5 \times 5 \times 5 = 125$, therefore $125 = 5^3$. The 3 is called the index.

Three laws of indices were introduced:

1. $a^m \times a^n = a^{m+n}$
2. $a^m \div a^n$ or $\frac{a^m}{a^n} = a^{m-n}$
3. $(a^m)^n = a^{mn}$

Positive indices

> **Worked examples**

1. Simplify $d^3 \times d^4$.

   $d^3 \times d^4 = d^{(3+4)}$
   $ = d^7$

2. Simplify $\frac{(p^2)^4}{p^2 \times p^4}$.

   $\frac{(p^2)^4}{p^2 \times p^4} = \frac{p^{(2 \times 4)}}{p^{(2+4)}}$
   $\phantom{\frac{(p^2)^4}{p^2 \times p^4}} = \frac{p^8}{p^6}$
   $\phantom{\frac{(p^2)^4}{p^2 \times p^4}} = p^{(8-6)}$
   $\phantom{\frac{(p^2)^4}{p^2 \times p^4}} = p^2$

Exercise 12.1

1. Simplify:
   - a $c^5 \times c^3$
   - b $m^4 \div m^2$
   - c $(b^3)^5 \div b^6$
   - d $\frac{m^4 n^9}{mn^3}$
   - e $\frac{6a^6 b^4}{3a^2 b^3}$
   - f $\frac{12x^5 y^7}{4x^2 y^5}$
   - g $\frac{4u^3 v^6}{8u^2 v^3}$
   - h $\frac{3x^6 y^5 z^3}{9x^4 y^2 z}$

2. Simplify:
   - a $4a^2 \times 3a^3$
   - b $2a^2 b \times 4a^3 b^2$
   - c $(2p^2)^3$
   - d $(4m^2 n^3)^2$
   - e $(5p^2)^2 \times (2p^3)^3$
   - f $(4m^2 n^2) \times (2mn^3)^3$
   - g $\frac{(6x^2 y^4)^2 \times (2xy)^3}{12x^6 y^8}$
   - h $(ab)^d \times (ab)^e$

12 ALGEBRAIC INDICES

The zero index

As shown in Chapter 7, the zero index indicates that a number or algebraic term is raised to the power of zero. A term raised to the power of zero is always equal to 1. This is shown below:

$$a^m \div a^n = a^{m-n} \qquad \text{therefore } \frac{a^m}{a^m} = a^{m-m}$$
$$= a^0$$
$$\text{However, } \frac{a^m}{a^m} = 1$$
$$\text{therefore } a^0 = 1$$

Exercise 12.2 Simplify:

a $c^3 \times c^0$ b $g^{-2} \times g^3 \div g^0$ c $(p^0)^3(q^2)^{-1}$ d $(m^3)^3(m^{-2})^5$

Negative indices

A negative index indicates that a number or an algebraic term is being raised to a negative power, e.g. a^{-4}.

As shown in Chapter 7, one of the laws of indices states that:

$$a^{-m} = \frac{1}{a^m}$$

This is proved as follows:

$$a^{-m} = a^{0-m}$$
$$= \frac{a^0}{a^m} \text{ (from the second law of indices)}$$
$$= \frac{1}{a^m}$$
$$\text{therefore } a^{-m} = \frac{1}{a^m}$$

Exercise 12.3 Simplify:

a $\dfrac{a^{-3} \times a^5}{(a^2)^0}$ b $\dfrac{(r^3)^{-2}}{(p^{-2})^3}$ c $(t^3 \div t^{-5})^2$ d $\dfrac{m^0 \div m^{-6}}{(m^{-1})^3}$

Exponential equations

Equations that involve indices as unknowns are known as **exponential equations**.

> ### Worked examples

a Find the value of x if $2^x = 32$.

32 can be expressed as a power of 2,

$32 = 2^5$.

Therefore $2^x = 2^5$

$x = 5$

Exponential equations

b Find the value of m if $3^{(m-1)} = 81$.

81 can be expressed as a power of 3,
$81 = 3^4$.

Therefore $3^{(m-1)} = 3^4$
$$m - 1 = 4$$
$$m = 5$$

Exercise 12.4

1 Find the value of x in each of the following:
  a $2^x = 4$ **b** $2^x = 16$
  c $4^x = 64$ **d** $10^x = 1000$
  e $5^x = 625$ **f** $3^x = 1$

2 Find the value of z in each of the following:
  a $2^{(z-1)} = 8$ **b** $3^{(z+2)} = 27$
  c $4^{2z} = 64$ **d** $10^{(z+1)} = 1$
  e $3^z = 9^{(z-1)}$ **f** $5^z = 125^z$

Student assessment 1

1 Simplify the following using indices:
  a $a \times a \times a \times b \times b$ **b** $d \times d \times e \times e \times e \times e$

2 Write out in full:
  a m^3 **b** r^4

3 Simplify the following using indices:
  a $a^4 \times a^3$ **b** $p^3 \times p^2 \times q^4 \times q^5$
  c $\dfrac{b^7}{b^4}$ **d** $\dfrac{(e^4)^5}{e^{14}}$

4 Simplify:
  a $r^4 \times t^0$ **b** $\dfrac{(a^3)^0}{b^2}$ **c** $\dfrac{(m^0)^5}{n^{-3}}$

5 Simplify:
  a $\dfrac{(p^2 \times p^{-5})^2}{p^3}$ **b** $\dfrac{(h^{-2} \times h^{-5})^{-1}}{h^0}$

6 Find the value of x in each of the following:
  a $2^{(2x+2)} = 128$ **b** $3^{(-x+4)} = 81$

13 Equations

An **equation** is formed when the value of an unknown quantity is needed.

Deriving and solving linear equations in one unknown

> **Worked example**
>
> Solve the following linear equations:
>
> a $3x + 8 = 14$
> $3x = 6$
> $x = 2$
>
> b $12 = 20 + 2x$
> $-8 = 2x$
> $-4 = x$
>
> c $3(p + 4) = 21$
> $3p + 12 = 21$
> $3p = 9$
> $p = 3$
>
> d $4(x - 5) = 7(2x - 5)$
> $4x - 20 = 14x - 35$
> $4x + 15 = 14x$
> $15 = 10x$
> $1.5 = x$

Exercise 13.1

Solve these linear equations:

1. a $5a - 2 = 18$ b $7b + 3 = 17$ c $9c - 12 = 60$
   d $6d + 8 = 56$ e $4e - 7 = 33$ f $12f + 4 = 76$

2. a $4a = 3a + 7$ b $8b = 7b - 9$
   c $7c + 5 = 8c$ d $5d - 8 = 6d$

3. a $3a - 4 = 2a + 7$ b $5b + 3 = 4b - 9$
   c $8c - 9 = 7c + 4$ d $3d - 7 = 2d - 4$

4. a $6a - 3 = 4a + 7$ b $5b - 9 = 2b + 6$
   c $7c - 8 = 3c + 4$ d $11d - 10 = 6d - 15$

5. a $\frac{a}{4} = 3$ b $\frac{1}{4}b = 2$ c $\frac{c}{5} = 2$
   d $\frac{1}{5}d = 3$ e $4 = \frac{e}{3}$ f $-2 = \frac{1}{8}f$

Deriving and solving linear equations in one unknown

6 a $\frac{a}{3}+1=4$ b $\frac{b}{5}+2=6$ c $8=2+\frac{c}{3}$

   d $-4=3+\frac{d}{5}$ e $9=5+\frac{2e}{3}$ f $-7=\frac{3f}{2}-1$

7 a $\frac{2a}{3}=3$ b $5=\frac{3b}{2}$ c $\frac{4c}{5}=2$

   d $7=\frac{5d}{8}$ e $1+\frac{3e}{8}=-5$ f $2=\frac{5f}{7}-8$

8 a $\frac{a+3}{2}=4$ b $\frac{b+5}{3}=2$ c $5=\frac{c-2}{3}$

   d $2=\frac{d-5}{3}$ e $3=\frac{2e-1}{5}$ f $6=\frac{4f-2}{5}$

9 a $3(a+1)=9$ b $5(b-2)=25$ c $8=2(c-3)$
   d $14=4(3-d)$ e $21=3(5-e)$ f $36=9(5-2f)$

10 a $\frac{a+2}{3}=\frac{a-3}{2}$ b $\frac{b-1}{4}=\frac{b+5}{3}$ c $\frac{2-c}{5}=\frac{7-c}{4}$

   d $\frac{8+d}{7}=\frac{7+d}{6}$ e $\frac{3-e}{4}=\frac{5-e}{2}$ f $\frac{10+f}{3}=\frac{5-f}{2}$

Exercise 13.2 Solve the linear equations:

1 a $3x=2x-4$ b $5y=3y+10$ c $2y-5=3y$
   d $p-8=3p$ e $3y-8=2y$ f $7x+11=5x$

2 a $3x-9=4$ b $4=3x-11$ c $6x-15=3x+3$
   d $4y+5=3y-3$ e $8y-31=13-3y$ f $4m+2=5m-8$

3 a $7m-1=5m+1$ b $5p-3=3+3p$ c $12-2k=16+2k$
   d $6x+9=3x-54$ e $8-3x=18-8x$ f $2-y=y-4$

4 a $\frac{x}{2}=3$ b $\frac{1}{2}y=7$ c $\frac{x}{4}=1$

   d $\frac{1}{4}m=3$ e $7=\frac{x}{5}$ f $4=\frac{1}{5}p$

5 a $\frac{x}{3}-1=4$ b $\frac{x}{5}+2=1$ c $\frac{2}{3}x=5$

   d $\frac{3}{4}x=6$ e $\frac{1}{5}x=\frac{1}{2}$ f $\frac{2x}{5}=4$

6 a $\frac{x+1}{2}=3$ b $4=\frac{x-2}{3}$ c $\frac{x-10}{3}=4$

   d $8=\frac{5x-1}{3}$ e $\frac{2(x-5)}{3}=2$ f $\frac{3(x-2)}{4}=4x-8$

7 a $6=\frac{2(y-1)}{3}$ b $2(x+1)=3(x-5)$ c $5(x-4)=3(x+2)$

   d $\frac{3+y}{2}=\frac{y+1}{4}$ e $\frac{7+2x}{3}=\frac{9x-1}{7}$ f $\frac{2x+3}{4}=\frac{4x-2}{6}$

113

13 EQUATIONS

> **Note**
> All diagrams are not drawn to scale.

Constructing equations

In many cases, when dealing with the practical applications of mathematics, equations need to be constructed first before they can be solved. Often the information is either given within the context of a problem or in a diagram.

➤ Worked examples

1. **a** Write an expression for the sum of the angles in the triangle.

    $(x + 30) + (x - 30) + 90$

    b Find the size of each of the angles in the triangle by constructing an equation and solving it to find the value of x.

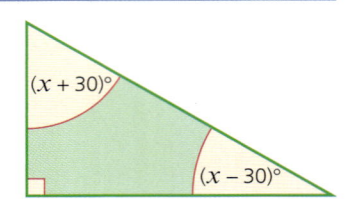

    The sum of the angles of a triangle is 180°.

    The sum of the angles of a triangle is 180°.

    $(x + 30) + (x - 30) + 90 = 180$
    $2x + 90 = 180$
    $2x = 90$
    $x = 45$

    The three angles are therefore: 90°, $x + 30 = 75°$ and $x - 30 = 15°$.
    Check: $90° + 75° + 15° = 180°$.

2. **a** Write an expression for the sum of the angles in the quadrilateral.

    $4x + 30 + 3x + 10 + 3x + 2x + 20$

    b Find the size of each of the angles in the quadrilateral by constructing an equation and solving it to find the value of x.

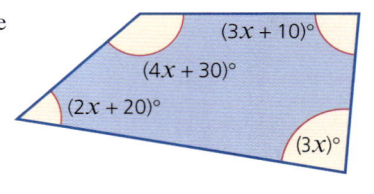

    The sum of the angles of a quadrilateral is 360°.

    The sum of the angles of a quadrilateral is 360°.

    $4x + 30 + 3x + 10 + 3x + 2x + 20 = 360$
    $12x + 60 = 360$
    $12x = 300$
    $x = 25$

    The angles are:

    $4x + 30 = (4 \times 25) + 30 = 130°$
    $3x + 10 = (3 \times 25) + 10 = 85°$
    $3x \quad\ \ = 3 \times 25 \quad\ \ = 75°$
    $2x + 20 = (2 \times 25) + 20 = 70°$
    $\qquad\qquad\qquad\text{Total} = 360°$

> **Note**
> There is more on angles in Chapter 18.

114

Constructing equations

Area of rectangle = base × height

3 Construct an equation and solve it to find the value of x in the diagram.

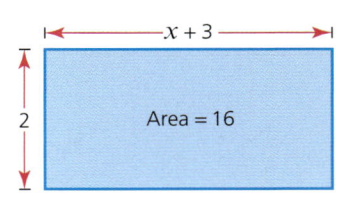

$2(x + 3) = 16$
$2x + 6 = 16$
$2x = 10$
$x = 5$

Exercise 13.3

In Q.1–3:
i Write an expression for the sum of the angles in each case, giving your answer in its simplest form.
ii construct an equation in terms of x
iii solve the equation
iv calculate the size of each of the angles
v check your answers.

1 a Triangle with angles $x°$, $(x+40)°$, $(x+20)°$

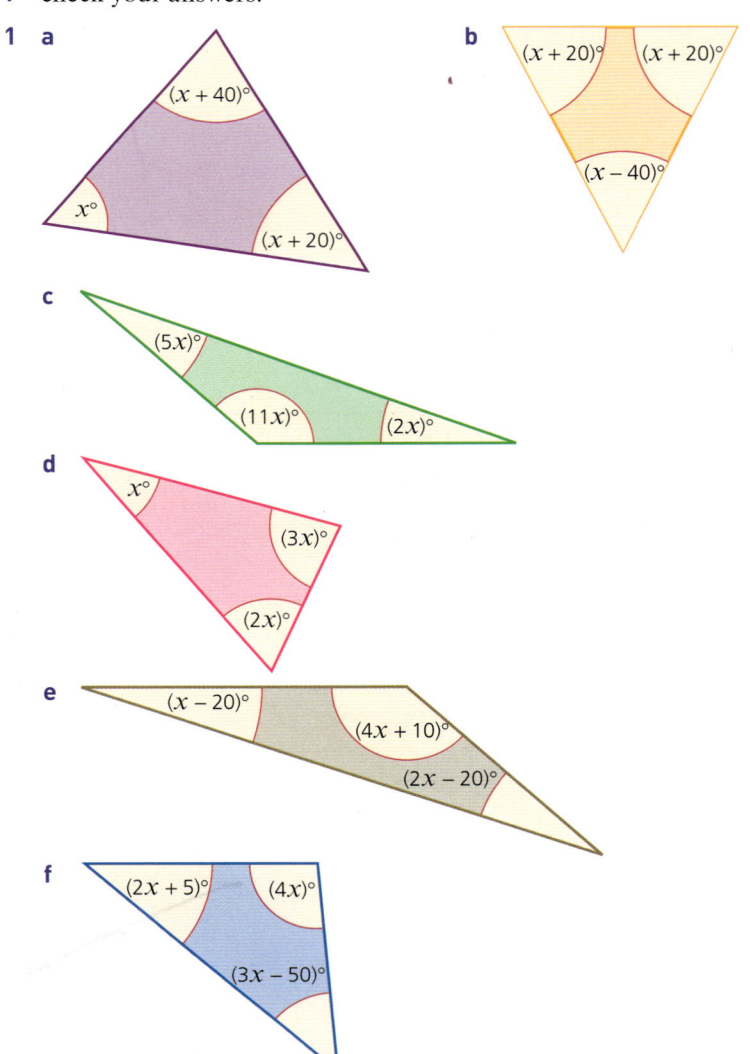

b Triangle with angles $(x+20)°$, $(x+20)°$, $(x-40)°$

c Triangle with angles $(5x)°$, $(11x)°$, $(2x)°$

d Triangle with angles $x°$, $(3x)°$, $(2x)°$

e Triangle with angles $(x-20)°$, $(4x+10)°$, $(2x-20)°$

f Triangle with angles $(2x+5)°$, $(4x)°$, $(3x-50)°$

13 EQUATIONS

Exercise 13.3 (cont)

2 a $(3x)°$, $(5x)°$, $(4x)°$

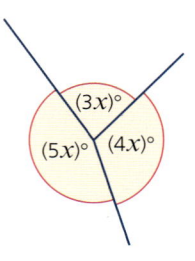

b $(3x)°$, $(4x+15)°$, $(4x+15)°$

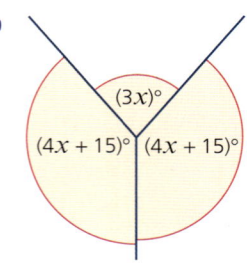

c $(6x+5)°$, $(2x+40)°$, $(x+10)°$, $(3x+5)°$

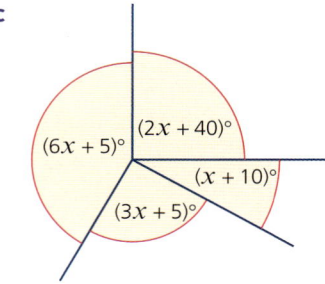

d $x°$, $(3x+15)°$, $(3x-5)°$, $(3x+20)°$

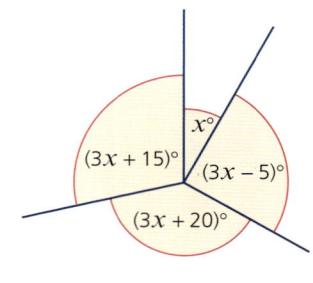

3 a $(4x)°$, $(3x-40)°$, $x°$, $(3x-40)°$

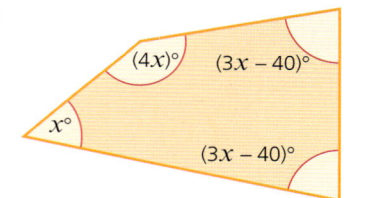

b $(3x)°$, $(3x+40)°$, $(3x+5)°$, $(x+15)°$

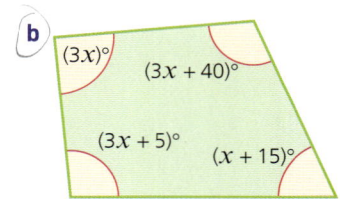

c $(5x-10)°$, $(5x+10)°$, $(4x+8)°$, $(2x)°$

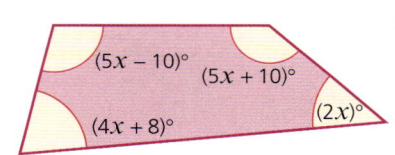

d $x°$, $(4x+10)°$, $(3x+15)°$, $(x+20)°$

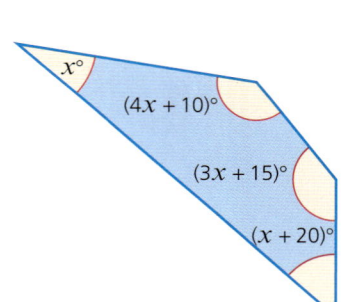

e $(x+23)°$, $(5x-5)°$

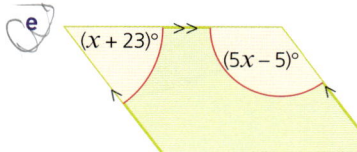

f $(2x+8)°$, $(4x-3)°$, $(3x-12)°$, $(2x-1)°$, $(3x+2)°$

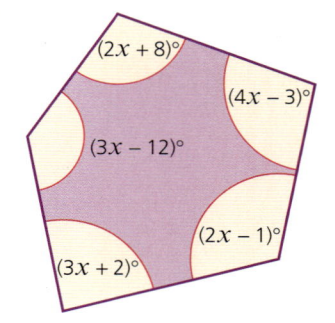

Constructing equations

4 By constructing an equation and solving it, find the value of x in each of these isosceles triangles:

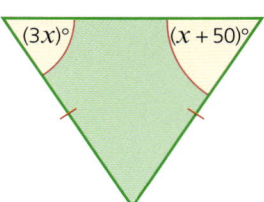

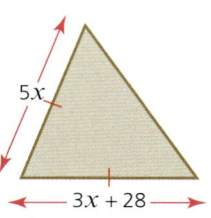

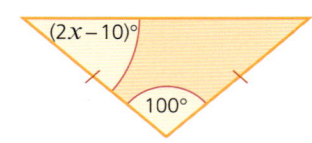

a [triangle with apex angle $x°$ and base angle $(4x)°$]

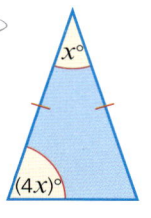

b [inverted triangle with top angles $(3x)°$ and $(x+50)°$]

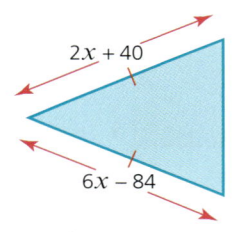

c [triangle with sides $5x$ and base $3x + 28$]

d [triangle with angles $(2x-10)°$ and $100°$]

e [triangle with sides $2x + 40$ and $6x - 84$]

f [triangle with apex angle $x°$ and base angle $70°$]

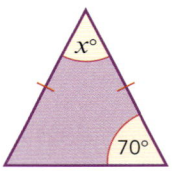

5 Using angle properties, calculate the value of x in each diagram:

a [two crossing lines with angles $(x+50)°$ and $(2x)°$]

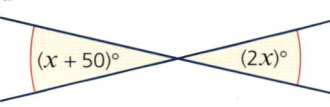

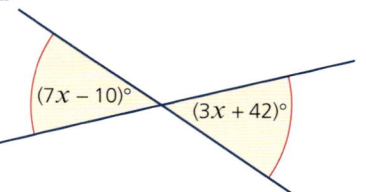

b [two crossing lines with angles $(7x-10)°$ and $(3x+42)°$]

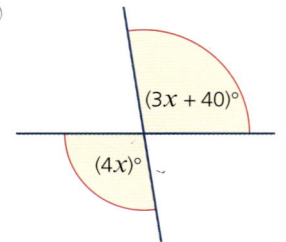

c [line crossed by another, angles $(3x+40)°$ and $(4x)°$]

d [two crossing lines with angles $(4x-55)°$ and $(2x+25)°$]

117

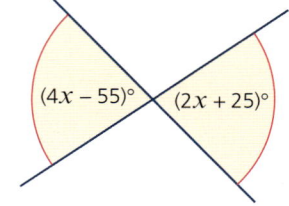

13 EQUATIONS

Exercise 13.3 (cont)

6 Calculate the value of x:

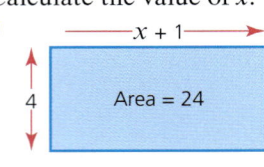

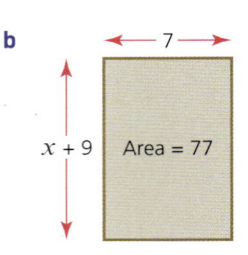

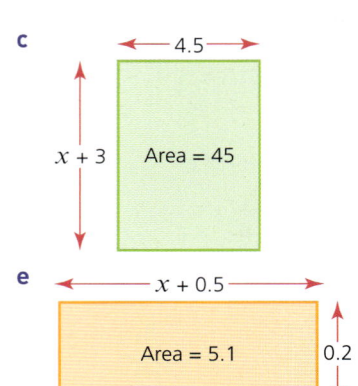

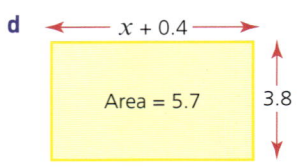

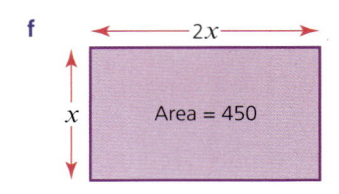

a. Rectangle: width $x+1$, height 4, Area = 24

b. Rectangle: width 7, height $x+9$, Area = 77

c. Rectangle: width 4.5, height $x+3$, Area = 45

d. Rectangle: width $x+0.4$, height 3.8, Area = 5.7

e. Rectangle: width $x+0.5$, height 0.2, Area = 5.1

f. Rectangle: width $2x$, height x, Area = 450

Sometimes a question is put into words and an equation must be formed from those words.

➜ Worked example

If I multiply a number by 4 and then add 6 the total is 26. What is the number?
Let the number be n.
  Then $4n + 6 = 26$
  $4n = 26 - 6$
  $4n = 20$
  $n = 5$

So the number is 5.

Exercise 13.4

In each case, find the number by forming an equation.

1. a If I multiply a number by 7 and add 1 the total is 22.
   b If I multiply a number by 9 and add 7 the total is 70.

2. a If I multiply a number by 8 and add 12 the total is 92.
   b If I add 2 to a number and then multiply by 3 the answer is 18.

3. a If I add 12 to a number and then multiply by 5 the answer is 100.
   b If I add 6 to a number and divide it by 4 the answer is 5.

4 a If I add 3 to a number and multiply by 4, the answer is the same as multiplying by 6 and adding 8.
  b If I add 1 to a number and then multiply by 3, the answer is the same as multiplying by 5 and subtracting 3.

Simultaneous equations

When the values of two unknowns are needed, two equations need to be formed and solved. The process of solving two equations and finding a common solution is known as **solving equations simultaneously**. The two most common ways of solving simultaneous equations algebraically are by **elimination** and by **substitution**.

By elimination

The aim of this method is to eliminate one of the unknowns by either adding or subtracting the two equations.

> **Worked examples**

Solve the following simultaneous equations by finding the values of x and x which satisfy both equations.

a $3x + y = 9$ (1)
   $5x - y = 7$ (2)

By adding equations (1) + (2) we eliminate the variable y:

$8x = 16$
$x = 2$

To find the value of y we substitute $x = 2$ into either equation (1) or (2). Substituting $x = 2$ into equation (1):

$3x + y = 9$

$6 + y = 9$

$y = 3$

To check that the solution is correct, the values of x and y are substituted into equation (2). If it is correct then the left-hand side of the equation will equal the right-hand side.

$5x - y = 7$
LHS $= 10 - 3 = 7$
$\qquad\quad$ = RHS

119

13 EQUATIONS

b $4x + y = 23$ (1)
   $x + y = 8$ (2)

By subtracting the equations, i.e. (1) − (2), we eliminate the variable y:

$3x = 15$

$x = 5$

By substituting $x = 5$ into equation (2), y can be calculated:

$x + y = 8$

$5 + y = 8$

$y = 3$

Check by substituting both values into equation (1):

$4x + y = 23$

LHS $= 20 + 3 = 23$

$=$ RHS

By substitution

The same equations can also be solved by the method known as substitution.

➡ Worked examples

a $3x + y = 9$ (1)
   $5x − y = 7$ (2)

Equation (2) can be rearranged to give: $y = 5x − 7$
This can now be substituted into equation (1):

$3x + (5x − 7) = 9$

$3x + 5x − 7 = 9$

$8x − 7 = 9$

$8x = 16$

$x = 2$

To find the value of y, $x = 2$ is substituted into either equation (1) or (2) as before, giving $y = 3$.

b $4x + y = 23$ (1)
   $x + y = 8$ (2)

Equation (2) can be rearranged to give $y = 8 − x$.
This can be substituted into equation (1):

$$4x + (8 - x) = 23$$
$$4x + 8 - x = 23$$
$$3x + 8 = 23$$
$$3x = 15$$
$$x = 5$$

y can be found as before, giving the result $y = 3$.

Exercise 13.5

Solve the simultaneous equations either by elimination or by substitution:

1.
   a. $x + y = 6$
      $x - y = 2$
   b. $x + y = 11$
      $x - y - 1 = 0$
   c. $x + y = 5$
      $x - y = 7$
   d. $2x + y = 12$
      $2x - y = 8$
   e. $3x + y = 17$
      $3x - y = 13$
   f. $5x + y = 29$
      $5x - y = 11$

2.
   a. $3x + 2y = 13$
      $4x = 2y + 8$
   b. $6x + 5y = 62$
      $4x - 5y = 8$
   c. $x + 2y = 3$
      $8x - 2y = 6$
   d. $9x + 3y = 24$
      $x - 3y = -14$
   e. $7x - y = -3$
      $4x + y = 14$
   f. $3x = 5y + 14$
      $6x + 5y = 58$

3.
   a. $2x + y = 14$
      $x + y = 9$
   b. $5x + 3y = 29$
      $x + 3y = 13$
   c. $4x + 2y = 50$
      $x + 2y = 20$
   d. $x + y = 10$
      $3x = -y + 22$
   e. $2x + 5y = 28$
      $4x + 5y = 36$
   f. $x + 6y = -2$
      $3x + 6y = 18$

4.
   a. $x - y = 1$
      $2x - y = 6$
   b. $3x - 2y = 8$
      $2x - 2y = 4$
   c. $7x - 3y = 26$
      $2x - 3y = 1$
   d. $x = y + 7$
      $3x - y = 17$
   e. $8x - 2y = -2$
      $3x - 2y = -7$
   f. $4x - y = -9$
      $7x - y = -18$

5.
   a. $x + y = -7$
      $x - y = -3$
   b. $2x + 3y = -18$
      $2x = 3y + 6$
   c. $5x - 3y = 9$
      $2x + 3y = 19$
   d. $7x + 4y = 42$
      $9x - 4y = -10$
   e. $4x - 4y = 0$
      $8x + 4y = 12$
   f. $x - 3y = -25$
      $5x - 3y = -17$

6.
   a. $2x + 3y = 13$
      $2x - 4y + 8 = 0$
   b. $2x + 4y = 50$
      $2x + y = 20$
   c. $x + y = 10$
      $3y = 22 - x$
   d. $5x + 2y = 28$
      $5x + 4y = 36$
   e. $2x - 8y = 2$
      $2x - 3y = 7$
   f. $x - 4y = 9$
      $x - 7y = 18$

7.
   a. $-4x = 4y$
      $4x - 8y = 12$
   b. $3x = 19 + 2y$
      $-3x + 5y = 5$
   c. $3x + 2y = 12$
      $-3x + 9y = -12$
   d. $3x + 5y = 29$
      $3x + y = 13$
   e. $-5x + 3y = 14$
      $5x + 6y = 58$
   f. $-2x + 8y = 6$
      $2x = 3 - y$

Further simultaneous equations

If neither x nor y can be eliminated by simply adding or subtracting the two equations, then it is necessary to multiply one or both of the equations. The equations are multiplied by a number in order to make the coefficients of x (or y) numerically equal.

13 EQUATIONS

→ Worked examples

a $3x + 2y = 22$ (1)

$x + y = 9$ (2)

To eliminate y, equation (2) is multiplied by 2:

$3x + 2y = 22$ (1)

$2x + 2y = 18$ (3)

By subtracting (3) from (1), the variable y is eliminated:

$x = 4$

Substituting $x = 4$ into equation (2), we have:

$x + y = 9$

$4 + y = 9$

$y = 5$

Check by substituting both values into equation (1):

$\quad 3x + 2y = 22$

LHS $= 12 + 10 = 22$

$\qquad\quad = $ RHS

b $5x - 3y = 1$ (1)

$3x + 4y = 18$ (2)

To eliminate the variable y, equation (1) is multiplied by 4, and equation (2) is multiplied by 3.

$20x - 12y = 4$ (3)

$9x + 12y = 54$ (4)

By adding equations (3) and (4) the variable y is eliminated:

$29x = 58$

$x = 2$

Substituting $x = 2$ into equation (2) gives:

$3x + 4y = 18$

$6 + 4y = 18$

$4y = 12$

$y = 3$

Check by substituting both values into equation (1):

$5x - 3y = 1$

LHS $= 10 - 9 = 1$

$\qquad\quad = $ RHS

Further simultaneous equations

Exercise 13.6

Solve the simultaneous equations either by elimination or by substitution.

1. a) $2a + b = 5$
    $3a - 2b = 4$
   b) $3b + 2c = 18$
    $2b - c = 5$
   c) $4c - d = 18$
    $2c + 2d = 14$
   d) $d + 5e = 17$
    $2d - 8e = -2$
   e) $3e - f = 5$
    $e + 2f = 11$
   f) $f + 3g = 5$
    $2f - g = 3$

2. a) $a + 2b = 8$
    $3a - 5b = -9$
   b) $4b - 3c = 17$
    $b + 5c = 10$
   c) $6c - 4d = -2$
    $5c + d = 7$
   d) $5d + e = 18$
    $2d + 3e = 15$
   e) $e + 2f = 14$
    $3e - f = 7$
   f) $7f - 5g = 9$
    $f + g = 3$

3. a) $3a - 2b = -5$
    $a + 5b = 4$
   b) $b + 2c = 3$
    $3b - 5c = -13$
   c) $c - d = 4$
    $3c + 4d = 5$
   d) $2d + 3e = 2$
    $3d - e = -8$
   e) $e - 2f = -7$
    $3e + 3f = -3$
   f) $f + g = -2$
    $3f - 4g = 1$

4. a) $2x + y = 7$
    $3x + 2y = 12$
   b) $5x + 4y = 21$
    $x + 2y = 9$
   c) $x + y = 7$
    $3x + 4y = 23$
   d) $2x - 3y = -3$
    $3x + 2y = 15$
   e) $4x = 4y + 8$
    $x + 3y = 10$
   f) $x + 5y = 11$
    $2x - 2y = 10$

5. a) $x + y = 5$
    $3x - 2y + 5 = 0$
   b) $2x - 2y = 6$
    $x - 5y = -5$
   c) $2x + 3y = 15$
    $2y = 15 - 3x$
   d) $x - 6y = 0$
    $3x - 3y = 15$
   e) $2x - 5y = -11$
    $3x + 4y = 18$
   f) $x + y = 5$
    $2x - 2y = -2$

6. a) $3y = 9 + 2x$
    $3x + 2y = 6$
   b) $x + 4y = 13$
    $3x - 3y = 9$
   c) $2x = 3y - 19$
    $3x + 2y = 17$
   d) $2x - 5y = -8$
    $-3x - 2y = -26$
   e) $5x - 2y = 0$
    $2x + 5y = 29$
   f) $8y = 3 - x$
    $3x - 2y = 9$

7. a) $4x + 2y = 5$
    $3x + 6y = 6$
   b) $4x + y = 14$
    $6x - 3y = 3$
   c) $10x - y = -2$
    $-15x + 3y = 9$
   d) $-2y = 0.5 - 2x$
    $6x + 3y = 6$
   e) $x + 3y = 6$
    $2x - 9y = 7$
   f) $5x - 3y = -0.5$
    $3x + 2y = 3.5$

Exercise 13.7

1. The sum of two numbers is 17 and their difference is 3. Find the two numbers by forming two equations and solving them simultaneously.

2. The difference between two numbers is 7. If their sum is 25, find the two numbers by forming two equations and solving them simultaneously.

123

13 EQUATIONS

Exercise 13.7 (cont)

3 Find the values of x and y.

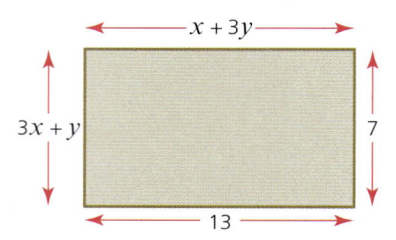

[Rectangle with top side $x + 3y$, left side $3x + y$, right side 7, bottom side 13]

4 Find the values of x and y.

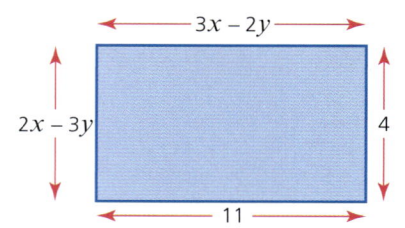

[Rectangle with top side $3x - 2y$, left side $2x - 3y$, right side 4, bottom side 11]

5 This year, a man's age m is three times his son's age s. Ten years ago, the man's age was five times the age his son was then. By forming two equations and solving them simultaneously, find both of their ages.

6 A grandfather is ten times as old as his granddaughter. He is also 54 years older than her. How old is each of them?

Student assessment 1

Solve the equations:

1 a $a + 9 = 15$ b $3b + 7 = -14$
   c $3 - 5c = 18$ d $4 - 7d = -24$

2 a $5a + 7 = 4a - 3$ b $8 - 3b = 4 - 2b$
   c $6 - 3c = c + 8$ d $4d - 3 = d + 9$

3 a $\frac{a}{5} = 2$ b $\frac{b}{7} = 3$
   c $4 = c - 2$ d $6 = \frac{1}{3}d$

4 a $\frac{a}{2} + 1 = 5$ b $\frac{b}{3} - 2 = 3$
   c $7 = \frac{c}{3} - 1$ d $1 = \frac{1}{3}d - 2$

5 a $\frac{a-2}{3} = \frac{a+2}{2}$ b $\frac{b+5}{4} = \frac{2+b}{3}$
   c $4(c - 5) = 3(c + 1)$ d $6(2 + 3d) = 5(4d - 2)$

Further simultaneous equations

6 Solve the simultaneous equations:
- **a** $a + 2b = 4$
  $3a + b = 7$
- **b** $b - 2c = -2$
  $3b + c = 15$
- **c** $2c - 3d = -5$
  $4c + d = -3$
- **d** $4d + 5e = 0$
  $d + e = -1$

7 Two students are buying school supplies. One buys a ruler and three pens, paying $7.70. The other student buys a ruler and five pens, paying $12.30. Calculate the cost of each of the items.

Student assessment 2

Solve the equations:
1
- **a** $x + 7 = 16$
- **b** $2x - 9 = 13$
- **c** $8 - 4x = 24$
- **d** $5 - 3x = -13$

2
- **a** $7 - m = 4 + m$
- **b** $5m - 3 = 3m + 11$
- **c** $6m - 1 = 9m - 13$
- **d** $18 - 3p = 6 + p$

3
- **a** $\frac{x}{-5} = 2$
- **b** $4 = \frac{1}{3}x$
- **c** $\frac{x+2}{3} = 4$
- **d** $\frac{2x-5}{7} = \frac{5}{2}$

4
- **a** $\frac{2}{3}(x - 4) = 8$
- **b** $4(x - 3) = 7(x + 2)$
- **c** $4 = \frac{2}{7}(3x + 8)$
- **d** $\frac{3}{4}(x - 1) = \frac{5}{8}(2x - 4)$

5 Solve the simultaneous equations:
- **a** $2x + 3y = 16$
  $2x - 3y = 4$
- **b** $4x + 2y = 22$
  $-2x + 2y = 2$
- **c** $x + y = 9$
  $2x + 4y = 26$
- **d** $2x - 3y = 7$
  $-3x + 4y = -11$

6 Two numbers added together equal 13. The difference between the two numbers is 6.5. Calculate each of the two numbers.

14 Sequences

Sequences

A **sequence** is an ordered set of numbers. Each number in a sequence is known as a **term**. The terms of a sequence form a pattern. For the sequence of numbers:

2, 5, 8, 11, 14, 17, ...

the difference between successive terms is +3. The **term-to-term rule** is therefore + 3.

→ Worked examples

1 Below is a sequence of numbers.

   5, 9, 13, 17, 21, 25, ...

   a What is the term-to-term rule for the sequence?

   The term-to-term rule is + 4.

   b Calculate the 10th term of the sequence.

   Continuing the pattern gives:

   5, 9, 13, 17, 21, 25, 29, 33, 37, 41, ...

   Therefore the 10th term is 41.

2 Below is a sequence of numbers.

   1, 2, 4, 8, 16, ...

   a What is the term-to-term rule for the sequence?

   The term-to-term rule is × 2.

   b Calculate the 10th term of the sequence.

   Continuing the pattern gives:

   1, 2, 4, 8, 16, 32, 64, 128, 256, 512, ...

   Therefore the 10th term is 512.

Exercise 14.1

For each of the sequences:

i State a rule to describe the sequence.

ii Calculate the 10th term.

a 3, 6, 9, 12, 15, ...
b 8, 18, 28, 38, 48, ...
c 11, 33, 55, 77, 99, ...
d 0.7, 0.5, 0.3, 0.1, ...
e $\frac{1}{2}, \frac{1}{3}, \frac{1}{4}, \frac{1}{5}, ...$
f $\frac{1}{2}, \frac{2}{3}, \frac{3}{4}, \frac{4}{5}, ...$

Sequences

g 1, 4, 9, 16, 25, ... **h** 4, 7, 12, 19, 28, ...
i 1, 8, 27, 64, ... **j** 5, 25, 125, 625, ...

Sometimes, the pattern in a sequence of numbers is not obvious. By looking at the differences between successive terms, a pattern can often be found.

→ Worked examples

1 Calculate the 8th term in the sequence

8, 12, 20, 32, 48, ...

The pattern in this sequence is not immediately obvious, so a row for the differences between successive terms can be constructed.

```
                    8      12      20      32      48
1st differences         4       8      12      16
```

The pattern in the differences row is + 4 and this can be continued to complete the sequence to the 8th term.

```
                 8   12   20   32   48   68   92   120
1st differences     4    8   12   16   20   24   28
```

So the 8th term is 120.

2 Calculate the 8th term in the sequence

3, 6, 13, 28, 55, ...

1st differences   3   7   15   27

The row of first differences is not sufficient to spot the pattern, so a row of 2nd differences is constructed.

```
                    3     6    13    28    55
1st differences        3     7    15    27
2nd differences           4     8    12
```

The pattern in the 2nd differences row can be seen to be + 4. This can now be used to complete the sequence.

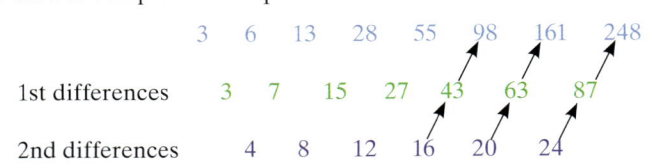

```
                 3    6   13   28   55   98   161   248
1st differences     3    7   15   27   43   63    87
2nd differences        4    8   12   16   20    24
```

So the 8th term is 248.

3 Calculate the 7th term in the sequence:

```
                    8    3    1    2    6
1st differences       −5   −2    1    4
2nd differences          3    3    3
```

127

14 SEQUENCES

The pattern of the second differences row is +3. This can now be used to continue the sequence:

	8		3		1		2		6		13		23
1st differences		−5		−2		1		4		7		10	
2nd differences			3		3		3		3		3		

The 7th term is therefore 23.

Exercise 14.2

For each of the sequences, calculate the next two terms:
- **a** 8, 11, 17, 26, 38, ...
- **b** 5, 7, 11, 19, 35, ...
- **c** 9, 3, 3, 9, 21, ...
- **d** −2, 5, 21, 51, 100, ...
- **e** 11, 9, 10, 17, 36, 79, ...
- **f** 4, 7, 11, 19, 36, 69, ...
- **g** −3, 3, 8, 13, 17, 21, 24, ...

The nth term

So far, the method used for generating a sequence relies on knowing the previous term to work out the next one. This method works but can be a little cumbersome if the 100th term is needed and only the first five terms are given! A more efficient rule is one which is related to a term's position in a sequence.

Worked examples

1 For the sequence shown, give an expression for the nth term.

Position	1	2	3	4	5	n
Term	3	6	9	12	15	?

By looking at the sequence it can be seen that the term is always $3 \times$ position.

Therefore the nth term can be given by the expression $3n$.

2 **a** For the sequence shown, give an expression for the nth term.

Position	1	2	3	4	5	n
Term	2	5	8	11	14	?

You will need to spot similarities between sequences. The terms of the above sequence are the same as the terms in example 1 above but with 1 subtracted each time.

The expression for the nth term is therefore $3n - 1$.

b Explain whether the term 165 is part of this sequence.

When $n = 55$ the term is $3 \times 55 - 1 = 164$

When $n = 56$ the term is $3 \times 56 - 1 = 167$

Therefore, 165 is not part of the sequence.

Exercise 14.3

1 For each of the sequences:
   i Write down the next two terms.
   ii Give an expression for the nth term.

   a 5, 8, 11, 14, 17, ...
   b 5, 9, 13, 17, 21, ...
   c 4, 9, 14, 19, 24, ...
   d 8, 10, 12, 14, 16, ...
   e 29, 22, 15, 8, 1, ...
   f 0, 4, 8, 12, 16, 20, ...
   g 1, 10, 19, 28, 37, ...
   h 15, 25, 35, 45, 55, ...
   i 9, 20, 31, 42, 53, ...
   j 1.5, 3.5, 5.5, 7.5, 9.5, 11.5, ...
   k 0.25, 1.25, 2.25, 3.25, 4.25, ...
   l 5, 4, 3, 2, 1, ...

2 The nth term for two different sequences are $2n + 8$ and $5n - 37$. Justifying your answers work out:
   a Which sequence, if any, the term 22 belongs to.
   b Which sequence, if any, the term 51 belongs to.
   c A term which belongs to both sequences.

Further sequences

To be able to spot rules for more complicated sequences, it is important to be aware of some other common types of sequence.

Worked examples

1

Position	1	2	3	4	5	n
Term	1	4	9	16		

   a Describe the sequence in words.
   The terms form the sequence of square numbers.
   i.e. $1 \times 1 = 1$, $2 \times 2 = 4$, $3 \times 3 = 9$, $4 \times 4 = 16$

   b Predict the 5th term.
   The 5th term is the fifth square number, i.e. $5 \times 5 = 25$.

   c Write the rule for the nth term.
   The nth term is $n \times n = n^2$.

2

Position	1	2	3	4	5	n
Term	1	8	27	64		

   a Describe the sequence in words.
   The terms form the sequence of cube numbers.
   i.e. $1 \times 1 \times 1 = 1$, $2 \times 2 \times 2 = 8$, $3 \times 3 \times 3 = 27$, $4 \times 4 \times 4 = 64$

   b Predict the 5th term.
   The 5th term is the fifth cube number, i.e. $5 \times 5 \times 5 = 125$.

   c Write the rule for the nth term.
   The nth term is $n \times n \times n = n^3$.

14 SEQUENCES

3 The table shows a sequence that is a pattern of growing triangles:

Position	1	2	3	4	5	n
Pattern	•	••	•••	••••		
Term	1	3	6	10		

a Predict the number of dots in the fifth position of the pattern.

The number of dots added each time is the same as the position number.

Therefore the number of dots in the fifth position is the number of dots in the fourth position + 5, i.e. 10 + 5 = 15.

b Calculate the nth term.

The rule can be deduced by looking at the dot patterns themselves.

The second pattern can be doubled and arranged as a rectangle as shown.

The total number of dots is $2 \times 3 = 6$.

The total number of black dots is therefore $\frac{1}{2} \times 2 \times 3 = 3$.

Notice that the height of the rectangle is equal to the position number (i.e. 2) and its length is one more than the position number (i.e. 3).

The third pattern can be doubled and arranged as a rectangle as shown.

The total number of dots is $3 \times 4 = 12$.

The total number of black dots is therefore $\frac{1}{2} \times 3 \times 4 = 6$.

Once again the height of the rectangle is equal to the position number (i.e. 3) and its length is one more than the position number (i.e. 4).

Therefore the nth pattern of dots can also be doubled and arranged into a rectangle with a height equal to n and a width equal to $n + 1$ as shown:

The total area is $n(n + 1)$.

The black area is therefore $\frac{1}{2}n(n+1)$.

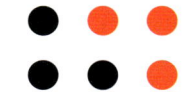

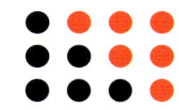

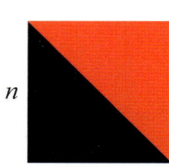

> **Note**
>
> The sequence of numbers 1, 3, 6, 10, 15, etc. is known as the sequence of **triangular numbers**. The formula for the nth triangular number is $\frac{1}{2}n(n+1)$.
>
> It is important to be able to identify these sequences as they are often used to form other sequences.

Further sequences

> **Worked examples**

1 A sequence of numbers is: 3, 6, 11, 18, 27, ...

   a Calculate the next two terms.

   The difference between the terms goes up by 2 each time.

   Therefore the next two terms are 38 and 51.

   b Calculate the rule for the nth term.

   This is not as difficult as it first seems if its similarity to the sequence of square numbers is noticed as shown:

Position	1	2	3	4	5	n
Square numbers	1	4	9	16	25	n^2
Term	3	6	11	18	27	

   The numbers in the given sequence are always 2 more than the sequence of square numbers.

   Therefore the rule for the nth term is $n^2 + 2$.

2 A sequence of numbers is: 0, 2, 5, 9, 14, ...

   a Calculate the next two terms.

   The difference between the terms goes up by 1 each time.

   Therefore the next two terms are 20 and 27.

   b Calculate the rule for the nth term.

   This too is not as difficult as it first seems if its similarity to the sequence of triangular numbers is noticed as shown:

Position	1	2	3	4	5	n
Triangular numbers	1	3	6	10	15	$\frac{1}{2}n(n+1)$
Term	0	2	5	9	14	

   The numbers in the given sequence are always 1 less than the sequence of triangular numbers. Therefore the rule for the nth term is $\frac{1}{2}n(n+1) - 1$.

Exercise 14.4

For each of the sequences in Q.1–5, consider their relation to sequences of square, cube or triangular numbers and then:
   i   Write down the next two terms.
   ii Write down the rule for the nth term.

1 2,   8,   18,   32, ...   2 2,   6,   12,   20, ...

3 –1, 6,   25,   62, ...   4 5,   8,   13,   20, ...

5 $\frac{1}{2}$, 4, $13\frac{1}{2}$, 32, ...

131

14 SEQUENCES

For each of the sequences in Q.6–8, consider their relation to the sequences above and write the rule for the nth term.

6   1,   7,   17,   31,   ...

7   1,   5,   11,   19,   ...

8   –2,   12,   50,   124,   ...

Student assessment 1

1 For each of the sequences:
   i Calculate the next two terms.   **ii** Explain the pattern in words.
   - **a** 9, 18, 27, 36, ...
   - **b** 54, 48, 42, 36, ...
   - **c** 18, 9, 4.5, ...
   - **d** 12, 6, 0, –6, ...
   - **e** 216, 125, 64, ...
   - **f** 1, 3, 9, 27, ...

2 For each of the sequences:
   i Calculate the next two terms.   **ii** Explain the pattern in words.
   - **a** 6, 12, 18, 24, ...
   - **b** 24, 21, 18, 15, ...
   - **c** 10, 5, 0, ...
   - **d** 16, 25, 36, 49, ...
   - **e** 1, 10, 100, ...
   - **f** 1, $\frac{1}{2}$, $\frac{1}{4}$, $\frac{1}{8}$, ...

3 For each of the sequences, give an expression for the nth term:
   - **a** 6, 10, 14, 18, 22, ...
   - **b** 13, 19, 25, 31, ...
   - **c** 3, 9, 15, 21, 27, ...
   - **d** 4, 7, 12, 19, 28, ...
   - **e** 0, 10, 20, 30, 40, ...
   - **f** 0, 7, 26, 63, 124, ...

4 For each of the sequences, give an expression for the nth term:
   - **a** 3, 5, 7, 9, 11, ...
   - **b** 7, 13, 19, 25, 31, ...
   - **c** 8, 18, 28, 38, ...
   - **d** 1, 9, 17, 25, ...
   - **e** –4, 4, 12, 20, ...
   - **f** 2, 5, 10, 17, 26, ...

5
   a Write down the first five terms of the sequence of square numbers.
   b Write down the first five terms of the sequence of cube numbers.
   c Write down the first five terms of the sequence of triangular numbers.

6 For each of the sequences:
   i Write the next two terms.   **ii** Write the rule for the nth term.
   - **a** 4, 7, 12, 19, ...
   - **b** 2, 16, 54, 128, ...
   - **c** $\frac{1}{2}$, $1\frac{1}{2}$, 3, 5, ...
   - **d** 0, 4, 10, 18, ...

15 Graphs in practical situations

Conversion graphs

A straight line graph can be used to convert one set of units to another. Examples include converting from one currency to another, converting miles to kilometres and converting temperatures from degrees Celsius to degrees Fahrenheit.

➜ Worked example

The graph below converts US dollars into Chinese yuan based on an exchange rate of $1 = 8.80 yuan.

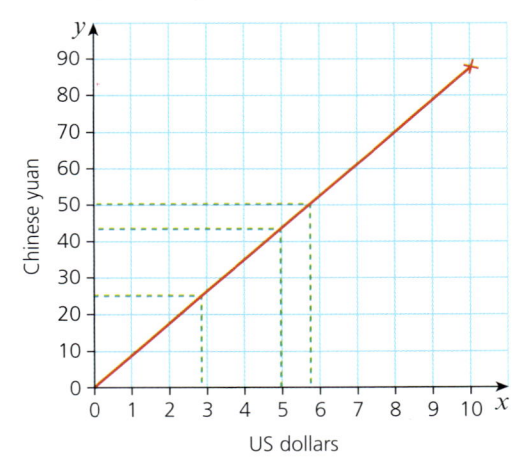

> **Note**
>
> ≈ is the symbol for 'is approximately equal to'.

a Using the graph, estimate the number of yuan equivalent to $5.

A line is drawn up from $5 until it reaches the plotted line, then across to the y-axis. From the graph it can be seen that $5 ≈ 44 yuan.

b Using the graph, what would be the cost in dollars of a drink costing 25 yuan?

A line is drawn across from 25 yuan until it reaches the plotted line, then down to the x-axis. From the graph it can be seen that the cost of the drink ≈ $2.80.

c If a meal costs 200 yuan, use the graph to estimate its cost in US dollars.

The graph does not go up to 200 yuan, therefore a factor of 200 needs to be used, e.g. 50 yuan. From the graph 50 yuan ≈ $5.70, therefore it can be deduced that 200 yuan ≈ $22.80 (i.e. 4 × $5.70).

15 GRAPHS IN PRACTICAL SITUATIONS

Exercise 15.1

> **Note**
> A diagram may help you answer these questions.

1. Given that 80 km = 50 miles, draw a conversion graph up to 100 km. Using your graph, estimate:
   a. how many miles in 50 km
   b. how many kilometres in 80 miles
   c. the speed in miles per hour (mph) equivalent to 100 km/h
   d. the speed in km/h equivalent to 40 mph.

2. You can roughly convert temperature in degrees Celsius to degrees Fahrenheit by doubling the degrees Celsius and adding 30.
   Draw a conversion graph up to 50 °C. Use your graph to estimate the following:
   a. the temperature in °F equivalent to 25 °C
   b. the temperature in °C equivalent to 100 °F
   c. the temperature in °F equivalent to 0 °C.

3. Given that 0 °C = 32 °F and 50 °C = 122 °F, on the graph you drew for Q.2, draw a true conversion graph.
   a. Use the true graph to calculate the conversions in Q.2.
   b. Where would you say the rough conversion is most useful?

4. Long-distance calls from New York to Harare are priced at 85 cents/min off-peak and $1.20/min at peak times.
   a. Draw, on the same axes, conversion graphs for the two different rates.
   b. From your graph, estimate the cost of an 8-minute call made off-peak.
   c. Estimate the cost of the same call made at peak rate.
   d. A caller has $4 of credit on his phone, estimate how much more time he can talk for if he rings at off-peak instead of at peak times.

5. A maths exam is marked out of 120. Draw a conversion graph and use it to change the following marks to percentages.
   a. 80   b. 110   c. 54   d. 72

Speed, distance and time

You may already be aware of the formula:

$$\text{Distance} = \text{speed} \times \text{time}$$

Rearranging the formula gives:

$$\text{Time} = \frac{\text{distance}}{\text{speed}} \quad \text{and} \quad \text{Speed} = \frac{\text{distance}}{\text{time}}$$

Where the speed is not constant:

$$\text{Average speed} = \frac{\text{total distance}}{\text{total time}}$$

Exercise 15.2

1. Find the average speed of an object moving:
   a. 30 m in 5 s
   b. 48 m in 12 s
   c. 78 km in 2 h
   d. 50 km in 2.5 h
   e. 400 km in 2 h 30 min
   f. 110 km in 2 h 12 min

Exercise 15.2 (cont)

2. How far will an object travel during:
   a. 10 s at 40 m/s
   b. 7 s at 26 m/s
   c. 3 hours at 70 km/h
   d. 4 h 15 min at 60 km/h
   e. 10 min at 60 km/h
   f. 1 h 6 min at 20 m/s?

3. How long will it take to travel:
   a. 50 m at 10 m/s
   b. 1 km at 20 m/s
   c. 2 km at 30 km/h
   d. 5 km at 70 m/s
   e. 200 cm at 0.4 m/s
   f. 1 km at 15 km/h?

Travel graphs

The graph of an object travelling at a constant speed is a straight line as shown (right).

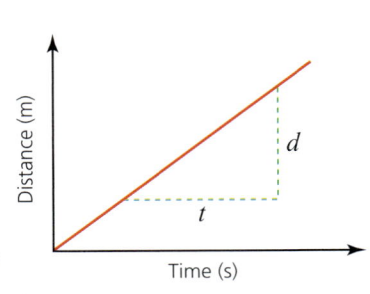

$$\text{gradient} = \frac{d}{t}$$

The units of the gradient are m/s, hence the gradient of a distance–time graph represents the speed at which the object is travelling. Another way of interpreting the gradient of a distance–time graph is that it represents the rate of change of distance with time.

➡ Worked example

The graph represents an object travelling at constant speed.

a. From the graph, calculate how long it took to cover a distance of 30 m.

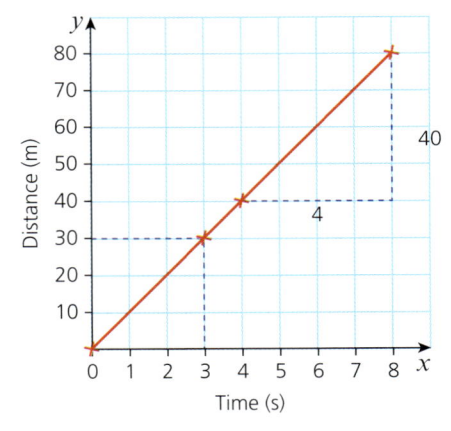

The time taken to travel 30 m was 3 seconds.

b. Calculate the gradient of the graph.

Taking two points on the line,

$$\text{gradient} = \frac{40\,\text{m}}{4\,\text{s}}$$

$$= 10\,\text{m/s}$$

15 GRAPHS IN PRACTICAL SITUATIONS

c Calculate the speed at which the object was travelling.

Gradient of a distance–time graph = speed.

Therefore the speed is 10 m/s.

Exercise 15.3

Note
A diagram may help you answer these questions.

1. Draw a distance–time graph for the first 10 seconds of an object travelling at 6 m/s.

2. Draw a distance–time graph for the first 10 seconds of an object travelling at 5 m/s. Use your graph to estimate:
   a the time taken to travel 25 m
   b how far the object travels in 3.5 seconds.

3. Two objects, A and B, set off from the same point and move in the same straight line. B sets off first, while A sets off 2 seconds later.

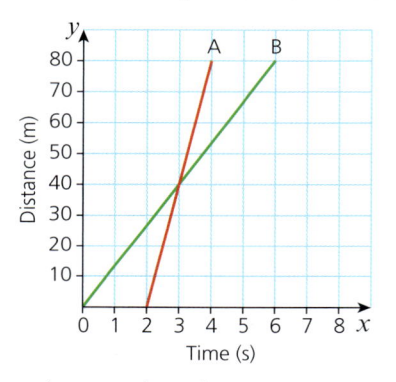

   Using the distance–time graph, estimate:
   a the rate of change of distance with time of each of the objects
   b how far apart the objects would be 20 seconds after the start.

4. Three objects, A, B and C, move in the same straight line away from a point X. Both A and C change their speed during the journey, while B travels at a constant speed throughout.

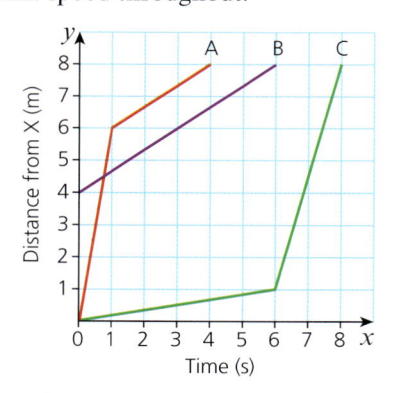

   From the distance–time graph, estimate:
   a the speed of object B
   b the two speeds of object A

Travel graphs

    c the average rate of change of distance with time of object C
    d how far object C is from X, 3 seconds from the start
    e how far apart objects A and C are, 4 seconds from the start.

The graphs of two or more journeys can be shown on the same axes. The shape of the graph gives a clear picture of the movement of each of the objects.

➜ Worked example

The journeys of two cars, X and Y, travelling between A and B, are represented on the distance–time graph. Car X and Car Y both reach point B, 100 km from A, at 11 00.

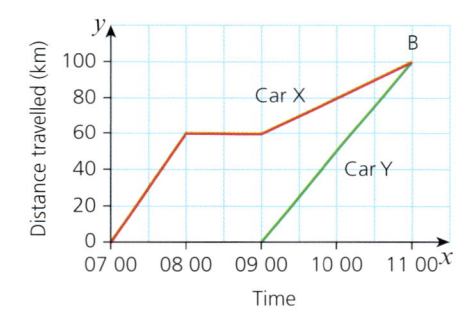

a Calculate the speed of Car X between 07 00 and 08 00.

$$\text{speed} = \frac{\text{distance}}{\text{time}}$$

$$\frac{60}{1} \text{ km/h} = 60 \text{ km/h}$$

b Calculate the speed of Car Y between 09 00 and 11 00.

$$\text{speed} = \frac{100}{2} \text{ km/h}$$
$$= 50 \text{ km/h}$$

c Explain what is happening to Car X between 08 00 and 09 00.

No distance has been travelled, therefore Car X is stationary.

Exercise 15.4

1 Two friends, Paul and Helena, arrange to meet for lunch at noon. They live 50 km apart and the restaurant is 30 km from Paul's home. The travel graph illustrates their journeys.

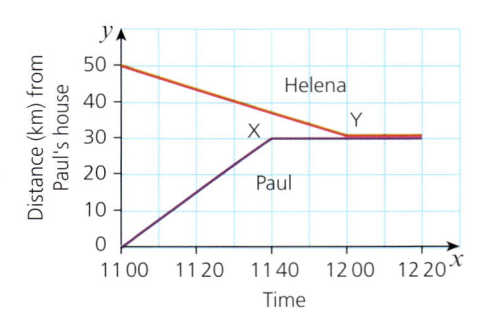

    a What is Paul's average speed between 11 00 and 11 40?

137

15 GRAPHS IN PRACTICAL SITUATIONS

Exercise 15.4 (cont)

    b What is Helena's average speed between 1100 and 1200?
    c What does the line XY represent?

2 A car travels at a speed of 60 km/h for 1 hour. It stops for 30 minutes, then continues at a constant speed of 80 km/h for a further 1.5 hours. Draw a distance–time graph for this journey.

3 A girl cycles for 1.5 hours at 10 km/h. She stops for an hour, then travels for a further 15 km in 1 hour. Draw a distance–time graph of the girl's journey.

4 Two friends leave their houses at 1600. The houses are 4 km apart and the friends travel towards each other on the same road. Fyodor walks at 7 km/h and Yin walks at 5 km/h.
    a On the same axes, draw a distance–time graph of their journeys.
    b From your graph, estimate the time at which they meet.
    c Estimate the distance from Fyodor's house to the point where they meet.

5 A train leaves a station P at 1800 and travels to station Q, 150 km away. It travels at a steady speed of 75 km/h. At 1810 another train leaves Q for P at a steady speed of 100 km/h.
    a On the same axes draw a distance–time graph to show both journeys.
    b From the graph, estimate the time at which the trains pass each other.
    c At what distance from station Q do the trains pass each other?
    d Which train arrives at its destination first?

6 A train sets off from town P at 0915 and heads towards town Q, 250 km away. Its journey is split into the three stages, a, b and c. At 0900 a second train leaves town Q heading for town P. Its journey is split into the two stages, d and e. Using the graph, calculate the following:
    a the speed of the first train during stages a, b and c
    b the speed of the second train during stages d and e.

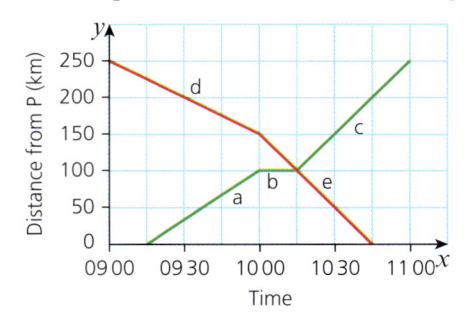

Travel graphs

Student assessment 1

1. Absolute zero (0 K) is equivalent to −273 °C and 0 °C is equivalent to 273 K. Draw a conversion graph which will convert K into °C. Use your graph to estimate:
   a the temperature in K equivalent to −40 °C
   b the temperature in °C equivalent to 100 K.

2. A plumber has a call-out charge of $70 and then charges a rate of $50 per hour.
   a Draw a conversion graph and estimate the cost of the following:
      i a job lasting $4\frac{1}{2}$ hours
      ii a job lasting $6\frac{3}{4}$ hours.
   b If a job cost $245, estimate from your graph how long it took to complete.

3. Joop lives 3.5 km from her school. She walks home at a constant speed of 9 km/h for the first 10 minutes. She then stops and talks to her friends for 5 minutes. She finally runs the rest of her journey home at a constant speed of 12 km/h.
   a Illustrate this information on a distance–time graph.
   b Use your graph to estimate the total time it took Joop to get home that day.

4. Look at the distance–time graphs A, B, C and D.
   a Two of the graphs are not possible.
      i Which two graphs are impossible?
      ii Explain why the two you have chosen are not possible.
   b Explain what the horizontal lines in the graphs say about the motion.

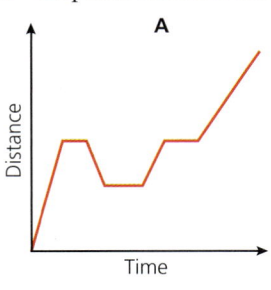

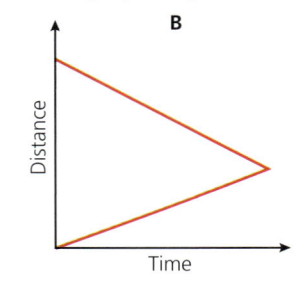

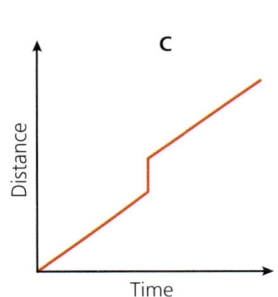

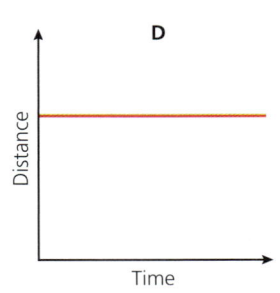

5. Paulo runs a 10 km race at an average speed of 9.6 km per hour.
   a How long did Paulo take to complete the race? Give your answer in hours, minutes and seconds.
   b What was his average speed in metres per second? Give your answer to 1 d.p.

16 Graphs of functions

Linear functions

A **linear function** produces a straight line when plotted. A straight line consists of an infinite number of points. However, to plot a linear function, only two points on the line are needed. Once these have been plotted, the line can be drawn through them and extended, if necessary, at both ends.

Worked examples

1 Plot the line $y = x + 3$.

   To identify two points, simply choose two values of x, substitute these into the equation and calculate the corresponding y-values. Sometimes a small table of results is clearer.

x	y
0	3
4	7

   Using the table, two points on the line are (0, 3) and (4, 7).

   Plot the points on a pair of axes and draw a line through them:

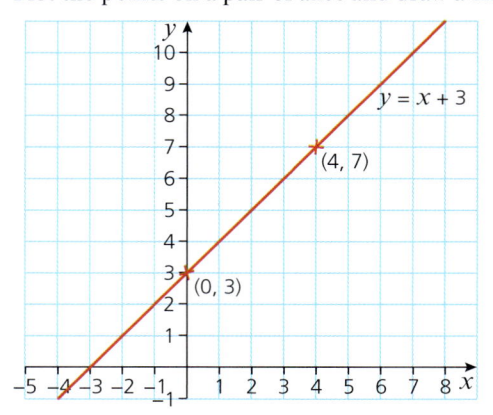

   It is good practice to check with a third point:

   Substituting $x = 2$ into the equation gives $y = 5$. As the point (2, 5) lies on the line, the line is drawn correctly.

Linear functions

2 Plot the line $2y + x = 6$.

It is often easier to plot a line if the function is first written with y as the subject:

$2y + x = 6$
$2y = -x + 6$
$y = -\frac{1}{2}x + 3$

Choose two values of x and find the corresponding values of y:

x	y
0	3
6	0

From the table, two points on the line are $(0, 3)$ and $(6, 0)$.

Plot the points on a pair of axes and draw a line through them:

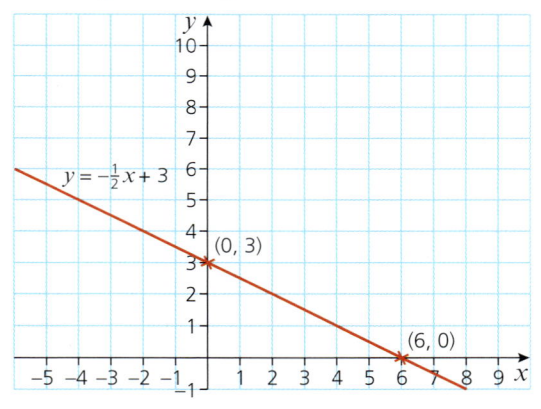

Check with a third point:

Substituting $x = 4$ into the equation gives $y = 1$. As the point $(4, 1)$ lies on the line, the line is drawn correctly.

Exercise 16.1

1 Plot the following straight lines.
  a $y = 2x + 4$
  b $y = 2x + 3$
  c $y = 2x - 1$
  d $y = x - 4$
  e $y = x + 1$
  f $y = x + 3$
  g $y = 1 - x$
  h $y = 3 - x$
  i $y = -(x + 2)$

2 Plot the following straight lines.
  a $y = 2x + 3$
  b $y = x - 4$
  c $y = 3x - 2$
  d $y = -2x$
  e $y = -x - 1$

16 GRAPHS OF FUNCTIONS

Graphical solution of simultaneous equations

When solving two equations simultaneously, you need to find a solution that works for both equations. Chapter 13 shows how to arrive at the solution algebraically. It is, however, possible to arrive at the same solution graphically.

➡ Worked example

a By plotting the graphs of both of the following equations on the same axes, find a common solution.

$$x + y = 4$$
$$x - y = 2$$

When both lines are plotted, the point at which they cross gives the common solution. This is because it is the only point which lies on both lines.

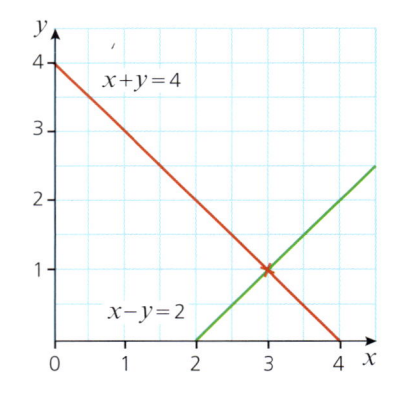

Therefore the common solution is (3, 1).

b Check your answer to part a by solving the equations algebraically.

$x + y = 4$ (1)

$x - y = 2$ (2)

$(1) + (2) \rightarrow 2x = 6$

$x = 3$

Substituting $x = 3$ into equation (1):

$3 + y = 4$

$y = 1$

Therefore the common solution occurs at (3, 1).

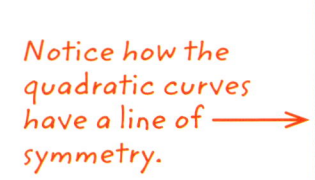

Quadratic functions

Exercise 16.2 Solve the simultaneous equations below:
  i by graphical means
  ii by algebraic means.

1 a $x + y = 5$
      $x - y = 1$
   b $x + y = 7$
      $x - y = 3$
   c $2x + y = 5$
      $x - y = 1$
   d $2x + 2y = 6$
      $2x - y = 3$
   e $x + 3y = -1$
      $x - 2y = -6$
   f $x - y = 6$
      $x + y = 2$

2 a $3x - 2y = 13$
      $2x + y = 4$
   b $4x - 5y = 1$
      $2x + y = -3$
   c $x + 5 = y$
      $2x + 3y - 5 = 0$
   d $x = y$
      $x + y + 6 = 0$
   e $2x + y = 4$
      $4x + 2y = 8$
   f $y - 3x = 1$
      $y = 3x - 3$

Quadratic functions

The general expression for a quadratic function takes the form $ax^2 + bx + c$, where a, b and c are constants. Some examples of quadratic functions are:

$$y = 2x^2 + 3x - 12 \qquad y = x^2 - 5x + 6 \qquad y = 3x^2 + 2x - 3$$

If a graph of a quadratic function is plotted, the smooth curve produced is called a **parabola**. For example:

$y = x^2$

x	-4	-3	-2	-1	0	1	2	3	4
y	16	9	4	1	0	1	4	9	16

$y = -x^2$

x	-4	-3	-2	-1	0	1	2	3	4
y	-16	-9	-4	-1	0	-1	-4	-9	-16

Notice how the quadratic curves have a line of symmetry.

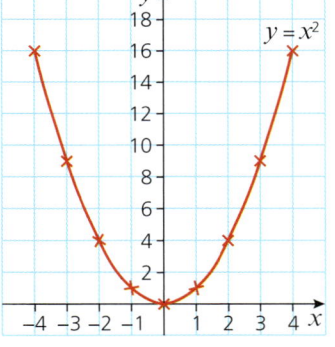

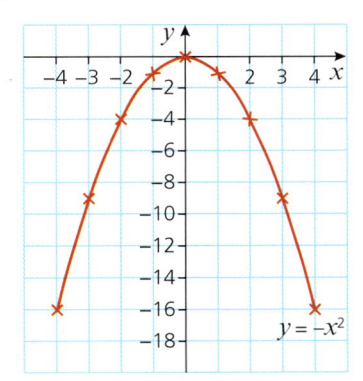

16 GRAPHS OF FUNCTIONS

> **Worked examples**

1 Plot a graph of the function $y = x^2 - 5x + 6$ for $0 \leqslant x \leqslant 5$.

First create a table of values for x and y:

x	0	1	2	3	4	5
$y = x^2 - 5x + 6$	6	2	0	0	2	6

These can then be plotted to give the graph:

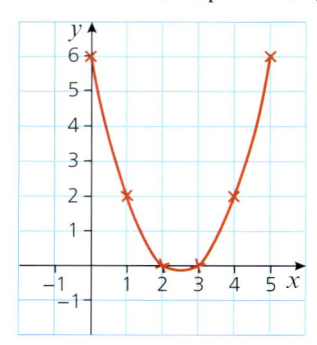

2 Plot a graph of the function $y = -x^2 + x + 2$ for $-3 \leqslant x \leqslant 4$.

Draw up a table of values:

x	−3	−2	−1	0	1	2	3	4
$y = -x^2 + x + 2$	−10	−4	0	2	2	0	−4	−10

Then plot the points and join them with a smooth curve:

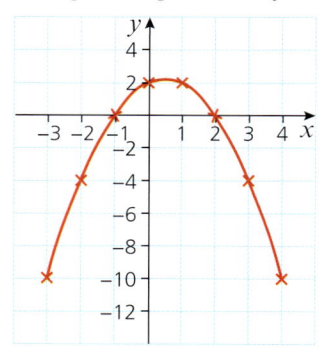

Exercise 16.3 For each of the following quadratic functions, construct a table of values for the stated range and then draw the graph.

a $y = x^2 + x - 2$, $-4 \leqslant x \leqslant 3$
b $y = -x^2 + 2x + 3$, $-3 \leqslant x \leqslant 5$
c $y = x^2 - 4x + 4$, $-1 \leqslant x \leqslant 5$
d $y = -x^2 - 2x - 1$, $-4 \leqslant x \leqslant 2$
e $y = x^2 - 2x - 15$, $-4 \leqslant x \leqslant 6$

Graphical solution of a quadratic equation

To solve an equation, you need to find the values of x when $y = 0$. On a graph, these are the values of x where the curve crosses the x-axis. These are known as the **roots** of the equation.

Worked examples

1 Draw a graph of $y = x^2 - 4x + 3$ for $-2 \leqslant x \leqslant 5$.

x	-2	-1	0	1	2	3	4	5
y	15	8	3	0	-1	0	3	8

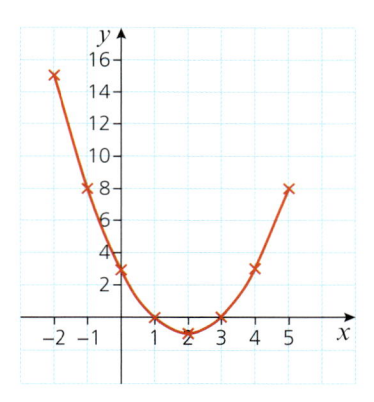

These are the values of x where the graph crosses the x-axis.

2 Use the graph to solve the equation $x^2 - 4x + 3 = 0$.

The solutions are $x = 1$ and $x = 3$

Exercise 16.4

Find the roots of each of the quadratic equations below by plotting a graph for the ranges of x stated.

a $x^2 - x - 6 = 0$, $-4 \leqslant x \leqslant 4$
b $-x^2 + 1 = 0$, $-4 \leqslant x \leqslant 4$
c $x^2 - 6x + 9 = 0$, $0 \leqslant x \leqslant 6$
d $-x^2 - x + 12 = 0$, $-5 \leqslant x \leqslant 4$
e $x^2 - 4x + 4 = 0$, $-2 \leqslant x \leqslant 6$

Note

A diagram may help you answer these questions.

In the previous worked example in which $y = x^2 - 4x + 3$, a solution was found to the equation $x^2 - 4x + 3 = 0$ by reading the values of x where the graph crossed the x-axis. The graph can, however, also be used to solve other related quadratic equations.

16 GRAPHS OF FUNCTIONS

Worked example

Look at how the given equation relates to the given graph.

Use the graph of $y = x^2 - 4x + 3$ to solve the equation $y = x^2 - 4x + 1 = 0$.

$x^2 - 4x + 1 = 0$ can be rearranged to give

$x^2 - 4x + 3 = 2$

Using the graph of $y = x^2 - 4x + 3$ and plotting the line $y = 2$ on the same axes gives the graph shown below.

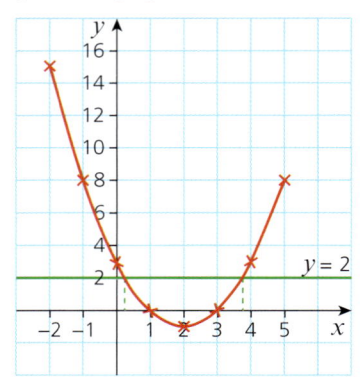

The points where the curve and the line cross give the solution to $x^2 - 4x + 3 = 2$, and hence also $x^2 - 4x + 1 = 0$.

Therefore the solutions to $x^2 - 4x + 1 = 0$ are $x \approx 0.3$ and $x \approx 3.7$.

Exercise 16.5

Using the graphs that you drew in Exercise 16.4, solve the following quadratic equations. Show your method clearly.

a $x^2 - x - 4 = 0$
b $-x^2 - 1 = 0$
c $x^2 - 6x + 8 = 0$
d $-x^2 - x + 9 = 0$
e $x^2 - 4x + 1 = 0$

The reciprocal function

If a graph of a **reciprocal function** is plotted, the curve produced is called a **hyperbola**.

Worked example

Plot the graph of $y = \frac{2}{x}$ for $-4 \leqslant x \leqslant 4$ using the table of values given below.

x	−4	−3	−2	−1	0	1	2	3	4
y	−0.5	−0.7	−1	−2	−	2	1	0.7	0.5

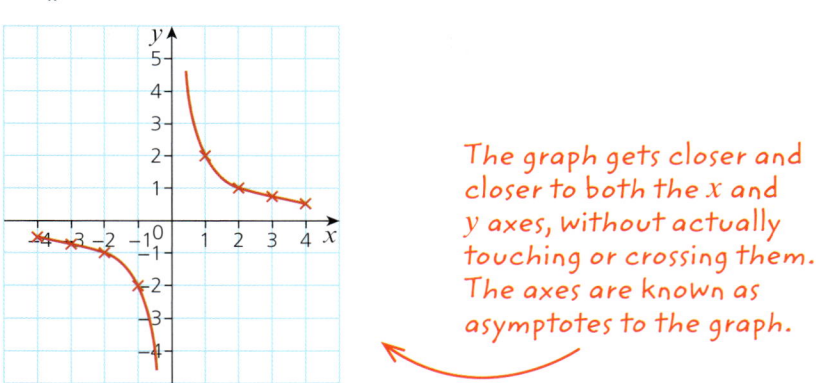

$y = \frac{2}{x}$ is a reciprocal function so the graph is a hyperbola.

The graph gets closer and closer to both the x and y axes, without actually touching or crossing them. The axes are known as asymptotes to the graph.

Exercise 16.6

1. Create a table of values and then use it to plot the graph of the function $y = \frac{1}{x}$ for $-4 \leqslant x \leqslant 4$.

2. Create a table of values and then use it to plot the graph of the function $y = \frac{3}{x}$ for $-4 \leqslant x \leqslant 4$.

Recognising and sketching functions

So far in this chapter, you have plotted graphs of functions. In other words, you have substituted values of x into the equation of a function, calculated the corresponding values of y, and plotted and joined the resulting (x, y) coordinates.

However, plotting an accurate graph is time-consuming and is not always necessary to answer a question. In many cases, a sketch of a graph is as useful and is considerably quicker.

When doing a sketch, certain key pieces of information need to be included. As a minimum, where the graph intersects both the x-axis and y-axis needs to be given.

Sketching linear functions

Straight line graphs can be sketched simply by working out where the line intersects both axes.

➔ Worked example

Sketch the graph of $y = -3x + 5$.

The graph intersects the y-axis when $x = 0$.

This is substituted in to the equation:

$y = -3(0) + 5$
$y = 5$

16 GRAPHS OF FUNCTIONS

The graph intersects the x-axis when $y = 0$.

This is then substituted in to the equation and solved:

$0 = -3x + 5$

$3x = 5$

$x = \frac{5}{3}$ (or $1\frac{2}{3}$)

Mark the two points and join them with a straight line:

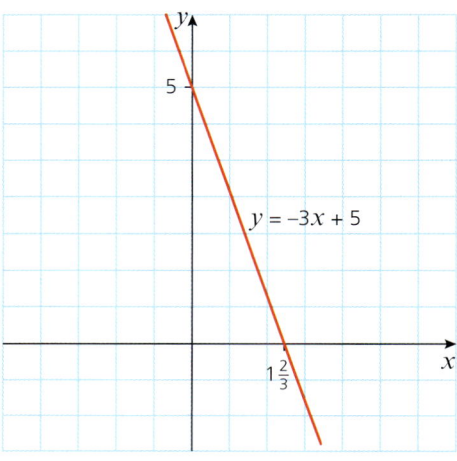

$y = -3x + 5$

Note that the sketch below, although it looks very different from the one above, is also acceptable as it shows the same intersections with the axes.

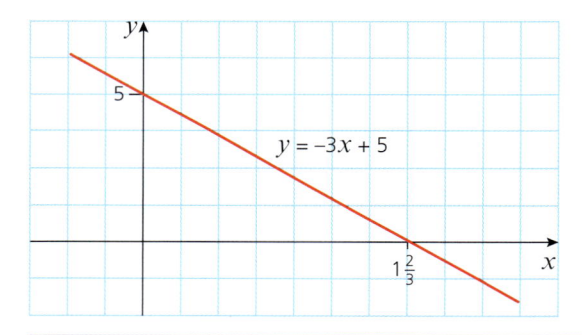

$y = -3x + 5$

Exercise 16.7

Sketch the following linear functions, showing clearly where the lines intersect both axes.

a $y = 2x - 4$
b $y = \frac{1}{2}x + 6$
c $y = -2x - 3$
d $y = -\frac{1}{3}x + 9$
e $2y + x - 2 = 0$
f $x = \frac{2y+4}{3}$

Sketching quadratic functions

You will have seen that plotting a quadratic function produces either a ∪- or a ∩-shaped curve, depending on whether the x^2 term is positive or negative.

Recognising and sketching functions

> Knowledge of turning points is not required, but it is useful for sketching.

Therefore, a quadratic graph has either a highest point or a lowest point, depending on its shape. These points are known as **turning points**.

To sketch a quadratic function, the key points that need to be included are the intersection with the y-axis and the intersections with the x-axis, if they exist.

→ Worked examples

1 a The graph of the quadratic equation $y = x^2 - 6x + 11$ has a lowest point at $(3, 2)$. Sketch the graph, showing clearly where it intersects the y-axis.

As the x^2 term is positive, the graph is ∪-shaped.
To find where the graph intersects the y-axis, substitute $x = 0$ into the equation.

$y = (0)^2 - 6(0) + 11$
$y = 11$

Therefore the graph can be sketched as follows:

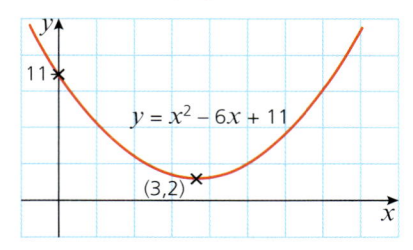

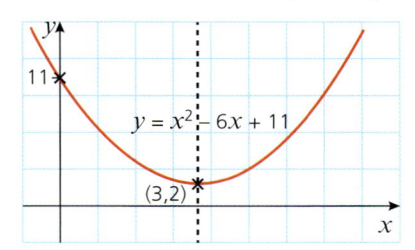

> **Note**
> Notice how the shape of a quadratic curve always has a line of symmetry through its turning point, i.e. it is always symmetrical.

b Draw the curve's line of symmetry on the sketch.

2 a The coordinates of the highest point of a quadratic graph are $(-4, 4)$. The equation of the function is $y = -x^2 - 8x - 12$. Sketch the graph.
As the x^2 term is negative, the graph is ∩-shaped.

To find where the graph intersects the y-axis, substitute $x = 0$ into the equation.

$y = -(0)^2 - 8(0) - 12$
$y = -12$

149

16 GRAPHS OF FUNCTIONS

Therefore the graph of $y = -x^2 - 8x - 12$ can be sketched as follows:

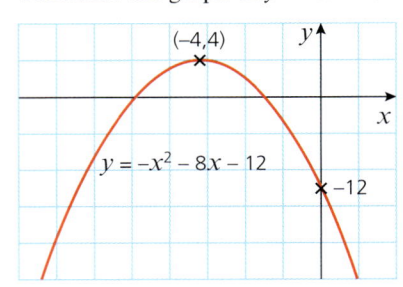

b Draw the curve's line of symmetry on the sketch.

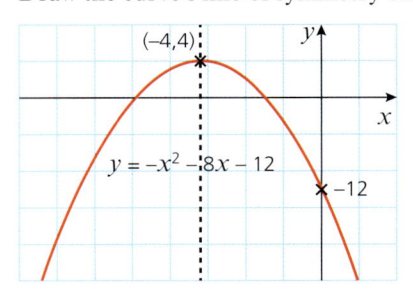

You will have seen in Chapter 11 that an expression such as $(x-2)(x+3)$ can be expanded to give $x^2 + x - 6$. Therefore $(x-2)(x+3)$ is also a quadratic expression. If a quadratic function is given in this form then the graph can still be sketched and, in particular, the points where it crosses the x-axis can be found too.

➡ Worked examples

1 Show that $(x+4)(x+2) = x^2 + 6x + 8$.

$(x+4)(x+2) = x^2 + 4x + 2x + 8$
$ = x^2 + 6x + 8$

2 Hence sketch the graph of $y = (x+4)(x+2)$.

The x^2 term is positive so the graph is ∪-shaped.

The graph intersects the y-axis when $x = 0$:

$y = (0+4)(0+2)$
$ = 4 \times 2$
$ = 8$

The intersection with the x-axis also needs to be calculated. At the x-axis, $y = 0$. Substituting $y = 0$ into the equation gives:

$(x+4)(x+2) = 0$

150

Recognising and sketching functions

For the product of two terms to be zero, one of the terms must be zero.

If $(x + 4) = 0$, then $x = -4$.

If $(x + 2) = 0$, then $x = -2$.

$x = -4$ and $x = -2$ are therefore where the graph intersects the x-axis.
The graph can be sketched as:

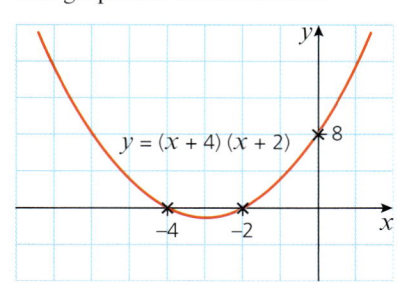

Exercise 16.8

1. For each part, the equation of a quadratic function is given as well as the coordinate of the point on the curve which the line of symmetry passes through. Sketch a graph for each function.
   a $y = x^2 - 10x + 27$;   line of symmetry passes through $(5, 2)$
   b $y = x^2 + 2x - 5$;   line of symmetry passes through $(-1, -6)$
   c $y = -x^2 + 4x - 3$;   line of symmetry passes through $(2, 1)$
   d $y = x^2 - 12x + 36$;   line of symmetry passes through $(6, 0)$
   e $y = 4x^2 - 20x$;   line of symmetry passes through $\left(\frac{5}{2}, -25\right)$

2. a Expand the brackets $(x + 3)(x - 3)$.
   b Use your expansion in part **a** to sketch the graph of $y = (x + 3)(x - 3)$. Label any point(s) of intersection with the axes.

3. a Expand the expression $-(x - 2)(x - 4)$.
   b Use your expansion in part **a** to sketch the graph of $y = -(x - 2)(x - 4)$. Label any point(s) of intersection with the axes.

4. a Expand the brackets $(-3x - 6)(x + 1)$.
   b Use your expansion in part **a** to sketch the graph of $y = (-3x - 6)(x + 1)$. Label any point(s) of intersection with the axes.

Student assessment 1

1. Plot these lines on the same pair of axes. Label each line clearly.
   a $x = -2$
   b $y = 3$
   c $y = 2x$
   d $y = -\frac{x}{2}$

2. Plot the graph of each linear equation.
   a $y = x + 1$
   b $y = 3 - 3x$
   c $y = 2x - 4$
   d $y = \frac{5}{2}x + 4$

3. Solve each pair of simultaneous equations graphically.
   a $x + y = 4$
      $x - y = 0$
   b $3x + y = 2$
      $x - y = 2$
   c $y + 4x + 4 = 0$
      $x + y = 2$
   d $x - y = -2$
      $3x + 2y + 6 = 0$

16 GRAPHS OF FUNCTIONS

4 a Copy and complete the table of values for the function $y = x^2 + 8x + 15$.

x	−7	−6	−5	−4	−3	−2	−1	0	1	2
y		3			3					

b Plot a graph of the function.

5 Plot the graph of each function for the given limits of x.
  a $y = x^2 - 3$; $-4 \leqslant x \leqslant 4$
  b $y = -x^2 - 2x - 1$; $-3 \leqslant x \leqslant 3$

6 a Plot the graph of the quadratic function $y = x^2 + 9x + 20$ for $-7 \leqslant x \leqslant -2$.
  b Showing your method clearly, use information from your graph to solve the equation $x^2 = -9x - 14$.

7 Sketch the graph of $y = \frac{1}{3}x - 5$. Label clearly any points of intersection with the axes.

Student assessment 2

1 Plot these lines on the same pair of axes. Label each line clearly.
  a $x = 3$ **b** $y = -2$ **c** $y = -3x$ **d** $y = \frac{x}{4} + 4$

2 Plot the graph of each linear equation.
  a $y = 2x + 3$
  b $y = 4 - x$
  c $y = 2x - 3$
  d $y = \frac{3}{2}x + \frac{5}{2}$

3 Solve each pair of simultaneous equations graphically.
  a $x + y = 6$
  $x - y = 0$
  b $x + 2y = 8$
  $x - y = -1$
  c $2x - y = -5$
  $x - 3y = 0$
  d $4x - 2y = -2$
  $3x - y + 2 = 0$

4 a Copy and complete the table of values for the function $y = -x^2 - 7x - 12$.

x	−7	−6	−5	−4	−3	−2	−1	0	1	2
y		−6				−2				

  b Plot a graph of the function.

5 Plot the graph of each function for the given limits of x.
  a $y = 1 - x^2$; $-4 \leqslant x \leqslant 4$
  b $y = x^2 - 3x - 10$; $-3 \leqslant x \leqslant 6$

6 a Plot the graph of the quadratic equation $y = -x^2 - x + 15$ for $-6 \leqslant x \leqslant 4$.
  b Showing your method clearly, use your graph to help you solve these equations.
    i $10 = x^2 + x$
    ii $x^2 = -x + 5$

7 Plot the graph of $y = \frac{2}{x}$ for $-4 \leqslant x \leqslant 4$.

8 Sketch the graph of $y = -\frac{5}{2}x + 10$. Label clearly any points of intersection with the axes.

Mathematical investigations and ICT 2

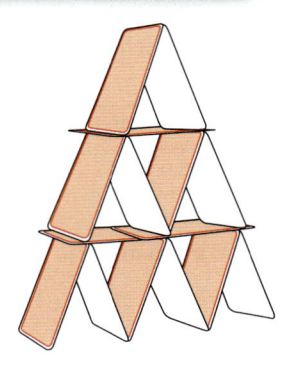

House of cards

The drawing shows a house of cards 3 layers high. 15 cards are needed to construct it.

1. How many cards are needed to construct a house 10 layers high?
2. Show that the general formula for the number of cards, c, needed to construct a house of cards n layers high, works for houses of cards up to 10 layers high.
3. Use the formula below to work out the number of cards needed for a house of 75 layers.

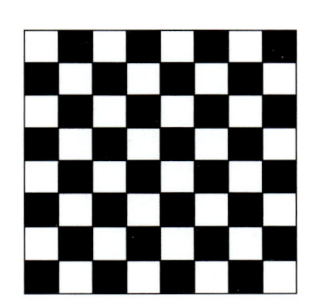

$$c = \tfrac{1}{2}n(3n+1)$$

Chequered boards

A chessboard is an 8×8 square grid with alternating black and white squares.

There are 64 unit squares of which 32 are black and 32 are white.

Consider boards of different sizes consisting of alternating black and white unit squares.

For example:

Total number of unit squares: 30

Number of black squares: 15

Number of white squares: 15

Total number of unit squares: 21

Number of black squares: 10

Number of white squares: 11

1. Investigate the number of black and white unit squares on different rectangular boards. Note: For consistency you may find it helpful to always keep the bottom right-hand square the same colour.
2. What are the numbers of black and white squares on a board $m \times n$ units?

MATHEMATICAL INVESTIGATIONS AND ICT 2

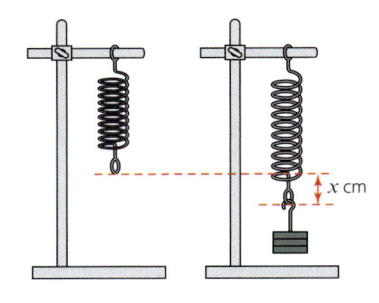

Modelling: Stretching a spring

A spring is attached to a clamp stand as shown.

Different weights are attached to the end of the spring. The table shows the mass (m) in grams of each weight and the amount by which the spring stretches (x) in centimetres.

Mass (g)	50	100	150	200	250	300	350	400	450	500
Extension (cm)	3.1	6.3	9.5	12.8	15.4	18.9	21.7	25.0	28.2	31.2

1. Plot a graph of mass against extension.
2. Describe the approximate relationship between the mass and the extension.
3. Draw a line of best fit through the data.
4. Calculate the equation of the line of best fit.
5. Use your equation to predict the extension of the spring for a mass of 275 g.
6. Explain why it is unlikely that the equation would be useful to find the extension when a mass of 5 kg is added to the spring.

ICT activity 1

You have seen that the solution of two simultaneous equations gives the coordinates of the point that satisfies both equations. If the simultaneous equations were plotted, the point at which the lines cross would correspond to the solution of the simultaneous equations.

For example:

Solving $x + y = 6$ and $x - y = 2$ produces the result $x = 4$ and $y = 2$, i.e. coordinates (4, 2).

Plotting the graphs of both lines confirms that the point of intersection occurs at (4, 2).

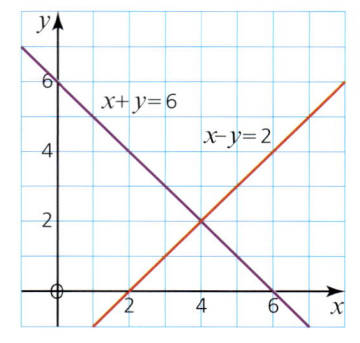

ICT activity 2

1. Use a graphing package to solve the following simultaneous equations graphically.
   a. $y = x$ and $x + y = 4$
   b. $y = 2x$ and $x + y = 3$
   c. $y = 2x$ and $y = 3$
   d. $y - x = 2$ and $y + \frac{1}{2}x = 5$
   e. $y + x = 5$ and $y + \frac{1}{2}x = 3$

2. Check your answers to Q.1 by solving each pair of simultaneous equations algebraically.

ICT activity 2

In this activity you will be using a graphing package or graphical calculator to find the solutions to quadratic and reciprocal functions.

You have seen that if a quadratic equation is plotted, its solution is represented by the points of intersection with the x-axis. For example, when plotting $y = x^2 - 4x + 3$, as shown below, the solution of $x^2 - 4x + 3 = 0$ occurs where the graph crosses the x-axis, i.e. at $x = 1$ and $x = 3$.

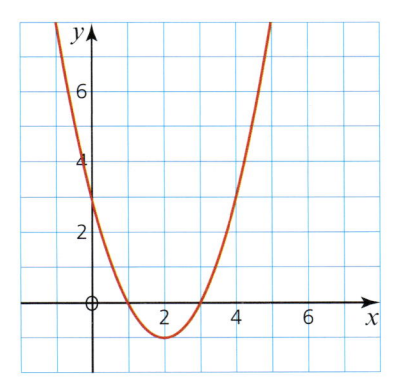

Use a graphing package or a graphical calculator to solve each equation graphically.

a. $x^2 + x - 2 = 0$
b. $x^2 - 7x + 6 = 0$
c. $x^2 + x - 12 = 0$
d. $2x^2 + 5x - 3 = 0$
e. $\frac{2}{x} - 2 = 0$
f. $\frac{2}{x} + 1 = 0$

TOPIC 3

Coordinate geometry

Contents

Chapter 17 Coordinates and straight line graphs (C3.1, C3.2, C3.3, C3.5, C3.6)

Learning objectives

C3.1 Use and interpret Cartesian coordinates in two dimensions.

C3.2 Draw straight line graphs for linear equations.

C3.3 Find the gradient of a straight line.

C3.5 Interpret and obtain the equation of a straight line graph in the form $y = mx + c$.

C3.6 Find the gradient and equation of a straight line parallel to a given line.

Position fixing

On a flat surface, two points at right angles will fix a position. These two points are called coordinates. On the surface of the Earth, position is fixed using latitude and longitude. Latitude is the distance from the equator. Longitude is measured at right angles to latitude.

In the early eighteenth century, however, only latitude could be calculated. There were several disasters caused by errors in determining a position at sea. One such disaster was the loss of 1400 lives and four ships in the English fleet of Sir Cloudesley Shovell in 1707. In 1714 the British government established the Board of Longitude and a large cash prize was offered for a practical method of finding the longitude of a ship at sea.

John Harrison, a self-educated English clockmaker, then invented the marine chronometer. This instrument allowed longitude to be calculated. It worked by comparing local noon with the time at a place given the longitude zero. Each hour was $360 \div 24 = 15$ degrees of longitude. Unlike latitude, which has the equator as a natural starting position, there is no natural starting position for longitude. The Greenwich meridian in London was chosen.

John Harrison (1693–1776)

17 Coordinates and straight line graphs

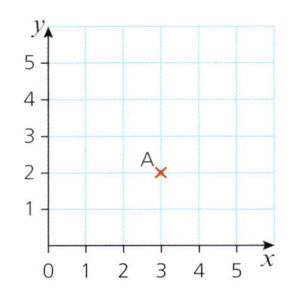

Coordinates

To fix a point in two dimensions (2D), its position is given in relation to a point called the **origin**. Through the origin, axes are drawn perpendicular to each other. The horizontal axis is known as the ***x*-axis**, and the vertical axis is known as the ***y*-axis**.

The *x*-axis is numbered from left to right. The *y*-axis is numbered from bottom to top.

The position of point *A* (left) is given by two coordinates: the *x*-coordinate first, followed by the *y*-coordinate. So the coordinates of point *A* are (3, 2).

A number line can extend in both directions by extending the *x*- and *y*-axes below zero, as shown in the grid (left).

Points *B*, *C* and *D* can be described by their coordinates:

- Point *B* is at (3, −3).
- Point *C* is at (−4, −3).
- Point *D* is at (−4, 3).

Exercise 17.1

1 Draw a pair of axes with both *x* and *y* from −8 to +8. Mark each of the following points on your grid:
   a *A* = (5, 2)   b *B* = (7, 3)   c *C* = (2, 4)
   d *D* = (−8, 5)   e *E* = (−5, −8)   f *F* = (3, −7)
   g *G* = (7, −3)   h *H* = (6, −6)

Draw a separate grid for each of Q.2–4 with *x*- and *y*-axes from −6 to +6. Plot and join the points in order to name each shape drawn.

2 *A* = (3, 2)   *B* = (3, −4)   *C* = (−2, −4)   *D* = (−2, 2)

3 *E* = (1, 3)   *F* = (4, −5)   *G* = (−2, −5)

4 *H* = (−6, 4)   *I* = (0, −4)   *J* = (4, −2)   *K* = (−2, 6)

Exercise 17.2

Draw a pair of axes with both *x* and *y* from −10 to +10.
1 Plot the points *P* = (−6, 4), *Q* = (6, 4) and *R* = (8, −2).
   a Plot point *S* such that *PQRS* when drawn is a parallelogram.
   b Draw diagonals *PR* and *QS*. What are the coordinates of their point of intersection?
   c What is the area of *PQRS*?

2 On the same axes, plot point M at (–8, 4) and point N at (4, 4).
   a Join points MNRS. What shape is formed?
   b What is the area of MNRS?
   c Explain your answer to **b**.

3 On the same axes, plot point J where point J has y-coordinate +10 and JRS, when joined, forms an isosceles triangle.
   What is the x-coordinate of all points on the line of symmetry of triangle JRS?

Exercise 17.3

1 a On a grid with axes numbered from –10 to +10, draw a hexagon ABCDEF with centre (0, 0), points A(0, 8) and B(7, 4) and two lines of symmetry.
   b Write down the coordinates of points C, D, E and F.

2 a On a similar grid to Q.1, draw an octagon PQRSTUVW which has point P(2, –8), point Q(–6, –8) and point R(–7, –5).
   b PQ = RS = TU = VW and QR = ST = UV = WP.
      List the coordinates of points S, T, U, V and W.
   c What are the coordinates of the centre of rotational symmetry of the octagon?

Reading scales

Exercise 17.4

1 The points A, B, C and D are not at whole number points on the number line. Point A is at 0.7.
   What are the positions of points B, C and D?

2 What are the positions of points I, J, K, L and M? (Each small square is 0.05, i.e. 2 squares is 0.1.)

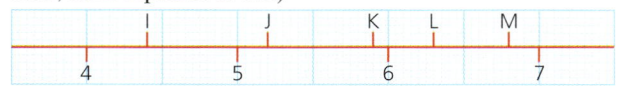

3 On this number line, point E is at 0.8 (1 small square represents 0.1).
   What are the positions of points F, G and H?

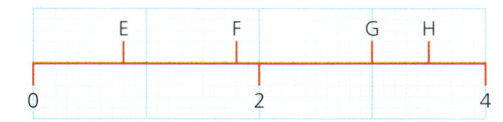

4 Point P is at position 0.4 and point W is at position 9.8 (each small square is 0.2).
   What are the positions of points Q, R, S, T, U and V?

17 COORDINATES AND STRAIGHT LINE GRAPHS

Exercise 17.5 Give the coordinates of points A, B, C, D, E, F, G and H.

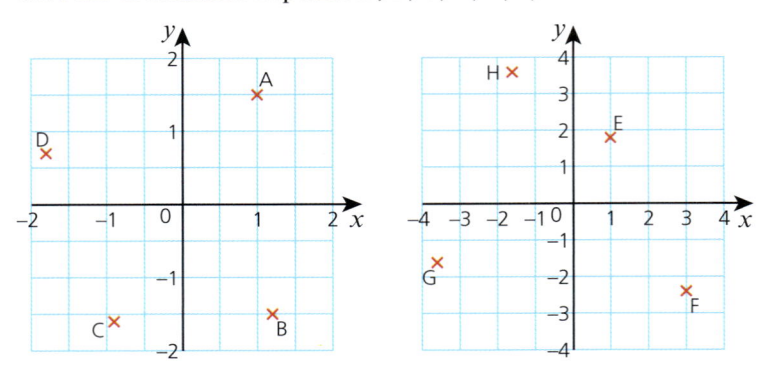

The gradient of a straight line

Lines are made of an infinite number of points. This chapter looks at those whose points form a straight line.
The graph shows three straight lines:

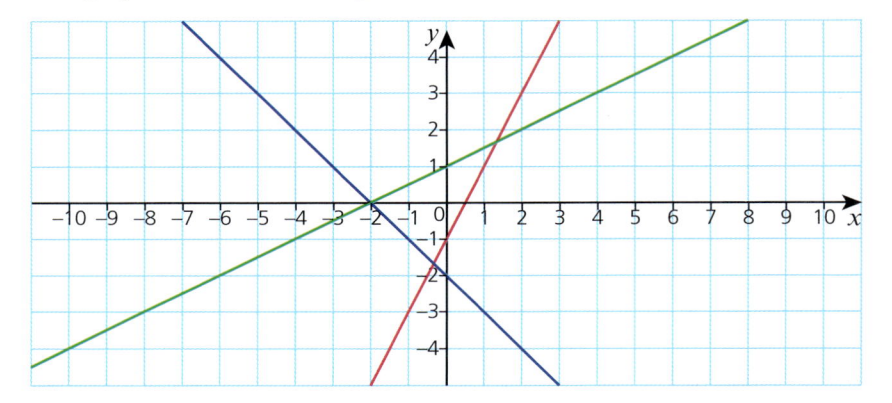

The lines have some properties in common (i.e. they are straight), but also have differences. One of their differences is that they have different slopes. The slope of a line is called its **gradient**.

Gradient

The gradient of a straight line is constant, i.e. it does not change. The gradient of a straight line can be calculated by using the coordinates of any two points on the line.

Gradient

> **Note**
>
> Notice how two points were chosen which lie where two lines cross. If this is not possible, choose two points which are as far apart as possible to reduce errors.

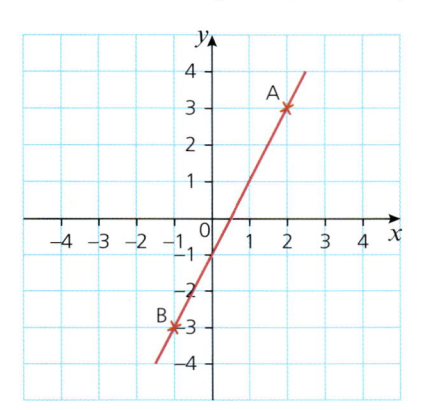

On this line two points, A and B, have been chosen:

The coordinates of the points are $A(2, 3)$ and $B(-1, -3)$. The gradient is calculated using the following formula:

$$\text{Gradient} = \frac{\text{vertical distance between two points}}{\text{horizontal distance between two points}}$$

Graphically this can be represented as follows:

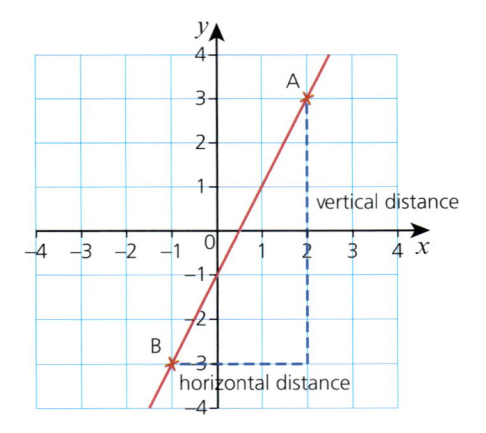

Therefore gradient $= \frac{3 - (-3)}{2 - (-1)} = \frac{6}{3} = 2$

In general, if the two points chosen have coordinates (x_1, y_1) and (x_2, y_2) the gradient is calculated as:

$$\text{Gradient} = \frac{y_2 - y_1}{x_2 - x_1}$$

17 COORDINATES AND STRAIGHT LINE GRAPHS

Worked example

Calculate the gradient of the line shown:

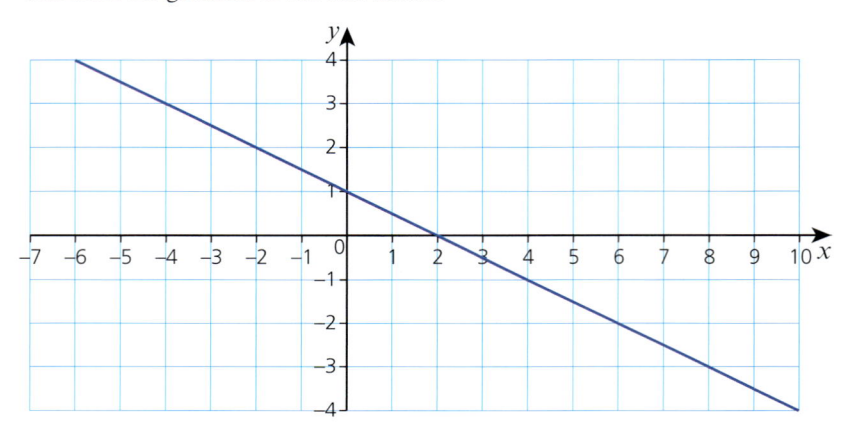

Choose two points on the line, e.g. (−4, 3) and (8, −3).

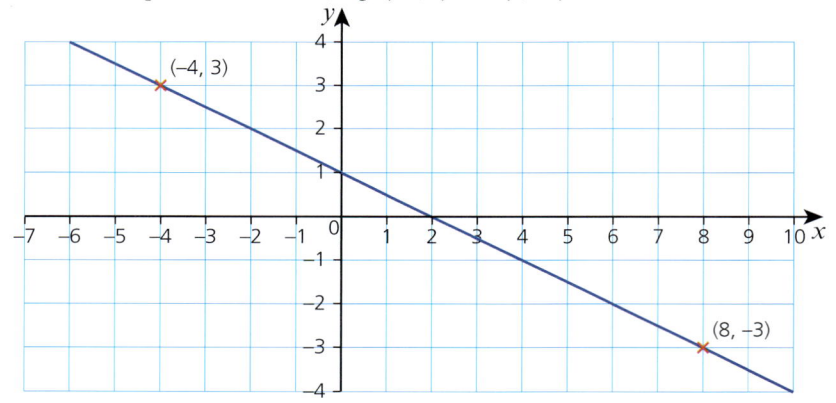

Let point 1 be (−4, 3) and point 2 be (8, −3).

$$\text{Gradient} = \frac{y_2 - y_1}{x_2 - x_1} = \frac{-3 - 3}{8 - (-4)}$$

$$= \frac{-6}{12} = -\frac{1}{2}$$

Note: The gradient is not affected by which point is chosen as point 1 and which is chosen as point 2. In the example above, if point 1 was (8, −3) and point 2 was (−4, 3), the gradient would be calculated as:

$$\text{Gradient} = \frac{y_2 - y_1}{x_2 - x_1} = \frac{3 - (-3)}{-4 - 8}$$

$$= \frac{6}{-12} = -\frac{1}{2}$$

Gradient

To check whether or not the sign of the gradient is correct, the following diagram is useful.

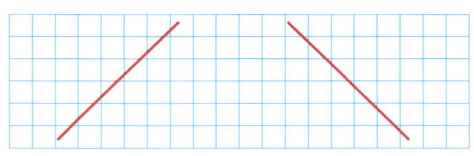

A line sloping this way will have a positive gradient.

A line sloping this way will have a negative gradient.

A large value for the gradient implies that the line is steep. The line on the right (below) will have a greater value for the gradient than the line on the left, as it is steeper.

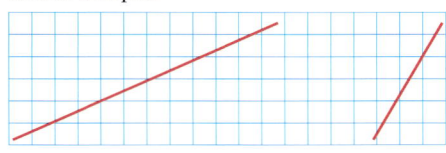

Exercise 17.6

1 For each of the following lines, select two points on the line and then calculate its gradient.

a

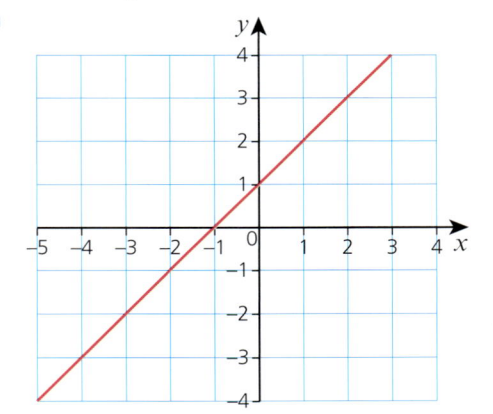

b

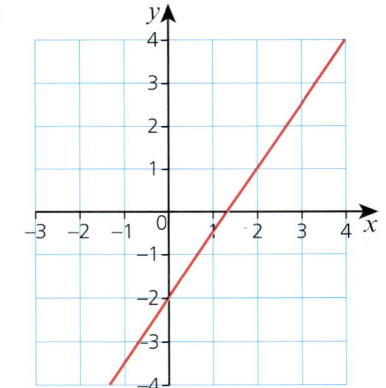

17 COORDINATES AND STRAIGHT LINE GRAPHS

Exercise 17.6 (cont)

c

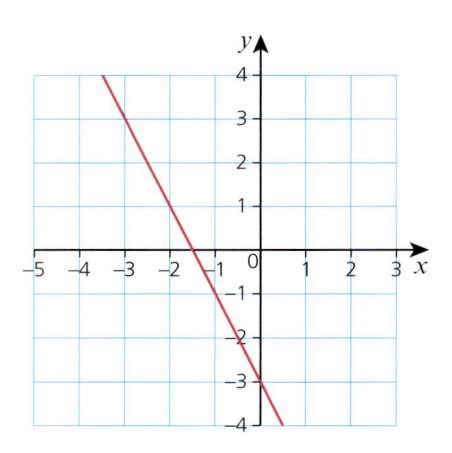

d

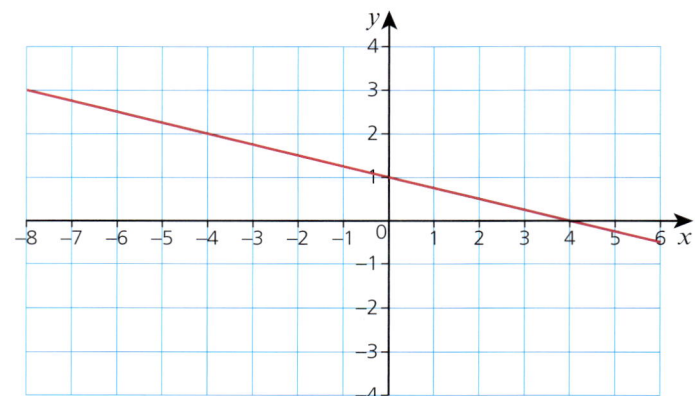

e

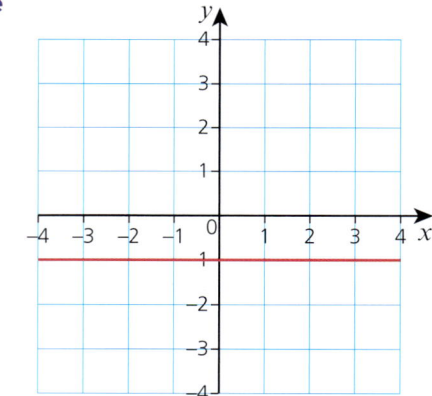

f

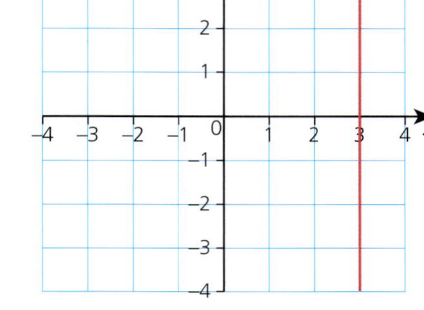

2 From your answers to Q.1, what conclusion can you make about the gradient of any horizontal line?

3 From your answers to Q.1, what conclusion can you make about the gradient of any vertical line?

4 The graph below shows six straight lines labelled A–F.

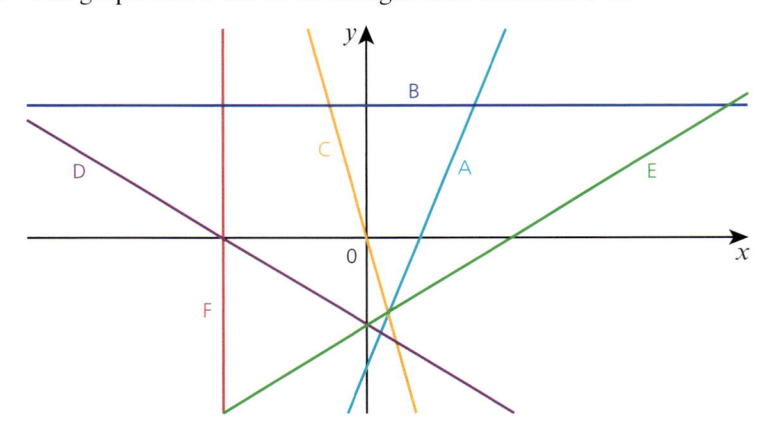

Six gradients are given below. Deduce which line has which gradient.

Gradient = $\frac{1}{2}$ Gradient is undefined   Gradient = 2

Gradient = –3   Gradient = 0   Gradient = $-\frac{1}{2}$

17 COORDINATES AND STRAIGHT LINE GRAPHS

The equation of a straight line

The coordinates of every point on a straight line all have a common relationship. This relationship when expressed algebraically as an equation in terms of x and/or y is known as the **equation of a straight line**.

Worked examples

1. By looking at the coordinates of some of the points on the line below, establish the equation of the straight line.

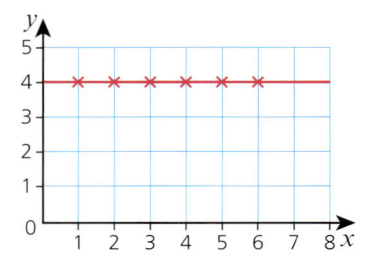

x	y
1	4
2	4
3	4
4	4
5	4
6	4

Some of the points on the line have been identified and their coordinates entered in a table (above). By looking at the table it can be seen that the only rule all the points have in common is that $y = 4$.

Hence the equation of the straight line is $y = 4$.

2. By looking at the coordinates of some of the points on the line below, establish the equation of the straight line.

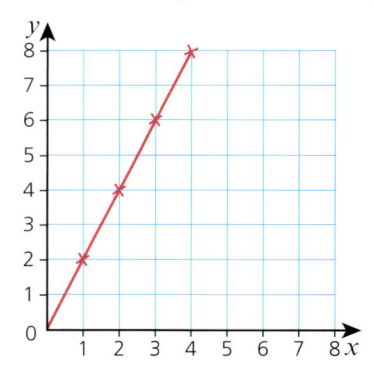

x	y
1	2
2	4
3	6
4	8

By looking at the table it can be seen that the relationship between the x- and y-coordinates is that each y-coordinate is twice the corresponding x-coordinate.

Hence the equation of the straight line is $y = 2x$.

The equation of a straight line

Exercise 17.7 For each of the following, identify the coordinates of some of the points on the line and use these to find the equation of the straight line.

a

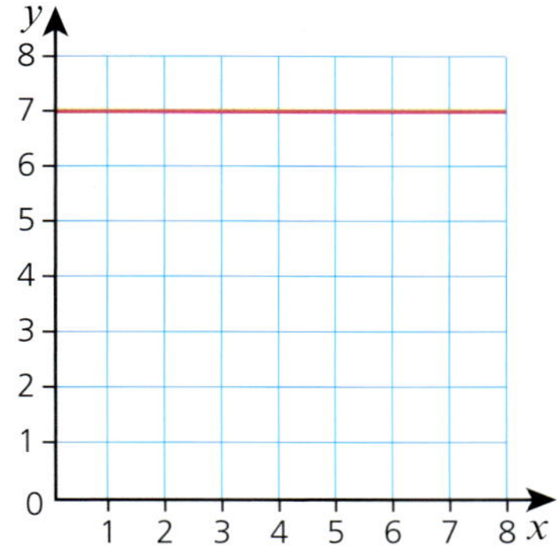

b

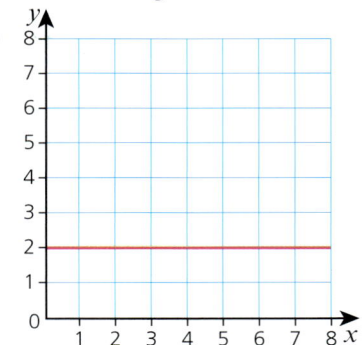

c

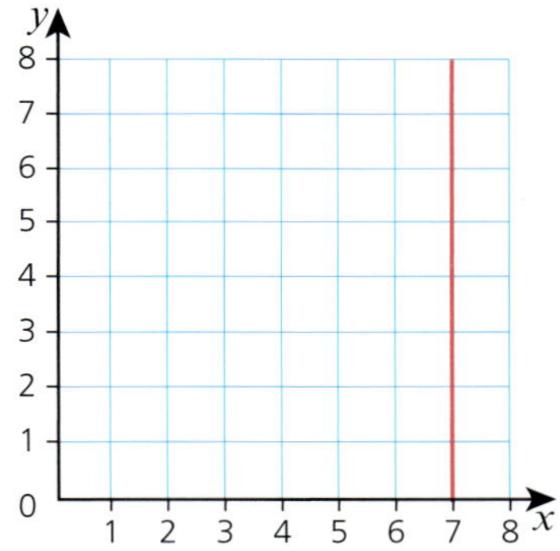

d

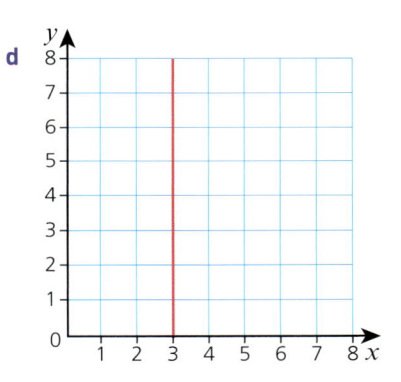

e

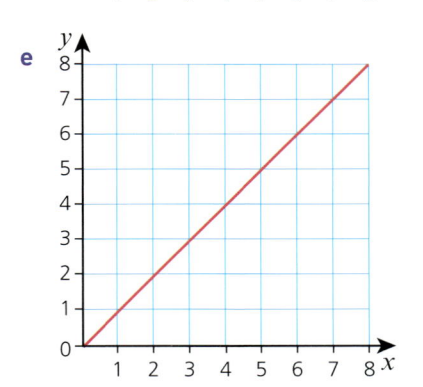

f

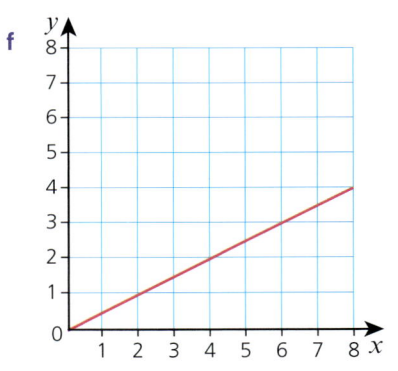

17 COORDINATES AND STRAIGHT LINE GRAPHS

Exercise 17.7 (cont) g

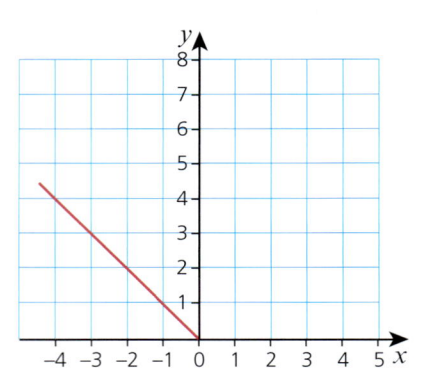

h

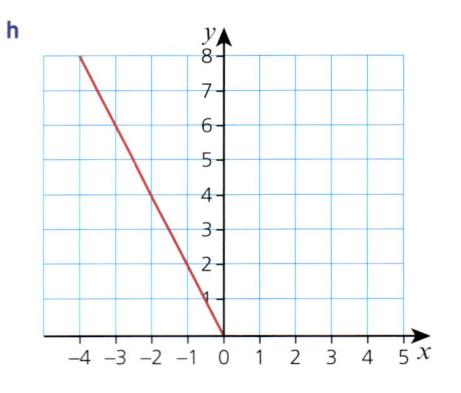

Exercise 17.8 1 For each of the following, identify the coordinates of some of the points on the line and use these to find the equation of the straight line.

a

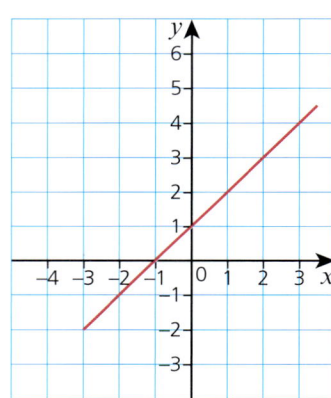

b

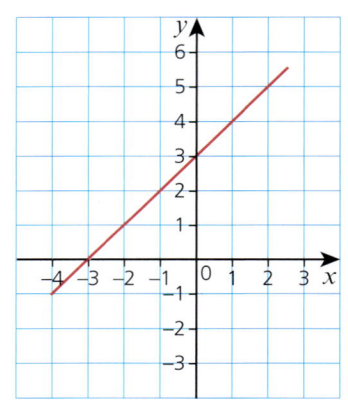

c

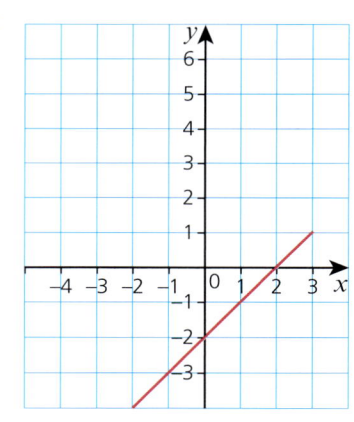

d

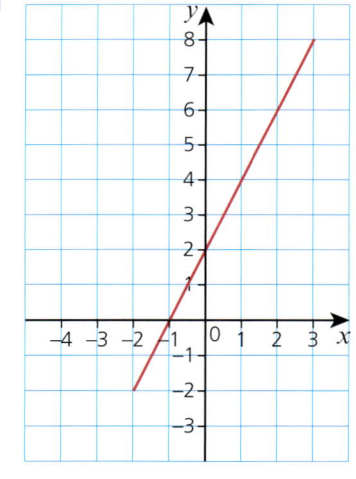

The equation of a straight line

e

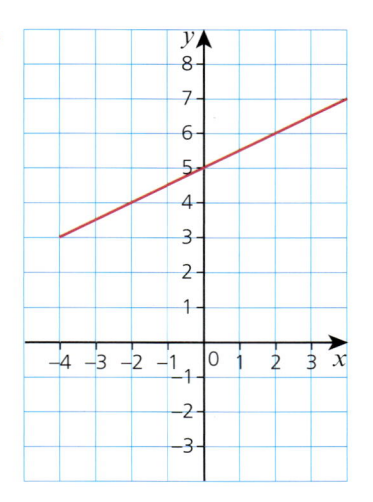

f

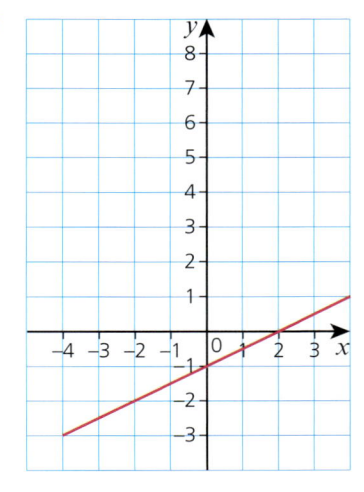

2 For each of the following, identify the coordinates of some of the points on the line and use these to find the equation of the straight line.

a

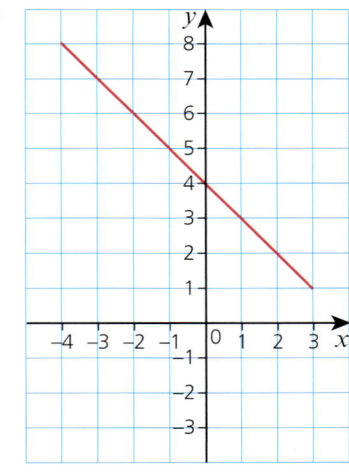

b

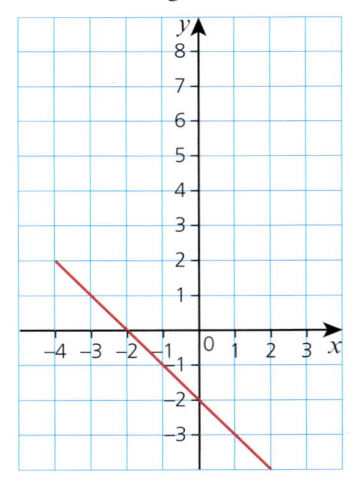

c

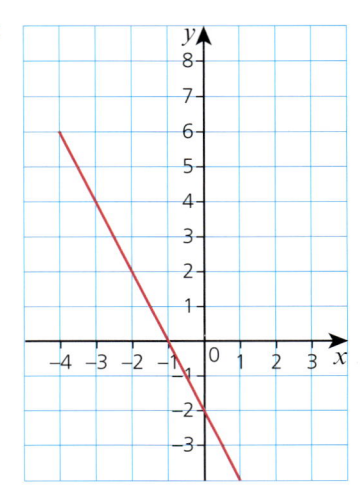

d

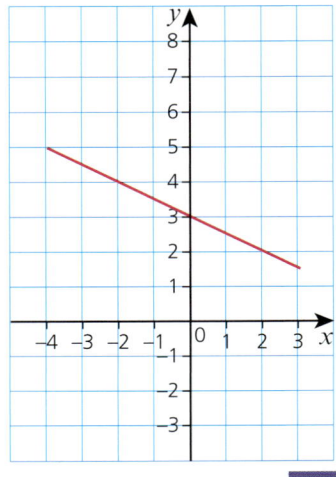

169

17 COORDINATES AND STRAIGHT LINE GRAPHS

Exercise 17.8 (cont)

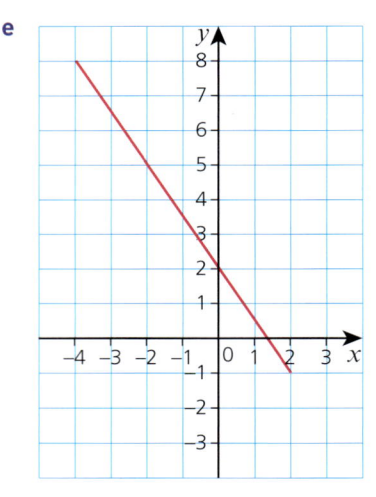

e

f

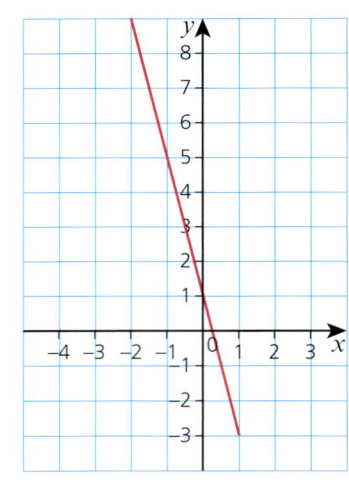

3 **a** For each of the graphs in Q.1 and 2, calculate the gradient of the straight line.
   b What do you notice about the gradient of each line and its equation?
   c What do you notice about the equation of the straight line and where the line intersects the y-axis?

4 Copy the diagrams in Q.1. Draw two lines on each diagram parallel to the given line.
   a Write the equation of these new lines in the form $y = mx + c$.
   b What do you notice about the equations of these new parallel lines?

5 In Q.2 you have an equation for these lines in the form $y = mx + c$. Copy the diagrams in Q.2. Change the value of the intercept c and then draw the new line.
   What do you notice about this new line and the first line?

The general equation of a straight line

In general, the equation of any straight line can be written in the form:

$$y = mx + c$$

where 'm' represents the gradient of the straight line and 'c' represents the intercept with the y-axis. This is shown in the diagram (left).

By looking at the equation of a straight line written in the form $y = mx + c$, it is therefore possible to deduce the line's gradient and intercept with the y-axis without having to draw it.

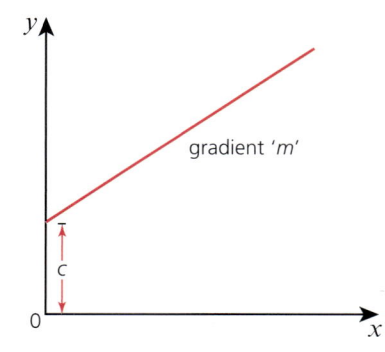

Parallel lines and their equations

→ Worked examples

1. Calculate the gradient and y-intercept of the following straight lines:
   a. $y = 3x - 2$
   gradient = 3
   y-intercept = –2

   b. $y = -2x + 6$
   gradient = –2
   y-intercept = 6

2. Calculate the gradient and y-intercept of the following straight lines:
   a. $2y = 4x + 2$

   This needs to be rearranged into **gradient–intercept form** (i.e. $y = mx + c$).

   $y - 2x + 1$ gradient = 2
   y-intercept = 1

   b. $y - 2x = -4$

   Rearranging into gradient–intercept form, we have:

   $y = 2x - 4$ gradient = 2
   y-intercept = –4

Exercise 17.9

For the following linear equations, calculate both the gradient and y-intercept.

a. $y = 2x + 1$
b. $y = 3x + 5$
c. $y = x - 2$
d. $y = \frac{1}{2}x + 4$
e. $y = -3x + 6$
f. $y = -\frac{2}{3}x + 1$
g. $y = -x$
h. $y = -x - 2$
i. $y = -(2x - 2)$

Parallel lines and their equations

Lines that are parallel, by their definition, must have the same gradient. Similarly, lines with the same gradient must be parallel. So a straight line with equation $y = -3x + 4$ must be parallel to a line with equation $y = -3x - 2$ as both have a gradient of –3.

→ Worked example

A straight line has equation $y = 2x + 4$. Another straight line has equation $y = -2x + 4$. Explain, giving reasons, whether the two lines are parallel to each other or not.

They are not parallel as one has a gradient of 2, the other has a gradient of –2.

Exercise 17.10

1. A straight line has equation $y = x + \frac{4}{3}$. Write down the equation of another straight line parallel to it.

2. A straight line has equation $y = -x + 6$. Which of the following lines is/are parallel to it?
   a. $y = -x - 2$
   b. $y = 8 - x$
   c. $y = x - 6$
   d. $y = -x$

171

17 COORDINATES AND STRAIGHT LINE GRAPHS

> **Worked example**

A straight line, A, has the equation $y = -3x + 6$. A second line, B, is parallel to line A and passes through the point with coordinates $(-4, 10)$.

Calculate the equation of line B.

As line B is a straight line it must take the form $y = mx + c$.

As it is parallel to line A, its gradient must be -3.

Because line B passes through the point $(-4, 10)$ these values can be substituted into the general equation of the straight line to give:

$$10 = -3 \times (-4) + c$$

Rearranging to find c gives: $c = -2$

The equation of line B is therefore $y = -3x - 2$.

Exercise 17.11

1 Find the equation of the line parallel to $y = 4x - 1$ that passes through $(0, 0)$.

2 Find the equations of lines parallel to $y = -3x + 1$ that pass through each of the following points:
   a $(0, 4)$
   b $(-2, 4)$
   c $\left(-\frac{5}{2}, 4\right)$

3 Find the equations of lines parallel to $x - 2y = 6$ that pass through each of the following points:
   a $(-4, 1)$
   b $\left(\frac{1}{2}, 0\right)$

Student assessment 1

1 Give the coordinates of points P, Q, R and S.

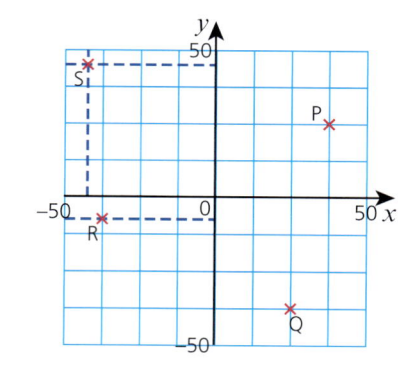

Parallel lines and their equations

2 For each of the following lines, select two points on the line and then calculate its gradient.

  a

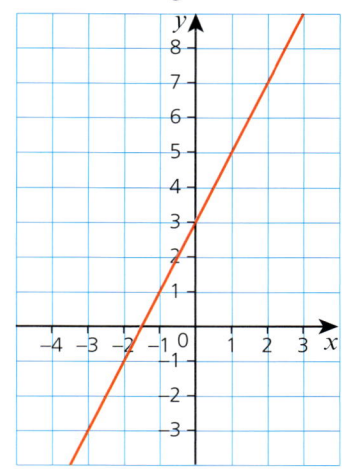

  b

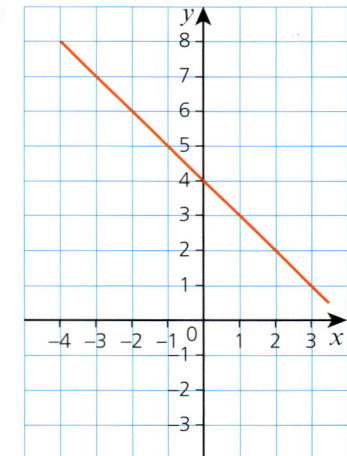

17 COORDINATES AND STRAIGHT LINE GRAPHS

3 Find the equation of the straight line for each of the following:

a

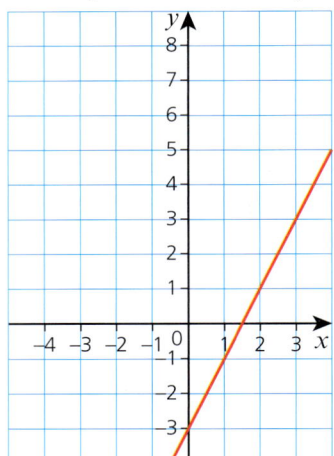

b

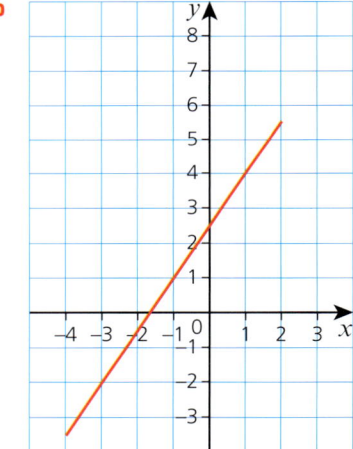

4 Write down the gradient and y-intercept for each of the following linear equations:

    a $y = \frac{1}{2}x$ **b** $y = 4x + 6$ **c** $y = -\frac{3}{2}x + \frac{5}{2}$

5 Write down the equation of the line parallel to the line $y = 5x + 6$ which passes through the origin.

Mathematical investigations and ICT 3

Plane trails

In an aircraft show, planes are made to fly with a coloured smoke trail. Depending on the formation of the planes, the trails can intersect in different ways.

In the diagram, the three smoke trails do not cross, as they are parallel.

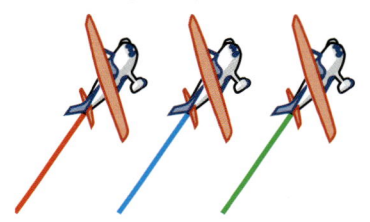

In the second diagram there are two crossing points.

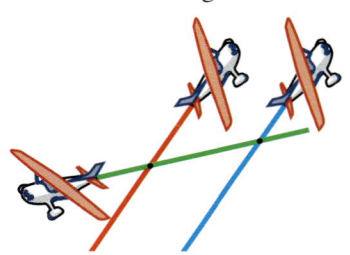

By flying differently, the three planes can produce trails that cross at three points.

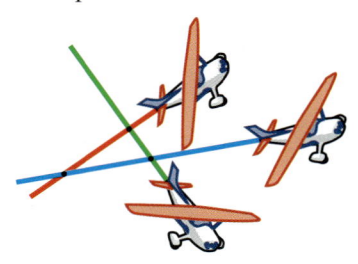

1. Investigate the connection between the maximum number of crossing points and the number of planes.
2. Record the results of your investigation in an ordered table.
3. Write an algebraic rule linking the number of planes (p) and the maximum number of crossing points (n).

TOPIC 4

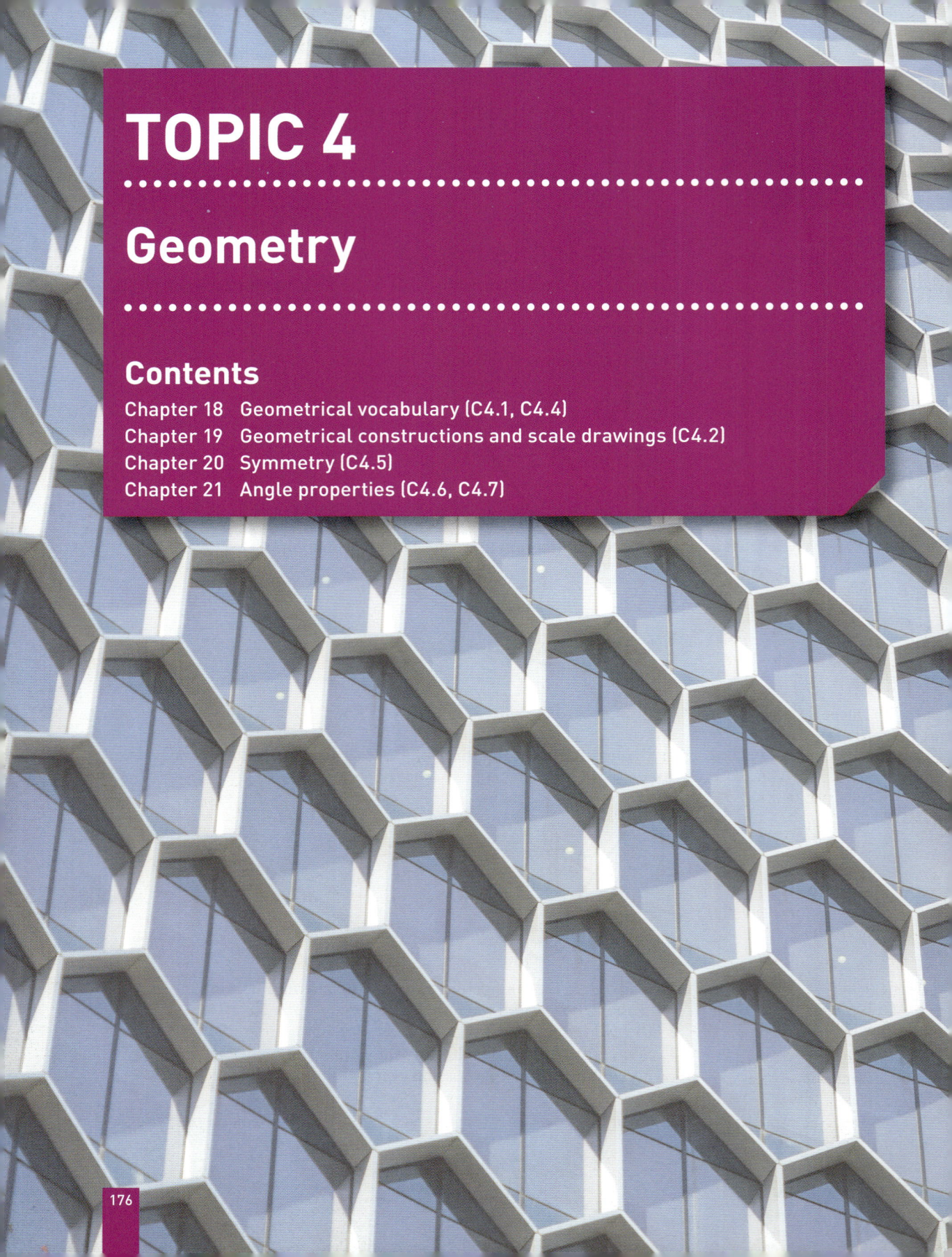

Geometry

Contents

Chapter 18 Geometrical vocabulary (C4.1, C4.4)
Chapter 19 Geometrical constructions and scale drawings (C4.2)
Chapter 20 Symmetry (C4.5)
Chapter 21 Angle properties (C4.6, C4.7)

Learning objectives

C4.1
1. Use and interpret the following geometrical terms:
   - point
   - vertex
   - line
   - parallel
   - perpendicular
   - bearing
   - right angle
   - acute, obtuse and reflex angles
   - interior and exterior angles
   - similar
   - congruent
   - scale factor.
2. Use and interpret the vocabulary of
   - triangles
   - special quadrilaterals
   - polygons
   - nets
   - simple solids.
3. Use and interpret the vocabulary of a circle.

C4.2
1. Measure and draw lines and angles.
2. Construct a triangle, given the length of all sides, using a ruler and pair of compasses only.
3. Draw, use and interpret nets.

C4.4
Calculate lengths of similar shapes.

C4.5
Recognise line symmetry and order of rotational symmetry in two dimensions.

C4.6
1. Calculate unknown angles and give simple explanations using the following geometrical properties:
   - Sum of angles at a point = 360°
   - Sum of angles at a point on a straight line = 180°
   - Vertically opposite angles are equal
   - Angle sum of a triangle = 180°
   - Angle sum of a quadrilateral = 360°.
2. Calculate unknown angles and give geometric explanations for angles formed within parallel lines:
   - Corresponding angles are equal.
   - Alternate angles are equal.
   - Co-interior angles sum to 180° (supplementary).
3. Know and use angle properties of regular polygons.

C4.7
Calculate unknown angles and give explanations using the following geometrical properties of circles:
- Angle in a semi-circle = 90°
- Angle between tangent and radius = 90°

The development of geometry

The beginnings of geometry can be traced back to around 2000BCE in ancient Mesopotamia and Egypt. Early geometry was a practical subject concerning lengths, angles, areas and volumes and was used in surveying, construction, astronomy and various crafts.

The earliest known texts on geometry are the Egyptian Rhind Papyrus (c.1650BCE), the Moscow Papyrus (c.1890BCE) and Babylonian clay tablets such as Plimpton 322 (c.1900BCE). For example, the Moscow Papyrus gives a formula for calculating the volume of a truncated pyramid, or frustum.

In the seventh century BCE, the Greek mathematician Thales of Miletus (which is now in Turkey) used geometry to solve problems such as calculating the height of pyramids and the distance of ships from the shore.

Euclid

In around 300BCE, Euclid wrote his book ***Elements***, perhaps the most successful textbook of all time. It introduced the concepts of definition, theorem and proof. Its contents are still taught in geometry classes today.

18 Geometrical vocabulary

Note
All diagrams are not drawn to scale.

Angles

Different types of angle have different names:

- **acute angles** lie between 0° and 90°
- **right angles** are exactly 90°
- **obtuse angles** lie between 90° and 180°
- **reflex angles** lie between 180° and 360°.

Two angles which add together to total 180° are called **supplementary angles**.

Two angles which add together to total 90° are called **complementary angles**.

Exercise 18.1

1 Draw and label one example of each of the following types of angle:

   right   acute   obtuse   reflex

2 Copy the angles below and write beneath each drawing the type of angle it shows:

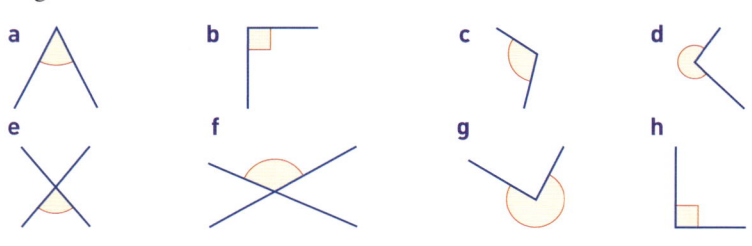

   a   b   c   d

   e   f   g   h

3 State whether the following pairs of angles are supplementary, complementary or neither:
   a 70°, 20°   b 90°, 90°   c 40°, 50°   d 80°, 30°
   e 15°, 75°   f 145°, 35°   g 133°, 57°   h 33°, 67°
   i 45°, 45°   j 140°, 40°

Angles can be labelled in several ways:

In the first case, the angle is labelled directly as x. In the second example, the angle can be labelled as angle PQR or angle RQP. In this case three points are chosen, with the angle in question being the middle one.

Perpendicular lines

Exercise 18.2 Sketch the shapes below. Name the angles marked with a single letter, in terms of three vertices.

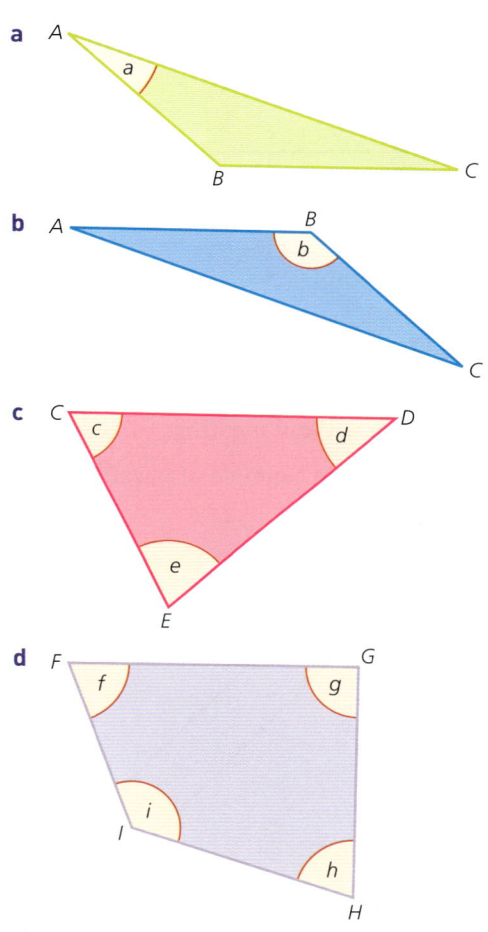

a

b

c

d

Perpendicular lines

To find the shortest **distance between two points**, you measure the length of the **straight line** which joins them.

Two lines which meet at right angles are **perpendicular** to each other.

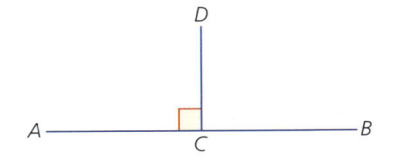

So in this diagram CD is perpendicular to AB, and AB is perpendicular to CD.

If the lines AD and BD are drawn to form a triangle, the line CD can be called the **height** or **altitude** of the triangle ABD.

18 GEOMETRICAL VOCABULARY

Exercise 18.3 For these diagrams, state which pairs of lines are perpendicular to each other.

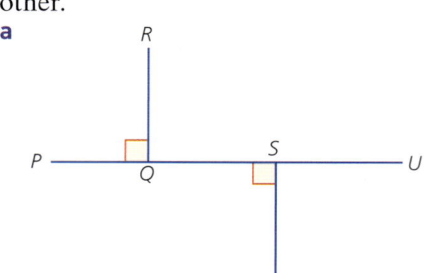

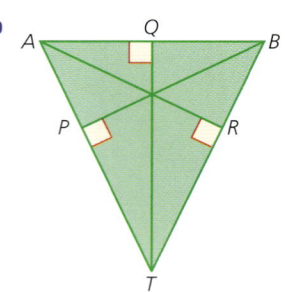

a

b

Parallel lines

Parallel lines are straight lines which can be continued to infinity in either direction without meeting.

Railway lines are an example of parallel lines. Parallel lines are marked with arrows as shown:

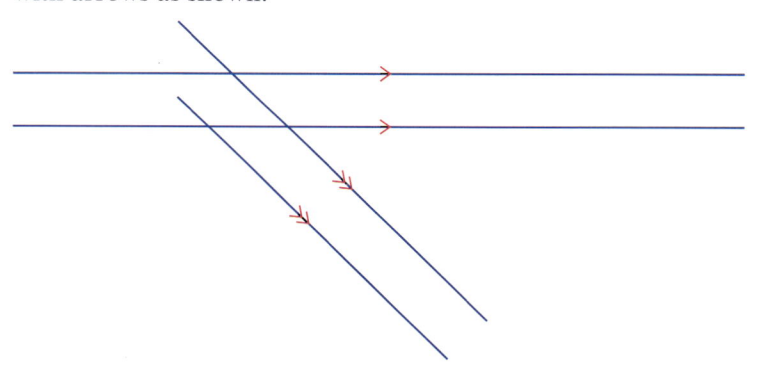

Vocabulary of the circle

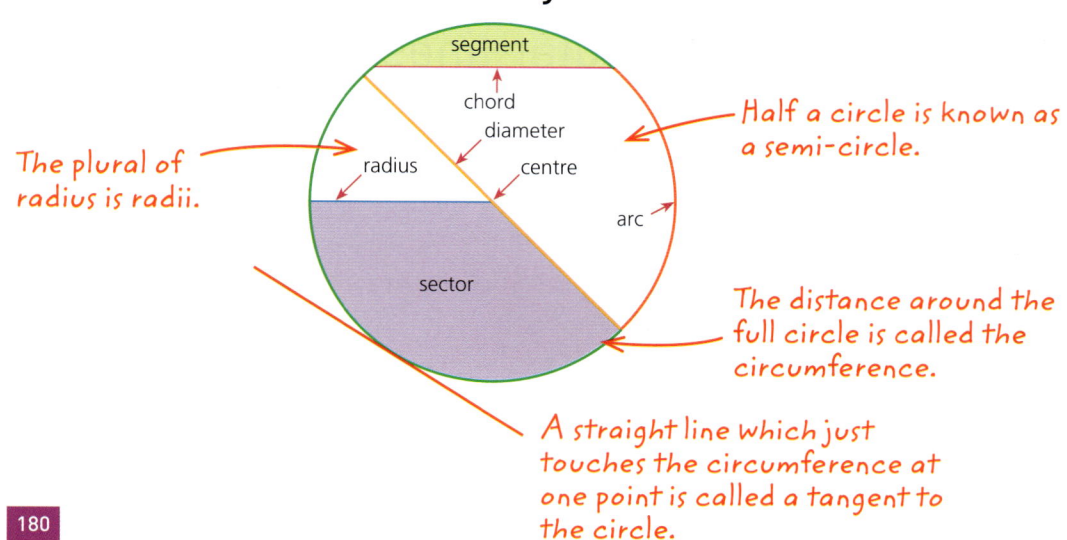

- segment
- chord
- diameter
- radius
- centre
- arc
- sector

The plural of radius is radii.

Half a circle is known as a semi-circle.

The distance around the full circle is called the circumference.

A straight line which just touches the circumference at one point is called a tangent to the circle.

Polygons

A **polygon** is a closed two-dimensional shape bounded by straight lines. Examples of polygons include triangles, quadrilaterals, pentagons and hexagons. These shapes all belong to the polygon family:

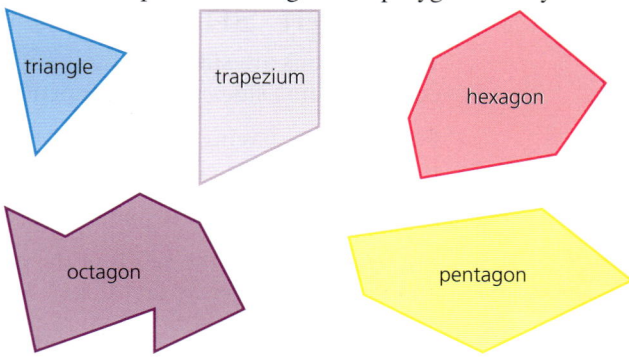

triangle, trapezium, hexagon, octagon, pentagon

A **regular polygon** is distinctive in that all its sides are of equal length and all its angles are of equal size. These shapes are some examples of regular polygons:

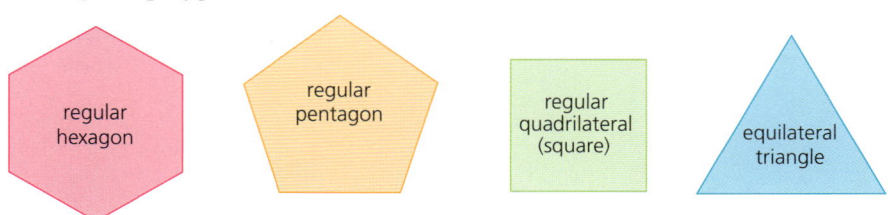

regular hexagon, regular pentagon, regular quadrilateral (square), equilateral triangle

A polygon where not all sides are the same length and angles are not the same size is called an **irregular polygon**.

The names of polygons are related to the number of angles they contain:

3 angles = **tri**angle
4 angles = **quad**rilateral (tetragon)
5 angles = **penta**gon
6 angles = **hexa**gon
7 angles = **hepta**gon

8 angles = **octa**gon
9 angles = **nona**gon
10 angles = **deca**gon
12 angles = **dodeca**gon

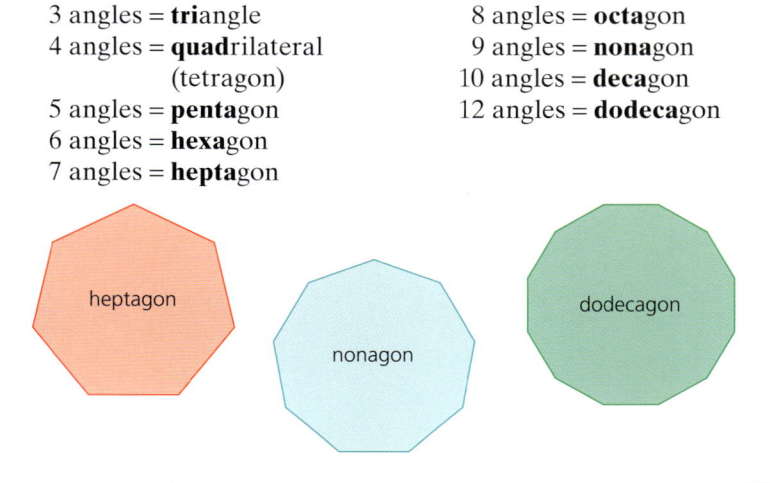

> **Note**
> A heptagon has seven sides.
> A nonagon has nine sides.
> A dodecagon has twelve sides.
> These names are not required for this syllabus.

heptagon, nonagon, dodecagon

181

18 GEOMETRICAL VOCABULARY

Exercise 18.4

1. Draw a sketch of each of the shapes listed on the previous page.
2. Draw accurately a regular hexagon, a regular pentagon and a regular octagon.

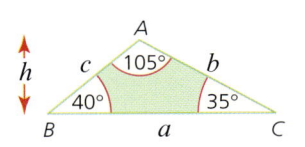

Similar shapes

Two polygons are **similar** if their angles are the same and corresponding sides are in proportion.

For triangles, having equal angles implies that corresponding sides are in proportion. The converse is also true.

In the diagrams (left), triangle ABC and triangle PQR are similar.

For similar figures the ratios of the lengths of the sides are the same and represent the scale factor, i.e.:

$$\frac{p}{a} = \frac{q}{b} = \frac{r}{c} = k \text{ (where } k \text{ is the \textbf{scale factor of enlargement})}$$

The heights of similar triangles are proportional also:

$$\frac{H}{h} = \frac{p}{a} = \frac{q}{b} = \frac{r}{c} = k$$

Exercise 18.5

1. **a** Explain why the two triangles are similar.

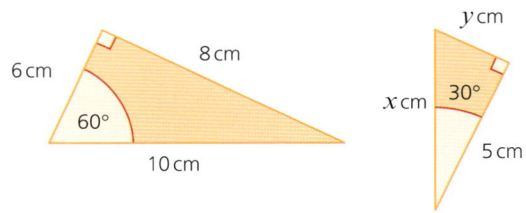

   b Calculate the scale factor which reduces the larger triangle to the smaller one.

   c Calculate the value of x and the value of y.

2. Which of the triangles below are similar?

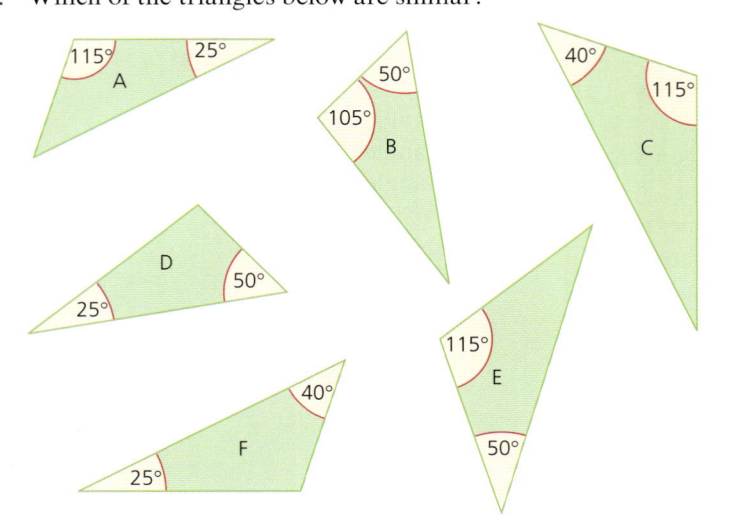

Congruent shapes

3 The triangles are similar.

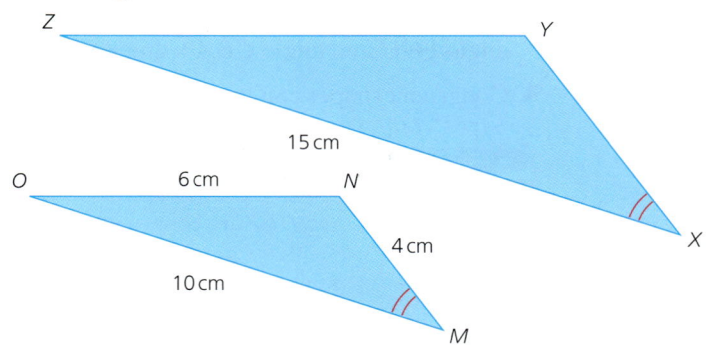

    a Calculate the length XY.   **b** Calculate the length YZ.

4 Calculate the lengths of sides p, q and r in the triangle:

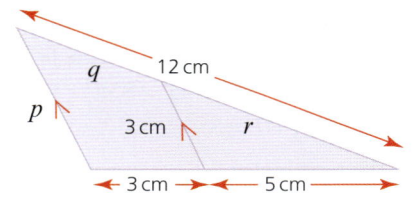

5 Calculate the lengths of sides e and f in the trapezium:

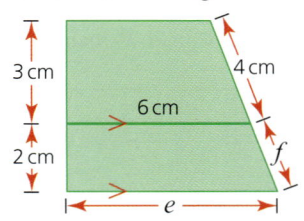

Congruent shapes

Two shapes are **congruent** if their corresponding sides are the same length and corresponding angles the same size, i.e. the shapes are exactly the same size and shape.

Shapes X and Y are congruent:

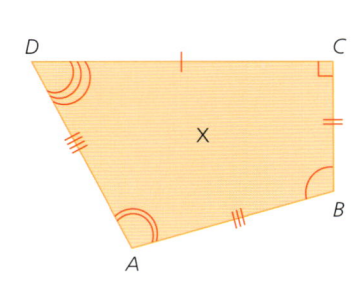

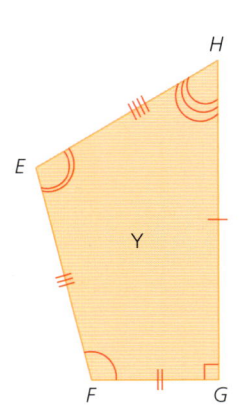

18 GEOMETRICAL VOCABULARY

Congruent shapes are by definition also similar, but similar shapes are not necessarily congruent.

They are congruent as $AB = EF$, $BC = FG$, $CD = GH$ and $DA = HE$. Also angle DAB = angle HEF, angle ABC = angle EFG, angle BCD = angle FGH and angle CDA = angle GHE.

Congruent shapes can therefore be reflections and rotations of each other.

➡ Worked example

Triangles ABC and DEF are congruent:

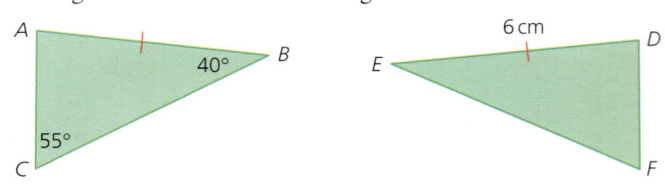

a Calculate the size of angle FDE.

As the two triangles are congruent, angle FDE = angle CAB.

Angle $CAB = 180° - 40° - 55° = 85°$

Therefore angle $FDE = 85°$.

b Deduce the length of AB.

As $AB = DE$, $AB = 6$ cm

Exercise 18.6

1 Look at the shapes on the grid. Which shapes are congruent to shape A?

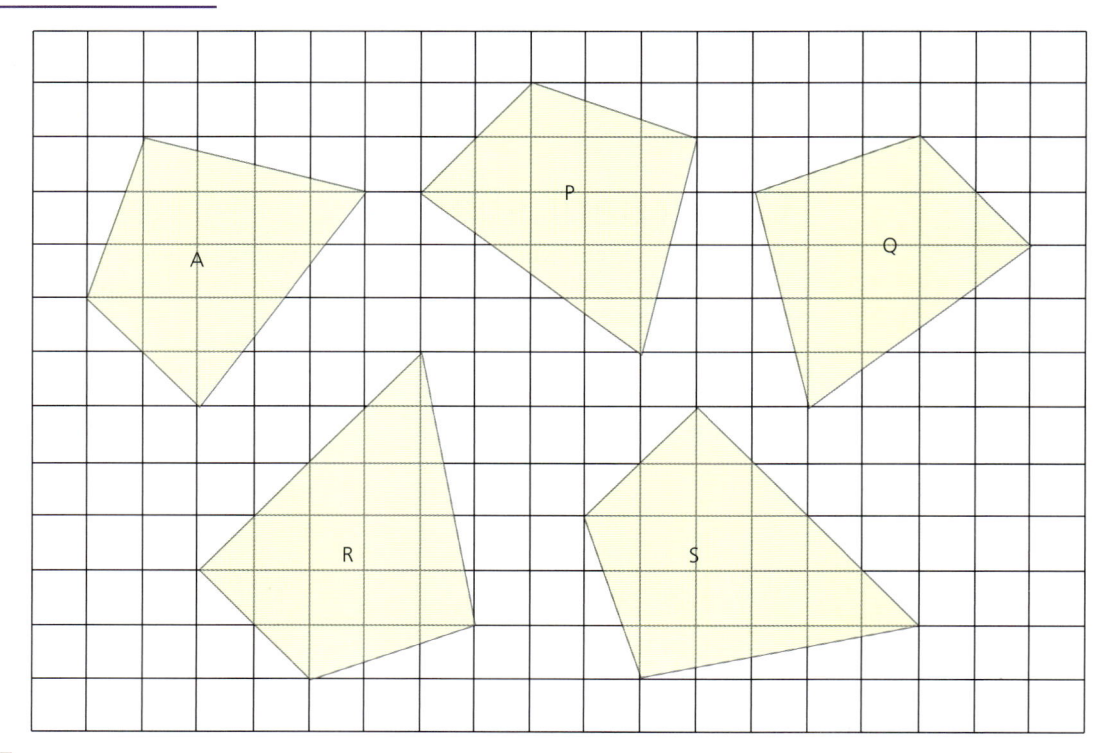

Congruent shapes

2 Two congruent shapes are shown. Calculate the value of x.

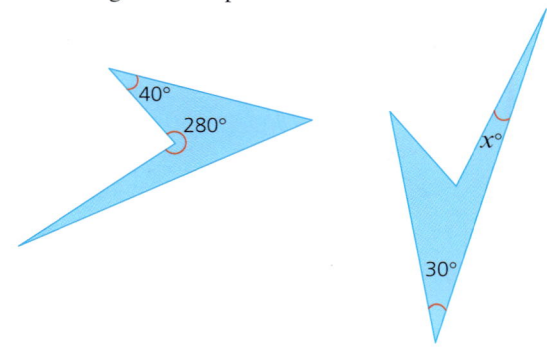

3 A quadrilateral is plotted on a pair of axes. The coordinates of its four vertices are (0, 1), (0, 5), (3, 4) and (3, 3). Another quadrilateral, congruent to the first, is also plotted on the same axes. Three of its vertices have coordinates (6, 5), (5, 2) and (4, 2). Calculate the coordinates of the fourth vertex.

4 Triangle P is drawn on a grid. One side of another triangle, Q, is also shown.

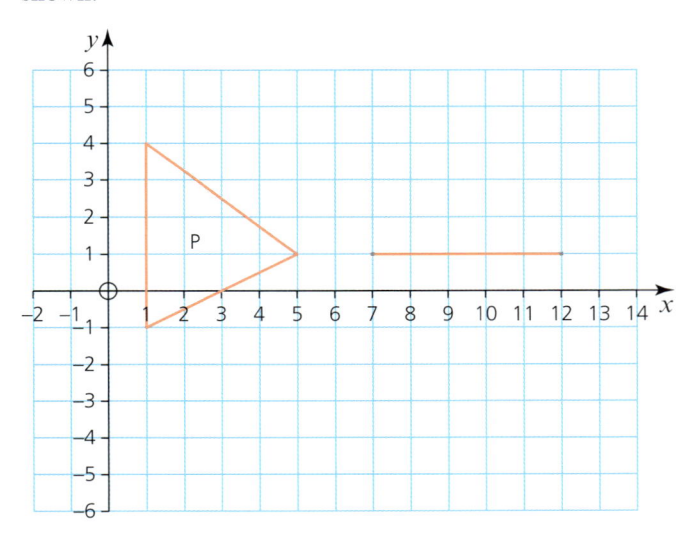

If triangles P and Q are congruent, give all the possible coordinates for the position of the missing vertex.

18 GEOMETRICAL VOCABULARY

Student assessment 1

1. Are the angles acute, obtuse, reflex or right angles?
   a 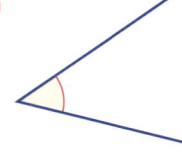
   b 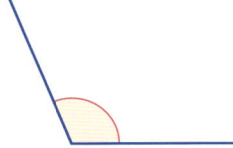
   c 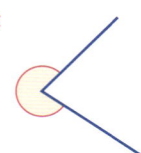
   d

2. Draw a circle of radius 3 cm. Mark on it:
   a a diameter   b a chord   c a sector.

3. Draw two congruent isosceles triangles with base angles of 45°.

4. Triangle X is drawn on a graph. One side of another triangle congruent to X is also shown:

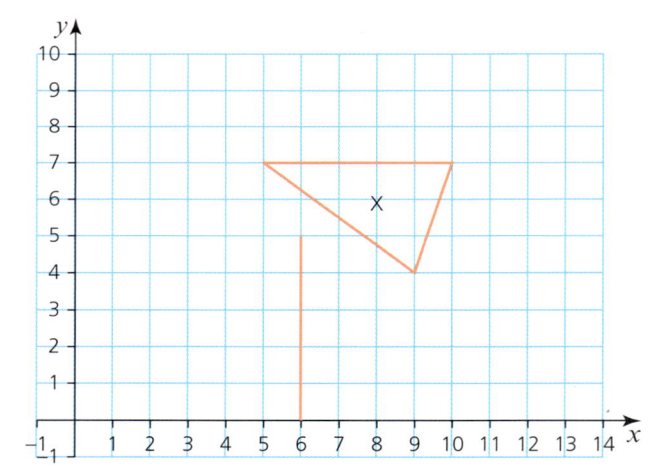

   Write the coordinates of all the points where the missing vertex could be.

Student assessment 2

1 Draw and label one pair of parallel lines intersecting another pair of parallel lines.

2 Make two statements about these two triangles:

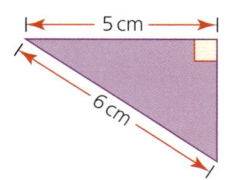

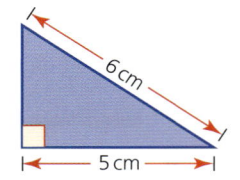

3 The diagram shows an equilateral triangle ABC. The midpoints L, M and N of each side are also joined.
   a Identify a trapezium congruent to trapezium $BCLN$.
   b Identify a triangle similar to triangle LMN.

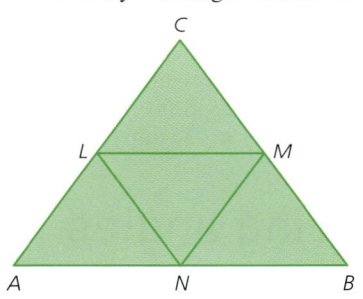

4 Decide whether each of the following statements are true or false.
   a All circles are similar.
   b All squares are similar.
   c All rectangles are similar.
   d All equilateral triangles are congruent.

19 Geometrical constructions and scale drawings

Measuring lines

A straight line can be drawn and measured accurately using a ruler.

Exercise 19.1

1 Using a ruler, measure the length of these lines to the nearest mm:

a
b
c
d
e
f

2 Draw lines of the following lengths using a ruler:
   a 3 cm   b 8 cm   c 4.6 cm
   d 94 mm   e 38 mm   f 61 mm

Measuring angles

An angle is a measure of **turn**. When drawn, it can be measured using either a protractor or an angle measurer. The units of turn are degrees (°). Measuring with a protractor needs care, as there are two scales marked on it – an inner one and an outer one.

➡ Worked examples

1 Measure the angle using a protractor:

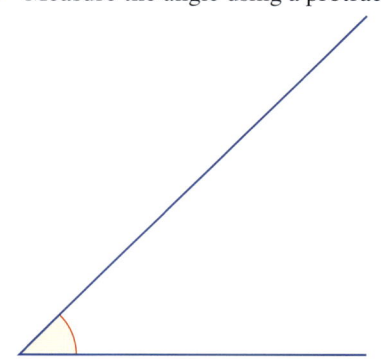

Place the protractor over the angle so that the cross lies on the point where the two lines meet.

Measuring angles

Align the 0° with one of the lines:

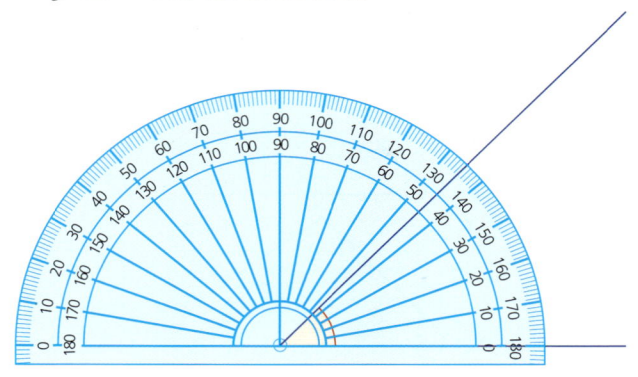

Decide which scale is appropriate. In this case, it is the inner scale as it starts at 0°.

Measure the angle using the inner scale.

The angle is 45°.

2 Draw an angle of 110°.

Start by drawing a straight line.

Place the protractor on the line so that the cross is on one of the end points of the line.

Ensure that the line is aligned with the 0° on the protractor:

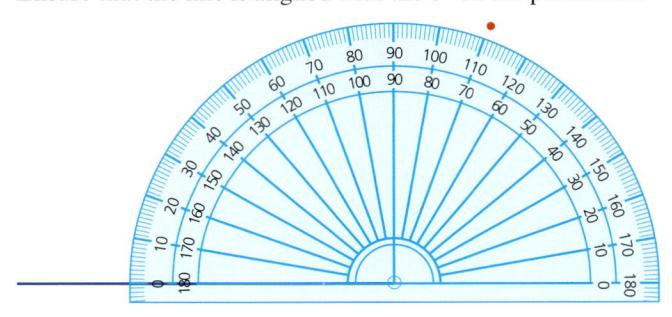

Decide which scale to use. In this case, it is the outer scale as it starts at 0°.

Mark where the protractor reads 110°.

Join the mark made to the end point of the original line.

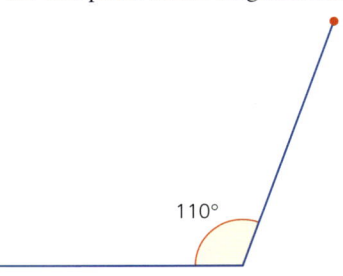

110°

19 GEOMETRICAL CONSTRUCTIONS AND SCALE DRAWINGS

Exercise 19.2

1 Measure each angle:

a

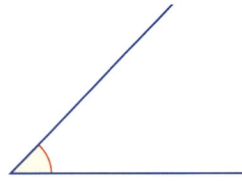

b

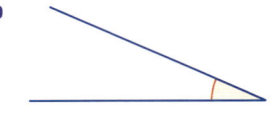

c

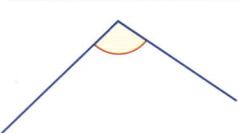

d

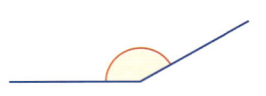

e

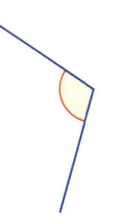

f

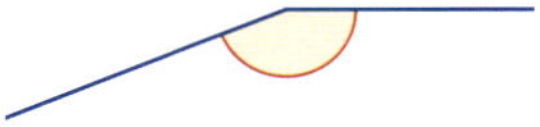

2 Measure each angle:

a

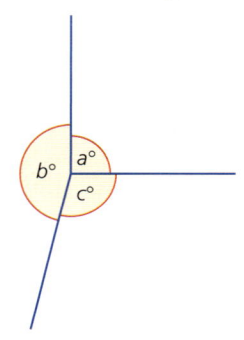

b

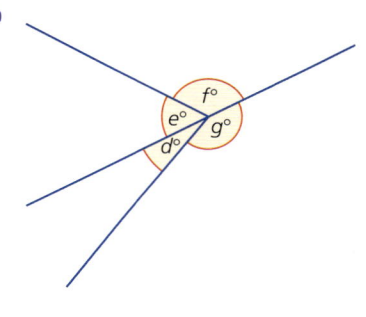

c

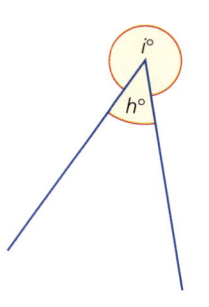

d

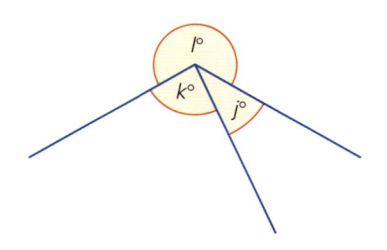

Constructing triangles

e

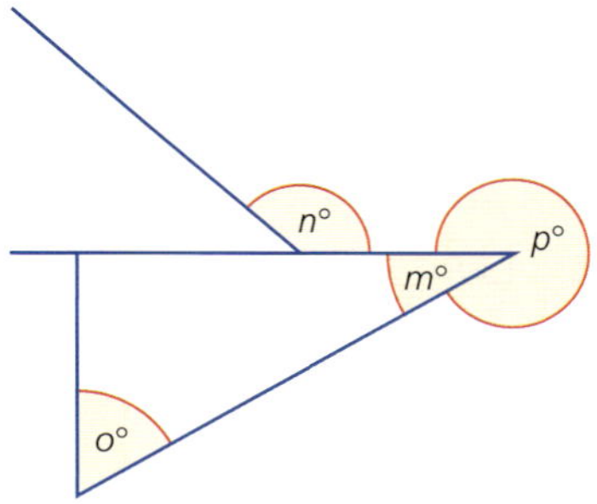

f

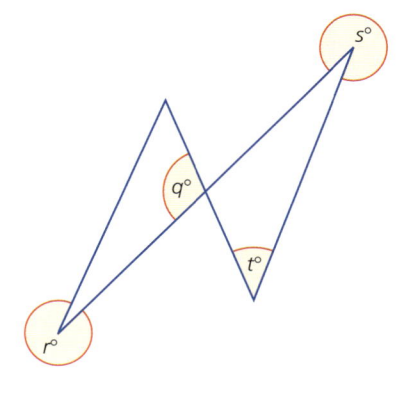

3 Draw angles of the following sizes:
- **a** 20°
- **b** 45°
- **c** 90°
- **d** 120°
- **e** 157°
- **f** 172°
- **g** 14°
- **h** 205°
- **i** 311°
- **j** 283°
- **k** 198°
- **l** 352°

Constructing triangles

Triangles can be drawn accurately by using a ruler and a pair of compasses. This is called **constructing** a triangle.

> ### Worked example
>
> The sketch shows the triangle ABC. 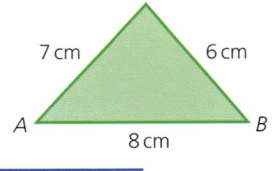
>
> Construct the triangle ABC given that:
>
> $AB = 8\,cm$, $BC = 6\,cm$ and $AC = 7\,cm$
>
> Draw the line AB using a ruler: 
>
> A ←——— 8 cm ———→ B
>
> Open up a pair of compasses to 6 cm. Place the compass point on B and draw an arc:

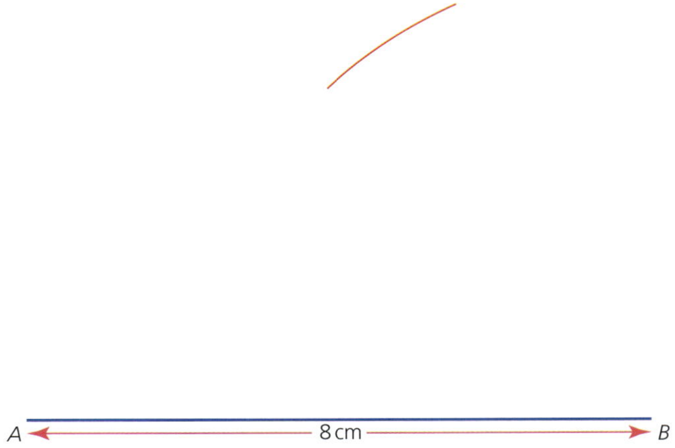

A ←——— 8 cm ———→ B

19 GEOMETRICAL CONSTRUCTIONS AND SCALE DRAWINGS

Note that every point on the arc is 6 cm away from B.

Open up the pair of compasses to 7 cm. Place the compass point on A and draw another arc, with centre A and radius 7 cm, ensuring that it intersects with the first arc. Every point on the second arc is 7 cm from A. Where the two arcs intersect is point C, as it is both 6 cm from B and 7 cm from A.

Join C to A and C to B:

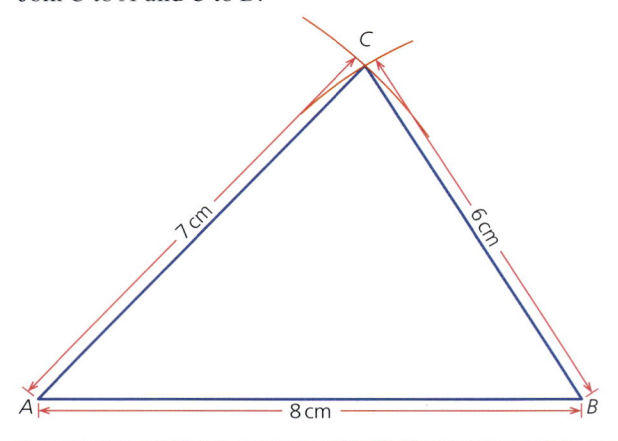

Exercise 19.3

Using only a ruler and a pair of compasses, construct the following triangles:
a   Triangle ABC where $AB = 10$ cm, $AC = 7$ cm and $BC = 9$ cm
b   Triangle LMN where $LM = 4$ cm, $LN = 8$ cm and $MN = 5$ cm
c   Triangle PQR, an equilateral triangle of side length 7 cm
d   i   Triangle ABC where $AB = 8$ cm, $AC = 4$ cm and $BC = 3$ cm
    ii Is this triangle possible? Explain your answer.

Scale drawings

Scale drawings are used when an accurate diagram, drawn in proportion, is needed. Common uses of scale drawings include maps and plans. The use of scale drawings involves understanding how to scale measurements.

➡ Worked examples

1   A map is drawn to a scale of 1 : 10000. If two objects are 1 cm apart on the map, how far apart are they in real life? Give your answer in metres.

   A scale of 1 : 10000 means that 1 cm on the map represents 10000 cm in real life.

   Therefore the distance = 10000 cm
                          = 100 m

Scale drawings

2 A model boat is built to a scale of 1 : 50. If the length of the real boat is 12 m, calculate the length of the model boat in cm.

A scale of 1 : 50 means that 50 cm on the real boat is 1 cm on the model boat.

12 m = 1200 cm

Therefore the length of the model boat = 1200 ÷ 50 cm
$$= 24 \text{ cm}$$

3 a Construct, to a scale of 1 : 1, a triangle ABC such that AB = 6 cm, AC = 5 cm and BC = 4 cm.

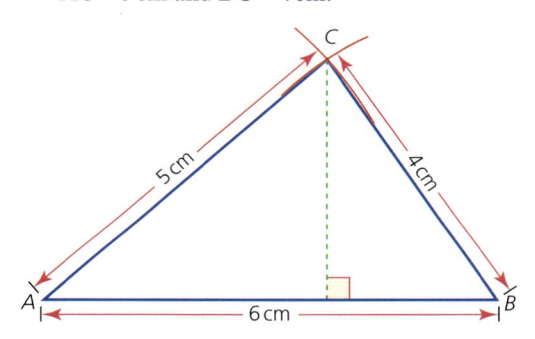

b Measure the perpendicular length of C from AB.

Perpendicular length is 3.3 cm.

c Calculate the area of the triangle.

$$\text{Area} = \frac{\text{base length} \times \text{perpendicular height}}{2}$$

$$\text{Area} = \frac{6 \times 3.3}{2} \text{cm} = 9.9 \text{ cm}^2$$

Exercise 19.4

1 In the following questions, both the scale to which a map is drawn and the distance between two objects on the map are given.

Find the real distance between the two objects, giving your answer in metres.
a 1 : 10 000, 3 cm   **b** 1 : 10 000, 2.5 cm
c 1 : 20 000, 1.5 cm   **d** 1 : 8000,   5.2 cm

2 In the following questions, both the scale to which a map is drawn and the true distance between two objects are given.

Find the distance between the two objects on the map, giving your answer in cm.
a 1 : 15 000, 1.5 km   **b** 1 : 50 000, 4 km
c 1 : 10 000, 600 m   **d** 1 : 25 000, 1.7 km

19 GEOMETRICAL CONSTRUCTIONS AND SCALE DRAWINGS

Exercise 19.4 (cont)

3   A rectangular pool measures 20 m by 36 m as shown below:

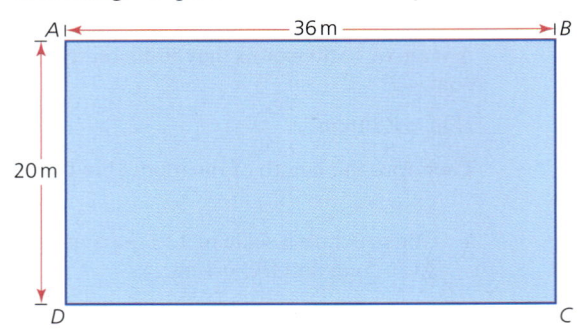

   a   Construct a scale drawing of the pool, using 1 cm for every 4 m.
   b   Ibrahim swims across the pool from *D* in a straight line so that he arrives at a point which is 40 m from *D* and 30 m from *C*. Work out the distance Ibrahim swam.

4   A triangular enclosure is shown in the diagram below:

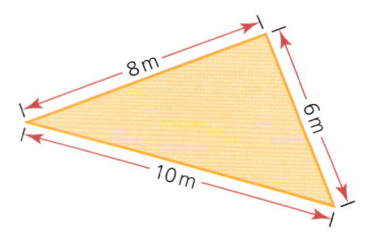

   a   Using a scale of 1 cm for each metre, construct a scale drawing of the enclosure.
   b   Calculate the true area of the enclosure.

5   An area of lawn is in the shape of a rhombus consisting of two equilateral triangles, of edge length 6.0 m, arranged side by side as shown. Construct the rhombus using a scale of 1 cm for each metre.

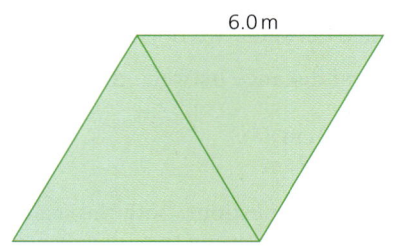

Nets

The diagram is the **net** of a cube. It shows the faces of the cube opened out into a two-dimensional plan. The net of a three-dimensional shape can be folded up to make that shape.

Nets

Exercise 19.5

1. The diagrams below show a cuboid and its net:

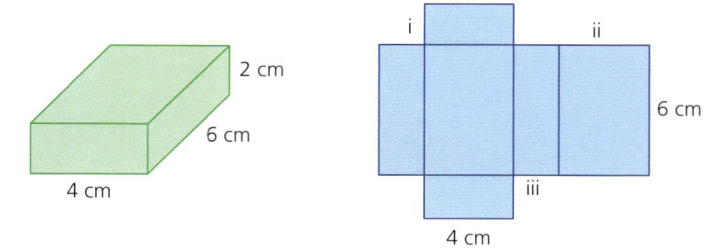

    a Write down the lengths of the sides marked i, ii and iii on the net.

    b Two other nets A and B are shown below:

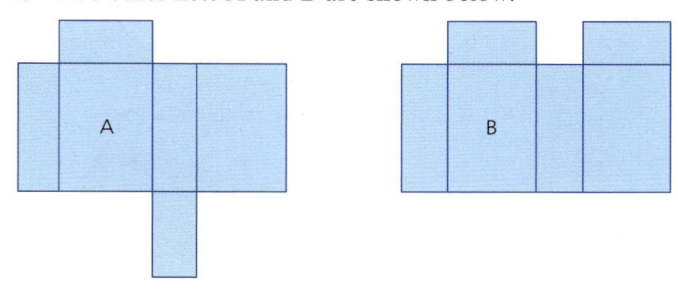

    i Which of the two nets cannot be folded to make a cuboid?

    ii Give a reason for your answer.

    c Draw a different possible net for the cuboid.

2. Two possible nets of a cube are shown below. On each one a face has been labelled X.

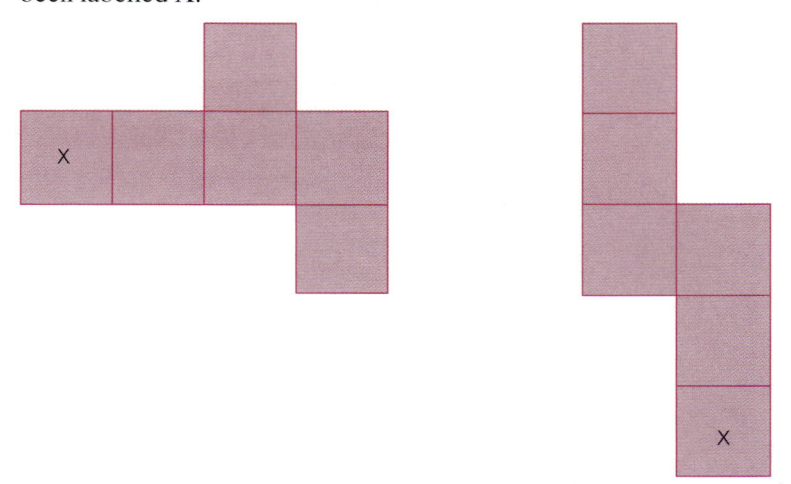

    Sketch each of the nets above and mark with the letter Y the face that would be opposite the face labelled X if the net was assembled to form a cube.

195

19 GEOMETRICAL CONSTRUCTIONS AND SCALE DRAWINGS

3 The net of a shape is given below:

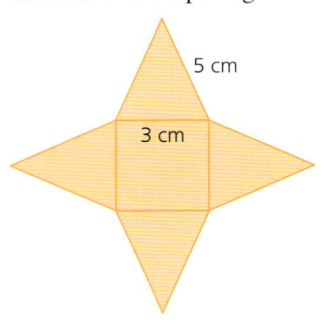

5 cm

3 cm

a Give the name of the 3D shape it makes.
b Using a ruler and a pair of compasses, construct a full-size net of the shape.

4 A triangular prism is given below:

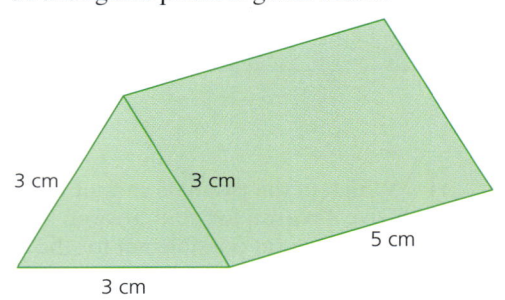

3 cm 3 cm

5 cm

3 cm

Using a ruler and a pair of compasses, construct a possible net of the prism.

Student assessment 1

1 a Using a ruler, measure the length of the line:

   b Draw a line 4.7 cm long.
2 a Using a protractor, measure the angle shown:

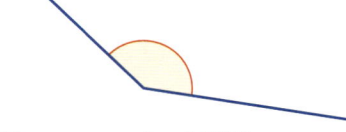

   b Draw an angle of 300°.
3 Construct triangle ABC such that $AB = 8$ cm, $AC = 6$ cm and $BC = 12$ cm.

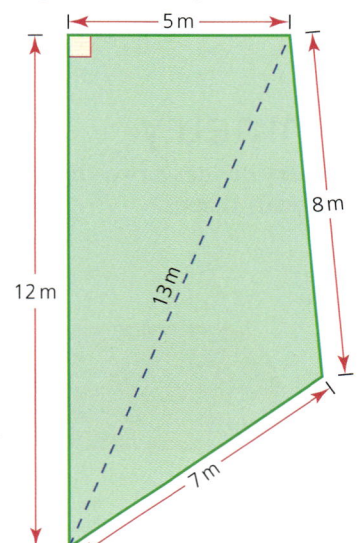

4 A plan of a living room is shown:

a Using a pair of compasses, construct a scale drawing of the room using 1 cm for every metre.
b Using a set square if necessary, calculate the total area of the actual living room.

5 Measure each of the five angles of the pentagon:

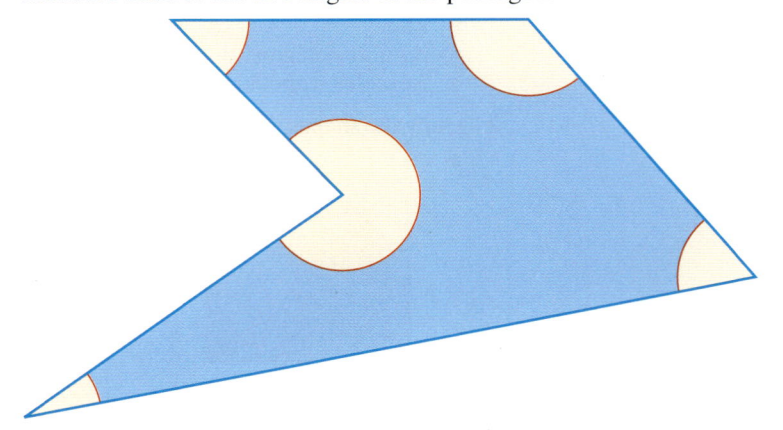

6 Draw, using a ruler and a protractor, a triangle with angles of 40°, 60° and 80°.

7 In the following questions, both the scale to which a map is drawn and the true distance between two objects are given.
Find the distance between the two objects on the map, giving your answer in cm.
   a 1 : 20 000,   4.4 km   **b** 1 : 50 000,   12.2 km

8 On squared paper, draw the net of a triangular prism.

20 Symmetry

Line symmetry

A **line of symmetry** divides a two-dimensional (flat) shape into two congruent (identical) shapes.

e.g.

1 line of symmetry   2 lines of symmetry   4 lines of symmetry

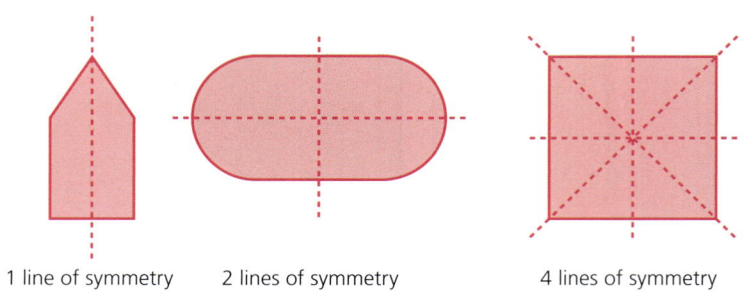

Exercise 20.1

1 Draw the following shapes and, where possible, show all their lines of symmetry:
   a square
   b rectangle
   c equilateral triangle
   d isosceles triangle
   e kite
   f regular hexagon
   g regular octagon
   h regular pentagon
   i isosceles trapezium
   j circle

2 Copy the shapes and, where possible, show all their lines of symmetry:
   a
   b
   c
   d

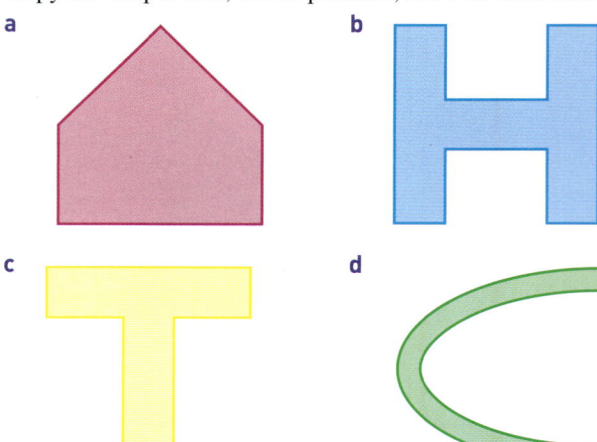

Line symmetry

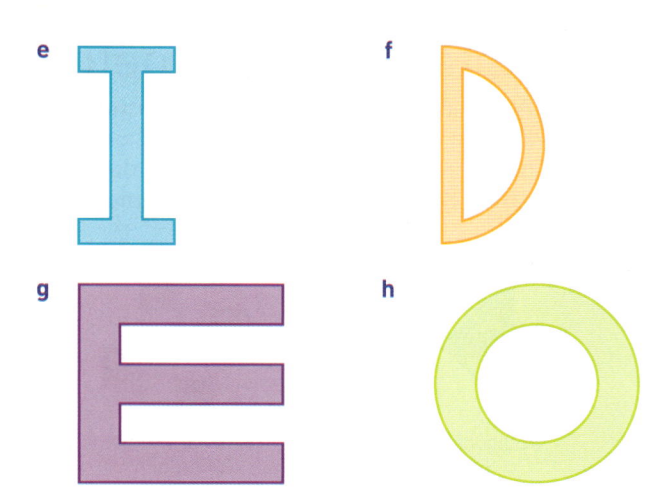

e   f

g   h

3 Copy the shapes and complete them so that the **bold** line becomes a line of symmetry:

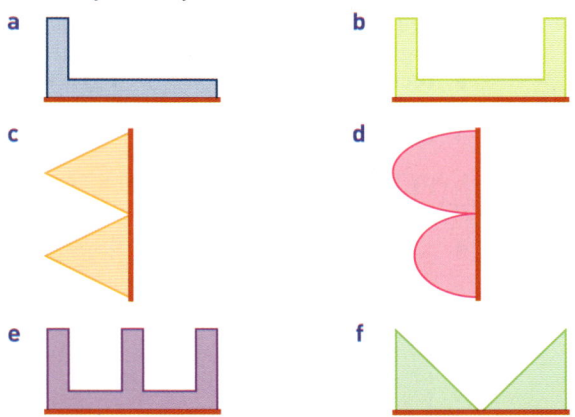

a   b

c   d

e   f

4 Copy the shapes and complete them so that the **bold** lines become lines of symmetry:

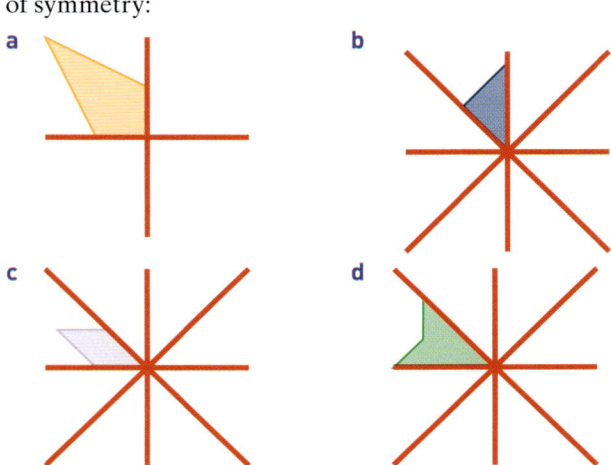

a   b

c   d

199

20 SYMMETRY

Rotational symmetry

A two-dimensional shape has **rotational symmetry** if, when rotated about a central point, it looks the same as its starting position. The number of times it looks the same during a complete revolution is called the **order of rotational symmetry**.

e.g.

rotational symmetry of order 2

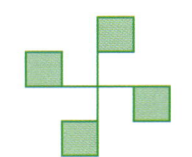

rotational symmetry of order 4

Exercise 20.2

1. Draw the following shapes. Identify the centre of rotation, and state the order of rotational symmetry:
   - a square
   - b equilateral triangle
   - c regular pentagon
   - d parallelogram
   - e rectangle
   - f rhombus
   - g regular hexagon
   - h regular octagon
   - i circle

2. Copy the shapes. Indicate the centre of rotation, and state the order of rotational symmetry:
   - a H
   - b N
   - c S
   - d X
   - e Z

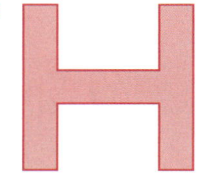

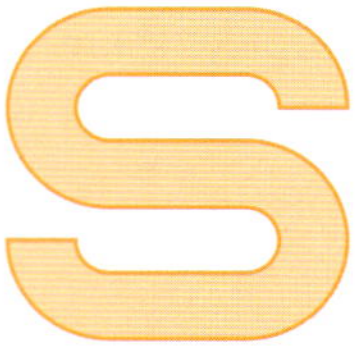

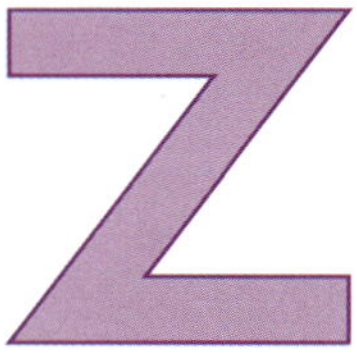

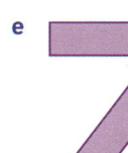

Rotational symmetry

Student assessment 1

1. Draw a shape with exactly:
   a one line of symmetry
   b two lines of symmetry
   c three lines of symmetry.
   Mark the lines of symmetry on each diagram.

2. Draw a shape with:
   a rotational symmetry of order 2
   b rotational symmetry of order 3.
   Mark the position of the centre of rotation on each diagram.

3. Copy and complete the following shapes so that the **bold** lines become lines of symmetry:

   a   b

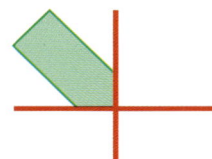

   c 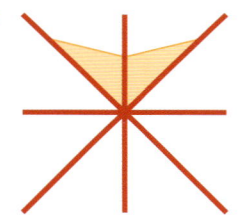   d

4. State the order of rotational symmetry for the completed drawings in Q.3.

21 Angle properties

> **Note**
> All diagrams are not drawn to scale.

Angles at a point and on a line

One complete revolution is equivalent to a rotation of 360° about a point. Similarly, half a complete revolution is equivalent to a rotation of 180° about a point. These facts can be seen clearly by looking at either a circular angle measurer or a semi-circular protractor.

Worked examples

1   Calculate the size of the angle $x°$ in the diagram below:

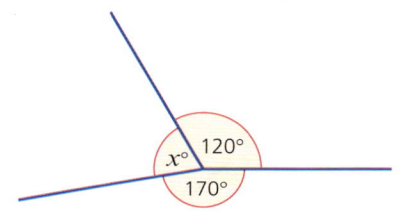

    The sum of all the **angles at a point** is 360°. Therefore:
    $120 + 170 + x = 360$
    $x = 360 - 120 - 170$
    $x = 70$

    Therefore the missing angle is 70°.

    Note that the size of the angle is **calculated** and *not* **measured**.

2   Calculate the size of angle $a°$ in the diagram below:

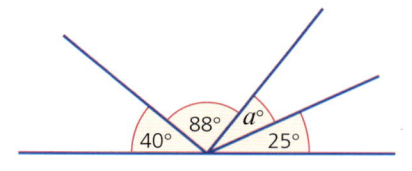

    The sum of all the **angles on a straight line** is 180°. Therefore:
    $40 + 88 + a + 25 = 180$
    $a = 180 - 40 - 88 - 25$
    $a = 27$

    Therefore the missing angle 27°.

Angles at a point and on a line

Exercise 21.1

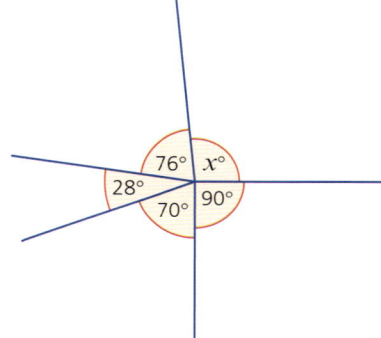

1 Calculate the value of x:

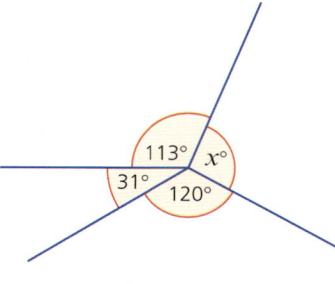

a 125°, 160°, $x°$

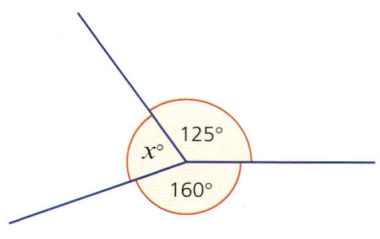

b 113°, 31°, 120°, $x°$

c 76°, $x°$, 28°, 70°, 90°

d 45°, 81°, 48°, 40°, $x°$

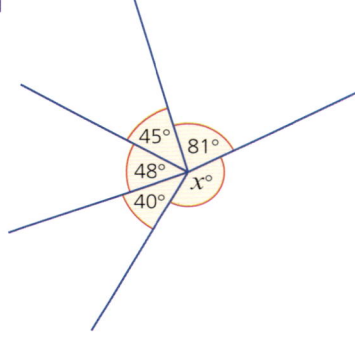

2 In the following questions, the angles lie about a point on a straight line. Find the value of y.

a 45°, $y°$, 24°

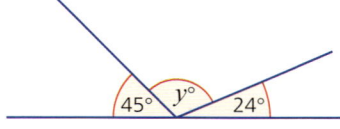

b 60°, $y°$, 43°, 40°

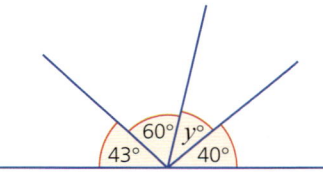

c $y°$, 76°, 32°, 50°

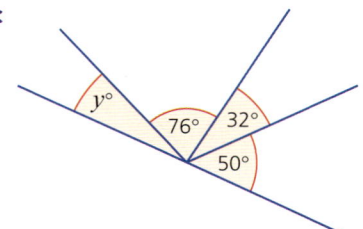

d $y°$, 34°, 21°, 63°

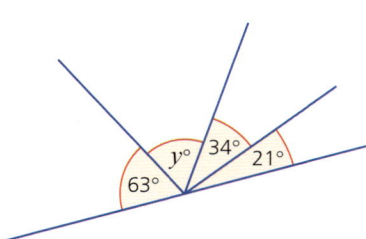

21 ANGLE PROPERTIES

Exercise 21.1 (cont)

3 Calculate the value of p in each diagram:

a

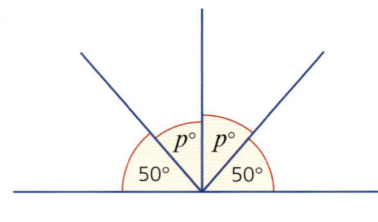

b

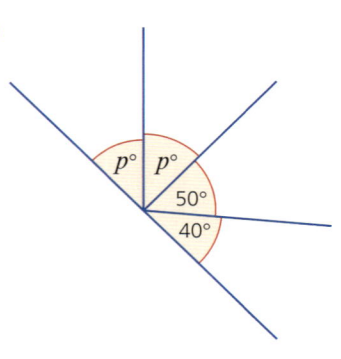

c

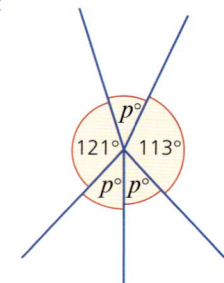

d

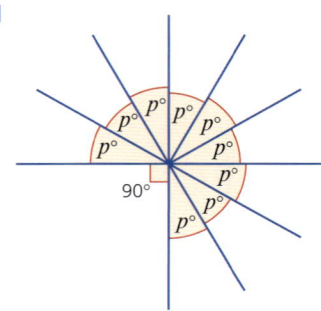

Angles formed by intersecting lines

Exercise 21.2

1 Draw a similar diagram to the one shown. Measure carefully each of the labelled angles and write them down.

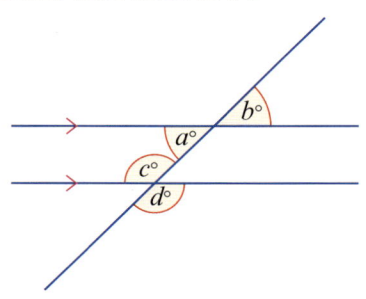

2 Draw a similar diagram to the one shown. Measure carefully each of the labelled angles and write them down.

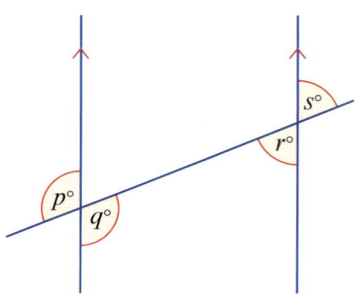

Angles formed by intersecting lines

3 Draw a similar diagram to the one shown. Measure carefully each of the labelled angles and write them down.

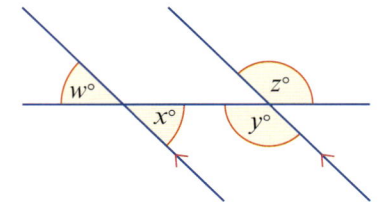

4 Write down what you have noticed about the angles you measured in Q.1–3.

When two straight lines cross, it is found that the angles opposite each other are the same size. They are known as **vertically opposite angles**. By using the fact that angles at a point on a straight line add up to 180°, it can be shown why vertically opposite angles must always be equal in size.

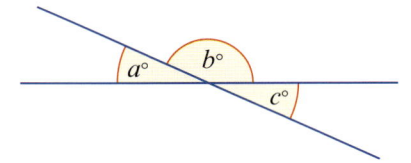

$a° + b° = 180°$

$c° + b° = 180°$

Therefore, $a°$ is equal to $c°$.

Exercise 21.3

1 Draw a similar diagram to the one shown. Measure carefully each of the labelled angles and write them down.

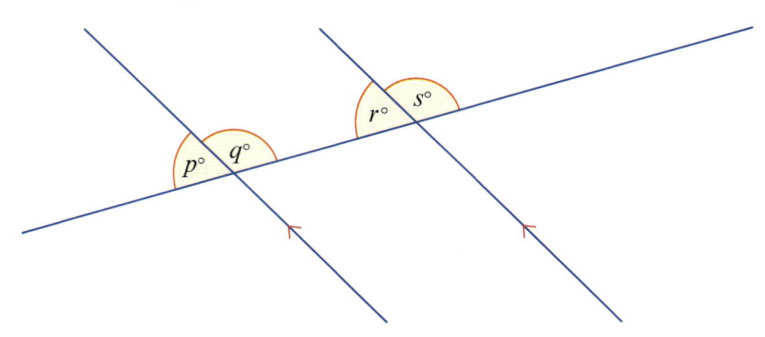

21 ANGLE PROPERTIES

Exercise 21.3 (cont)

2 Draw a similar diagram to the one shown. Measure carefully each of the labelled angles and write them down.

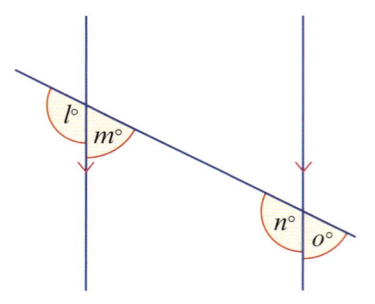

3 Draw a similar diagram to the one shown. Measure carefully each of the labelled angles and write them down.

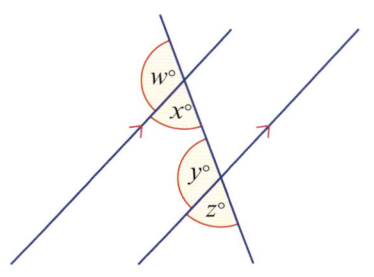

4 Write down what you have noticed about the angles you measured in Q.1–3.

Angles formed within parallel lines

When a line intersects two parallel lines, as in the diagram below, it is found that certain angles are the same size.

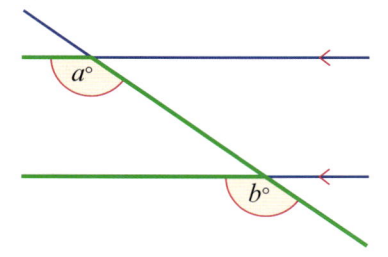

The angles $a°$ and $b°$ are equal and are known as **corresponding angles**. Corresponding angles can be found by looking for an 'F' formation in a diagram.

A line intersecting two parallel lines also produces another pair of equal angles, known as **alternate angles**. These can be shown to be equal by using the fact that both vertically opposite and corresponding angles are equal.

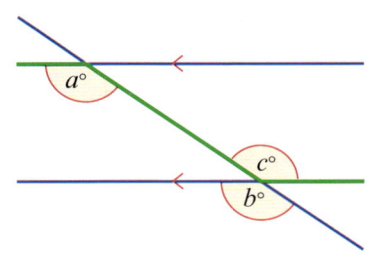

Angles formed within parallel lines

In the diagram, $a° = b°$ (corresponding angles). But $b° = c°$ (vertically opposite). It can therefore be deduced that $a° = c°$.

Angles $a°$ and $c°$ are alternate angles. These can be found by looking for a 'Z' formation in a diagram.

Exercise 21.4

In each of the following questions, some of the angles are given. Deduce, giving your reasons, the size of the other labelled angles.

a

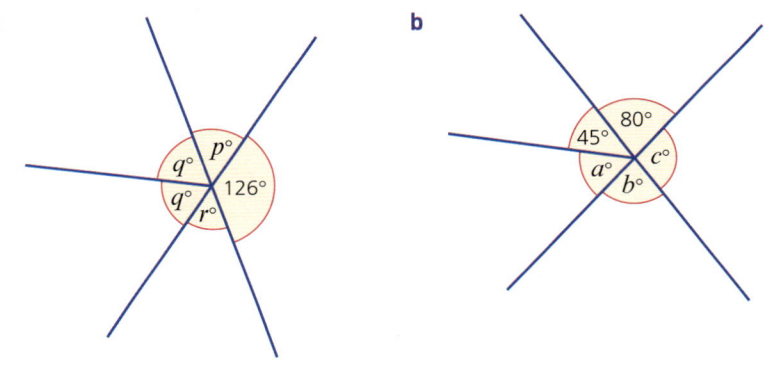

b

c

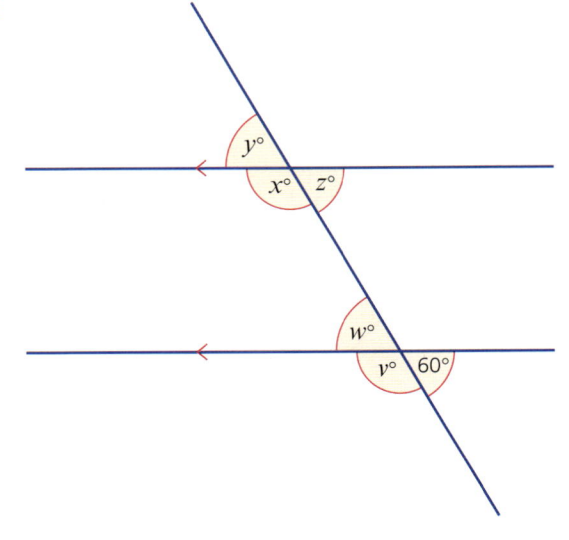

21 ANGLE PROPERTIES

Exercise 21.4 (cont)

d

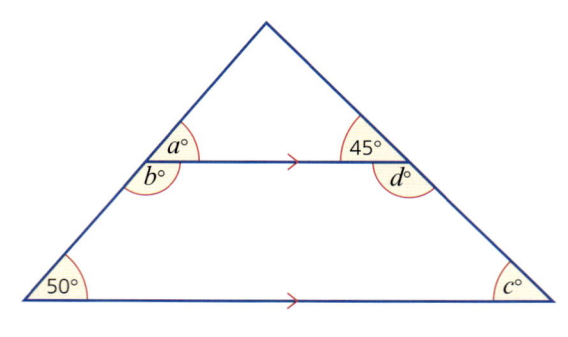

e

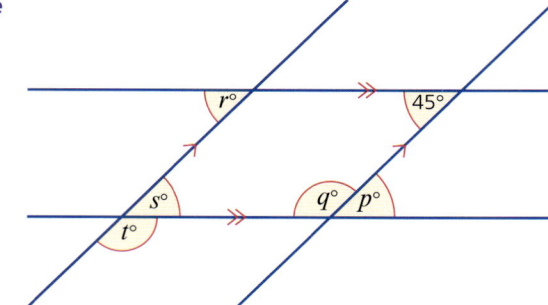

f

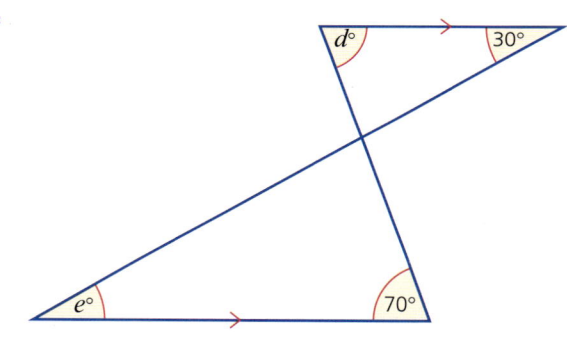

g

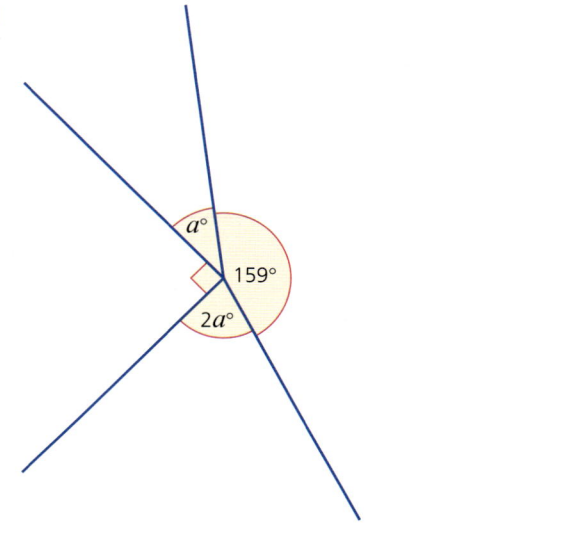

Angle properties of triangles

h

3a°

2a°

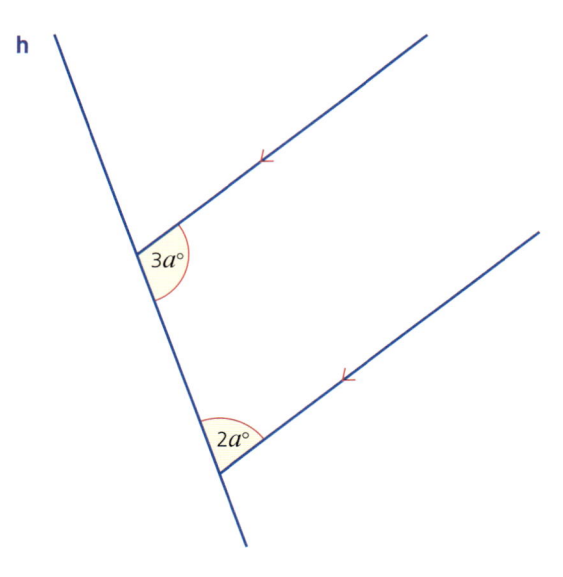

In the Q.h above you will have noticed that the angles 3a° and 2a° add up to 180°.

This can be proved as shown below:

$a° + b° = 180°$ (angles on a straight line)

$a° = c°$ (corresponding angles are equal)

Therefore $c° + b° = 180°$.

$b°$ and $c°$ are known as **co-interior** angles.

Co-interior angles face each other within parallel lines and add up to 180°.

Pairs of angles which add up to 180° are also called supplementary angles.

Angle properties of triangles

A **triangle** is a plane (two-dimensional) shape consisting of three angles and three sides. There are six main types of triangle. Their names refer to the sizes of their angles and/or the lengths of their sides, and are as follows:

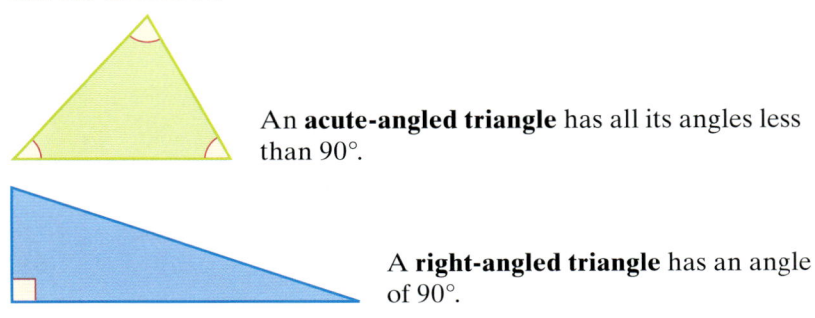

An **acute-angled triangle** has all its angles less than 90°.

A **right-angled triangle** has an angle of 90°.

209

21 ANGLE PROPERTIES

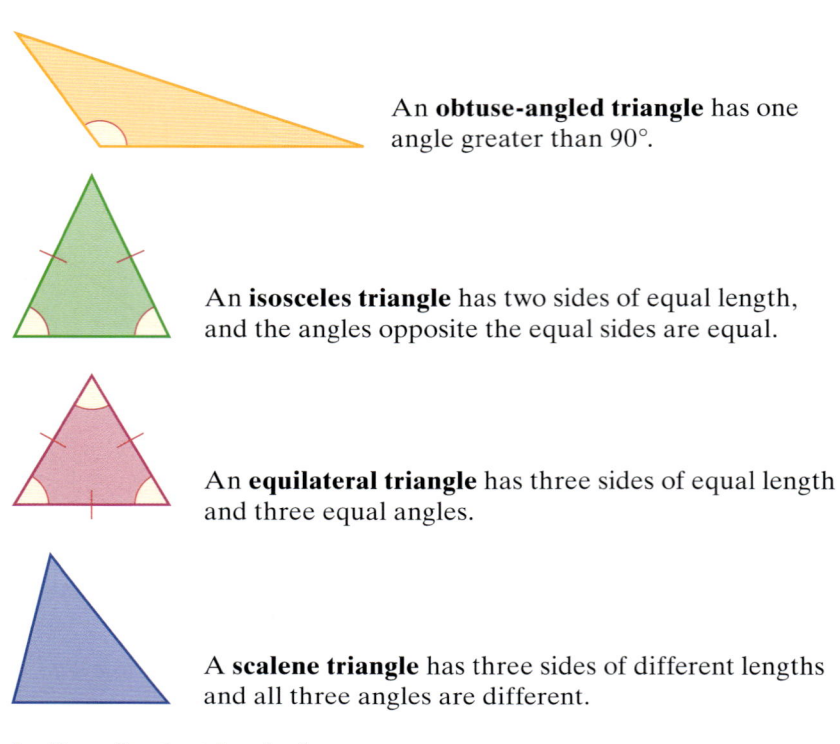

An **obtuse-angled triangle** has one angle greater than 90°.

An **isosceles triangle** has two sides of equal length, and the angles opposite the equal sides are equal.

An **equilateral triangle** has three sides of equal length and three equal angles.

A **scalene triangle** has three sides of different lengths and all three angles are different.

Exercise 21.5

1. Describe the triangles in two ways.

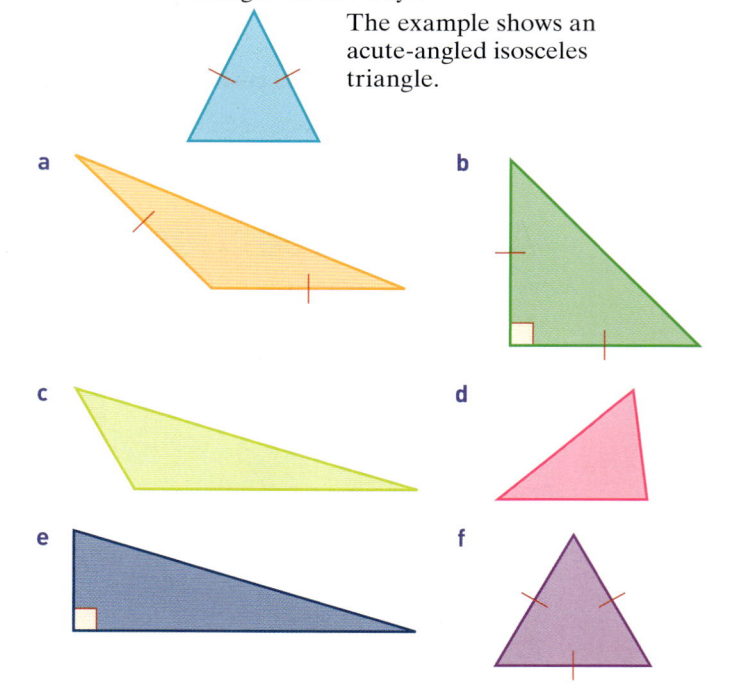

   The example shows an acute-angled isosceles triangle.

   a b

   c d

   e f

Angle properties of triangles

2. Draw the following triangles using a ruler and compasses:
   a. an acute-angled isosceles triangle of sides 5 cm, 5 cm and 6 cm, and altitude 4 cm
   b. a right-angled scalene triangle of sides 6 cm, 8 cm and 10 cm
   c. an equilateral triangle of side 7.5 cm
   d. an obtuse-angled isosceles triangle of sides 13 cm, 13 cm and 24 cm, and altitude 5 cm.

Exercise 21.6

1. a. Draw five different triangles. Label their angles $x°$, $y°$ and $z°$. As accurately as you can, measure the three angles of each triangle and add them together.
   b. What do you notice about the sum of the three angles of each of your triangles?

2. a. Draw a triangle on a piece of paper and label the angles $a°$, $b°$ and $c°$. Cut it out, then tear off the corners of the triangle and arrange them as shown below:

   b. What do you notice about the total angle that $a°$, $b°$ and $c°$ make?

The sum of the interior angles of a triangle

It can be seen from the previous questions that triangles of any shape have one thing in common. That is, that the sum of their three angles is constant: 180°.

➔ Worked example

Calculate the size of the angle $x°$ in the triangle below:

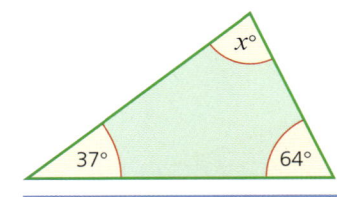

$37 + 64 + x = 180$
$x = 180 - 37 - 64$
$x = 79$

Therefore the missing angle is 79°.

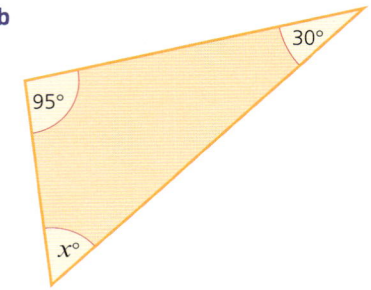

Exercise 21.7

1. For each triangle, use the information given to calculate the value of x.
   a.
   b.

211

Exercise 21.7 (cont)

c

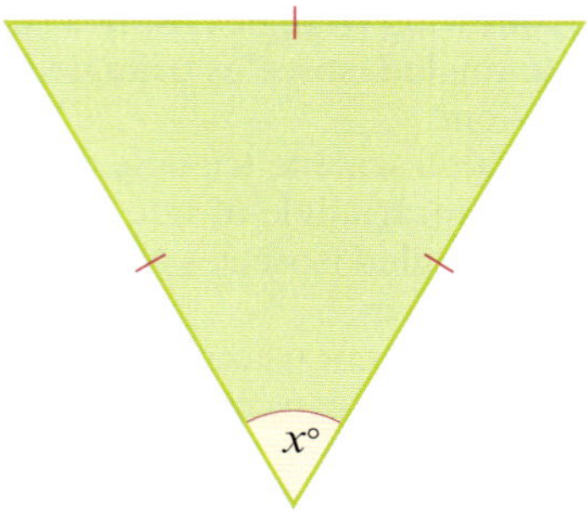
$x°$

d

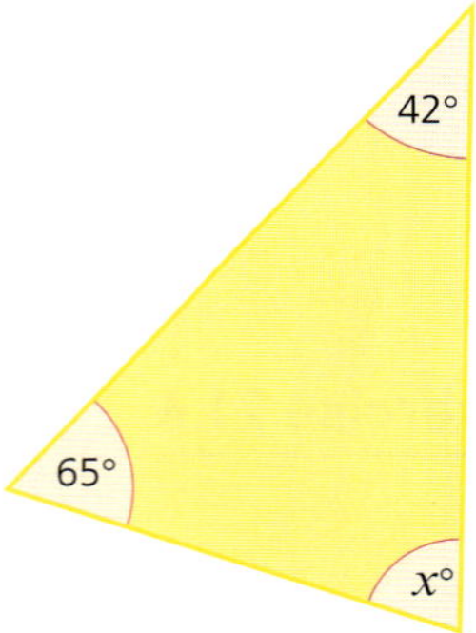
42°
65°
$x°$

e

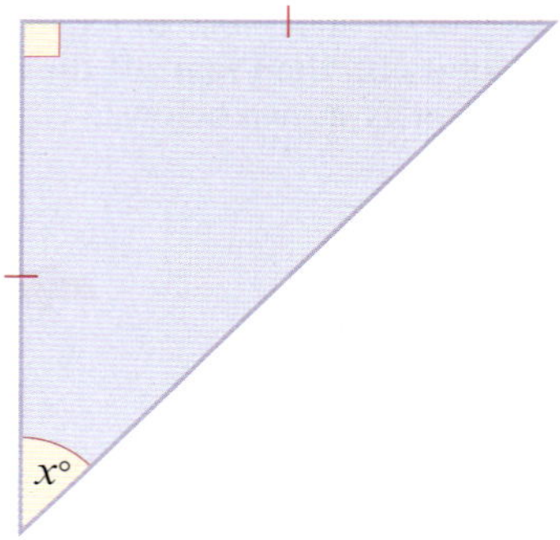
$x°$

f

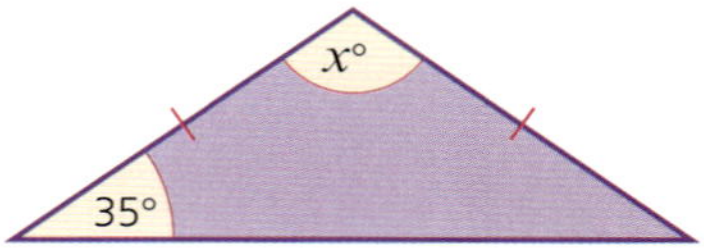
$x°$
35°

2 In each diagram, calculate the size of the labelled angles.

a

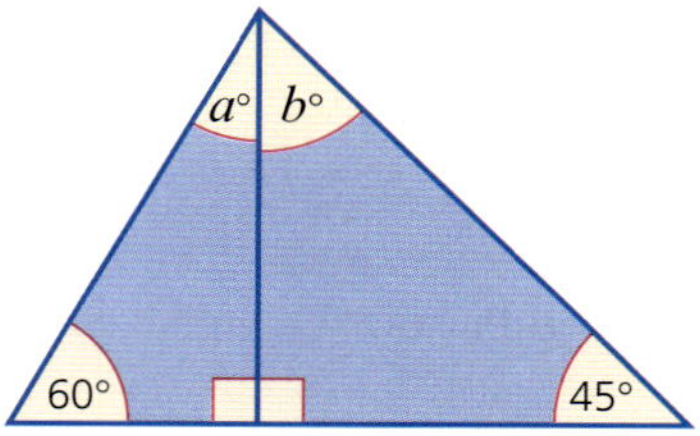
$a°$
$b°$
60°
45°

b

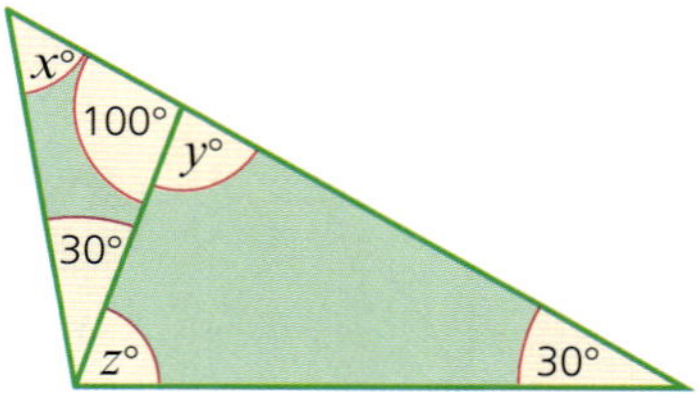
$x°$
100°
$y°$
30°
$z°$
30°

c

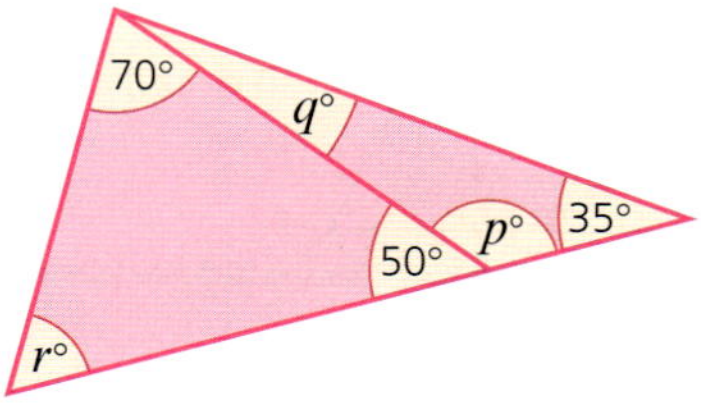
70°
$q°$
50°
$p°$
35°
$r°$

d

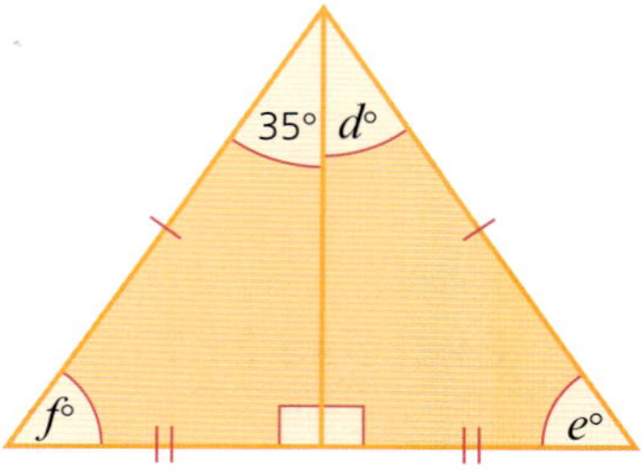
35°
$d°$
$f°$
$e°$

Angle properties of quadrilaterals

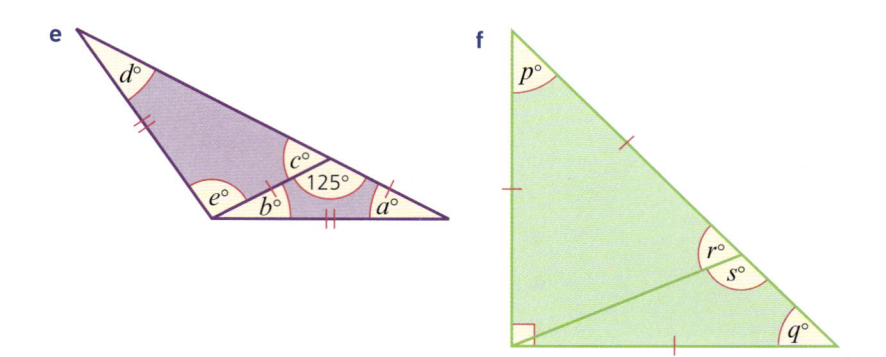

Angle properties of quadrilaterals

A **quadrilateral** is a plane shape consisting of four angles and four sides. There are several types of quadrilateral. The main ones, and their properties, are described below.

- Two pairs of parallel sides.
- All sides are equal.
- All angles are equal.
- Diagonals intersect at right angles.

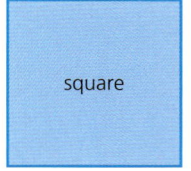

square

- Two pairs of parallel sides.
- Opposite sides are equal.
- All angles are equal.

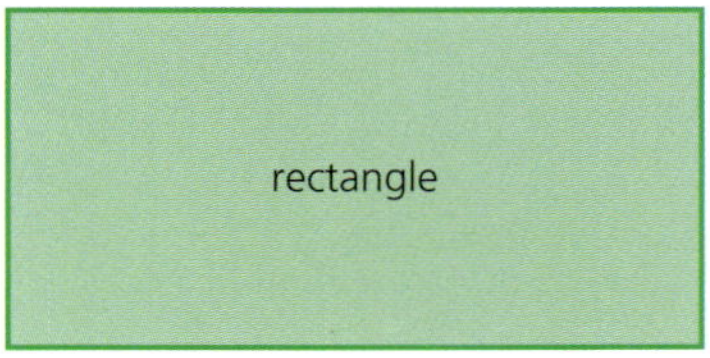

rectangle

- Two pairs of parallel sides.
- All sides are equal.
- Opposite angles are equal.
- Diagonals intersect at right angles.

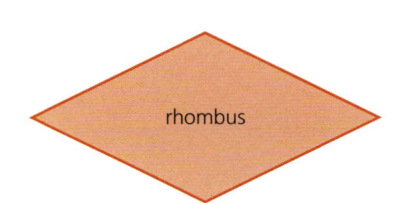

rhombus

- Two pairs of parallel sides.
- Opposite sides are equal.
- Opposite angles are equal.

parallelogram

213

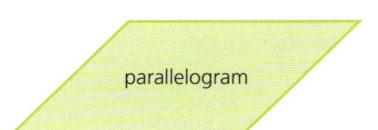

21 ANGLE PROPERTIES

- One pair of parallel sides.
- An **isosceles trapezium** has one pair of parallel sides and the other pair of sides are equal in length.

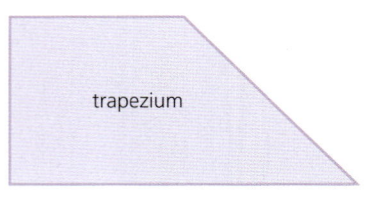

trapezium

- Two pairs of equal sides.
- One pair of equal angles.
- Diagonals intersect at right angles.

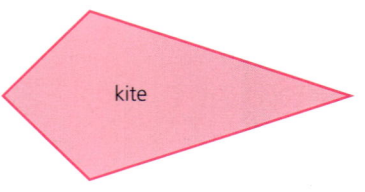

kite

Exercise 21.8

1 Copy the diagrams and name each shape according to the definitions given above.

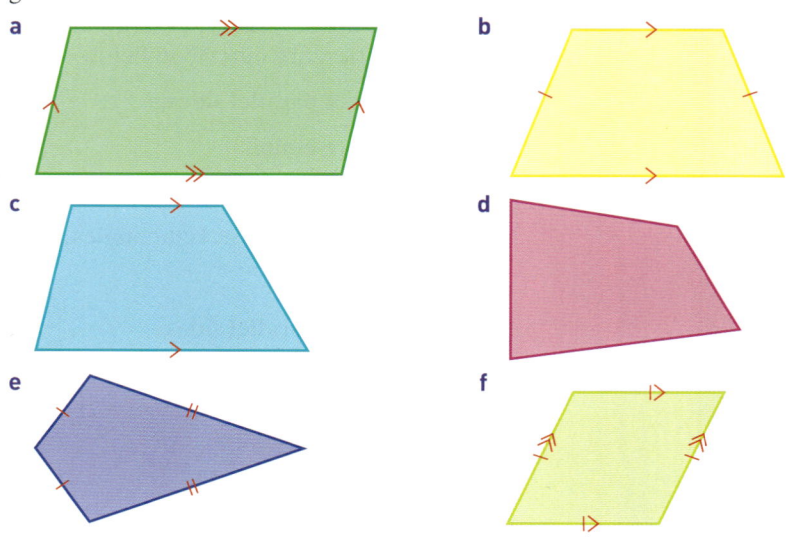

a

b

c

d

e

f

2 Copy and complete the table. The first line has been started for you.

	Rectangle	Square	Parallelogram	Kite	Rhombus	Equilateral triangle
Opposite sides equal in length	Yes		Yes			—
All sides equal in length						
All angles right angles						
Both pairs of opposite sides parallel						—
Diagonals equal in length						—
Diagonals intersect at right angles						—
All angles equal						

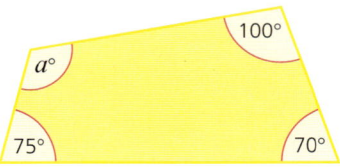

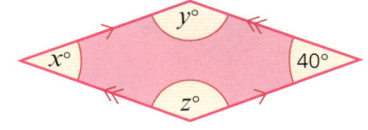

Angle properties of quadrilaterals

The sum of the interior angles of a quadrilateral

In the quadrilaterals shown, a straight line is drawn from one of the corners (vertices) to the opposite corner. The result is to split each quadrilateral into two triangles.

As already shown earlier in the chapter, the sum of the angles of a triangle is 180°. Therefore, as a quadrilateral can be drawn as two triangles, the sum of the four angles of any quadrilateral must be 360°.

➡ Worked example

Calculate the size of angle $p°$ in the quadrilateral below:

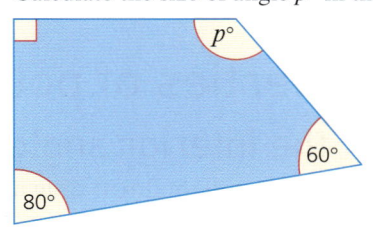

$90 + 80 + 60 + p = 360$
$p = 360 - 90 - 80 - 60$

Therefore the missing angle is 130°.

Exercise 21.9

For each diagram, calculate the size of the labelled angles.

a

b

21 ANGLE PROPERTIES

Exercise 21.9 (cont)

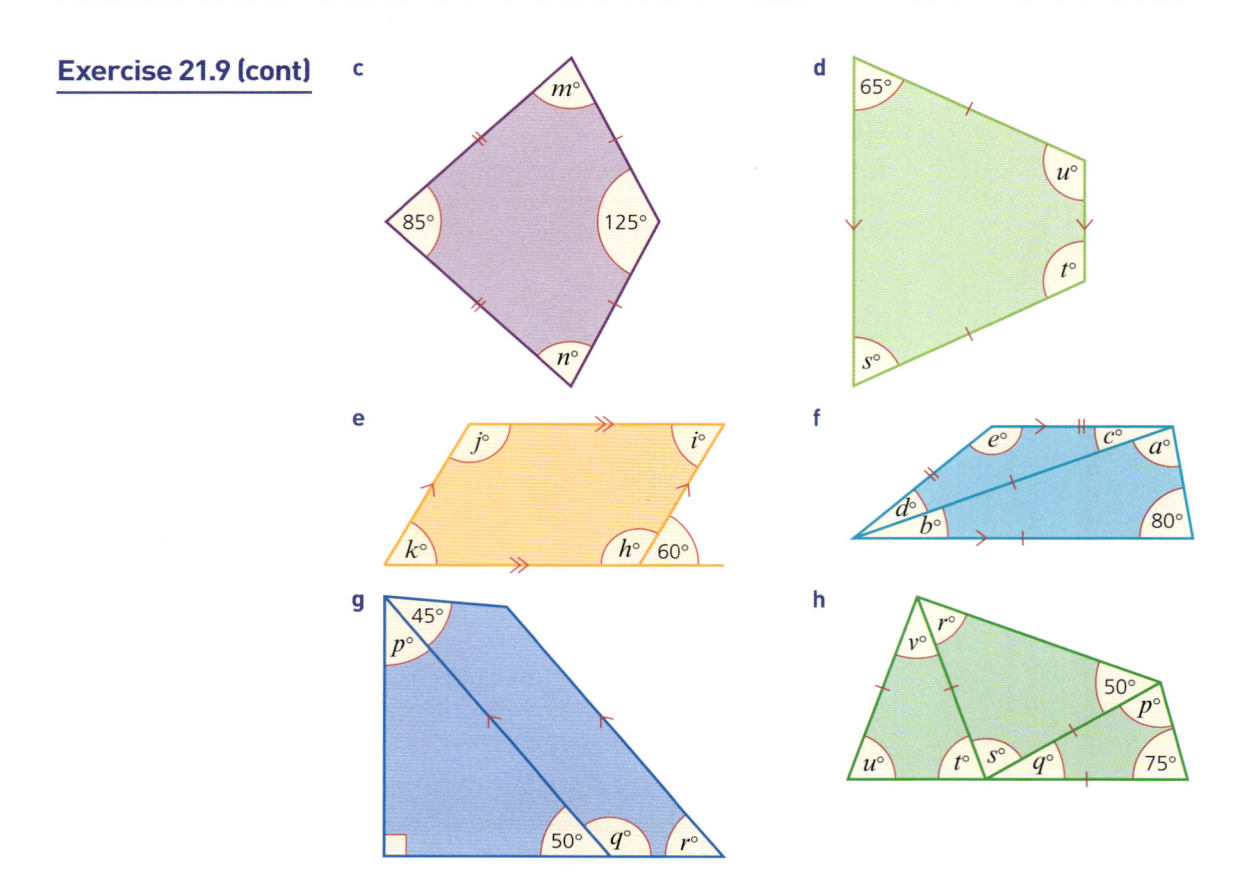

c, d, e, f, g, h (diagrams)

Angle properties of polygons
The sum of the interior angles of a polygon

In the polygons shown, a straight line is drawn from each vertex to vertex A.

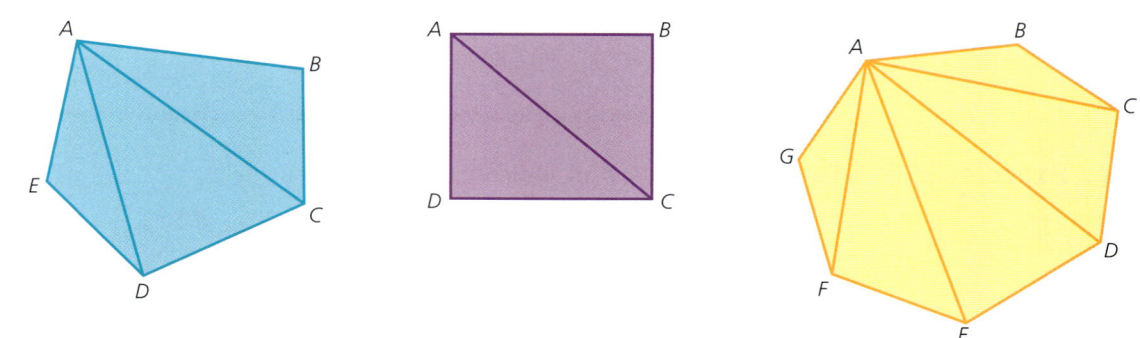

As can be seen, the number of triangles is always two less than the number of sides the polygon has, i.e. if there are n sides, there will be $(n-2)$ triangles.

Angle properties of polygons

Since the angles of a triangle add up to 180°, the sum of the **interior angles** of a polygon is therefore $180(n-2)°$.

➡ Worked example

Find the sum of the interior angles of a regular pentagon and hence the size of each interior angle.

For a pentagon, $n = 5$.
Therefore the sum of the interior angles $= 180 \times (5-2)°$
$= 180 \times 3°$
$= 540°$

For a regular pentagon the interior angles are of equal size.
Therefore each angle $= \frac{540°}{5} = 108°$.

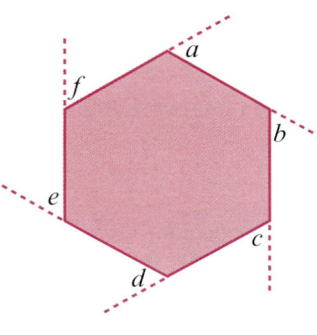

The sum of the exterior angles of a polygon

The angles marked a, b, c, d, e and f represent the **exterior angles** of the regular hexagon (left).

For any convex polygon the sum of the exterior angles is 360°.

If the polygon is regular and has n sides, then each exterior angle $= \frac{360°}{n}$.

➡ Worked examples

1 Find the exterior angle of a nine-sided regular polygon.

$\frac{360°}{9} = 40°$

Therefore, each exterior angle is 40°.

2 Calculate the number of sides a regular polygon has, if each exterior angle is 15°.

$15 = \frac{360°}{n}$

$n = \frac{360°}{15}$

$= 24$

The polygon has 24 sides.

Exercise 21.10

1 Find the sum of the interior angles of the following polygons:
   a a hexagon
   c a seven-sided polygon
   b a nine-sided polygon

2 Find the size of each interior angle of the following regular polygons:
   a an octagon
   c a decagon
   b a square
   d a twelve-sided regular polygon

Note

A seven-sided regular polygon is a heptagon.
A nine-sided regular polygon is a nonagon.
A twelve-sided regular polygon is a dodecagon.
These names are not required for this syllabus.

217

21 ANGLE PROPERTIES

Exercise 21.10 (cont)

3. Find the size of each exterior angle of the following regular polygons:
   a. a pentagon
   c. a seven-sided regular polygon
   b. a twelve-sided regular polygon

4. The exterior angles of regular polygons are given. In each case calculate the number of sides the polygon has.
   a. 20°
   b. 36°
   c. 10°
   d. 45°
   e. 18°
   f. 3°

5. The interior angles of regular polygons are given. In each case calculate the number of sides the polygon has.
   a. 108° b. 150° c. 162°
   d. 156° e. 171° f. 179°

6. Calculate the number of sides a regular polygon has if an interior angle is five times the size of an exterior angle.

7. Copy and complete the table for regular polygons:

Number of sides	Name	Sum of exterior angles	Size of an exterior angle	Sum of interior angles	Size of an interior angle
3					
4					
5					
6					
7	heptagon				
8					
9	nonagon				
10					
12	dodecagon				

8. Two students Kwasi and Chioma are looking at a regular polygon. Kwasi states that the exterior angles of the regular polygon are each 50°. Chioma states that they are 45°.
Explain which of the students is definitely wrong.

The angle in a semi-circle

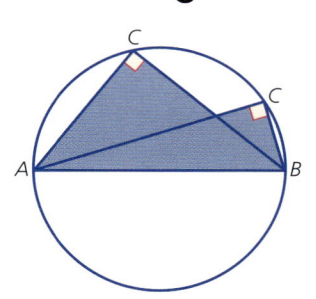

If AB represents the diameter of the circle, then the angle at C is 90°.

The angle in a semi-circle

Exercise 21.11 In each of the following diagrams, O marks the centre of the circle. Calculate the value of x in each case.

a
b
c
d
e
f

The angle between a tangent and a radius of a circle

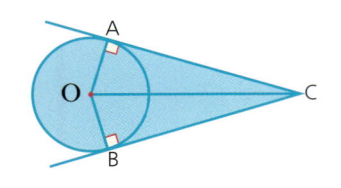

The angle between a tangent at a point and the radius to the same point on the circle is a right angle.

Triangles OAC and OBC (left) are congruent as angle OAC and angle OBC are right angles, $OA = OB$ because they are both radii and OC is common to both triangles.

219

21 ANGLE PROPERTIES

Exercise 21.12

1 In each of the following diagrams, O marks the centre of the circle. Calculate the value of x in each case.

a

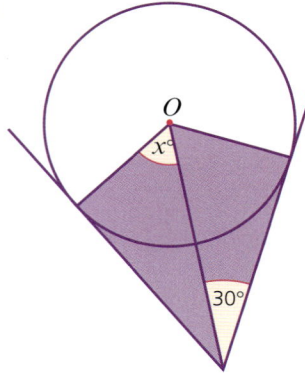

b

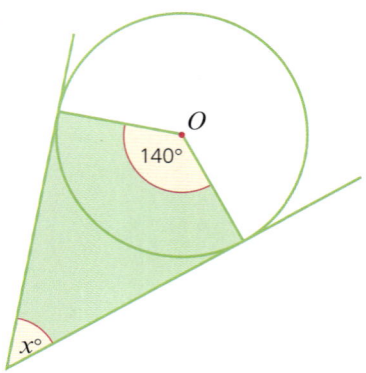

c

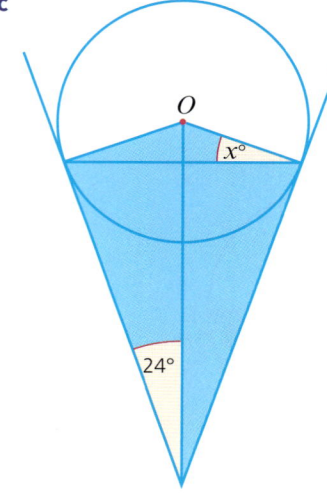

Student assessment 1

1 For each diagram, calculate the size of the labelled angles.

a

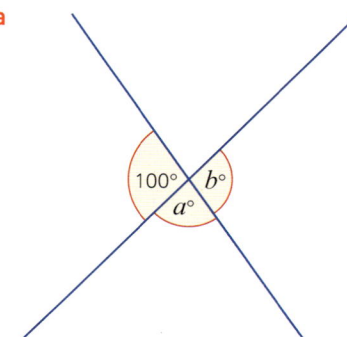

b

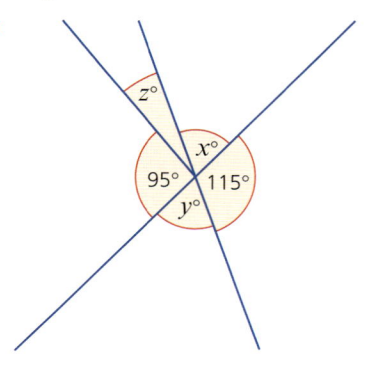

The angle in a semi-circle

c

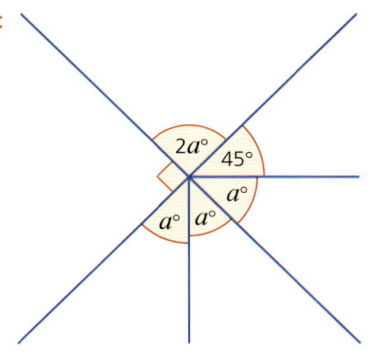

2a°, 45°, a°, a°, a°

d

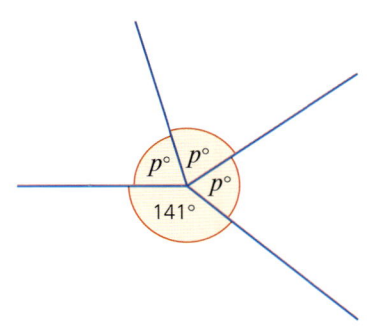

p°, p°, p°, 141°

2 For each diagram, calculate the size of the labelled angles.

a

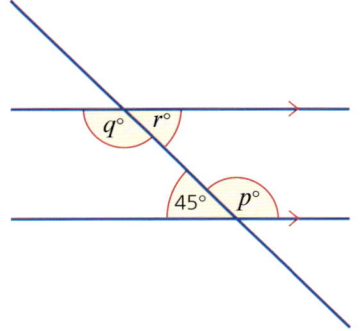

q°, r°, 45°, p°

b

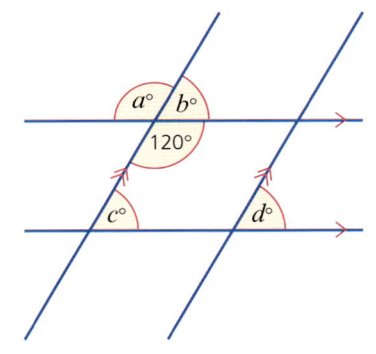

a°, b°, 120°, c°, d°

3 For each diagram, calculate the size of the labelled angles.

a

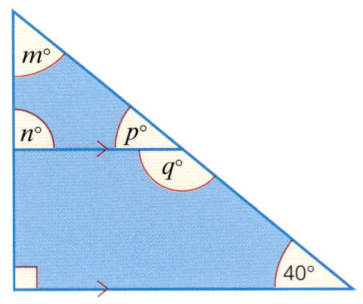

m°, n°, p°, q°, 40°

b

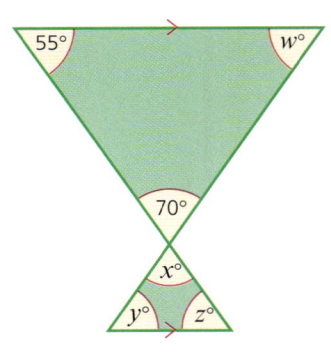

55°, w°, 70°, x°, y°, z°

c

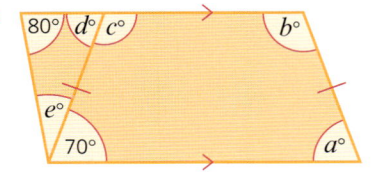

80°, d°, c°, b°, e°, 70°, a°

d

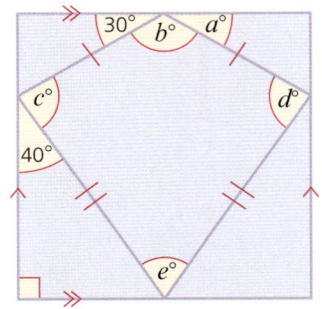

30°, b°, a°, c°, d°, 40°, e°

221

21 ANGLE PROPERTIES

Student assessment 2

1. Draw a diagram of an octagon to help illustrate the fact that the sum of the internal angles of an octagon is given by $180 \times (8 - 2)°$.

2. Find the size of each interior angle of a 20-sided regular polygon.

3. What is the sum of the interior angles of a nonagon?

4. What is the sum of the exterior angles of a polygon?

5. What is the size of the exterior angle of a regular pentagon?

6. If AB is the diameter of the circle and $AC = 5$ cm and $BC = 12$ cm, calculate:

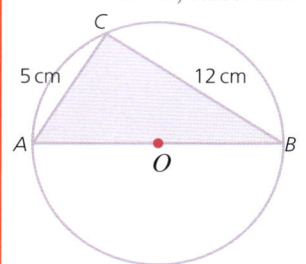

   a the size of angle ACB
   b the length of the radius of the circle.

In Q.7–10, O marks the centre of the circle. Calculate the value of x in each case.

7.

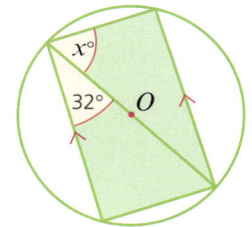

8.

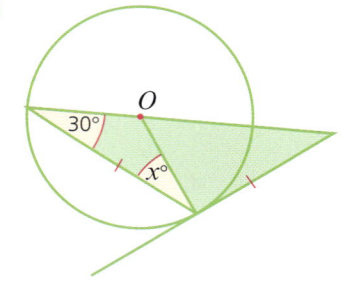

The angle in a semi-circle

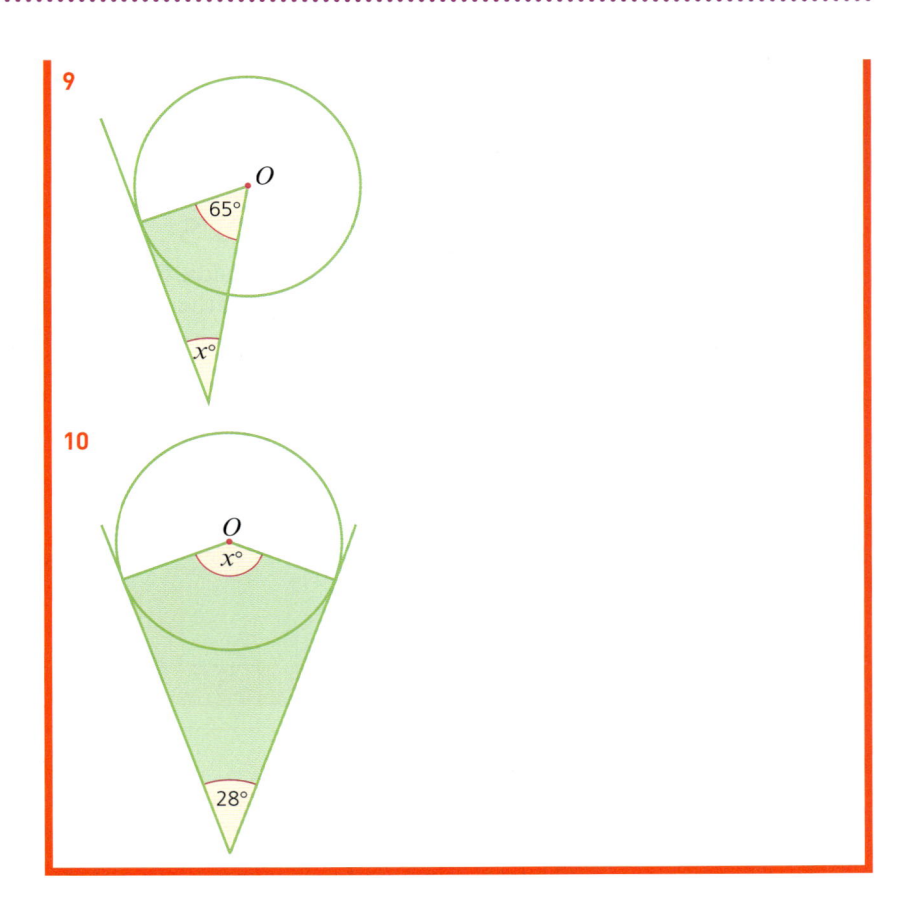

9

10

Mathematical investigations and ICT 4

Fountain borders

The Alhambra Palace in Granada, Spain, has many fountains which pour water into pools. Many of the pools are surrounded by beautiful ceramic tiles. This investigation looks at the number of square tiles needed to surround a particular shape of pool.

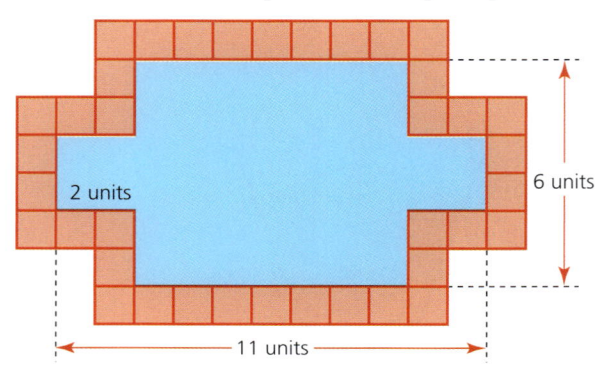

The diagram above shows a rectangular pool of 11×6 units, in which a square of dimension 2×2 units is taken from each corner.

The total number of unit square tiles needed to surround the pool is 38.

The shape of the pool can be generalised as shown below:

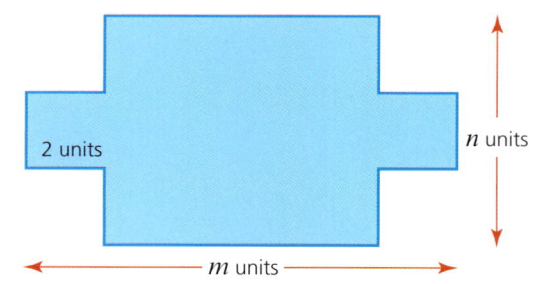

1. Investigate the number of unit square tiles needed for different sized pools. Record your results in an ordered table.
2. From your results, write an algebraic rule in terms of m and n for the number of tiles T needed to surround a pool.
3. Justify, in words and using diagrams, why your rule works.

Tiled walls

Many cultures have used tiles to decorate buildings. Putting tiles on a wall takes skill. These days, to make sure that each tile is in the correct position, 'spacers' are used between the tiles.

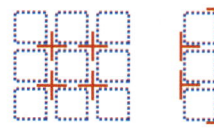

You can see from the diagram that there are +-shaped and T-shaped spacers.

1. Draw other sized squares and rectangles, and investigate the relationship between the dimensions of each shape (length and width) and the number of +-shaped and T-shaped spacers.
2. Record your results in an ordered table.
3. Write an algebraic rule for the number of +-shaped spacers c in a rectangle l tiles long by w tiles wide.
4. Write an algebraic rule for the number of T-shaped spacers t in a rectangle l tiles long by w tiles wide.

ICT activity

In this activity, you will use a spreadsheet to calculate the sizes of interior and exterior angles of regular polygons.

Set up a spreadsheet as shown below:

> **Note**
>
> If you don't know the names of some of these polygons, you can research them (and others) on the internet. These names are not required for this syllabus.

	A	B	C	D	E	F
1			Regular Polygons			
2	Number of sides	Name	Sum of exterior angles	Size of an exterior angle	Size of an interior angle	Sum of interior angles
3	3					
4	4					
5	5					
6	6					
7	7					
8	8					
9	9					
10	10					
11	12					
12	20					

Use formulae to generate the results in these columns

1. By using formulae, use the spreadsheet to generate the results for the sizes of the interior and exterior angles.
2. Write down the general formulae you would use to calculate the sizes of the interior and exterior angles of an n-sided regular polygon.

TOPIC 5

Mensuration

Contents

Chapter 22 Measures (C5.1)
Chapter 23 Perimeter, area and volume (C5.2, C5.3, C5.4, C5.5)

Learning objectives

C5.1
Use metric units of mass, length, area, volume and capacity in practical situations and convert quantities into larger or smaller units.

C5.2
Carry out calculations involving the perimeter and area of a rectangle, triangle, parallelogram and trapezium.

C5.3
1 Carry out calculations involving the circumference and area of a circle.
2 Carry out calculations involving arc length and sector area as fractions of the circumference and area of a circle, where the sector angle is a factor of 360°.

C5.4
Carry out calculations and solve problems involving the surface area and volume of a:
- cuboid
- prism
- cylinder
- sphere
- pyramid
- cone.

C5.5
1 Carry out calculations and solve problems involving perimeters and areas of:
   - compound shapes
   - parts of shapes.
2 Carry out calculations and solve problems involving surface areas and volumes of:
   - compound solids
   - parts of solids.

Measurement

A measurement is the ratio of a physical quantity, such as a length, time or temperature, to a unit of measurement, such as the metre, the second or the degree Celsius. So if someone is 1.68 m tall they are 1.68 times bigger than the standard measure called a metre.

The International System of Units (or SI units from the French language name *Système International d'Unités*) is the world's most widely used system of units. The SI units for the seven basic physical quantities are:

- the metre (m) – the SI unit of length
- the kilogram (kg) – the SI unit of mass
- the second (s) – the SI unit of time
- the ampere (A) – the SI unit of electric current
- the kelvin (K) – the SI unit of temperature
- the mole (mol) – the SI unit of amount of substance
- the candela (cd) – the SI unit of luminous intensity.

This system was a development of the metric system which was first used in the 1790s during the French Revolution. This early system used just the metre and the kilogram and was intended to give fair and consistent measures in France.

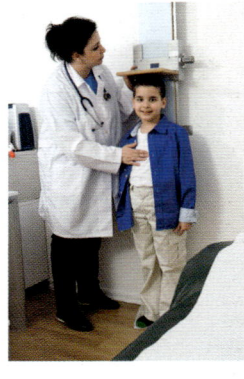

227

22 Measures

Metric units

The metric system uses a variety of units for length, mass and capacity.

- The common units of length are: kilometre (km), metre (m), centimetre (cm) and millimetre (mm).
- The common units of mass are: tonne (t), kilogram (kg), gram (g) and milligram (mg).
- The common units of capacity are: litre (L or l) and millilitre (ml).

> **Note**
>
> 'centi' comes from the Latin *centum* meaning 'hundred' (a centimetre is one hundredth of a metre).
> 'milli' comes from the Latin *mille* meaning 'thousand' (a millimetre is one thousandth of a metre).
> 'kilo' comes from the Greek *khilloi* meaning 'thousand' (a kilometre is one thousand metres).

It may be useful to have some practical experience of estimating lengths, volumes and capacities before starting the following exercises.

Exercise 22.1

1 Copy and complete the sentences:
   a There are ... centimetres in one metre.
   b There are ... millimetres in one metre.
   c One metre is one ... of a kilometre.
   d There are ... kilograms in one tonne.
   e There are ... grams in one kilogram.
   f One milligram is one ... of a gram.
   g One thousand kilograms is one ... .
   h One thousandth of a gram is one ... .
   i One thousand millilitres is one ... .
   j One thousandth of a litre is one ... .

2 Which of the units given would be used to measure the following?
   mm, cm, m, km, mg, g, kg, ml, litres
   a your height
   b the length of your finger
   c the mass of a shoe
   d the amount of liquid in a cup
   e the height of a van
   f the mass of a ship
   g the capacity of a swimming pool
   h the length of a highway
   i the capacity of the petrol tank of a car.

3 Use a ruler to draw lines of these lengths:
   a 6 cm
   b 18 cm
   c 41 mm
   d 8.7 cm
   e 67 mm

4 Draw four lines and label them A, B, C and D.
   a Estimate their lengths in mm.
   b Measure them to the nearest mm.

5 Copy the sentences and put in the correct unit:
   a A tree in the school grounds is 28 ... tall.
   b The distance to the nearest big city is 45 ... .
   c The depth of a lake is 18 ... .
   d A person's mass is about 60 ... .
   e The capacity of a bowl is 5 ... .
   f The distance Ahmet can run in 10 seconds is about 70 ... .
   g The mass of my car is about 1.2 ... .
   h Ayse walks about 1700 ... to school.
   i A melon has a mass of 650 ... .
   j The amount of blood in your body is 5 ... .

Converting from one unit to another

Length

$1\,km = 1000\,m$

Therefore $1\,m = \frac{1}{1000}\,km$

$1\,m = 1000\,mm$

Therefore $1\,mm = \frac{1}{1000}\,m$

$1\,m = 100\,cm$

Therefore $1\,cm = \frac{1}{100}\,m$

$1\,cm = 10\,mm$

Therefore $1\,mm = \frac{1}{10}\,cm$

➔ Worked examples

1 Change 5.8 km into m.
  Since 1 km = 1000 m,
  5.8 km is 5.8 × 1000 m
  5.8 km = 5800 m

2 Change 4700 mm to m.
  Since 1 m is 1000 mm,
  4700 mm is 4700 ÷ 1000 m
  4700 mm = 4.7 m

3 Convert 2.3 km into cm.
  2.3 km is 2.3 × 1000 m = 2300 m
  2300 m is 2300 × 100 cm
  2.3 km = 230 000 cm

22 MEASURES

Exercise 22.2

1 Put in the missing unit to make the statements correct:
   a 3 cm = 30 ...
   b 25 ... = 2.5 cm
   c 3200 m = 3.2 ...
   d 7.5 km = 7500 ...
   e 300 ... = 30 cm
   f 6000 mm = 6 ...
   g 3.2 m = 3200 ...
   h 4.2 ... = 4200 mm
   i 1 million mm = 1 ...
   j 2.5 km = 2500 ...

2 Convert to millimetres:
   a 2 cm
   b 8.5 cm
   c 23 cm
   d 1.2 m
   e 0.83 m
   f 0.05 m
   g 62.5 cm
   h 0.087 m
   i 0.004 m

3 Convert to metres:
   a 3 km
   b 4700 mm
   c 560 cm
   d 6.4 km
   e 0.8 km
   f 96 cm
   g 62.5 cm
   h 0.087 km
   i 0.004 km

4 Convert to kilometres:
   a 5000 m
   b 6300 m
   c 1150 m
   d 2535 m
   e 250 000 m
   f 500 m
   g 70 m
   h 8 m
   i 1 million m
   j 700 million m

Mass

1 tonne is 1000 kg

Therefore 1 kg = $\frac{1}{1000}$ tonne

1 kilogram is 1000 g

Therefore 1 g = $\frac{1}{1000}$ kg

1 g is 1000 mg

Therefore 1 mg = $\frac{1}{1000}$ g

Worked examples

1 Convert 8300 kg to tonnes.

   Since 1000 kg = 1 tonne, 8300 kg is 8300 ÷ 1000 tonnes

   8300 kg = 8.3 tonnes

2 Convert 2.5 g to mg.

   Since 1 g is 1000 mg, 2.5 g is 2.5 × 1000 mg

   2.5 g = 2500 mg

Exercise 22.3

1 Convert:
   a 3.8 g to mg
   b 28 500 kg to tonnes
   c 4.28 tonnes to kg
   d 320 mg to g
   e 0.5 tonnes to kg

Area and volume conversions

2 An item has a mass of 630 g, while another item has a mass of 720 g. Express the total mass in kg.

3 a Express the total mass in kg:
1.2 tonne, 760 kg, 0.93 tonne and 640 kg
b Express the total mass in g:
460 mg, 1.3 g, 1260 mg and 0.75 g
c A small cat weighs 2800 g and a large cat weighs 6.5 kg. What is the total weight in kg of the two animals?
d In one bag of shopping, Imran has items of total mass 1350 g. In another bag there are items of total mass 3.8 kg. What is the mass in kg of both bags of shopping?
e Find the total mass in kg of the fruit listed:
apples 3.8 kg, peaches 1400 g, bananas 0.5 kg, oranges 7500 g, grapes 0.8 kg

Capacity

1 litre is 1000 millilitres

Therefore 1 ml = $\frac{1}{1000}$ litre

But capacity is a type of volume and can therefore be expressed, for example, in cm^3 or m^3

Exercise 22.4

1 Convert to litres:
  a 8400 ml   **b** 650 ml
  c 87 500 ml   **d** 50 ml
  e 2500 ml

2 Convert to millilitres:
  a 3.2 litres   **b** 0.75 litre
  c 0.087 litre   **d** 8 litres
  e 0.008 litre   **f** 0.3 litre

3 Calculate the following and give the totals in millilitres:
  a 3 litres + 1500 ml   **b** 0.88 litre + 650 ml
  c 0.75 litre + 6300 ml   **d** 450 ml + 0.55 litre

4 Calculate the following and give the totals in litres:
  a 0.75 litre + 450 ml   **b** 850 ml + 490 ml
  c 0.6 litre + 0.8 litre   **d** 80 ml + 620 ml + 0.7 litre

Area and volume conversions

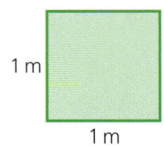

Converting between units for area and volume is not as straightforward as converting between units for length.

The diagram (left) shows a square of side length 1 m.

Area of the square = 1 m^2

However, if the lengths of the sides are written in cm, each of the sides is 100 cm.

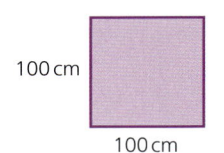

22 MEASURES

Area of the square = 100 × 100 = 10 000 cm²

Therefore an area of 1 m² = 10 000 cm².

Similarly, a square of side length 1 cm is the same as a square of side length 10 mm. Therefore an area of 1 cm² is equivalent to an area of 100 mm².

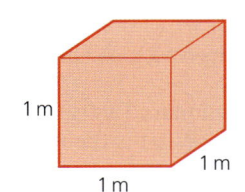

The diagram (left) shows a cube of side length 1 m.

Volume of the cube = 1 m³

Once again, if the lengths of the sides are written in cm, each of the sides are 100 cm.

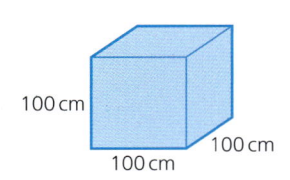

Volume of the cube = 100 × 100 × 100 = 1 000 000 cm³

Therefore a volume of 1 m³ = 1 000 000 cm³.

Similarly, a cube of side length 1 cm is the same as a cube of side length 10 mm.

Therefore a volume of 1 cm³ is equivalent to a volume of 1000 mm³.

A volume of 1 m³ is equivalent to a capacity of 1000 litres.

As 1 m³ = 1 000 000 cm³, it follows that a volume of 1 cm³ is equivalent to a capacity of 1 ml.

Exercise 22.5

1 Convert the following areas:
   a 10 m² to cm²
   b 2 m² to mm²
   c 5 km² to m²
   d 3.2 km² to m²
   e 8.3 cm² to mm²

2 Convert the following areas:
   a 500 cm² to m²
   b 15 000 mm² to cm²
   c 1000 m² to km²
   d 40 000 mm² to m²
   e 2 500 000 cm² to km²

3 Convert the following volumes:
   a 2.5 m³ to cm³
   b 3.4 cm³ to mm³
   c 2 km³ to m³
   d 0.2 m³ to cm³
   e 0.03 m³ to mm³

4 Convert the following volumes:
   a 150 000 cm³ to m³
   b 24 000 mm³ to cm³
   c 850 000 m³ to km³
   d 300 mm³ to cm³
   e 15 cm³ to m³

5 Covert the following volumes and capacities.
   a 1.2 litres to cm³
   b 0.5 m³ to litres
   c 4250 ml to cm³
   d 220 litres to m³

6 A water tank in the shape of a cuboid has dimensions 120 × 80 × 50 cm. It is 75% full.
   How many litres of water does the water tank have?

Area and volume conversions

Student assessment 1

1. Convert the lengths to the units indicated:
   a. 2.6 cm to mm
   b. 62.5 cm to mm
   c. 0.88 m to cm
   d. 0.007 m to mm
   e. 4800 mm to m
   f. 7.81 km to m
   g. 6800 m to km
   h. 0.875 km to m
   i. 2 m to mm
   j. 0.085 m to mm

2. Convert the masses to the units indicated:
   a. 4.2 g to mg
   b. 750 mg to g
   c. 3940 g to kg
   d. 4.1 kg to g
   e. 0.72 tonnes to kg
   f. 4100 kg to tonnes
   g. 6 280 000 mg to kg
   h. 0.83 tonnes to g
   i. 47 million kg to tonnes
   j. 1 kg to mg

3. Add the masses, giving your answer in kg:
   3.1 tonnes, 4860 kg and 0.37 tonnes

4. Convert the liquid measures to the units indicated:
   a. 1800 ml to litres
   b. 3.2 litres to ml
   c. 0.083 litres to ml
   d. 250 000 ml to litres

5. Convert the following areas:
   a. 56 cm^2 to mm^2
   b. 2.05 m^2 to cm^2

6. Convert the following volumes:
   a. 8670 cm^3 to m^3
   b. 444 000 cm^3 to m^3

Student assessment 2

1. Convert the lengths to the units indicated:
   a. 4.7 cm to mm
   b. 0.003 m to mm
   c. 3100 mm to cm
   d. 6.4 km to m
   e. 49 000 m to km
   f. 4 m to mm
   g. 0.4 cm to mm
   h. 0.034 m to mm
   i. 460 mm to cm
   j. 50 000 m to km

2. Convert the masses to the units indicated:
   a. 3.6 mg to g
   b. 550 mg to g
   c. 6500 g to kg
   d. 6.7 kg to g
   e. 0.37 tonnes to kg
   f. 1510 kg to tonnes
   g. 380 000 kg to tonnes
   h. 0.077 kg to g
   i. 6 million mg to kg
   j. 2 kg to mg

3. Subtract 1570 kg from 2 tonnes.

4. Convert the measures of capacity to the units indicated:
   a. 3400 ml to litres
   b. 6.7 litres to ml
   c. 0.73 litres to ml
   d. 300 000 ml to litres

5. Convert the following areas:
   a. 0.03 m^2 to mm^2
   b. 0.005 km^2 to m^2

6. Convert the following volumes:
   a. 100 400 cm^3 to m^3
   b. 5005 m^3 to km^3

23 Perimeter, area and volume

Note

All diagrams are not drawn to scale.

The perimeter and area of a rectangle

The **perimeter** of a shape is the distance around the outside of the shape. Perimeter can be measured in mm, cm, m, km, etc.

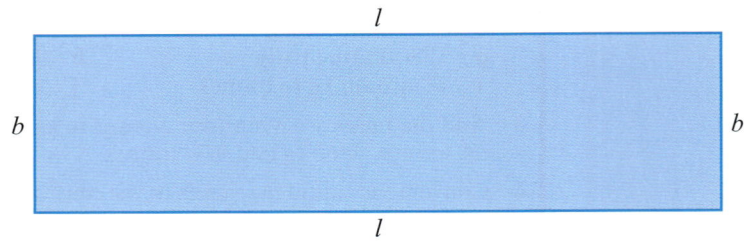

The perimeter of the rectangle above of **length** l and **breadth** b is:

Perimeter = $l + b + l + b$

This can be rearranged to give:

Perimeter = $2l + 2b$

This can be factorised to give:

Perimeter = $2(l + b)$

The **area** of a shape is the amount of surface that it covers. Area is measured in mm^2, cm^2, m^2, km^2, etc.

The area A of the rectangle above is given by the formula:
$A = lb$

➔ Worked example

Find the area of the rectangle.

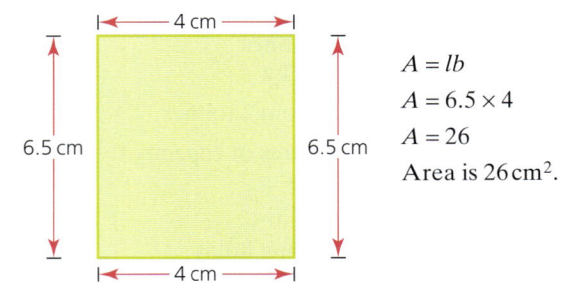

$A = lb$
$A = 6.5 \times 4$
$A = 26$
Area is $26\,cm^2$.

The perimeter and area of a rectangle

Exercise 23.1 Calculate the area and perimeter of the rectangles described in the table.

	Length	Breadth	Area	Perimeter
a	6 cm	4 cm		
b	5 cm	9 cm		
c	4.5 cm	6 cm		
d	3.8 m	10 m		
e	5 m	4.2 m		
f	3.75 cm	6 cm		
g	3.2 cm	4.7 cm		
h	18.7 m	5.5 cm		
i	85 cm	1.2 m		
j	3.3 m	75 cm		

Worked example

Calculate the breadth of a rectangle with an area of 200 cm² and length of 25 cm.

$A = lb$ $200 = 25b$

$b = 8$

So the breadth is 8 cm.

Exercise 23.2

1 Use the formula for the area of a rectangle to find the value of A, l or b as indicated in the table.

	Length	Breadth	Area
a	8.5 cm	7.2 cm	A cm²
b	25 cm	b cm	250 cm²
c	l cm	25 cm	400 cm²
d	7.8 m	b m	78 m²
e	l cm	8.5 cm	102 cm²
f	22 cm	b cm	330 cm²
g	l cm	7.5 cm	187.5 cm²

2 Find the area and perimeter of each of these squares or rectangles:
   a the floor of a room which is 8 m long by 7.5 m wide
   b a stamp which is 35 mm long by 25 mm wide
   c a wall which is 8.2 m long by 2.5 m high
   d a field which is 130 m long by 85 m wide
   e a chessboard of side 45 cm

23 PERIMETER, AREA AND VOLUME

Exercise 23.2 (cont)

f a page of a book which is 25 cm wide by 35 cm long
g an airport runway which is 3.5 km long by 800 m wide
h a street which is 1.2 km long by 25 m wide
i a sports hall floor which is 65 m long by 45 m wide
j the surface of a tile which is a square of side 125 mm

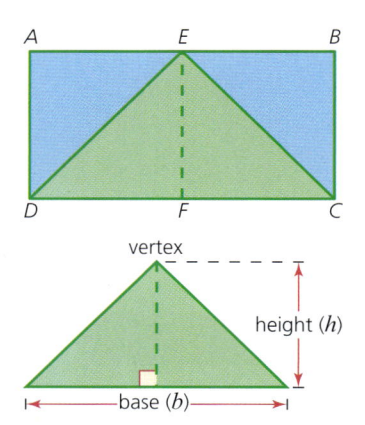

The area of a triangle

Rectangle *ABCD* has triangle *CDE* drawn inside it.

Point *E* is a **vertex** of the triangle.

EF is the **height** or **altitude** of the triangle.

CD is the length of the rectangle, but is called the **base** of the triangle.

It can be seen from the diagram that triangle *DEF* is half the area of the rectangle *AEFD*.

Also, triangle *CFE* is half the area of rectangle *EBCF*.

It follows that triangle *CDE* is half the area of rectangle *ABCD*.

Area of a triangle is $A = \frac{1}{2}bh$, where *b* is the base and *h* is the height.

> **Note**
>
> It does not matter which side is called the base, but the height **must** be measured at right angles from the base to the opposite vertex.

Exercise 23.3 Calculate the areas of the triangles:

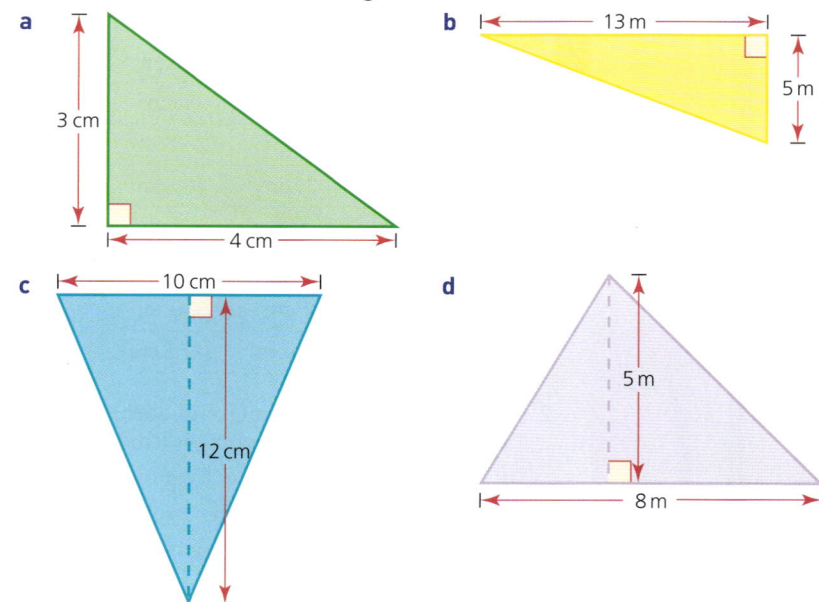

a 3 cm, 4 cm (right triangle)
b 13 m, 5 m
c 10 cm, 12 cm
d 5 m, 8 m

236

e

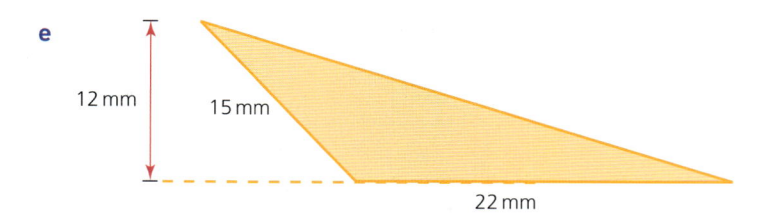

12 mm   15 mm

22 mm

Compound shapes

Sometimes, being asked to work out the perimeter and area of a shape can seem difficult. However, calculations can often be made easier by splitting a shape up into simpler shapes. A shape that can be split into simpler ones is known as a **compound shape**.

➡ Worked example

The diagram shows a pentagon and its dimensions. Calculate the area of the shape.

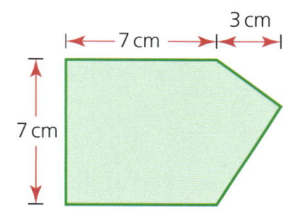

3 cm
7 cm
7 cm

The area of the pentagon is easier to calculate if it is split into two simpler shapes; a square and a triangle:

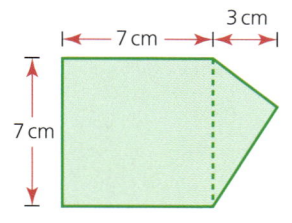

3 cm
7 cm
7 cm

The area of the square is $7 \times 7 = 49\,\text{cm}^2$.

The area of the triangle is $\frac{1}{2} \times 7 \times 3 = 10.5\,\text{cm}^2$.

Therefore the total area of the pentagon is $49 + 10.5 = 59.5\,\text{cm}^2$.

237

23 PERIMETER, AREA AND VOLUME

Exercise 23.4 Calculate the areas of the compound shapes:

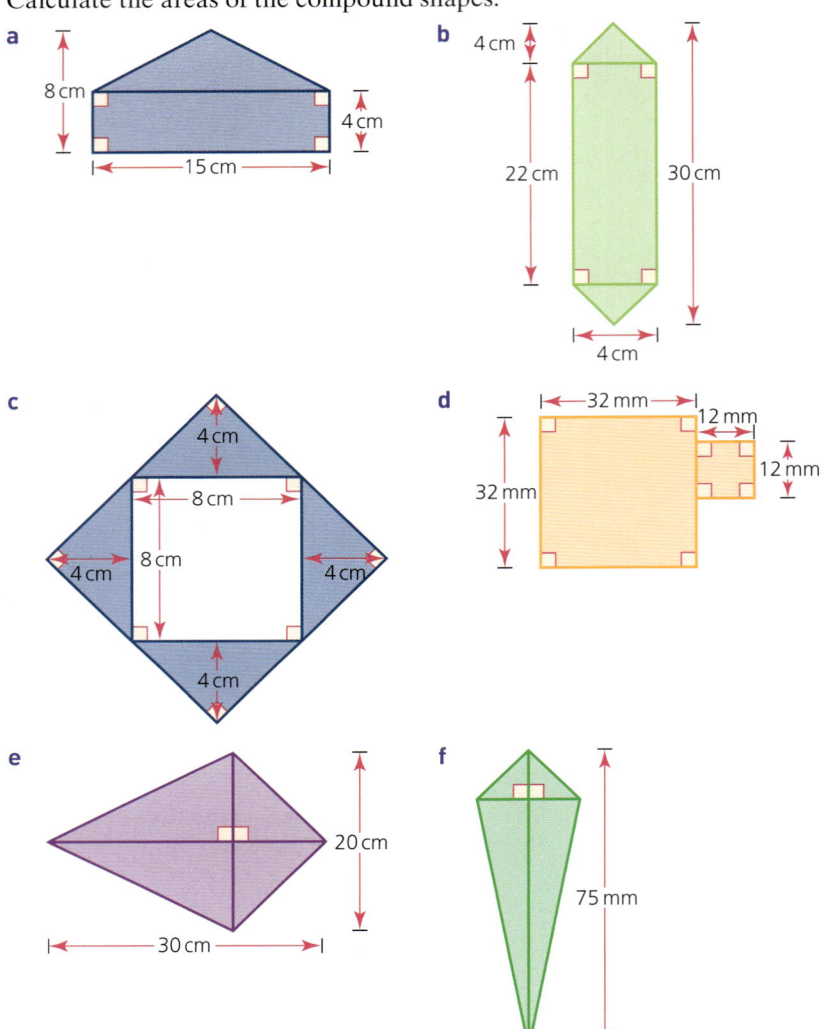

a, b, c, d, e, f

The area of a parallelogram and a trapezium

A **parallelogram** can be rearranged to form a rectangle in the following way:

The area of a parallelogram and a trapezium

Therefore:

area of parallelogram = base length × perpendicular height

A **trapezium** can be split into two triangles:

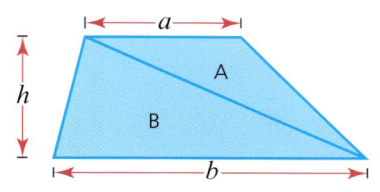

Area of triangle $A = \frac{1}{2} \times a \times h$

Area of triangle $B = \frac{1}{2} \times b \times h$

Area of trapezium

$= $ area of triangle A + area of triangle B

$= \frac{1}{2}ah + \frac{1}{2}bh$

$= \frac{1}{2}h(a+b)$

➔ Worked examples

1 Calculate the area of the parallelogram:

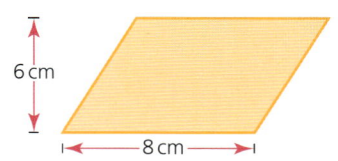

Area = base length × perpendicular height

$= 8 \times 6$

$= 48 \, cm^2$

2 Calculate the shaded area in the shape:

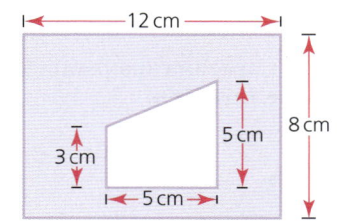

23 PERIMETER, AREA AND VOLUME

$$\text{Area of rectangle} = 12 \times 8$$
$$= 96\,\text{cm}^2$$
$$\text{Area of trapezium} = \tfrac{1}{2} \times 5(3+5)$$
$$= 2.5 \times 8$$
$$= 20\,\text{cm}^2$$
$$\text{Shaded area} = 96 - 20$$
$$= 76\,\text{cm}^2$$

Exercise 23.5

Find the area of these shapes:

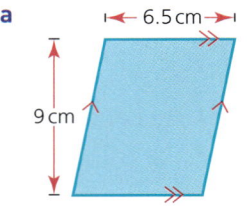

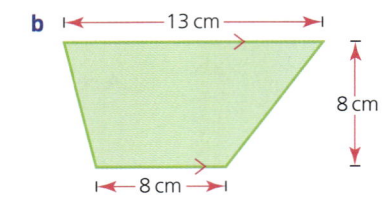

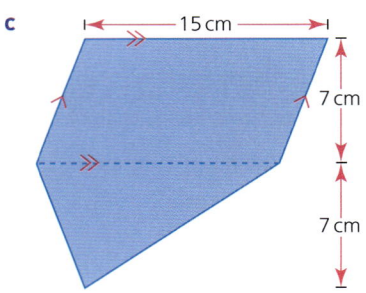

a Parallelogram with base 6.5 cm and height 9 cm.

b Trapezium with parallel sides 13 cm and 8 cm, and height 8 cm.

c Shape with top 15 cm, and right side divided into 7 cm and 7 cm.

Exercise 23.6

1 Calculate the value of a.

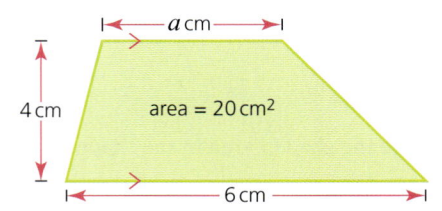

Trapezium with top a cm, bottom 6 cm, height 4 cm, area = 20 cm².

2 If the areas of the trapezium and parallelogram in the diagram are equal, calculate the value of x.

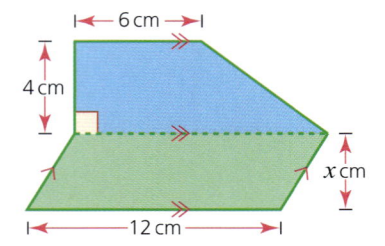

Diagram with 6 cm top, 4 cm height, 12 cm bottom, and x cm.

The circumference and area of a circle

3 The end view of a house is as shown in the diagram.

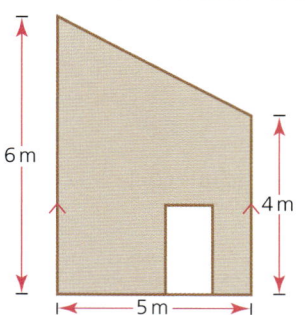

If the door has a width and height of 0.75 m and 2 m, respectively, calculate the area of brickwork.

4 A garden in the shape of a trapezium is split into three parts: flower beds in the shape of a triangle and a parallelogram, and a section of grass in the shape of a trapezium. The area of the grass is two and a half times the total area of the flower beds. Calculate:

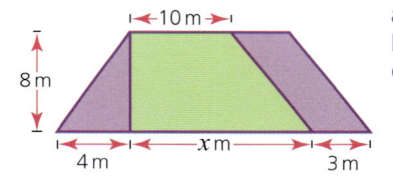

a the area of each flower bed
b the area of grass
c the value of x.

The circumference and area of a circle

Note

Use the π-button on the calculator unless a question says otherwise.

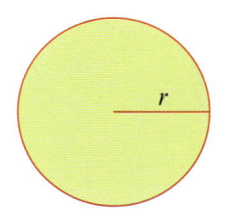

The **circumference of a circle** is $2\pi r$.
$C = 2\pi r$

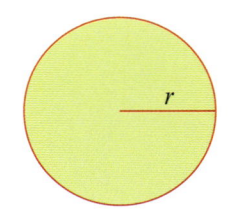

The **area of a circle** is πr^2.
$A = \pi r^2$

→ Worked examples

1 Calculate the circumference of this circle, giving your answer to 3 s.f.

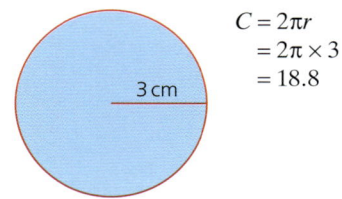

$C = 2\pi r$
$= 2\pi \times 3$
$= 18.8$

The circumference is 18.8 cm.

241

23 PERIMETER, AREA AND VOLUME

The answer 18.8 cm is only correct to 3 s.f. and as such is only an approximation. An **exact** answer involves leaving the answer in terms of π, i.e.

$C = 2\pi r$

$= 2\pi \times 3$

$= 6\pi$ cm

2 If the circumference of this circle is 12 cm, calculate the radius, giving your answer:
i to 3 s.f. ii in terms of π.

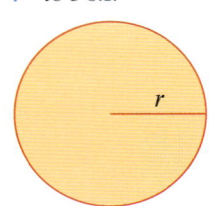

a $C = 2\pi r$

$r = \dfrac{C}{2\pi}$

$r = \dfrac{12}{2\pi}$

$= 1.91$

The radius is 1.91 cm.

b $r = \dfrac{C}{2\pi}$

$= \dfrac{12}{2\pi}$

$= \dfrac{6}{\pi}$ cm

3 Calculate the area of this circle, giving your answer:
i to 3 s.f. ii in exact form.

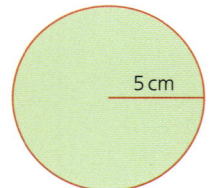

5 cm

a $A = \pi r^2$

$= \pi \times 5^2$

$= 78.5$

The area is 78.5 cm².

b $A = \pi r^2$

$= \pi \times 5^2$

$= 25\pi$ cm²

4 The area of a circle is 34 cm², calculate the radius, giving your answer:
i to 3 s.f. ii in terms of π.

242

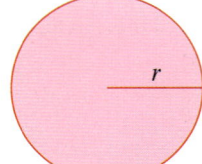

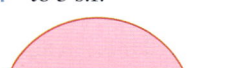

The circumference and area of a circle

    a $A = \pi r^2$ b $r = \sqrt{\frac{A}{\pi}}$

       $r = \sqrt{\frac{A}{\pi}}$ $= \sqrt{\frac{34}{\pi}}$ cm

       $r = \sqrt{\frac{34}{\pi}} = 3.29$

    The radius is 3.29 cm.

Exercise 23.7

1. Calculate the circumference of each circle, giving your answers to 2 d.p.

    a   4 cm   b   3.5 cm

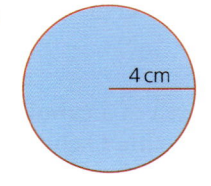

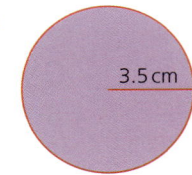

    c   9.2 cm   d   0.5 m

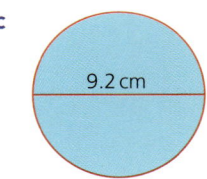

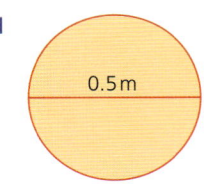

2. Calculate the area of each circle in Q.1. Give your answers to 2 d.p.

3. Calculate the radius of a circle when the circumference is:
    a   15 cm   b π cm
    c   4 m   d   8 mm

4. Calculate the diameter of a circle when the area is:
    a   16 cm^2 b 9π cm^2
    c   8.2 m^2 d   14.6 mm^2

Exercise 23.8

1. The wheel of a child's toy car has an outer radius of 25 cm. Calculate:
    a   how far the car has travelled after one complete turn of the wheel
    b   how many times the wheel turns for a journey of 1 km.

2. If the wheel of a bicycle has a diameter of 60 cm, calculate how far a cyclist will have travelled after the wheel has rotated 100 times.

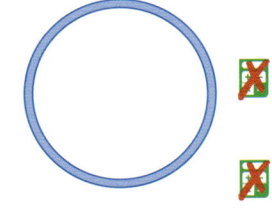

3. A circular ring (left) has a cross-section. If the outer radius is 22 mm and the inner radius is 20 mm, calculate the cross-sectional area of the ring. Give your answer in terms of π.

4. Four circles are drawn in a line and enclosed by a rectangle, as shown. If the radius of each circle is 3 cm, calculate the unshaded area within the rectangle, giving your answer in terms of π.

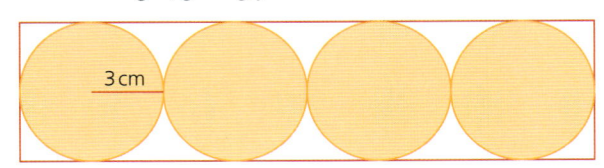

243

23 PERIMETER, AREA AND VOLUME

Exercise 23.8 (cont)

5 A garden is made up of a rectangular patch of grass and two semi-circular vegetable patches. If the dimensions of the rectangular patch are 16 m (length) and 8 m (width) respectively, give your answers in terms of π.

   a the perimeter of the garden   b the total area of the garden.

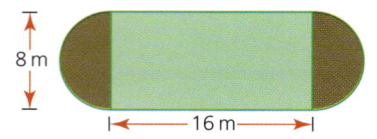

The surface area of a cuboid and a cylinder

To calculate the surface area of a **cuboid**, start by looking at its individual faces. These are either squares or rectangles. The surface area of a cuboid is the sum of the areas of its faces.

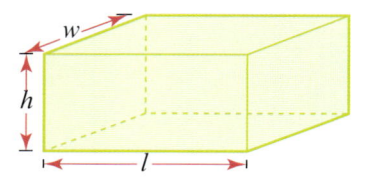

Area of top = wl Area of bottom = wl

Area of front = lh Area of back = lh

Area of left side = wh Area of right side = wh

Total surface area

$= 2wl + 2lh + 2wh$

$= 2(wl + lh + wh)$

For the surface area of a **cylinder**, it is best to visualise the net of the solid. It is made up of one rectangular piece and two circular pieces:

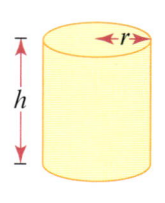

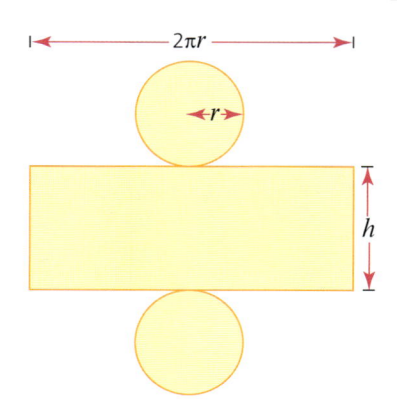

The surface area of a cuboid and a cylinder

$$\text{Area of circular pieces} = 2 \times \pi r^2$$
$$\text{Area of rectangular piece} = 2\pi r \times h$$
$$\text{Total surface area} = 2\pi r^2 + 2\pi r h$$
$$= 2\pi r(r + h)$$

→ Worked examples

1 Calculate the surface area of the cuboid.

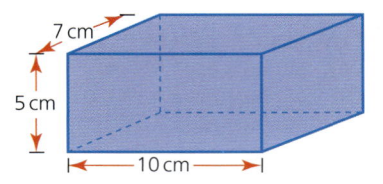

Total area of top and bottom = $2 \times 7 \times 10 = 140\,\text{cm}^2$

Total area of front and back = $2 \times 5 \times 10 = 100\,\text{cm}^2$

Total area of both sides = $2 \times 5 \times 7 = 70\,\text{cm}^2$

Total surface area = $140 + 100 + 70$

$= 310\,\text{cm}^2$

2 If the height of a cylinder is 7 cm and the radius of its circular top is 3 cm, calculate its surface area.

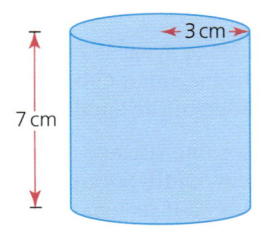

Total surface area = $2\pi r(r + h)$
$= 2\pi \times 3 \times (3 + 7)$
$= 6\pi \times 10$
$= 60\pi$
$= 188.50\,\text{cm}^2$ (2 d.p.)

The total surface area is $188.50\,\text{cm}^2$.

Exercise 23.9

1 These are the dimensions of some cuboids. Calculate the surface area of each one.
   a $l = 12\,\text{cm}$, $w = 10\,\text{cm}$, $h = 5\,\text{cm}$
   b $l = 4\,\text{cm}$, $w = 6\,\text{cm}$, $h = 8\,\text{cm}$
   c $l = 4.2\,\text{cm}$, $w = 7.1\,\text{cm}$, $h = 3.9\,\text{cm}$
   d $l = 5.2\,\text{cm}$, $w = 2.1\,\text{cm}$, $h = 0.8\,\text{cm}$

Note
A diagram may help you answer these questions.

23 PERIMETER, AREA AND VOLUME

Exercise 23.9 (cont)

2 These are the dimensions of some cuboids. Calculate the height of each one.
   a $l = 5$ cm, $w = 6$ cm,   surface area = 104 cm^2
   b $l = 2$ cm, $w = 8$ cm,   surface area = 112 cm^2
   c $l = 3.5$ cm, $w = 4$ cm,   surface area = 118 cm^2
   d $l = 4.2$ cm, $w = 10$ cm, surface area = 226 cm^2

3 These are the dimensions of some cylinders. Calculate the surface area of each one.
   a $r = 2$ cm, $h = 6$ cm
   b $r = 4$ cm, $h = 7$ cm
   c $r = 3.5$ cm, $h = 9.2$ cm
   d $r = 0.8$ cm, $h = 4.3$ cm

4 These are the dimensions of some cylinders. Calculate the height of each one. Give your answers to 1 d.p.
   a $r = 2.0$ cm, surface area = 40 cm^2
   b $r = 3.5$ cm, surface area = 88 cm^2
   c $r = 5.5$ cm, surface area = 250 cm^2
   d $r = 3.0$ cm, surface area = 189 cm^2

Exercise 23.10

1 Two cubes are placed next to each other. The length of each edge of the larger cube is 4 cm.

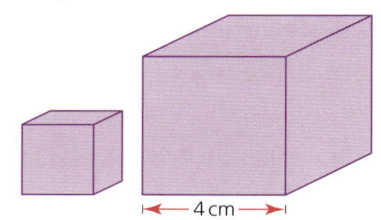

   If the ratio of their surface areas is 1 : 4, calculate:
   a the surface area of the small cube
   b the length of an edge of the small cube.

2 Two cuboids have the same surface area. The dimensions of one of them are: length = 3 cm, width = 4 cm and height = 2 cm. Calculate the height of the other cuboid if its length is 1 cm and its width is 4 cm.

3 A cube and a cylinder have the same surface area. If the cube has an edge length of 6 cm and the cylinder a radius of 2 cm, calculate:
   a the surface area of the cube
   b the height of the cylinder.

4 Two cylinders have the same surface area. The shorter of the two has a radius of 3 cm and a height of 2 cm, and the taller cylinder has a radius of 1 cm. Calculate: 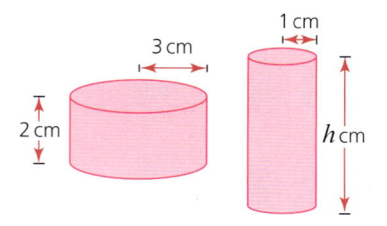
   a the surface area of one of the cylinders in terms of π
   b the height of the taller cylinder.

246

The volume and surface area of a prism

A **prism** is any three-dimensional object which has a constant cross-sectional area. Some examples of common types of prism are:

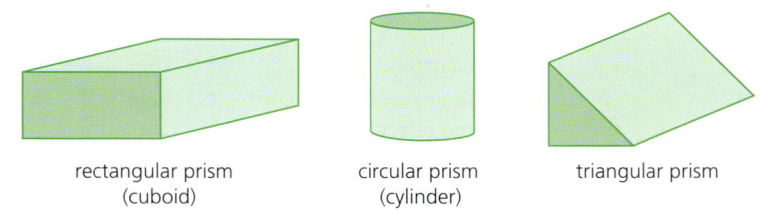

rectangular prism (cuboid)   circular prism (cylinder)   triangular prism

When each of the shapes is cut parallel to the shaded face, the cross-section is constant and the shape is therefore classified as a prism.

Volume of a prism = area of cross-section × length
Surface area of a prism = sum of the area of each of its faces

Worked examples

1   Calculate the volume of the cylinder in the diagram:

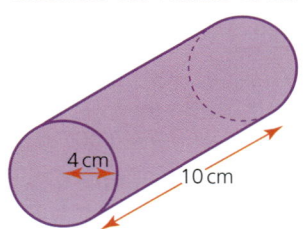

Volume = area of cross-section × length
       = $\pi \times 4^2 \times 10$

Volume = 502.7 cm³ (1 d.p.)

As an exact value the volume would be left as 160π cm³.

2   For the L-shaped prism in the diagram, calculate:
   a   the volume

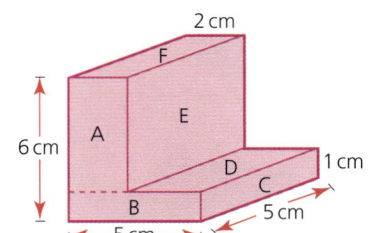

The cross-sectional area can be split into two rectangles:

23 PERIMETER, AREA AND VOLUME

Area of rectangle A = 5 × 2
$= 10 \, cm^2$
Area of rectangle B = 5 × 1
$= 5 \, cm^2$

Total cross-sectional area = $10 \, cm^2 + 5 \, cm^2 = 15 \, cm^2$

Volume of prism = 15 × 5
$= 75 \, cm^3$

b the surface area.

Area of rectangle A = 5 × 2 = $10 \, cm^2$
Area of rectangle B = 5 × 1 = $5 \, cm^2$
Area of rectangle C = 5 × 1 = $5 \, cm^2$
Area of rectangle D = 3 × 5 = $15 \, cm^2$
Area of rectangle E = 5 × 5 = $25 \, cm^2$
Area of rectangle F = 2 × 5 = $10 \, cm^2$
Area of back is the same as area of rectangle A + area of rectangle B = $15 \, cm^2$
Area of left face is the same as area of rectangle C + area of rectangle E = $30 \, cm^2$
Area of base = 5 × 5 = $25 \, cm^2$

Total surface area = 10 + 5 + 5 + 15 + 25 + 10 + 15 + 30 + 25
$= 140 \, cm^2$

Exercise 23.11

1. Calculate the volume of each of the following cuboids, where w, l and h represent the width, length and height, respectively.
   a $w = 2 \, cm$, $l = 3 \, cm$, $h = 4 \, cm$
   b $w = 6 \, cm$, $l = 1 \, cm$, $h = 3 \, cm$
   c $w = 6 \, cm$, $l = 23 \, mm$, $h = 2 \, cm$
   d $w = 42 \, mm$, $l = 3 \, cm$, $h = 0.007 \, m$

2. Calculate the volume of each of the following cylinders, where r represents the radius of the circular face and h the height of the cylinder.
   a $r = 4 \, cm$, $h = 9 \, cm$ b $r = 3.5 \, cm$, $h = 7.2 \, cm$
   c $r = 25 \, mm$, $h = 10 \, cm$ d $r = 0.3 \, cm$, $h = 17 \, mm$

3. Calculate the volume and total surface area of each of these right-angled triangular prisms:

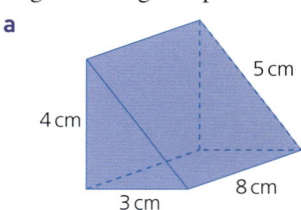

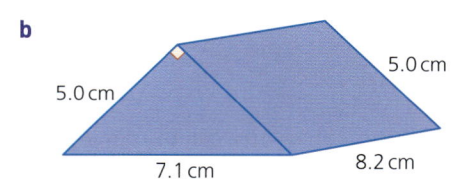

   a

   4 cm, 3 cm, 5 cm, 8 cm

   b

   5.0 cm, 5.0 cm, 7.1 cm, 8.2 cm

The volume and surface area of a prism

4 The diagram below shows the net of a right-angled triangular prism.

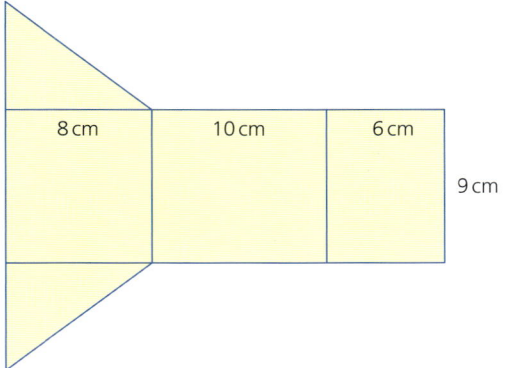

Calculate:
a the surface area of the prism   b the volume of the prism.

5 Calculate the volume of each prism. All dimensions given are in centimetres.

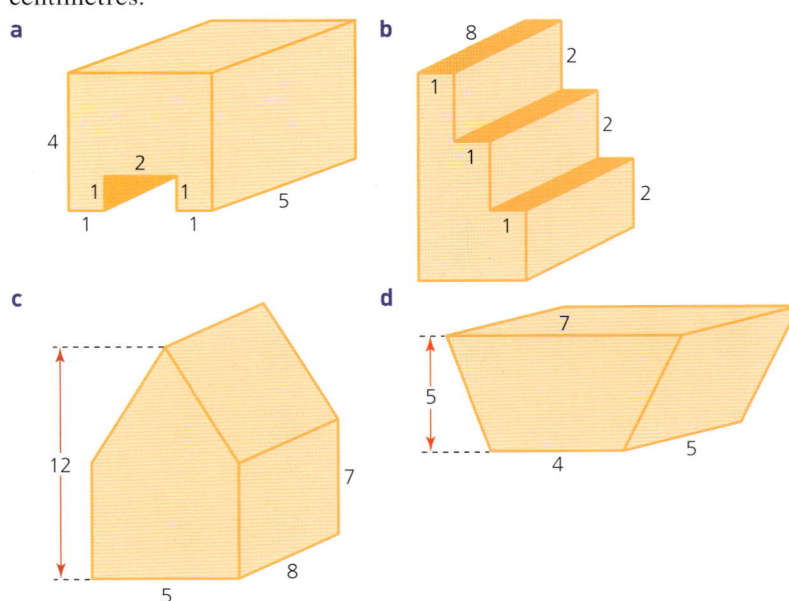

Exercise 23.12

1 The diagram shows a plan view of a cylinder inside a box the shape of a cube. The radius of the cylinder is 8 cm.

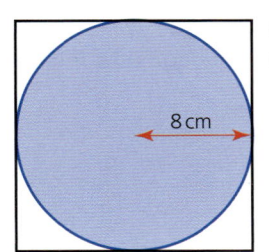

Calculate the percentage volume of the cube not occupied by the cylinder.

23 PERIMETER, AREA AND VOLUME

Exercise 23.12 (cont)

2 A chocolate bar is made in the shape of a triangular prism. The triangular face of the prism is equilateral and has an edge length of 4 cm and a perpendicular height of 3.5 cm. The manufacturer also sells these in special packs of six bars arranged as a hexagonal prism, as shown.

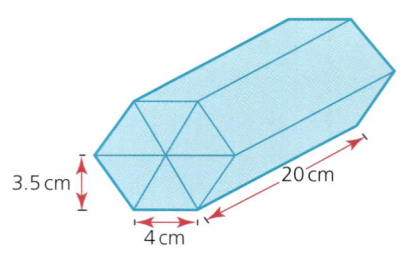

If the prisms are 20 cm long, calculate:
  a the cross-sectional area of the pack
  b the volume of the pack.

3 A cuboid and a cylinder have the same volume. The radius and height of the cylinder are 2.5 cm and 8 cm, respectively. If the length and width of the cuboid are each 5 cm, calculate its height to 1 d.p.

4 A section of steel pipe is shown in the diagram below. The inner radius is 35 cm and the outer radius is 36 cm. Calculate the volume of steel used in making the pipe if it has a length of 130 m. Give your answer in terms of π.

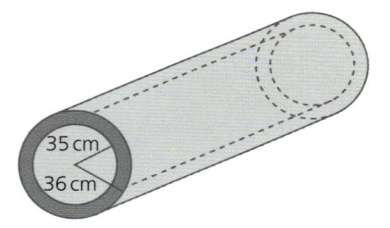

Arc length

An **arc** is part of the circumference of a circle between two radii.

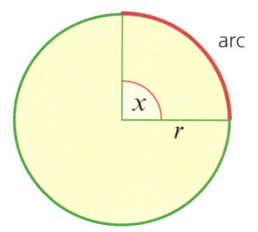

The length of an arc is proportional to the size of the angle x between the two radii. The length of the arc as a fraction of the circumference of the whole circle is therefore equal to the fraction that x is of 360°.

Arc length = $\frac{x}{360} \times 2\pi r$

Arc length

> A minor arc is the smaller of two arcs in a diagram. The larger arc is called the major arc. This is not required for the Core syllabus, but is useful to know.

→ Worked examples

1. Find the length of the minor arc in the circle (right).
   a Give your answer to 3 s.f.
   Arc length $= \frac{60}{360} \times 2 \times \pi \times 6$
   $= 6.28$ cm
   b Give your answer in terms of π.
   Arc length $= \frac{60}{360} \times 2 \times \pi \times 6$
   $= 2\pi$ cm

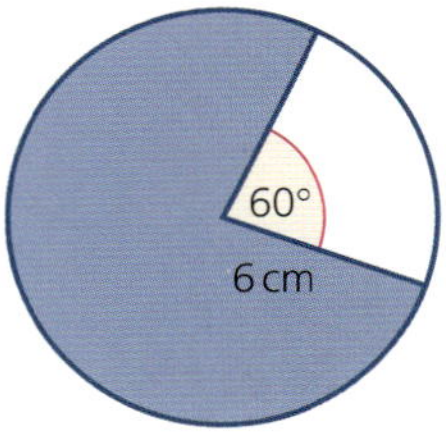

2. In the circle, the length of the minor arc is 3π cm and the radius is 9 cm.
   a Calculate the angle x.
   Arc length $= \frac{x}{360} \times 2\pi r$

   $3\pi = \frac{x}{360} \times 2 \times \pi \times 9$

   $x = \frac{3\pi \times 360}{2 \times \pi \times 9}$

   $= 60°$

   b Calculate the length of the major arc. 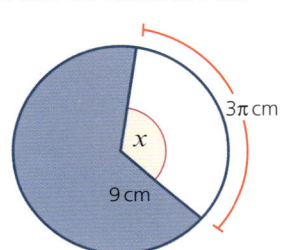
   $C = 2\pi r$
   $= 2 \times \pi \times 9 = 18\pi$
   Major arc = circumference − minor arc
   $= 18\pi - 3\pi = 15\pi$ cm

Exercise 23.13

> A sector is the region of a circle enclosed by two radii and an arc.

1. For each of these sectors, give the length of the arc to 3 s.f. O is the centre of the circle.

   a 45°, 8 cm

   b 8°, 15 cm

   c 120°, 6 cm

   d 270°, 5 cm

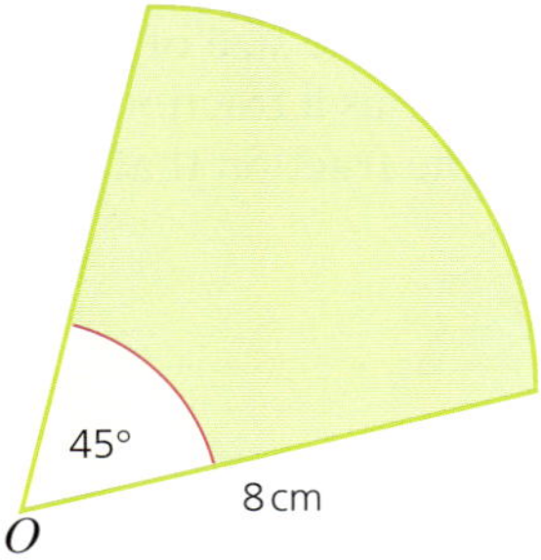

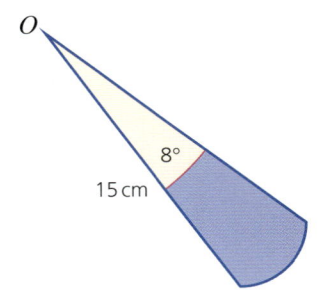

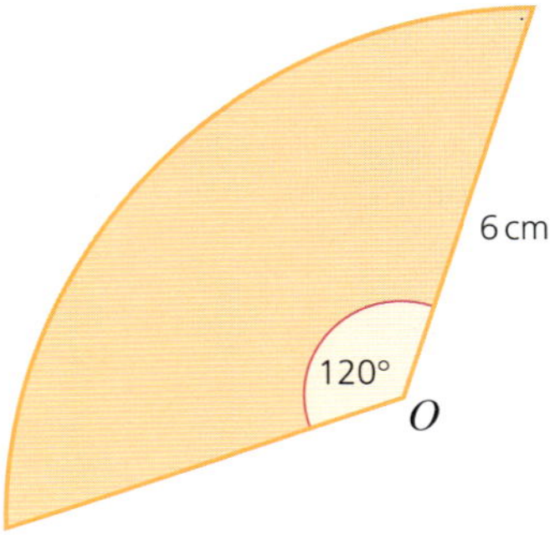

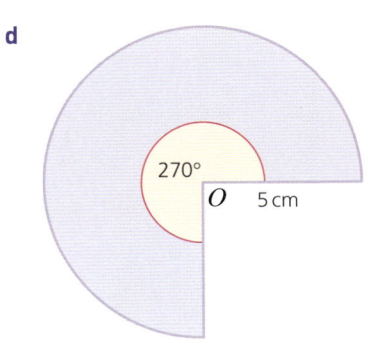

23 PERIMETER, AREA AND VOLUME

Exercise 23.13 (cont)

2. Calculate the angle x for each sector. The radius r and arc length a are given in each case.
   a $\quad r = 15\,\text{cm}, \ a = 3\pi\,\text{cm}$
   b $\quad r = 12\,\text{cm}, \ a = 6\pi\,\text{cm}$
   c $\quad r = 24\,\text{cm}, \ a = 8\pi\,\text{cm}$
   d $\quad r = \frac{3}{2}\,\text{cm}, \ a = \frac{\pi}{3}\,\text{cm}$

3. Calculate the radius r for each sector. The angle x and arc length a are given in each case.
   a $\quad x = 90°, \quad a = 16\,\text{cm}$
   b $\quad x = 36°, \quad a = 24\,\text{cm}$
   c $\quad x = 20°, \quad a = 6.5\,\text{cm}$
   d $\quad x = 72°, \quad a = 17\,\text{cm}$

Exercise 23.14

1. Calculate the perimeter of each of these shapes. Give your answers in terms of π.
   a
   b

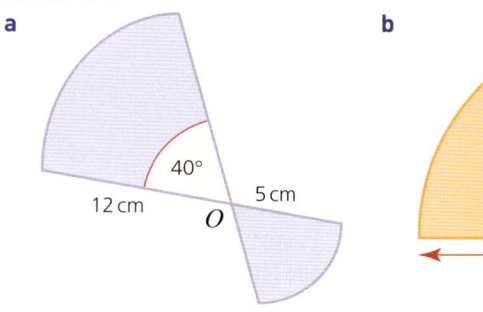

2. For the diagram, calculate:
   a the radius of the smaller sector
   b the perimeter of the shape

The area of a sector

A **sector** is the region of a circle enclosed by two radii and an arc. Its area is proportional to the size of the angle x between the two radii. The area of the sector as a fraction of the area of the whole circle is therefore equal to the fraction that x is of 360°.

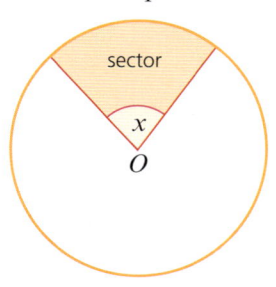

Area of sector $= \frac{x}{360}\pi r^2$

The area of a sector

> ### Worked examples

1. Calculate the area of the sector, giving your answer:
   a to 3 s.f.
   $$\text{Area} = \frac{x}{360} \times \pi r^2$$
   $$= \frac{45}{360} \times \pi \times 12^2$$
   $$= 56.5 \text{ cm}^2$$

   b in terms of π.
   $$\text{Area} = \frac{45}{360} \times \pi \times 12^2$$
   $$= 18\pi \text{ cm}^2$$

2. Calculate the radius of the sector, giving your answer to 3 s.f.
   $$\text{Area} = \frac{x}{360} \times \pi r^2$$
   $$50 = \frac{30}{360} \times \pi \times r^2$$
   $$\frac{50 \times 360}{30\pi} = r^2$$
   $$r = 13.8$$

   The radius is 13.8 cm.

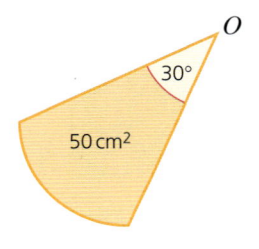

Exercise 23.15

1. Calculate the area of each of the sectors described in the table, using the values of the angle x and radius r:

	a	b	c	d
x	60	120	2	72
r (cm)	8	14	18	14

2. Calculate the radius for each of the sectors described in the table, using the values of the angle x and the area A:

	a	b	c	d
x	40	12	72	18
A (cm²)	120	42	4	400

3. Calculate the value of the angle x for each of the sectors described in the table, using the values of the radius r and area A:

	a	b	c	d
r	12 cm	20 cm	2 cm	0.5 m
A	8π cm²	40π cm²	$\frac{\pi}{2}$ cm²	$\frac{\pi}{60}$ m²

23 PERIMETER, AREA AND VOLUME

Exercise 23.16

1. A rotating sprinkler is placed in one corner of a garden. It has a reach of 8 m and rotates through an angle of 30°. Calculate the area of garden not being watered. Give your answer in terms of π.

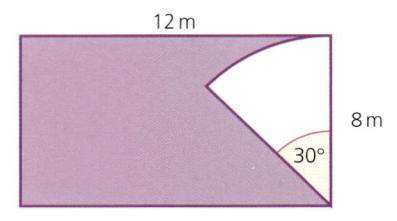

2. Two sectors, AOB and COD, share the same centre O. The area of AOB is three times the area of COD. Calculate:
   a the area of sector AOB
   b the area of sector COD
   c the radius r cm of sector COD.

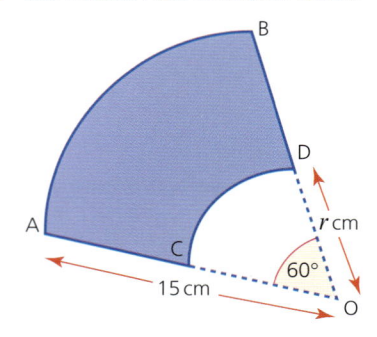

3. A circular cake is cut. One of the slices is shown. Calculate:
   a the length a cm of the arc
   b the total surface area of all the sides of the slice
   c the volume of the slice.

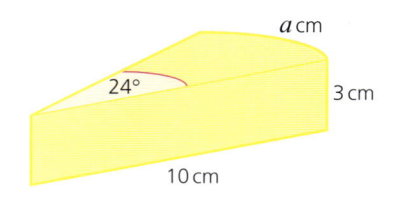

The volume of a sphere

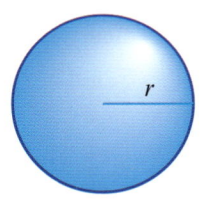

Volume of sphere = $\frac{4}{3}\pi r^3$

You should know how to use this formula, but you do not need to memorise it.

The volume of a sphere

> **Worked examples**

1. Calculate the volume of the sphere, giving your answer:
   a to 3 s.f.
   b in terms of π.

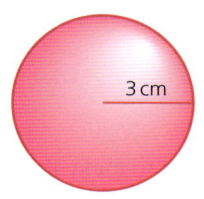

   (sphere with radius 3 cm)

   Volume of sphere = $\frac{4}{3}\pi r^3$ Volume of sphere = $\frac{4}{3}\pi \times 3^3$

   $= \frac{4}{3} \times \pi \times 3^3$ $= 36\pi$ cm^3

   $= 113.1$

   The volume is 113 cm^3.

2. Given that the volume of a sphere is 150 cm^3, calculate its radius to 3 s.f.

   $V = \frac{4}{3}\pi r^3$

   $r^3 = \frac{3 \times V}{4 \times \pi}$

   $r^3 = \frac{3 \times 150}{4 \times \pi}$

   $r = \sqrt[3]{35.8} = 3.30$

   The radius is 3.30 cm.

Exercise 23.17

1. The radius of four spheres is given. Calculate the volume of each one.
   a $r = 6$ cm   b $r = 9.5$ cm
   c $r = 8.2$ cm   d $r = 0.7$ cm

2. The volume of four spheres is given. Calculate the radius of each one, giving your answers in centimetres and to 3 s.f.
   a $V = 130$ cm^3 b $V = 720$ cm^3
   c $V = 0.2$ m^3 d $V = 1000$ mm^3

Exercise 23.18

1. Given that sphere B has twice the volume of sphere A, calculate the radius of sphere B. Give your answer to 3 s.f.

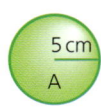

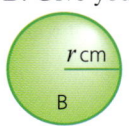

   (sphere A with radius 5 cm; sphere B with radius r cm)

255

23 PERIMETER, AREA AND VOLUME

Exercise 23.18 (cont)

2 Calculate the volume of material used to make the half sphere bowl in the diagram, given the inner radius of the bowl is 5 cm and its outer radius is 5.5 cm. Give your answer in terms of π.

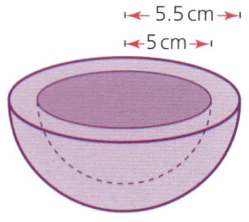

Note

A half sphere is called a hemisphere. This term is not required for the Core syllabus.

3 The volume of material used to make the sphere and half sphere bowl is the same. Given that the radius of the sphere is 7 cm and the inner radius of the bowl is 10 cm, calculate to 1 d.p. the outer radius r cm of the bowl.

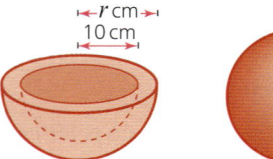

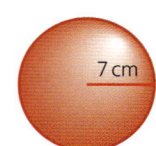

4 A ball is placed inside a box into which it will fit tightly. If the radius of the ball is 10 cm, calculate the percentage volume of the box not occupied by the ball.

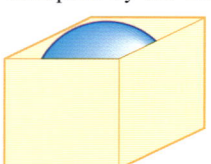

The surface area of a sphere

Surface area of sphere = $4\pi r^2$

You should know how to use this formula, but you do not need to memorise it.

Exercise 23.19

1 The radius of four spheres is given. Calculate the surface area of each one.
   a $r = 6$ cm
   b $r = 4.5$ cm
   c $r = 12.25$ cm
   d $r = \frac{1}{3}$ cm

2 The surface area of four spheres is given. Calculate the radius of each one.
   a $A = 50$ cm^2
   b $A = 16.5$ cm^2
   c $A = 120$ mm^2
   d $A = \pi$ cm^2

The volume of a pyramid

3 Sphere A has a radius of 8 cm and sphere B has a radius of 16 cm. Calculate the ratio of their surface areas in the form $1 : n$.

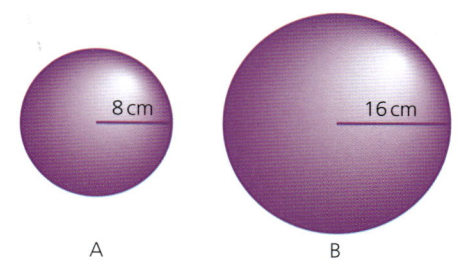

4 The diameter of half a sphere is 10 cm, and it is attached to a cylinder of equal diameter as shown. If the total length of the shape is 20 cm, calculate the surface area of the whole shape.

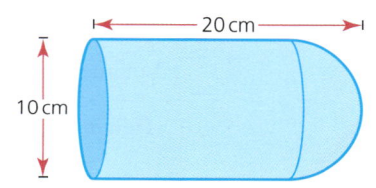

The volume of a pyramid

A **pyramid** is a three-dimensional shape in which each of its faces must be plane. A pyramid has a polygon for its base and the other faces are triangles with a common vertex, known as the **apex**. Its individual name is taken from the shape of the base.

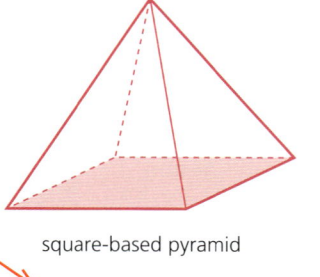

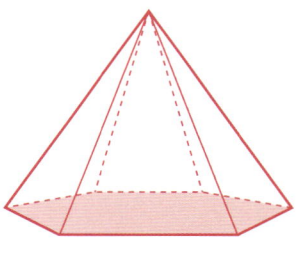

A plane is a two-dimensional (2D) flat surface.

square-based pyramid

hexagonal-based pyramid

Volume of any pyramid = $\frac{1}{3}$ × area of base × perpendicular height

You should know how to use this formula, but you do not need to memorise it.

257

23 PERIMETER, AREA AND VOLUME

> **Worked examples**

1 A rectangular-based pyramid has a perpendicular height of 5 cm and base dimensions as shown. Calculate the volume of the pyramid.

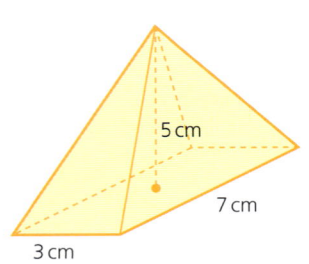

Volume = $\frac{1}{3}$ × base area × height

= $\frac{1}{3}$ × 3 × 7 × 5 = 35

The volume is 35 cm³.

2 The pyramid shown has a volume of 60 cm³. Calculate its perpendicular height h cm.

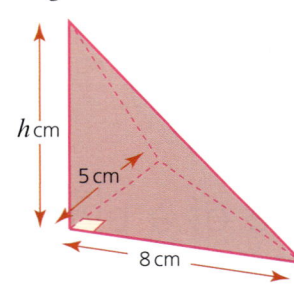

Volume = $\frac{1}{3}$ × base area × height

Height = $\frac{3 \times \text{volume}}{\text{base area}}$

$h = \frac{3 \times 60}{\frac{1}{2} \times 8 \times 5}$

$h = 9$

The height is 9 cm.

Exercise 23.20   Find the volume of each of the following pyramids:

a

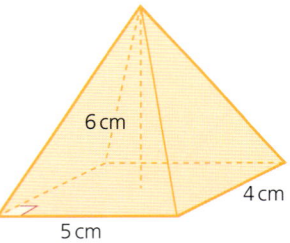

b   Base area = 50 cm²

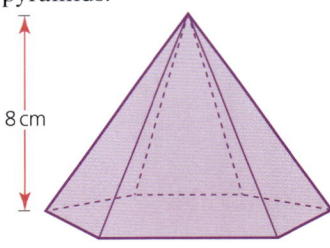

c

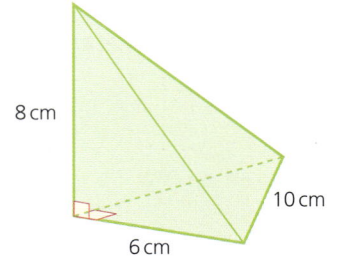

d

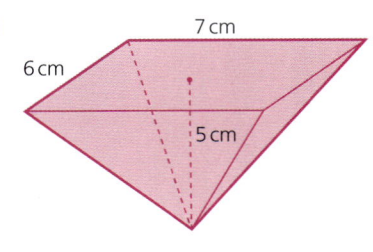

The surface area of a pyramid

The surface area of a pyramid is found by adding together the areas of all faces.

Exercise 23.21

1 Calculate the surface area of a regular tetrahedron with edge length 2 cm.

> **Note**
> A tetrahedron is a triangular pyramid. It has three sides and a base, all of which are equilateral triangles.

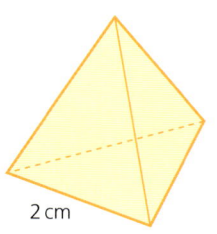

2 cm

2 The rectangular-based pyramid shown has a sloping edge length of 12 cm. Calculate its surface area.

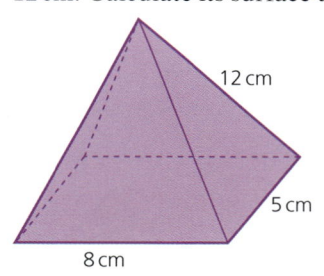

12 cm
5 cm
8 cm

3 Two square-based pyramids are glued together as shown. Given that all the triangular faces are identical, calculate the surface area of the whole shape.

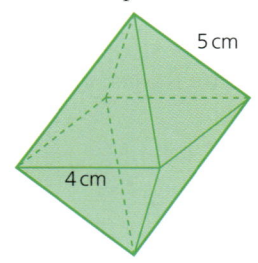

5 cm
4 cm

The volume of a cone

A **cone** is a pyramid with a circular base. The formula for its volume is therefore the same as for any other pyramid.

Volume = $\frac{1}{3}$ × base area × height

$= \frac{1}{3}\pi r^2 h$

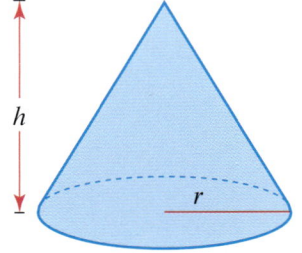

You should know how to use this formula, but you do not need to memorise it.

259

23 PERIMETER, AREA AND VOLUME

Worked examples

1 Calculate the volume of the cone.

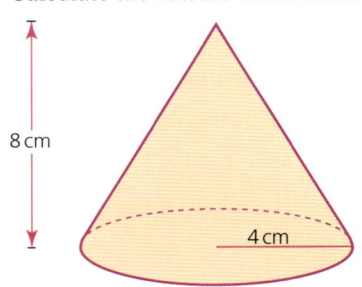

Volume = $\frac{1}{3}\pi r^2 h$

$= \frac{1}{3} \times \pi \times 4^2 \times 8$

$= 134.0$ (1 d.p.)

The volume is 134 cm³ (3 s.f.).

2 The sector below forms a cone as shown.

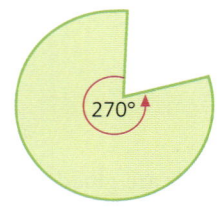

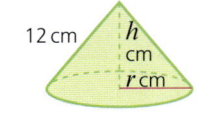

a Calculate, in terms of π, the base circumference of the cone.
The base circumference of the cone is equal to the arc length of the sector.

The radius of the sector is equal to the slant height of the cone (i.e. 12 cm).

Sector arc length = $\frac{x}{360} \times 2\pi r$

$= \frac{270}{360} \times 2\pi \times 12 = 18\pi$

So the base circumference is 18π cm.

b Calculate, in exact form, the base radius of the cone.

The base of a cone is circular, therefore:

$C = 2\pi r$

$r = \frac{C}{2\pi}$

$= \frac{18\pi}{2\pi} = 9$

So the radius is 9 cm.

The volume of a cone

c Calculate the exact height of the cone.

The vertical height of the cone can be calculated using Pythagoras' theorem on the right-angled triangle enclosed by the base radius, vertical height and the sloping face.

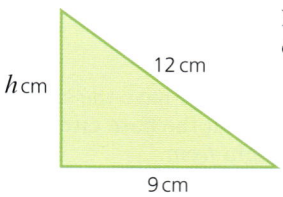

Note that the length of the sloping face is equal to the radius of the sector.

$12^2 = h^2 + 9^2$

$h^2 = 12^2 - 9^2$

$h^2 = 63$

$h = \sqrt{63} = 7.937... = 7.94$ to 3 s.f.

Therefore the vertical height is $3\sqrt{7}$ cm.

d Calculate the volume of the cone, leaving your answer to 3 s.f.

Volume $= \frac{1}{3} \times \pi r^2 h$

$= \frac{1}{3} \pi \times 9^2 \times \sqrt{63}$

$= 27\sqrt{63}\pi$ cm^3

$= 673$ cm^3

In these examples, the previous answer was used to calculate the next stage of the question. By using exact values each time, we avoid rounding errors in the calculation.

Exercise 23.22

1 Calculate the volume of the cones described in the table. Use the values for the base radius r and the vertical height h given in each case.

	r	h
a	3 cm	6 cm
b	6 cm	7 cm
c	8 mm	2 cm
d	6 cm	44 mm

2 Calculate the base radius of the cones described in the table. Use the values for the volume V and the vertical height h given in each case.

	V	h
a	600 cm^3	12 cm
b	225 cm^3	18 mm
c	1400 mm^3	2 cm
d	0.04 m^3	145 mm

261

23 PERIMETER, AREA AND VOLUME

Exercise 23.22 (cont)

3 The base circumference C and the length of the sloping face l of four cones is given in the table. Calculate in each case:
   i   the base radius
   ii the vertical height
   iii the volume.

   Give all answers to 3 s.f.

	C	l
a	50 cm	15 cm
b	100 cm	18 cm
c	0.4 m	75 mm
d	240 mm	6 cm

Exercise 23.23

1 The two cones A and B have the same volume. Using the dimensions shown and given that the base circumference of cone B is 60 cm, calculate the height h cm.

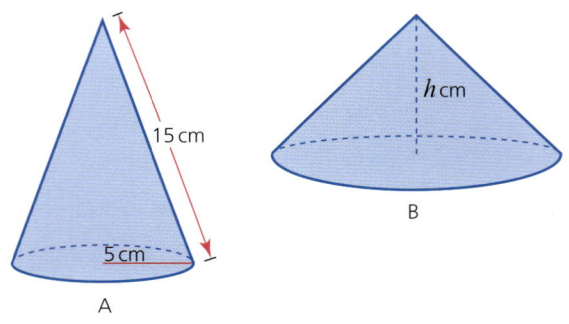

2 A cone is placed inside a cuboid as shown. The base diameter of the cone is 12 cm and the height of the cuboid is 16 cm.

   Calculate the volume of the cuboid not occupied by the cone.

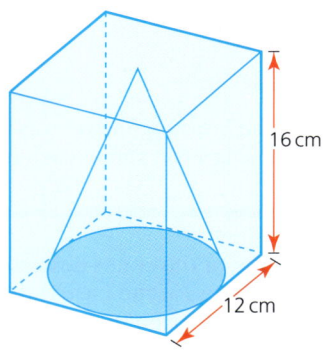

3 An ice cream consists of half a sphere and a cone.

   Calculate its total volume, give your answer in terms of π.

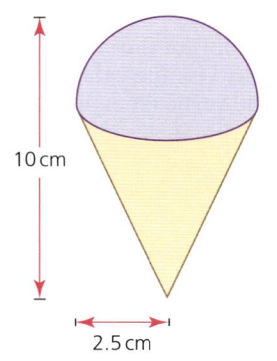

The surface area of a cone

4 A cone is placed on top of a cylinder.
Using the dimensions given, calculate the total volume of the shape.

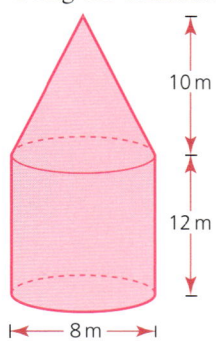

10 m
12 m
8 m

5 A large cone is made of solid metal and has a base diameter of 16 cm and a height of 24 cm.
A small cone, with a base diameter of 4 cm is removed from the top of the large cone.
  a Calculate the height of the smaller cone.
  b Calculate the volume of the smaller cone.
  c If the bottom part of the large cone is melted down, how many of the smaller cones could be made from it?

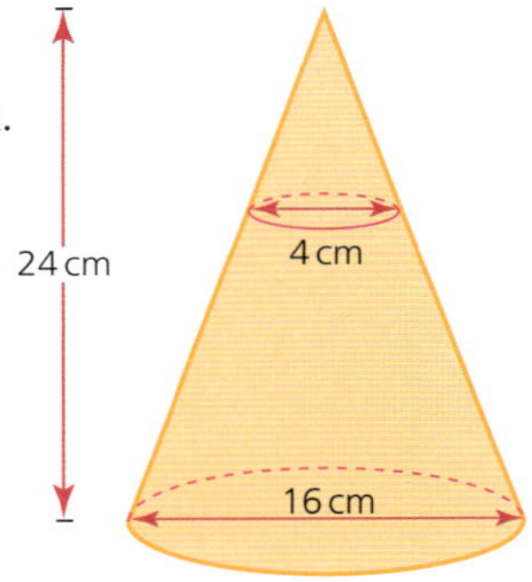

24 cm, 4 cm, 16 cm

6 Two cones, A and B, are placed either end of a cylindrical tube as shown. Given that the volumes of A and B are in the ratio 2 : 1, calculate:
  a the volume of cone A 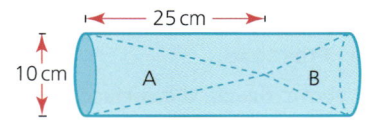
  b the height of cone B
  c the volume of the cylinder.

25 cm, 10 cm

The surface area of a cone

The surface area of a cone comprises the area of the circular base and the area of the curved face. The area of the curved face is equal to the area of the sector from which it is formed.

➔ Worked example

Calculate the total surface area of the cone.

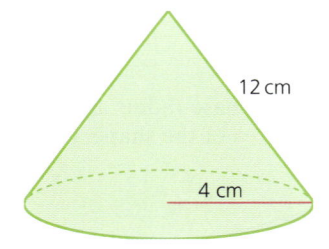

12 cm
4 cm

Surface area of base = $\pi r^2 = 16\pi \text{ cm}^2$

263

23 PERIMETER, AREA AND VOLUME

The curved surface area can best be visualised if drawn as a sector as shown in the diagram. The radius of the sector is equivalent to the slant height of the cone. The curved perimeter of the sector is equivalent to the base circumference of the cone.

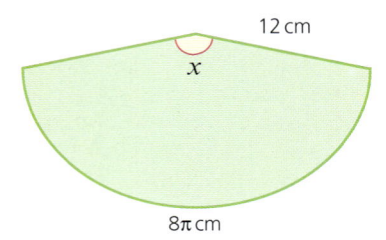

$$\frac{x}{360} = \frac{8\pi}{24\pi}$$

Therefore $x = 120°$

Area of sector = $\frac{120}{360} \times \pi \times 12^2 = 48\pi \, \text{cm}^2$

Total surface area = $48\pi + 16\pi$

$= 64\pi$

$= 201$ (3 s.f.)

The total surface area is 201 cm².

The area of the sector was calculated to be $60\pi \, \text{cm}^2$. This is therefore also the area of the curved surface of the cone.

The curved surface of a cone can also be calculated using the formula Area = $\pi r l$, where r represents the radius of the circular base and l represents the slant length of the cone.

In the example above, the curved surface area = $\pi \times 5 \times 12$

$= 64\pi \, \text{cm}^2$

Exercise 23.24

Note
"Give your answers in exact form" means you need to provide them in terms of π.

1 Calculate the total surface area of the cones. Give your answers in exact form.

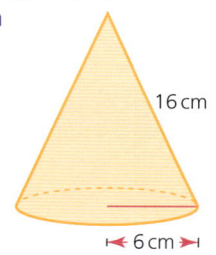

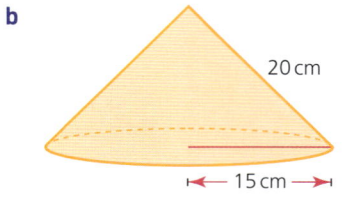

   a 16 cm, 6 cm

   b 20 cm, 15 cm

2 Two cones with the same base radius are stuck together as shown. Calculate the surface area of the shape, giving your answer in exact form.

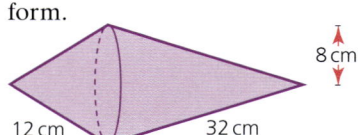

   12 cm, 32 cm, 8 cm

Student assessment 1

1. A rowing lake, rectangular in shape, is 2.5 km long by 500 m wide. Calculate the surface area of the water in km².

2. A rectangular floor 12 m long by 8 m wide is to be covered in ceramic tiles 40 cm long by 20 cm wide.
   a Calculate the number of tiles required to cover the floor.
   b The tiles are bought in boxes of 18 at a cost of $30 per box. What is the cost of the tiles needed to cover the floor if only whole boxes can be bought?

3. A flower bed is in the shape of a right-angled triangle of sides 3 m, 4 m and 5 m. Sketch the flower bed, and calculate its area and perimeter.

4. A drawing of a building shows a rectangle 50 cm high and 10 cm wide with a triangular tower 20 cm high and 10 cm wide at the base on top of it. Find the area of the drawing of the building.

5. The squares of a chessboard are each of side 7.5 cm. What is the area of the chessboard?

Student assessment 2

1. Calculate the circumference and area of each of the following circles. Give your answers to 1 d.p.
   a 5.5 cm
   b 16 mm

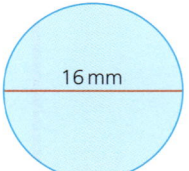

2. A semi-circular shape is cut out of the side of a rectangle as shown. Calculate the shaded area to 3 s.f.

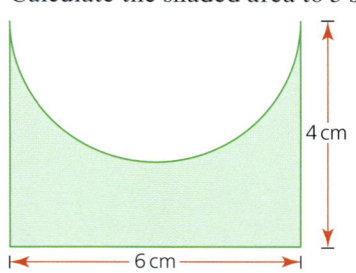

   4 cm
   6 cm

23 PERIMETER, AREA AND VOLUME

3 For the shape shown in the diagram, calculate the area of:
  a the semi-circle   **b** the trapezium
  c the whole shape.

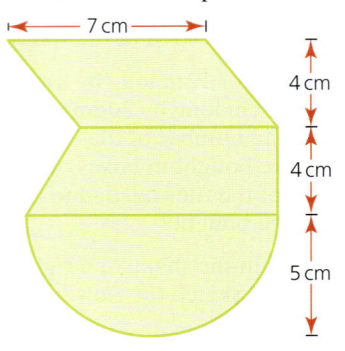

4 A cylindrical tube has an inner diameter of 6 cm, an outer diameter of 7 cm and a length of 15 cm.

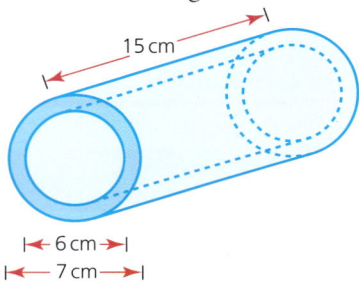

Calculate the following to 3 s.f.:
  a the surface area of the shaded end
  b the inside surface area of the tube
  c the total surface area of the tube.

5 Calculate the volume of each of the following cylinders:
  a 3 mm, 12 mm   **b** 2.5 cm, 2 cm

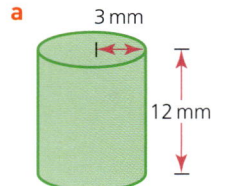

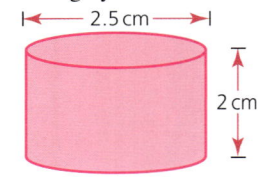

6 The diagram below shows the net of a right-angled triangular prism.

Calculate:
a the surface area of the prism
b the volume of the prism.

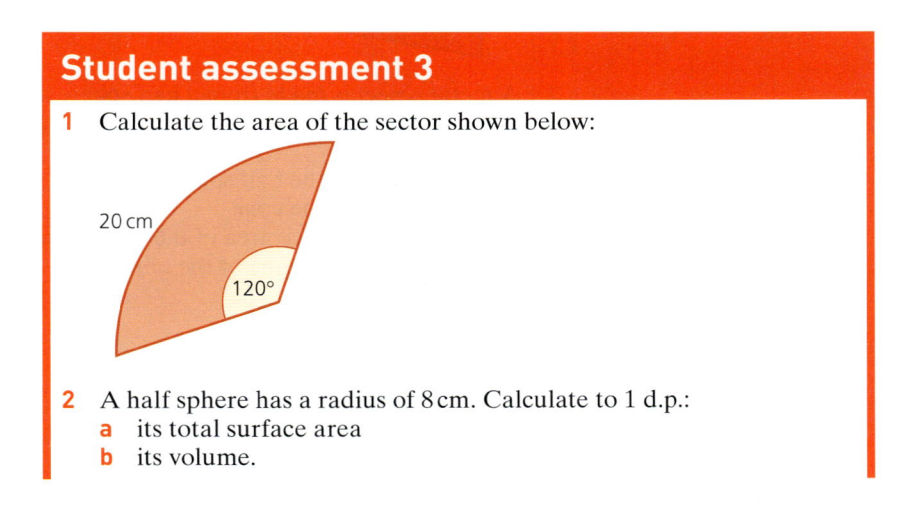

Student assessment 3

1 Calculate the area of the sector shown below:

2 A half sphere has a radius of 8 cm. Calculate to 1 d.p.:
a its total surface area
b its volume.

23 PERIMETER, AREA AND VOLUME

3 A large cone has a small cone cut from its top as shown.
   a Show that the vertical height of the small cone is 7.5 cm.
   b Calculate the volume of the truncated cone.

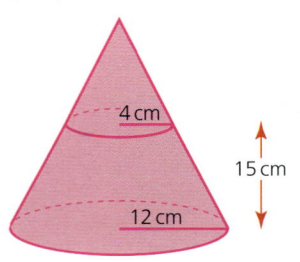

4 The prism has a cross-sectional area in the shape of a sector. Calculate:
   a the radius r cm
   b the cross-sectional area of the prism
   c the total surface area of the prism
   d the volume of the prism.

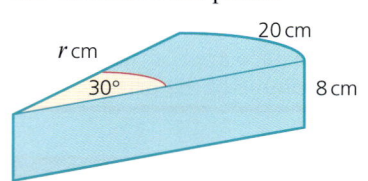

5 A metal object is made from a half sphere and a cone, both of base radius 12 cm. The height of the object when upright is 36 cm. Calculate:
   a the volume of the half sphere
   b the volume of the cone
   c the curved surface area of the half sphere
   d the total surface area of the object.

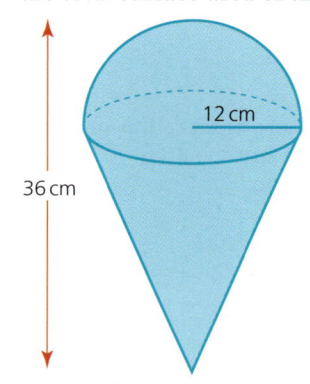

Mathematical investigations and ICT 5

Metal trays

A rectangular sheet of metal measures 30 cm by 40 cm.

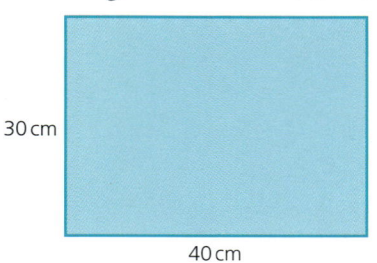

The sheet has squares of equal size cut from each corner. It is then folded to form a metal tray as shown.

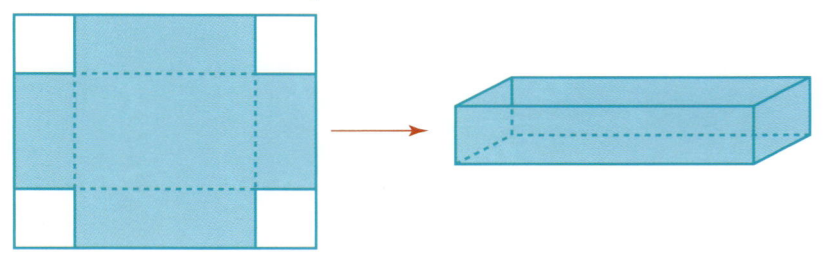

1. **a** Calculate the length, width and height of the tray if a square of side length 1 cm is cut from each corner of the sheet of metal.
   b Calculate the volume of this tray.

2. **a** Calculate the length, width and height of the tray if a square of side length 2 cm is cut from each corner of the sheet of metal.
   b Calculate the volume of this tray.

3. Using a spreadsheet if necessary, investigate the relationship between the volume of the tray and the size of the square cut from each corner. Enter your results in an ordered table.

4. Calculate, to 1 d.p., the side length of the square that produces the tray with the greatest volume.

5. State the greatest volume to the nearest whole number.

TOPIC 6

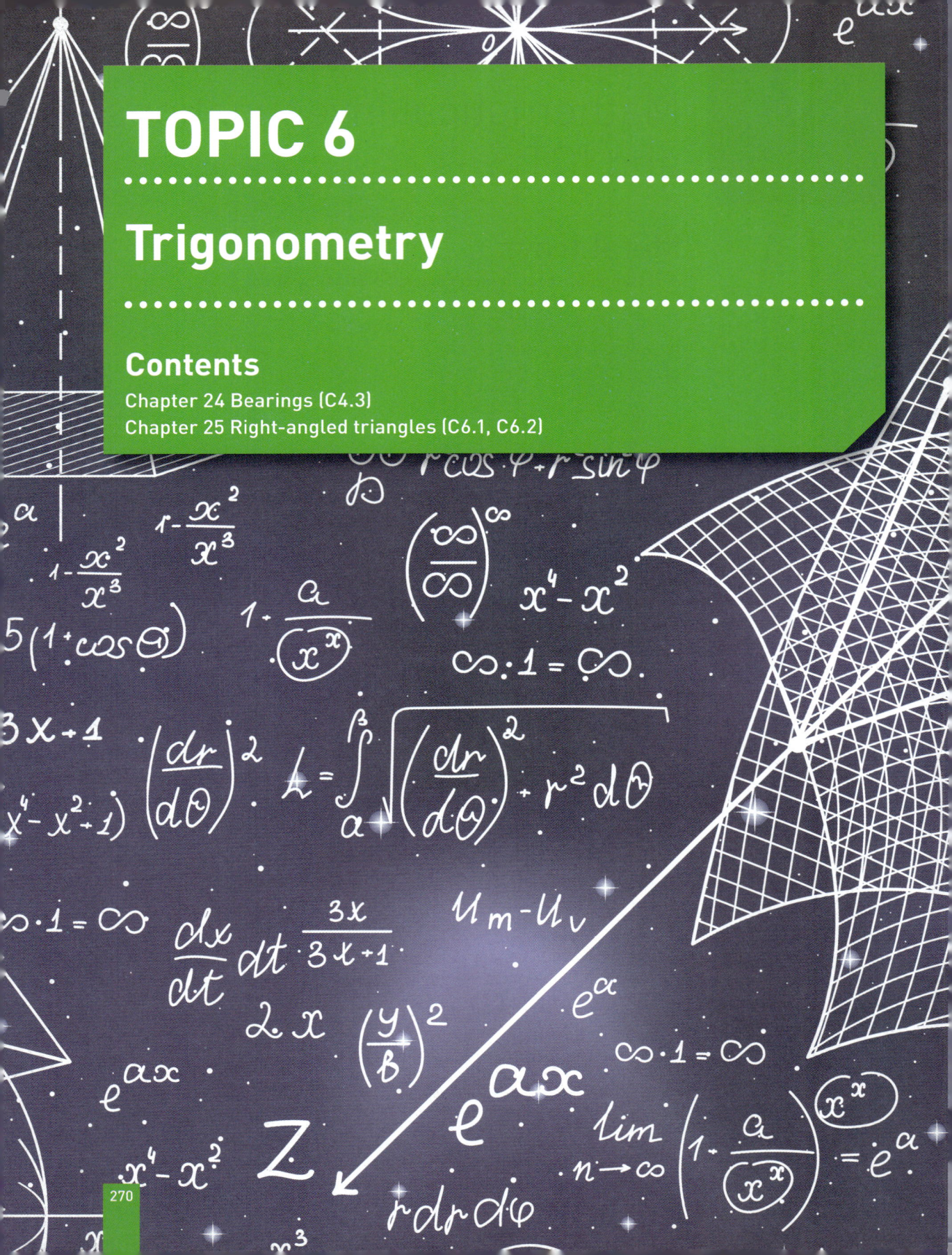

Trigonometry

Contents

Chapter 24 Bearings (C4.3)
Chapter 25 Right-angled triangles (C6.1, C6.2)

Learning objectives

C4.3
1. Draw and interpret scale drawings.
2. Use and interpret three-figure bearings.

C6.1
Know and use Pythagoras' theorem.

C6.2
1. Know and use the sine, cosine and tangent ratios for acute angles in calculations involving sides and angles of a right-angled triangle.
2. Solve problems in two dimensions using Pythagoras' theorem and trigonometry.

The development of trigonometry

In about 2000BC, astronomers in Sumer in ancient Mesopotamia introduced angle measure. They divided the circle into 360 degrees. They and the ancient Babylonians studied the ratios of the sides of similar triangles. They discovered some properties of these ratios. However, they did not develop these into a method for finding sides and angles of triangles – what we now call trigonometry.

The ancient Greeks, among them Euclid and Archimedes, developed trigonometry further. They studied the properties of chords in circles and produced proofs of the trigonometric formulae we use today.

The modern sine function was first defined in an ancient Hindu text, the *Surya Siddhanta*, and further work was done by the Indian mathematician and astronomer Aryabhata in the fifth century.

By the tenth century, Islamic mathematicians were using all six trigonometric functions (sine, cosine, tangent and their reciprocals). They made tables of trigonometric values and were applying them to problems in the geometry of the sphere.

Aryabhata (476–550)

As late as the sixteenth century, trigonometry was not well known in Europe. Nicolaus Copernicus decided it was necessary to explain the basic concepts of trigonometry in his book to enable people to understand his theory that the Earth went around the Sun.

Soon after, however, the need for accurate maps of large areas for navigation meant that trigonometry grew into a major branch of mathematics.

24 Bearings

> **Note**
> All diagrams are not drawn to scale.

Bearings

In the days when sailing ships travelled the oceans of the world, compass bearings like the ones in the diagram (below) were used.

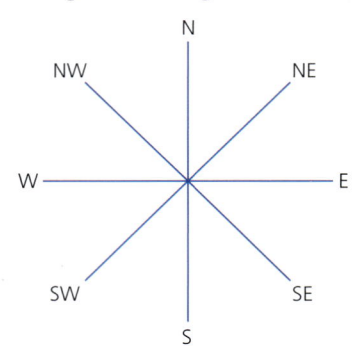

As the need for more accurate direction arose, extra points were added to N, E, S, W, NE, SE, SW and NW. Midway between north and north-east was north-north-east, and midway between north-east and east was east-north-east, and so on. This gave 16 points of the compass. This was later extended even further, eventually to 64 points.

As the speed of travel increased, a new system was required. The new system was the **three-figure bearing** system. North was given the **bearing** zero. 360° in a clockwise direction was one full rotation.

Exercise 24.1

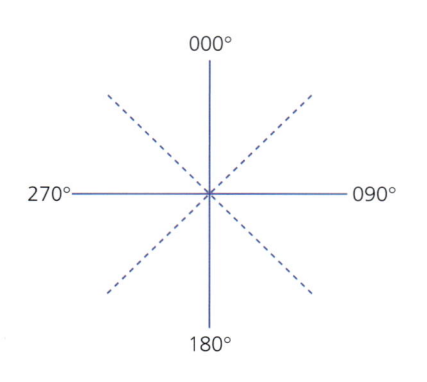

1. Copy the three-figure bearing diagram (left). On your diagram, mark the bearings for the compass points north-east, south-east, south-west and north-west.

2. Draw diagrams to show the following compass bearings and journeys. Use a scale of 1 cm : 1 km. North can be taken to be a line vertically up the page.
   a. Start at point A. Travel 7 km on a bearing of 135° to point B. From B, travel 12 km on a bearing of 250° to point C. Measure the distance and bearing of A from C.
   b. Start at point P. Travel 6.5 km on a bearing of 225° to point Q. From Q, travel 7.8 km on a bearing of 105° to point R. From R, travel 8.5 km on a bearing of 090° to point S. What are the distance and bearing of P from S?
   c. Start from point M. Travel 11.2 km on a bearing of 270° to point N. From point N, travel 5.8 km on a bearing of 170° to point O. What are the bearing and distance of M from O?

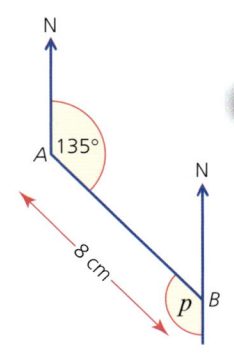

Back bearings

Worked examples

1 The bearing of B from A is 135° and the distance from A to B is 8 cm, as shown. The bearing of A from B is called the **back bearing**.

Since the two north lines are parallel:

$p = 135°$ (alternate angles), so the back bearing is $(180 + 135)°$.

That is, 315°.

Note: There are a number of methods of solving this type of problem.

2 The bearing of B from A is 245°. What is the bearing of A from B?

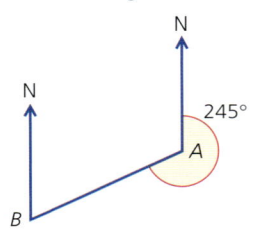

Since the two north lines are parallel:

$b = (245 - 180)° = 65°$ (alternate angles), so the bearing is 065°.

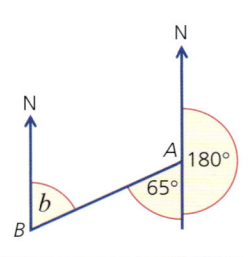

Exercise 24.2

Note
A diagram may help you answer these questions.

1 Given the following bearings of point B from point A, draw diagrams and use them to **calculate** the bearing of A from B.
   a bearing 130°
   b bearing 145°
   c bearing 220°
   d bearing 200°
   e bearing 152°
   f bearing 234°
   g bearing 163°
   h bearing 214°

2 Given the following bearings of point D from point C, draw diagrams and use them to **calculate** the bearing of C from D.
   a bearing 300°
   b bearing 320°
   c bearing 290°
   d bearing 282°

24 BEARINGS

Student assessment 1

1. From the top of a tall building in a town it is possible to see five towns. The bearing and distance of each one are given in the table:

Town	Distance (km)	Bearing
Bourn	8	070°
Catania	12	135°
Deltaville	9	185°
Etta	7.5	250°
Freetown	11	310°

Choose an appropriate scale and draw a diagram to show the position of each town. What are the distance and bearing of the following?
   a Bourn from Deltaville
   b Etta from Catania

2. A coastal radar station picks up a distress call from a ship. It is 50 km away on a bearing of 345°. The radar station contacts a lifeboat at sea which is 20 km away on a bearing of 220°.
Make a scale drawing and use it to find the distance and bearing of the ship from the lifeboat.

3. A climber gets to the top of Mont Blanc. He can see in the distance a number of ski resorts. He uses his map to find the bearing and distance of the resorts, and records them in a table:

Resort	Distance (km)	Bearing
Val d'Isère	30	082°
Les Arcs	40	135°
La Plagne	45	205°
Méribel	35	320°

Choose an appropriate scale and draw a diagram to show the position of each resort. What are the distance and bearing of the following?
   a Val d'Isère from La Plagne
   b Méribel from Les Arcs

4. An aircraft is seen on radar at airport X. The aircraft is 210 km away from the airport on a bearing of 065°. The aircraft is diverted to airport Y, which is 130 km away from airport X on a bearing of 215°. Use an appropriate scale and make a scale drawing to find the distance and bearing of airport Y from the aircraft.

25 Right-angled triangles

> **Note**
> All diagrams are not drawn to scale.

Trigonometric ratios

There are three basic trigonometric ratios: **sine**, **cosine** and **tangent**.

Each of these relates an angle of a right-angled triangle to a ratio of the lengths of two of its sides.

The sides of the triangle have names, two of which are dependent on their position in relation to a specific angle.

The longest side (always opposite the right angle) is called the **hypotenuse**. The side opposite the angle is called the **opposite** side and the side next to the angle is called the **adjacent** side.

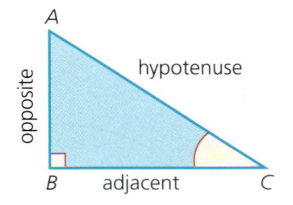

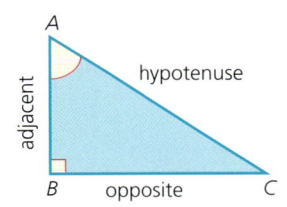

Note that, when the chosen angle is at A, the sides labelled opposite and adjacent change (above right).

Tangent

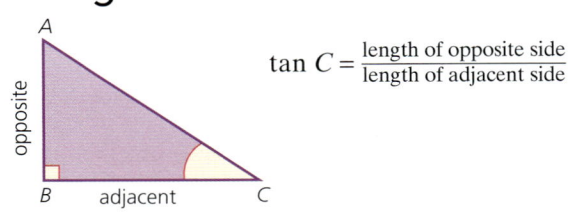

$$\tan C = \frac{\text{length of opposite side}}{\text{length of adjacent side}}$$

275

25 RIGHT-ANGLED TRIANGLES

→ Worked examples

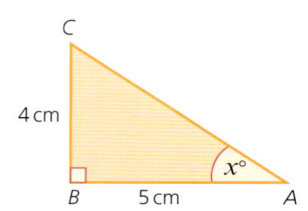

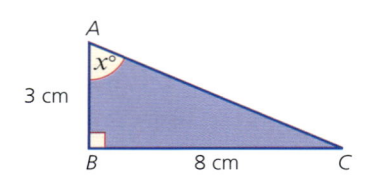

1 Calculate the size of angle BAC in each triangle.

Triangle 1: $\tan x = \dfrac{\text{opposite}}{\text{adjacent}} = \dfrac{4}{5}$

$x = \tan^{-1}\left(\dfrac{4}{5}\right)$

$x = 38.7$ (3 s.f.)

angle $BAC = 38.7°$ (3 s.f.)

Triangle 2: $\tan x = \dfrac{8}{3}$

$x = \tan^{-1}\left(\dfrac{8}{3}\right)$

$x = 69.4$ (1 d.p.)

angle $BAC = 69.4°$ (1 d.p.)

Answers to angles should be given to one decimal place, unless stated otherwise.

2 Calculate the length of the opposite side QR (right).

$\tan 42° = \dfrac{p}{6}$

$6 \times \tan 42° = p$

$p = 5.40$ (3 s.f.)

$QR = 5.40$ cm (3 s.f.)

3 Calculate the length of the adjacent side XY.

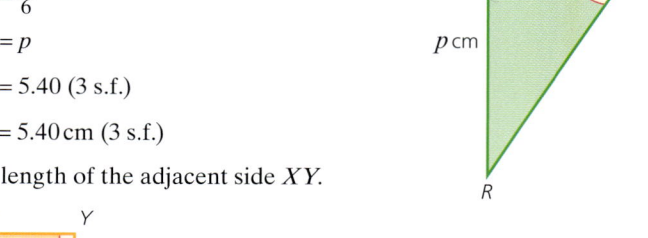

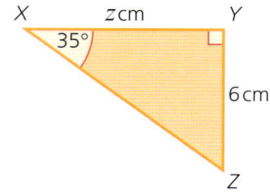

$\tan 35° = \dfrac{6}{z}$

$z \times \tan 35° = 6$

$z = \dfrac{6}{\tan 35°}$

$z = 8.57$ (3 s.f.)

$XY = 8.57$ cm (3 s.f.)

Tangent

Exercise 25.1 Calculate the length of the side marked x cm in each of the diagrams in Q.1 and 2. Give your answers to 1 d.p.

1 a Triangle ABC, right angle at B, angle 20° at A, AB = 5 cm, BC = x cm.

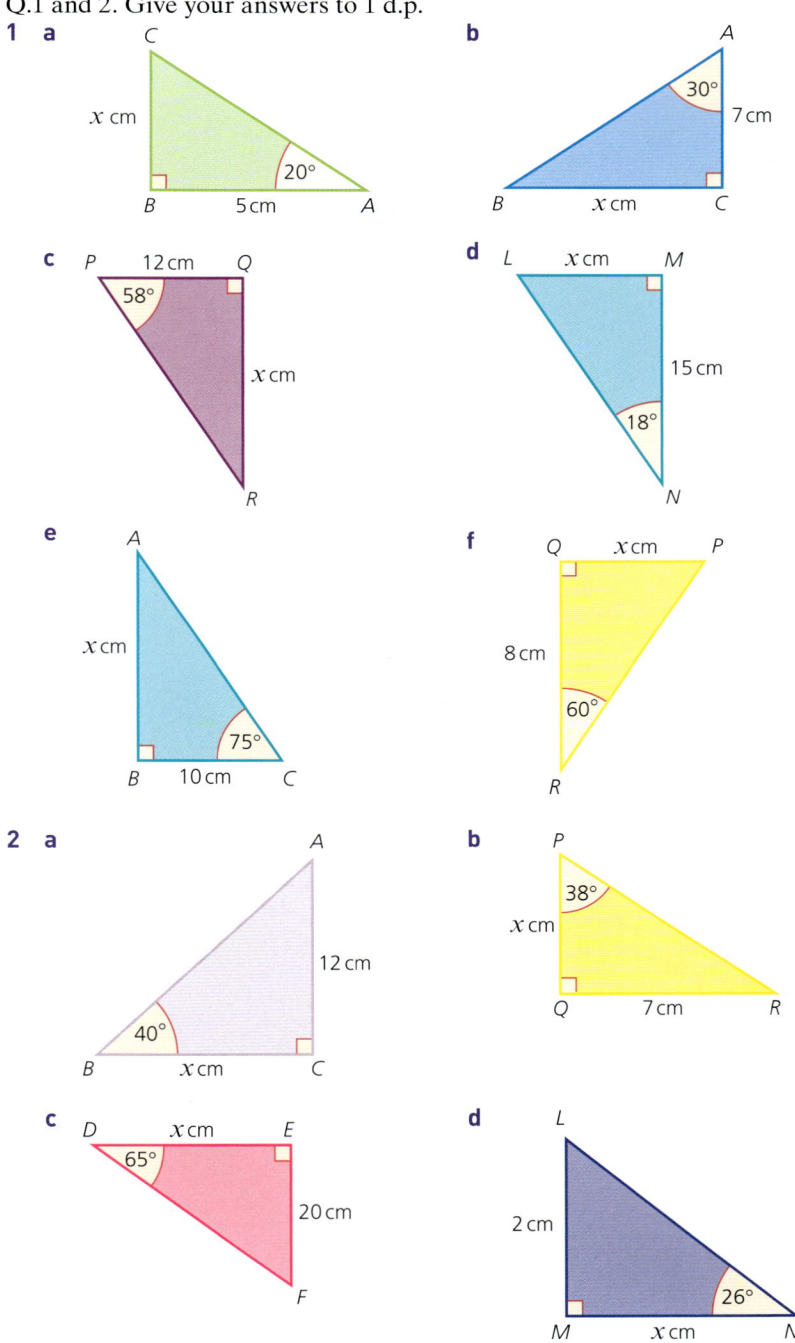

b Triangle ABC, right angle at C, angle 30° at A, AC = 7 cm, BC = x cm.

c Triangle PQR, right angle at Q, angle 58° at P, PQ = 12 cm, QR = x cm.

d Triangle LMN, right angle at M, angle 18° at N, MN = 15 cm, LM = x cm.

e Triangle ABC, right angle at B, angle 75° at C, BC = 10 cm, AB = x cm.

f Triangle QPR, right angle at Q, angle 60° at R, QR = 8 cm, QP = x cm.

2 a Triangle ABC, right angle at C, angle 40° at B, AC = 12 cm, BC = x cm.

b Triangle PQR, right angle at Q, angle 38° at P, QR = 7 cm, PQ = x cm.

c Triangle DEF, right angle at E, angle 65° at D, DE = x cm, EF = 20 cm.

d Triangle LMN, right angle at M, angle 26° at N, LM = 2 cm, MN = x cm.

Exercise 25.1 (cont)

e

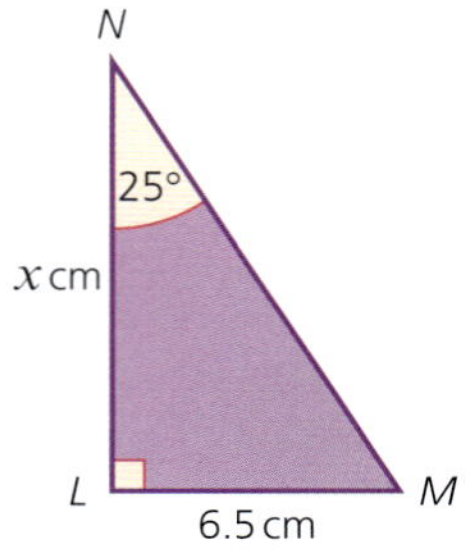

f

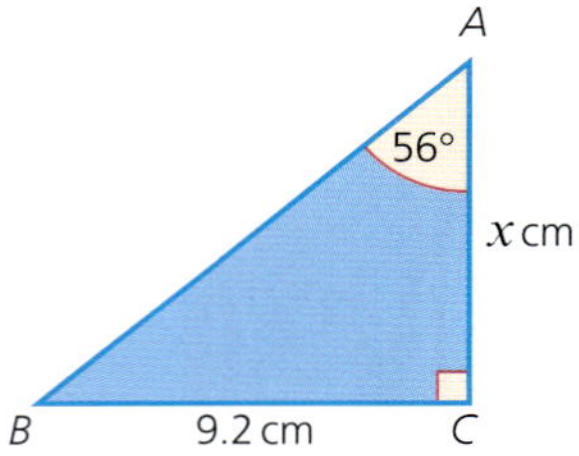

3 Calculate the size of the marked angle $x°$ in each diagram. Give your answers to 1 d.p.

a

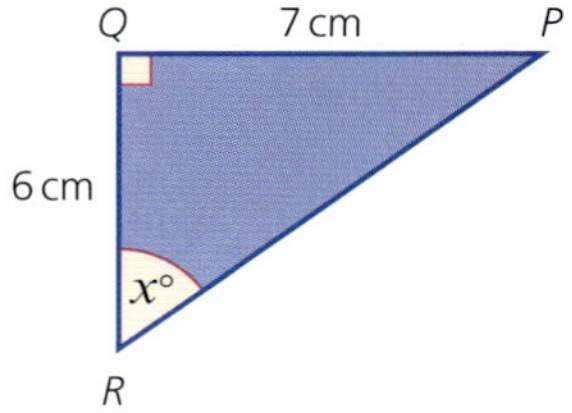

b

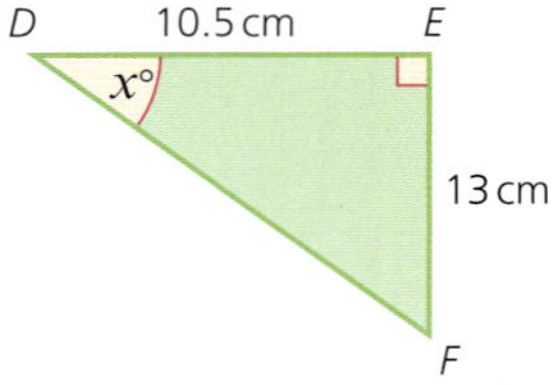

c

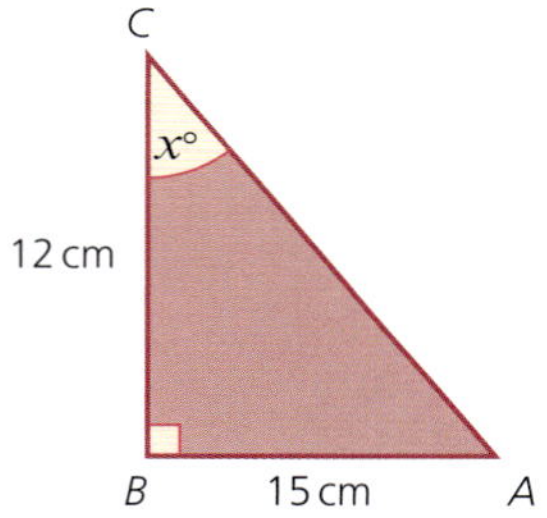

d

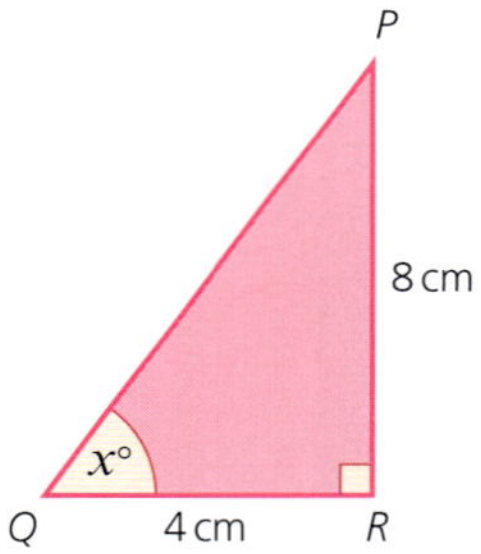

e

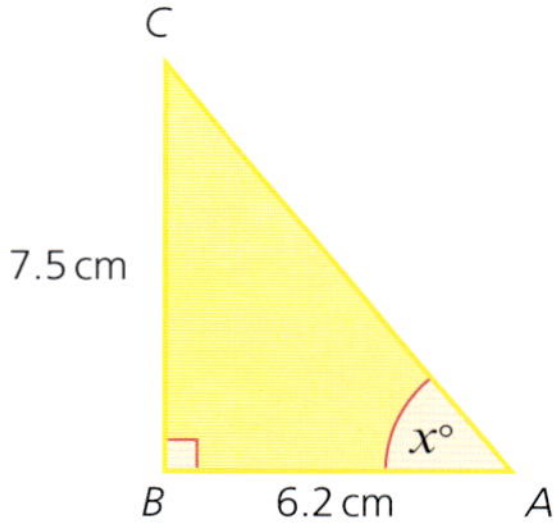

f

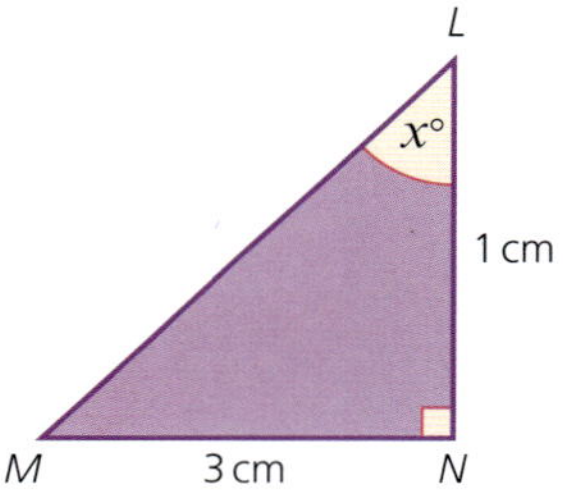

Sine

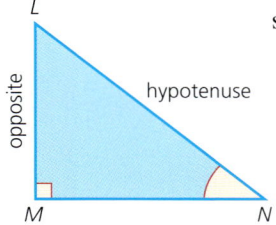

$$\sin N = \frac{\text{length of opposite side}}{\text{length of hypotenuse}}$$

→ Worked examples

1 Calculate the size of angle BAC.

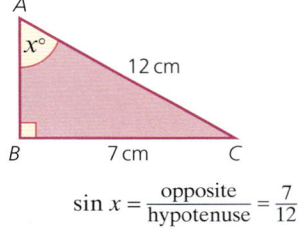

$$\sin x = \frac{\text{opposite}}{\text{hypotenuse}} = \frac{7}{12}$$

$$x = \sin^{-1}\left(\frac{7}{12}\right)$$

$$x = 35.7 \text{ (1 d.p.)}$$

angle $BAC = 35.7°$ (1 d.p.)

2 Calculate the length of the hypotenuse PR.

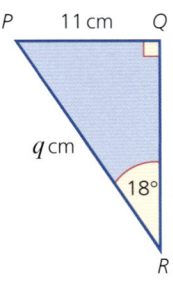

$$\sin 18° = \frac{11}{q}$$

$$q \times \sin 18° = 11$$

$$q = \frac{11}{\sin 18°}$$

$$q = 35.6 \text{ (3 s.f.)}$$

$PR = 35.6$ cm (3 s.f.)

25 RIGHT-ANGLED TRIANGLES

Exercise 25.2

1. Calculate the length of the marked side in each diagram. Give your answers to 1 d.p.

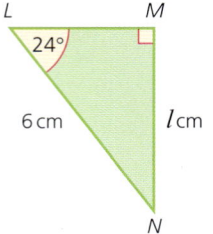

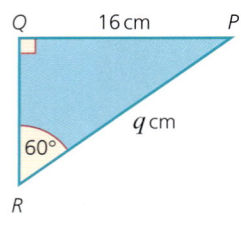

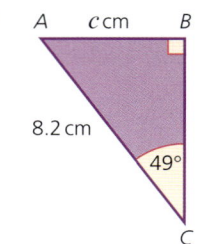

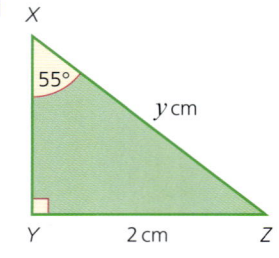

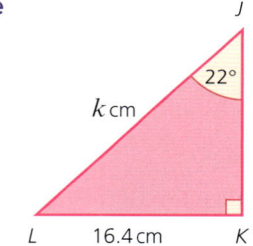

   a Triangle LMN with right angle at M, angle 24° at L, LN = 6 cm, MN = l cm.

   b Triangle QPR with right angle at Q, QP = 16 cm, angle 60° at R, RP = q cm.

   c Triangle ABC with right angle at B, AC = 8.2 cm, angle 49° at C, AB = c cm.

   d Triangle XYZ with right angle at Y, angle 55° at X, YZ = 2 cm, XZ = y cm.

   e Triangle JKL with right angle at K, angle 22° at J, LK = 16.4 cm, JL = k cm.

   f Triangle ABC with right angle at B, AC = 45 cm, angle 45° at C, AB = c cm.

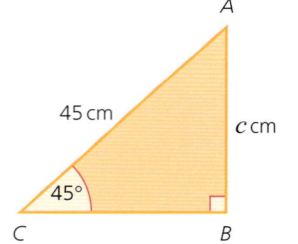

2. Calculate the size of the angle marked $x°$ in each diagram. Give your answers to 1 d.p.

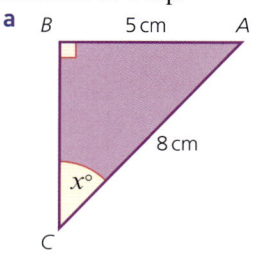

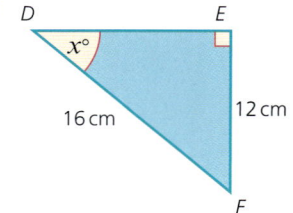

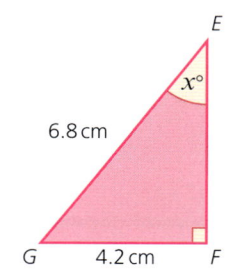

   a Triangle ABC with right angle at B, BA = 5 cm, CA = 8 cm, angle $x°$ at C.

   b Triangle DEF with right angle at E, angle $x°$ at D, DF = 16 cm, EF = 12 cm.

   c Triangle EFG with right angle at F, GE = 6.8 cm, GF = 4.2 cm, angle $x°$ at E.

   d Triangle LMN with right angle at L, LM = 7.1 cm, MN = 9.3 cm, angle $x°$ at N.

280

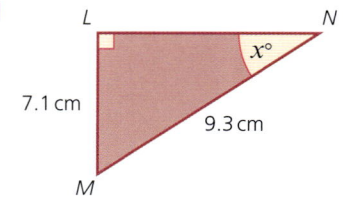

Exercise 25.2 (cont)

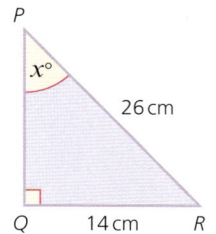

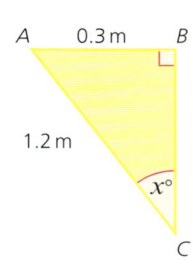

e [Triangle PQR with right angle at Q, PR = 26 cm, QR = 14 cm, angle x° at P]

f [Triangle ABC with right angle at B, AB = 0.3 m, BC = 1.2 m, angle x° at C]

Cosine

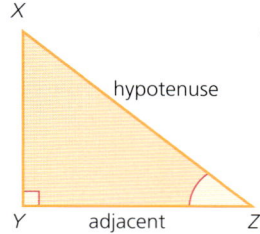

$$\cos Z = \frac{\text{length of adjacent side}}{\text{length of hypotenuse}}$$

[Triangle XYZ with right angle at Y, hypotenuse XZ, adjacent YZ]

→ Worked examples

1 Calculate the length XY.

$\cos 62° = \dfrac{\text{adjacent}}{\text{hypotenuse}} = \dfrac{z}{20}$

$z = 20 \times \cos 62°$

$z = 9.39$ (3 s.f.)

$XY = 9.39$ cm (3 s.f.)

[Triangle XYZ with right angle at Y, angle 62° at X, XZ = 20 cm, XY = z cm]

2 Calculate the size of angle ABC.

$\cos x = \dfrac{5.3}{12}$

$x = \cos^{-1}\left(\dfrac{5.3}{12}\right)$

$x = 63.8$ (1 d.p.)

angle $ABC = 63.8°$ (1 d.p.)

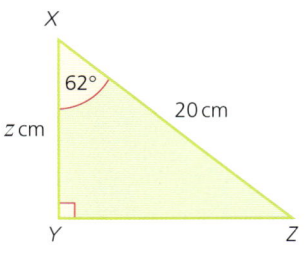

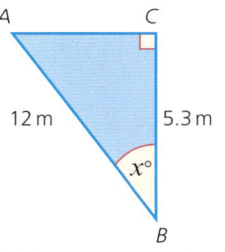

[Triangle ABC with right angle at C, AB = 12 m, CB = 5.3 m, angle x° at B]

281

25 RIGHT-ANGLED TRIANGLES

Exercise 25.3 Calculate the marked side or angle in each diagram. Give your answers to 1 d.p.

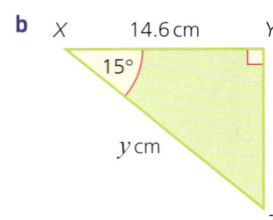

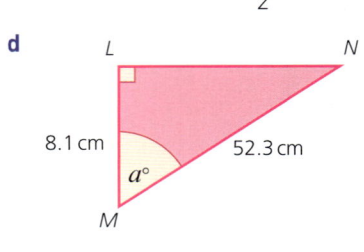

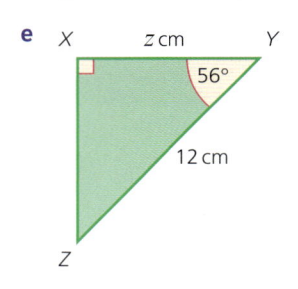

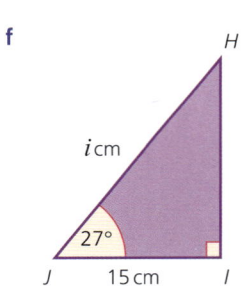

a Triangle ABC, right angle at B, AC = 40 cm, angle C = 26°, BC = a cm

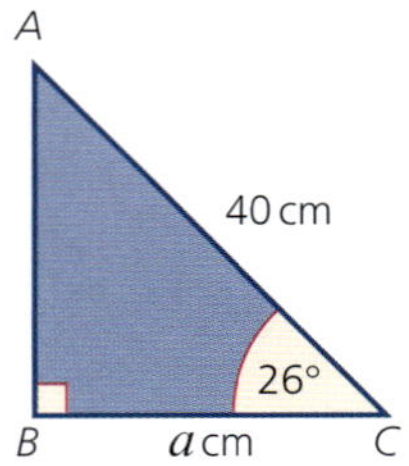

b Triangle XYZ, right angle at Y, XY = 14.6 cm, angle X = 15°, XZ = y cm

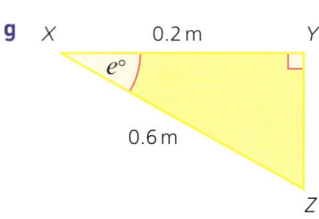

c Triangle EFG, right angle at F, EF = 12 cm, EG = 18 cm, angle E = $x°$

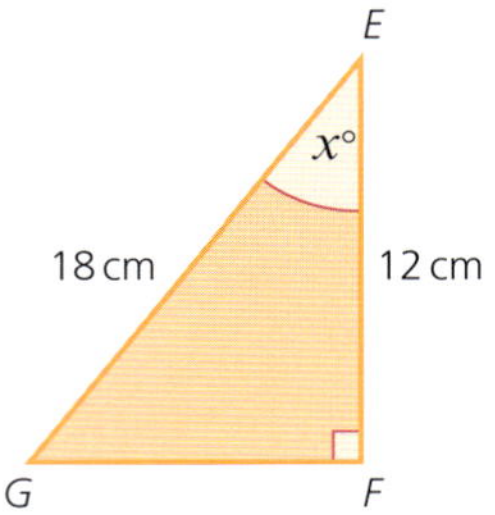

d Triangle LMN, right angle at L, LM = 8.1 cm, MN = 52.3 cm, angle M = $a°$

e Triangle XYZ, right angle at X, XY = z cm, angle Y = 56°, YZ = 12 cm

f Triangle HIJ, right angle at I, HJ = i cm, angle J = 27°, JI = 15 cm

g Triangle XYZ, right angle at Y, XY = 0.2 m, YZ = 0.6 m, angle X = $e°$

h Triangle ABC, right angle at C, AB = 13.7 cm, angle B = 81°, BC = a cm

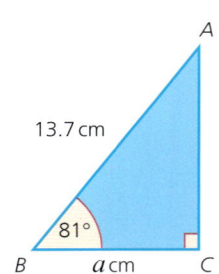

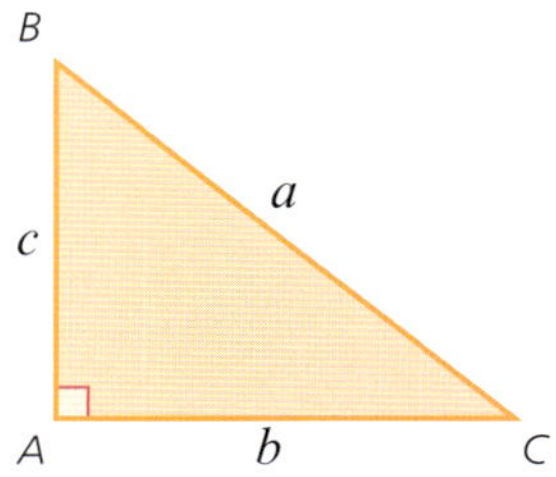

Pythagoras' theorem

Pythagoras' theorem states the relationship between the lengths of the three sides of a right-angled triangle.

Pythagoras' theorem states that:

$$a^2 = b^2 + c^2$$

Pythagoras' theorem

→ Worked examples

1 Calculate the length of the side BC.

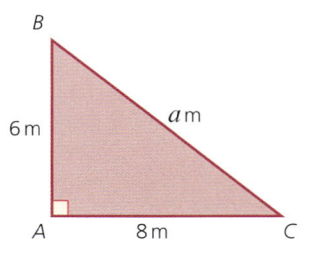

Using Pythagoras:

$a^2 = b^2 + c^2$

$a^2 = 8^2 + 6^2$

$a^2 = 64 + 36 = 100$

$a = \sqrt{100}$

$a = 10$

$BC = 10\,\text{m}$

2 Calculate the length of the side AC.

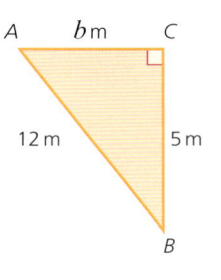

Using Pythagoras:

$a^2 = b^2 + c^2$

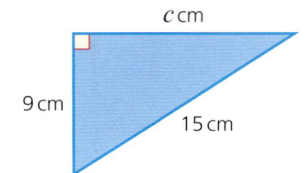

$12^2 = b^2 + 5^2$

$b^2 = 12^2 - 5^2$ $b = \sqrt{119}$

$= 144 - 25$ $b = 10.9$ (3 s.f.)

$= 119$ $AC = 10.9\,\text{m}$ (3 s.f.)

Exercise 25.4

In each of the diagrams in Q.1 and 2, use Pythagoras' theorem to calculate the length of the marked side.

1 a (4 cm, 3 cm, a cm)

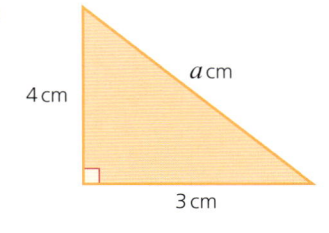

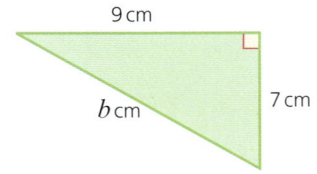

b (9 cm, 7 cm, b cm)

c (9 cm, 15 cm, c cm)

d (20 cm, 15 cm, d cm)

283

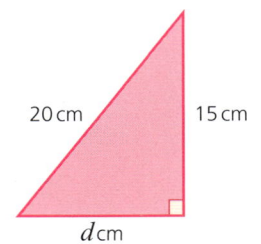

25 RIGHT-ANGLED TRIANGLES

Exercise 25.4 (cont)

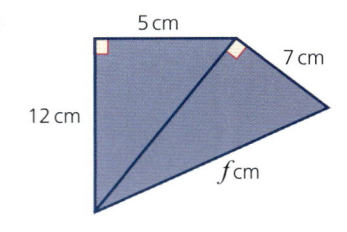

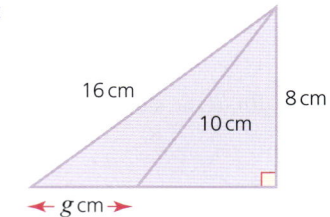

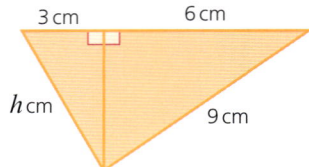

2 a) [Quadrilateral with sides 4 cm, 9 cm, 5 cm and diagonal e cm, with right angles shown]

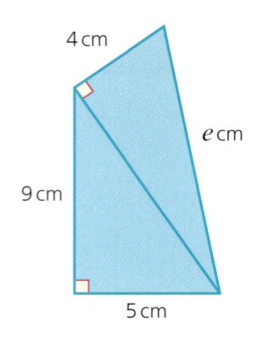

b) [Quadrilateral with sides 5 cm, 7 cm, 12 cm and diagonal f cm, with right angles shown]

c) [Triangle with 16 cm, 10 cm, 8 cm and base g cm]

d) [Triangle with 3 cm, 6 cm, 9 cm and h cm]

e) [Triangle with 4 cm, 8 cm, 12 cm and k cm]

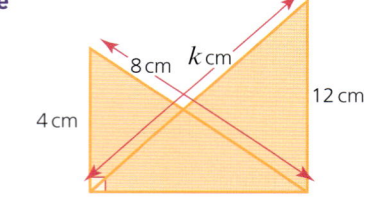

3 Villages *A*, *B* and *C* lie on the edge of the Namib desert. Village *A* is 30 km due north of village *C*. Village *B* is 65 km due east of *A*.

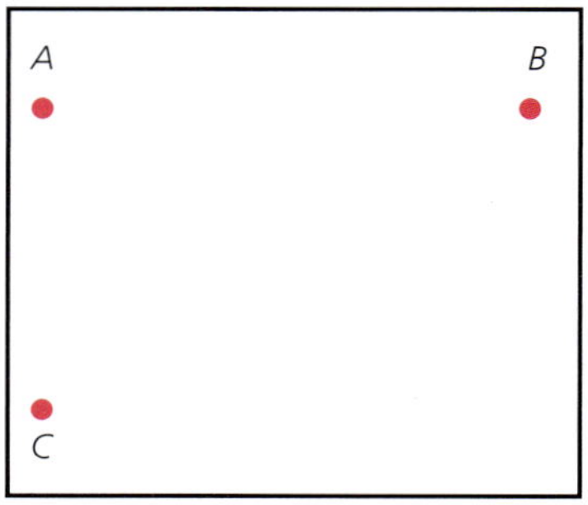

Calculate the shortest distance between villages *C* and *B*, giving your answer to the nearest 0.1 km.

4 Town *X* is 54 km due west of town *Y*. The shortest distance between town *Y* and town *Z* is 86 km. If town *Z* is due south of *X*, calculate the distance between *X* and *Z*, giving your answer to the nearest kilometre.

Pythagoras' theorem

5 Village *B* (below) is on a bearing of 135° and at a distance of 40 km from village *A*. Village *C* is on a bearing of 225° and at a distance of 62 km from village *A*.

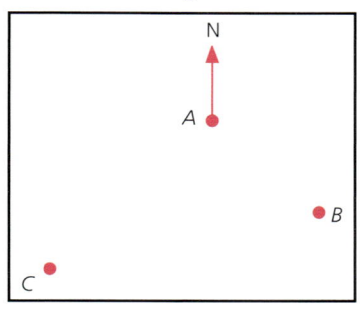

  a Show that triangle *ABC* is right-angled.
  b Calculate the distance from *B* to *C*, giving your answer to the nearest 0.1 km.

6 Two boats set off from *X* at the same time. Boat *A* sets off on a bearing of 325° and with a velocity of 14 km/h. Boat B sets off on a bearing of 235° and with a velocity of 18 km/h.

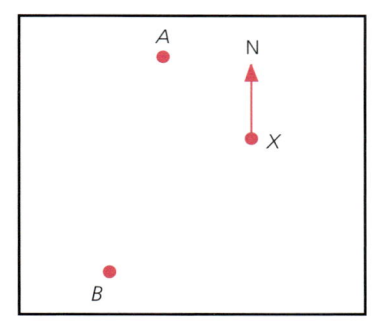

Calculate the distance between the boats after they have been travelling for 2.5 hours. Give your answer to the nearest kilometre.

7 A boat sets off on a trip from *S*. It heads towards *B*, a point 6 km away and due north. At *B* it changes direction and heads towards point *C*, also 6 km away and due east of *B*. At *C* it changes direction once again and heads on a bearing of 135° towards *D* which is 13 km from *C*.
  a Calculate the distance between *S* and *C* to the nearest 0.1 km.
  b Calculate the distance the boat will have to travel if it is to return to *S* from *D*.

8 Two trees are standing on flat ground. The height of the smaller tree is 7 m. The distance between the top of the smaller tree and the base of the taller tree is 15 m.
The distance between the top of the taller tree and the base of the smaller tree is 20 m.

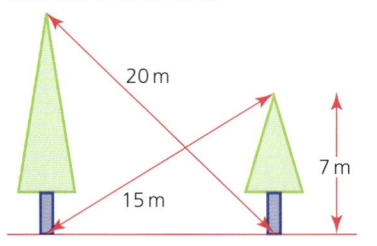

Calculate the height of the taller tree.

285

25 RIGHT-ANGLED TRIANGLES

Exercise 25.5

For the whole of Exercise 25.5, give your answers to 1 d.p.

1. By using Pythagoras' theorem, trigonometry or both, calculate the marked value in each diagram.

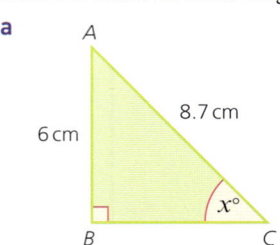

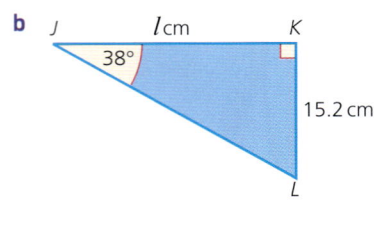

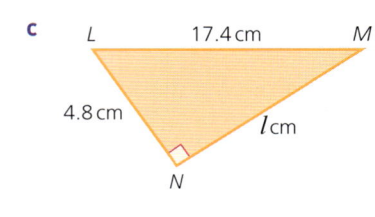

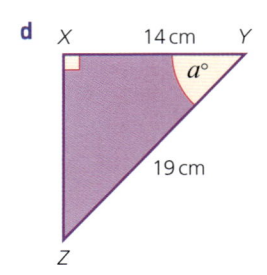

   a Triangle ABC with right angle at B, AB = 6 cm, AC = 8.7 cm, angle at C = $x°$.

   b Triangle JKL with right angle at K, JK = l cm, KL = 15.2 cm, angle at J = 38°.

   c Triangle LMN with right angle at N, LM = 17.4 cm, LN = 4.8 cm, MN = l cm.

   d Triangle XYZ with right angle at X, XY = 14 cm, YZ = 19 cm, angle at Y = $a°$.

2. The following triangles (not drawn to scale) have dimensions as shown.

   i prove whether they are right-angled triangles or not

   ii if a triangle is right-angled calculate the size of the angle marked $x°$

   a Triangle with sides 25 mm, 60 mm, 65 mm, angle $x°$ between the 25 mm and 65 mm sides.

   b Triangle with sides 21 mm, 28 mm, 34 mm, angle $x°$ between the 28 mm and 34 mm sides.

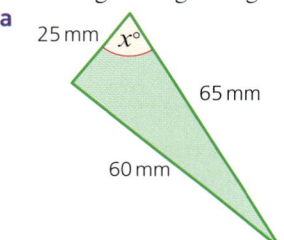

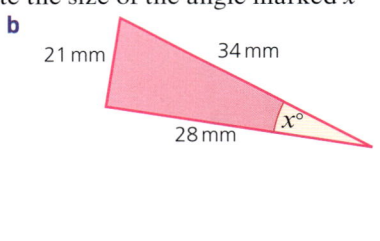

3. A sailing boat sets off from a point X and heads towards Y, a point 17 km north. At point Y it changes direction and heads towards point Z, a point 12 km away on a bearing of 090°. Once at Z the crew want to sail back to X. Calculate:

   a the distance ZX

   b the bearing of X from Z.

Pythagoras' theorem

4 An aeroplane sets off from *G* on a bearing of 024° towards *H*, a point 250 km away.

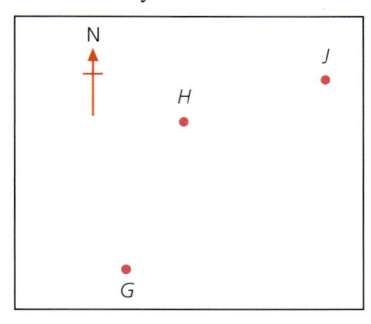

At *H* it changes course and heads towards *J* on a bearing of 055° and a distance of 180 km away.

- **a** How far is *H* to the north of *G*?
- **b** How far is *H* to the east of *G*?
- **c** How far is *J* to the north of *H*?
- **d** How far is *J* to the east of *H*?
- **e** What is the shortest distance between *G* and *J*?
- **f** What is the bearing of *G* from *J*?

5 Two trees are standing on flat ground. The angle of elevation of their tops from a point *X* on the ground is 40°. The horizontal distance between *X* and the small tree is 8 m and the distance between the tops of the two trees is 20 m.

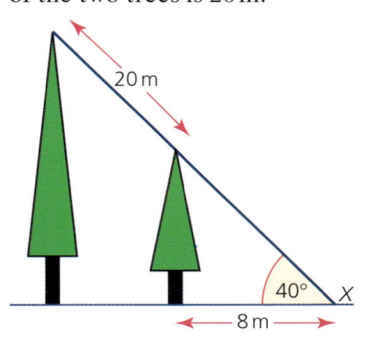

Calculate the horizontal distance between the trees.

6 *PQRS* is a quadrilateral. The sides *RS* and *QR* are the same length. The sides *QP* and *RS* are parallel.

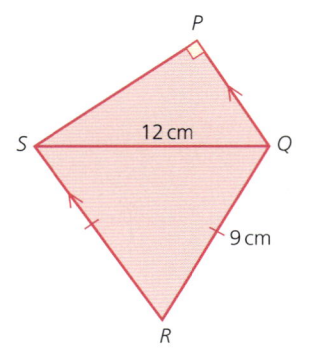

Calculate:
- **a** angle *SQR*
- **b** length *PQ*
- **c** the area of *PQRS*.

287

25 RIGHT-ANGLED TRIANGLES

Student assessment 1

1. Calculate the length of the side marked with a letter in each diagram. Give your answers correct to 1 d.p.

   a. Right-angled triangle with legs 12 cm and 16 cm, hypotenuse a cm.

   b. Right-angled triangle with legs 12.5 cm and 30 cm, hypotenuse b cm.

   c. Right-angled triangle with hypotenuse 1.5 cm, one leg 1.2 cm, other leg c cm.

   d. Right-angled triangle with one leg 7.5 cm, hypotenuse 19.5 cm, other leg d cm.

   e. Isosceles triangle with two equal sides 15 cm, base 15 cm, height e cm.

Pythagoras' theorem

2 Calculate the size of the angle marked $x°$ in each diagram. Give your answers correct to the nearest degree.

a [triangle with 15 cm, 9 cm, angle $x°$ at top, right angle at right]

b [triangle with 4.2 cm, 6.3 cm, angle $x°$ at top left, right angle at bottom left]

c [triangle with 3 cm (top), 5 cm (left), right angle at top left, angle $x°$ at bottom]

d [triangle with 14.8 cm, 12.3 cm, angle $x°$ at right, right angle at bottom left]

3 Calculate the length of the side marked q cm in each diagram. Give your answers correct to 1 d.p.

a [right triangle with legs 3 cm and 4 cm, hypotenuse q cm]

b [right triangle with 10 cm, 12 cm, q cm]

c [triangle with 3 cm, 6 cm, 65°, right angle, q cm]

d [figure with 48 cm, 18 cm, 25°, q cm]

4 A rectangular rug measures 3.9 m by 2.4 m. Calculate the distance between the opposite corners. Give your answer correct to 3 s.f.

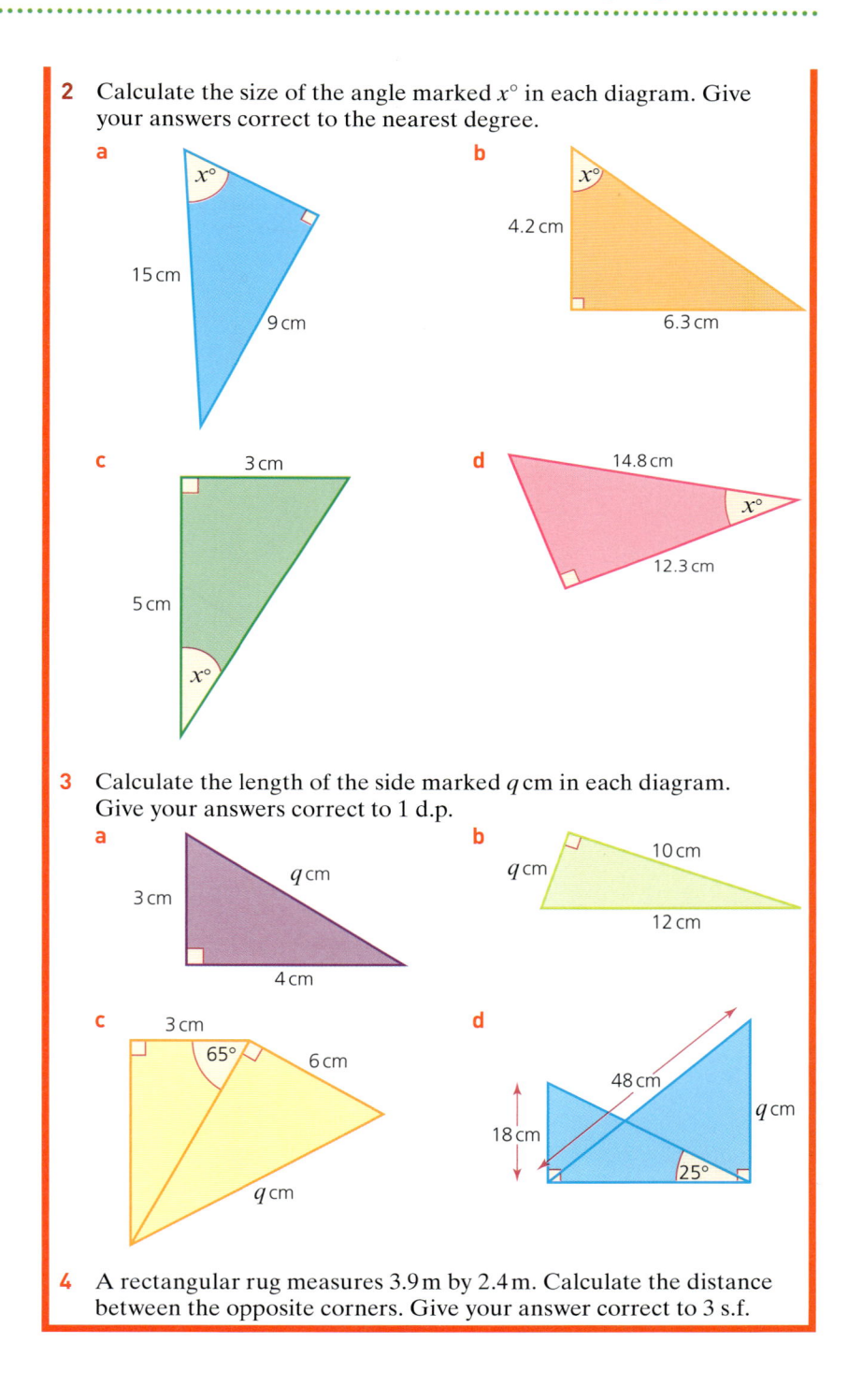

25 RIGHT-ANGLED TRIANGLES

Student assessment 2

1. A map shows three towns A, B and C. Town A is due north of C. Town B is due east of A. The distance AC is 75 km and the bearing of C from B is 245°. Calculate, giving your answers to the nearest 100 m:
   a the distance AB
   b the distance BC.

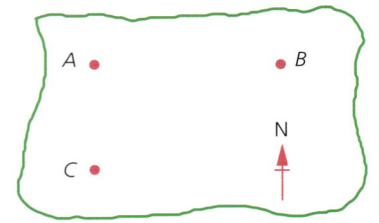

2. Two trees stand 16 m apart. Their tops make an angle of $x°$ at point A on the ground.

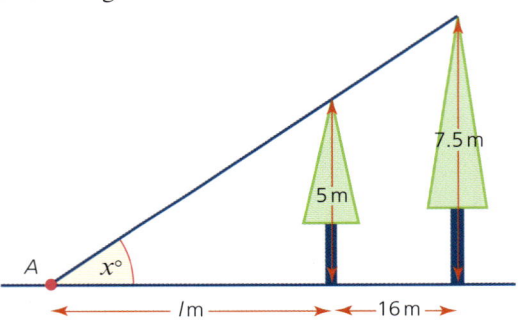

   a Calculate the value of l.
   b Calculate the value of x.

3. Two boats, X and Y, sailing in a race, are shown in the diagram:

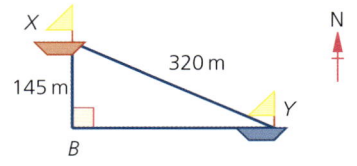

   Boat X is 145 m due north of a buoy B. Boat Y is due east of buoy B. Boats X and Y are 320 m apart. Calculate:
   a the distance BY
   b the bearing of Y from X
   c the bearing of X from Y.

Mathematical investigations and ICT 6

Pythagoras and circles

The explanation for Pythagoras' theorem usually shows a right-angled triangle with squares drawn on each of its three sides, as in the diagram.

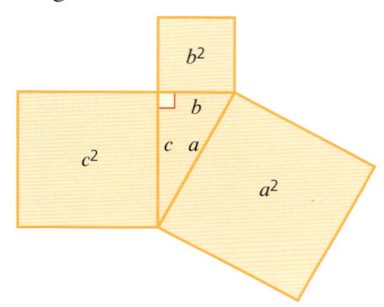

In this example, the area of the square on the hypotenuse, a^2, is equal to the sum of the areas of the squares on the other two sides, $b^2 + c^2$.

This gives the formula $a^2 = b^2 + c^2$.

1. Draw a right-angled triangle.

2. Using a pair of compasses, construct a semi-circle off each side of the triangle. Your diagram should look similar to the one below.

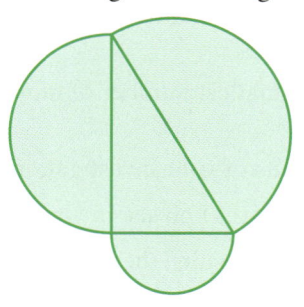

3. By measuring the diameter of each semi-circle, calculate their areas.

4. Is the area of the semi-circle on the hypotenuse the sum of the areas of the semi-circles drawn on the other two sides? Does Pythagoras' theorem still hold for semi-circles?

5. Does Pythagoras' theorem still hold if equilateral triangles are drawn on each side?

6. Investigate for other regular polygons.

MATHEMATICAL INVESTIGATIONS AND ICT 6

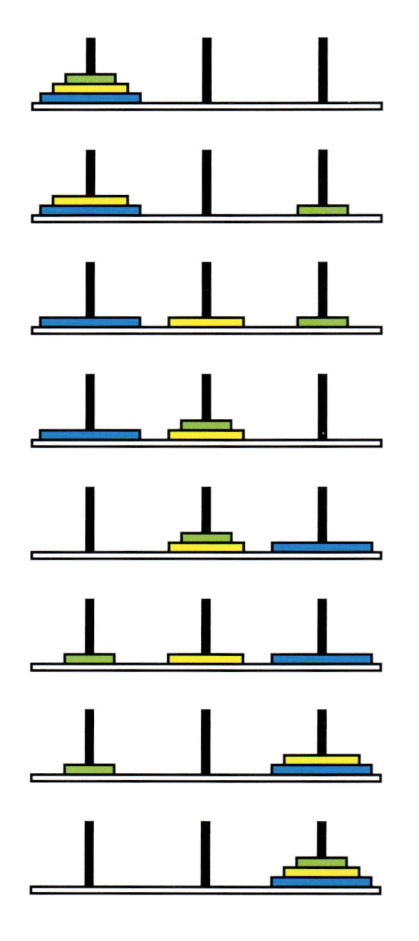

Towers of Hanoi

This investigation is based on an old Vietnamese legend. The legend is as follows:

> At the beginning of time, a temple was created by the Gods. Inside the temple stood three giant rods. On one of these rods, 64 gold discs, all of different diameters, were stacked in descending order of size, i.e. the largest at the bottom rising to the smallest at the top. Priests at the temple were responsible for moving the discs onto the remaining two rods until all 64 discs were stacked in the same order on one of the other rods. When this task was completed, time would cease and the world would come to an end.

The discs however could only be moved according to certain rules. These were:
- Only one disc could be moved at a time.
- A disc could only be placed on top of a larger one.

The diagrams (left) show the smallest number of moves required to transfer three discs from the rod on the left to the rod on the right.

With three discs, the smallest number of moves is seven.

1. What is the smallest number of moves needed for two discs?

2. What is the smallest number of moves needed for four discs?

3. Investigate the smallest number of moves needed to move different numbers of discs.

4. Display the results of your investigation in an ordered table.

5. Describe any patterns you see in your results.

6. Predict, from your results, the smallest number of moves needed to move ten discs.

7. Determine a formula for the smallest number of moves for n discs.

8. Assume the priests have been transferring the discs at the rate of one per second and assume the Earth is approximately 4.54 billion years old (4.54×10^9 years). According to the legend, is the world coming to an end soon? Justify your answer with relevant calculations.

Pythagorean triples

The triangle below is a right-angled triangle because $3^2 + 4^2 = 5^2$.

The numbers 3, 4 and 5 are known as a Pythagorean triple.

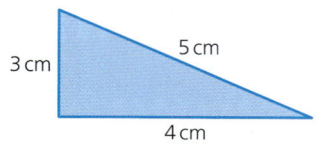

1 Can you find two more Pythagorean triples?

2 Using the internet as a research tool, research Pythagorean triples and write a short report about what you have found out.

TOPIC 7

Vectors and transformations

Contents

Chapter 26 Transformations (C7.1)

Learning objectives

C7.1
Recognise, describe and draw the following transformations:
1. Reflection of a shape in a vertical or horizontal line.
2. Rotation of a shape about the origin, vertices or midpoints of edges of the shape, through multiples of 90°.
3. Enlargement of a shape from a given centre by a given scale factor.
4. Translation of a shape by a given vector $\begin{pmatrix} x \\ y \end{pmatrix}$.

The development of vectors

The study of vectors arose from coordinates in two dimensions. Around 1636, René Descartes and Pierre de Fermat founded analytic geometry by linking the solutions to an equation with two variables with points on a curve.

In 1804, Czech mathematician Bernhard Bolzano worked on the mathematics of points, lines and planes and his work formed the beginnings of work on vectors. Later in the nineteenth century, this was further developed by German mathematician August Möbius and Italian mathematician Giusto Bellavitis.

Bernhard Bolzano (1781–1848)

26 Transformations

An object undergoing a **transformation** changes in either position or shape. In its simplest form, this change can occur because of a **reflection**, **rotation**, **translation** or **enlargement**. When an object undergoes a transformation, its new position or shape is called the **image**.

Reflection

When an object is reflected, it undergoes a 'flip' movement about a dashed (broken) line known as the **mirror line**, as shown in the diagram.

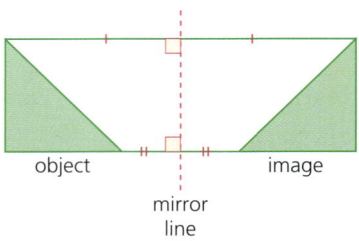

A point on the object and its equivalent point on the image are equidistant from the mirror line. This distance is measured at right angles to the mirror line. The line joining the point to its image is perpendicular to the mirror line.

Exercise 26.1

For questions 1–5, copy each diagram and draw the object's image under reflection in the dashed line(s).

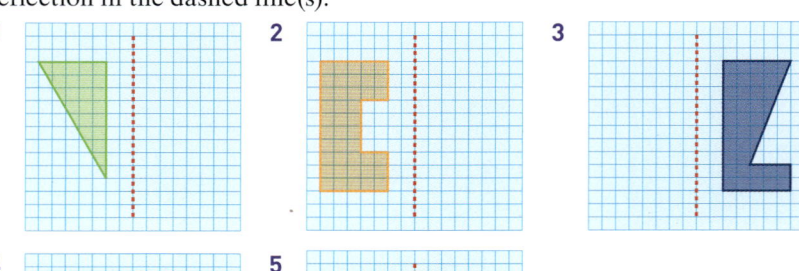

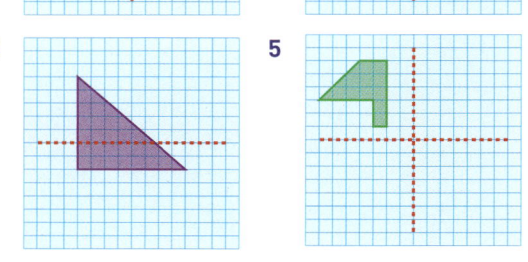

1

2

3

4

5

Rotation

Exercise 26.2 For questions 1–3, copy each diagram and draw the position of the mirror line(s).

1.

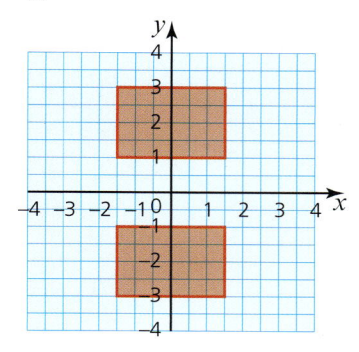

2.

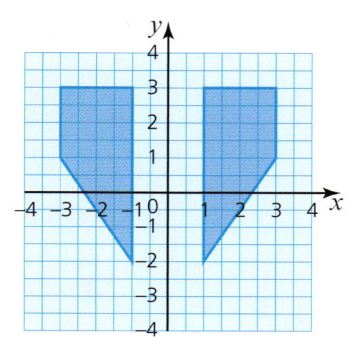

3.

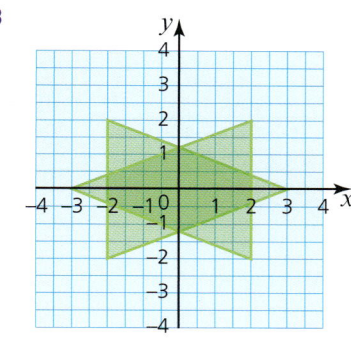

Rotation

When an object is rotated, it undergoes a 'turning' movement about a specific point known as the **centre of rotation**. To describe a rotation, it is necessary to identify not only the position of the centre of rotation but also the angle and direction of the turn, as shown in the diagram (right).

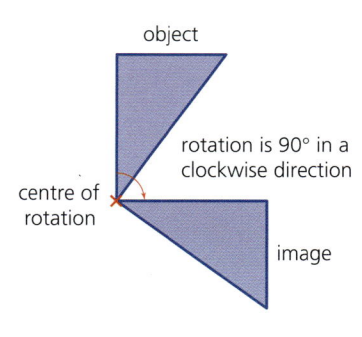

Exercise 26.3 For questions 1–6, the object and centre of rotation have been given. Copy each diagram and draw the object's image under the stated rotation about the marked point.

1. rotation 180°

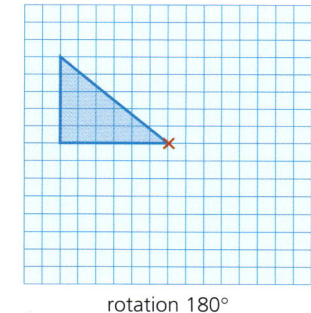

2. rotation 90° clockwise

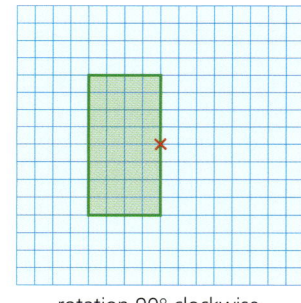

26 TRANSFORMATIONS

Exercise 26.3 (cont)

3 rotation 180°

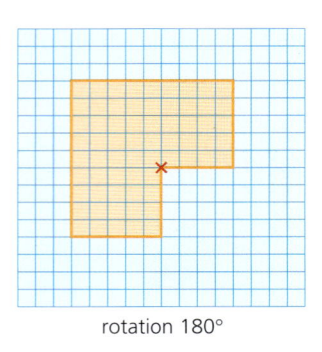

4 rotation 90° clockwise

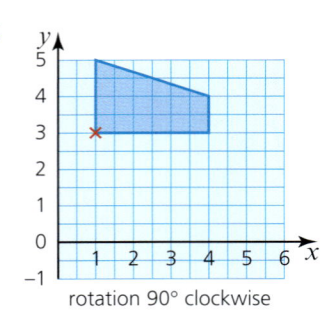

5 rotation 90° anticlockwise

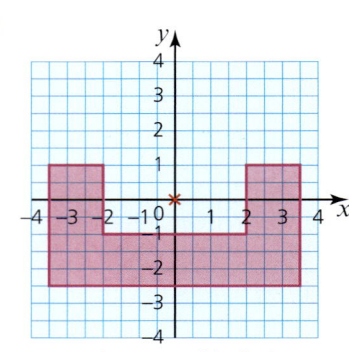

6 rotation 90° clockwise

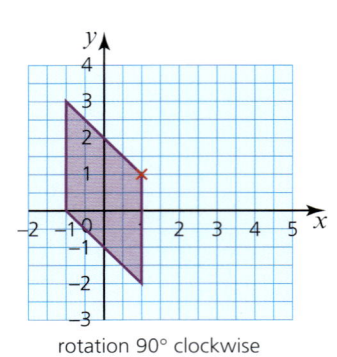

Exercise 26.4

For questions 1–6, the object (unshaded) and image (shaded) have been drawn. Copy each diagram, then:
  a mark the centre of rotation
  b calculate the angle and direction of rotation.

1

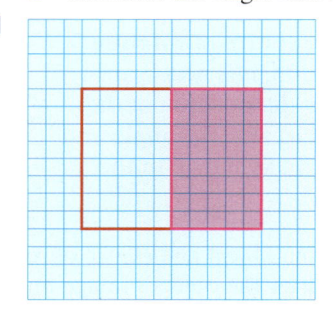

2

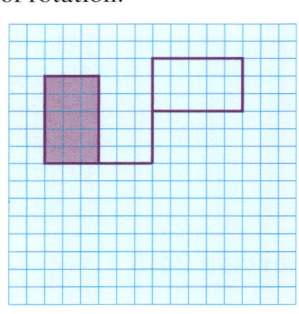

3

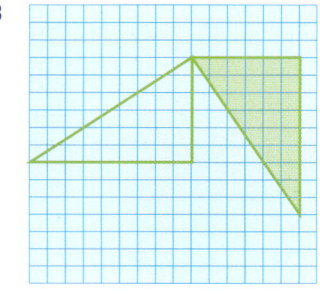

4

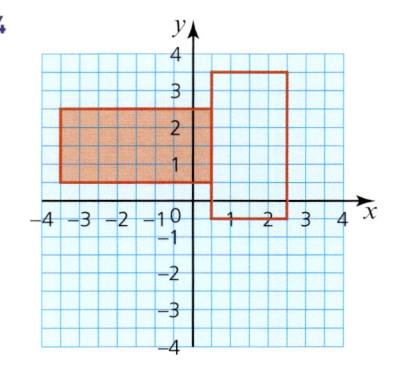

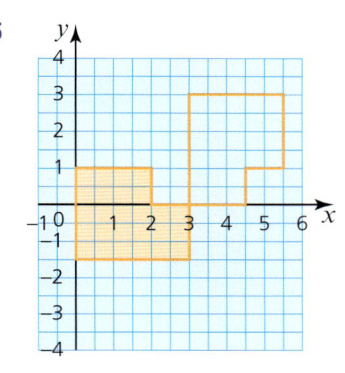

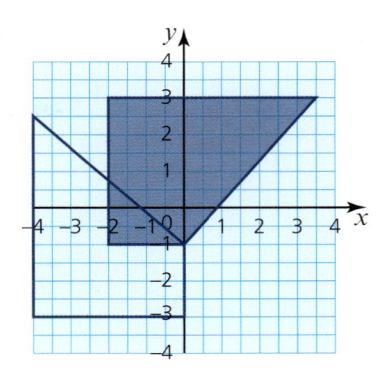

Translation

When an object is translated, it undergoes a 'straight sliding' movement. To describe a translation, it is necessary to give the **translation vector**. As no rotation is involved, each point on the object moves in the same way to its corresponding point on the image, e.g.:

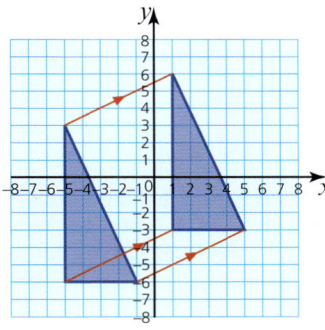

Vector = $\begin{pmatrix} 6 \\ 3 \end{pmatrix}$

Vector = $\begin{pmatrix} -4 \\ 5 \end{pmatrix}$

The translation vector consists of two numbers arranged vertically, one above the other.

The top number indicates how far the object moves horizontally and the bottom number indicates how far it moves vertically, i.e. $\begin{pmatrix} x \\ y \end{pmatrix}$.

Like coordinates, a positive *x*-value represents a horizontal move to the right, whilst a negative *x*-value represents a horizontal move to the left.

A positive *y*-value represents a vertical move to the upwards, whilst a negative *y*-value represents a vertical move downwards.

26 TRANSFORMATIONS

Exercise 26.5 For questions 1–4, object A has been translated to each of images B and C. Give the translation vectors in each case.

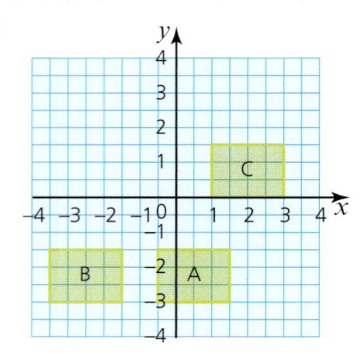

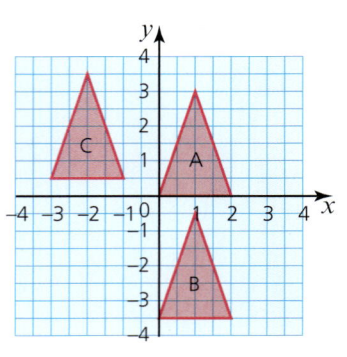

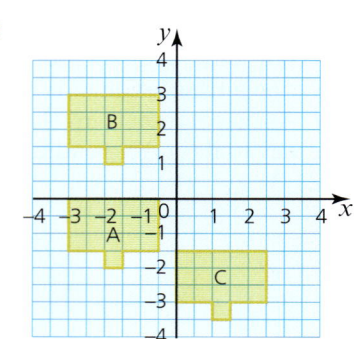

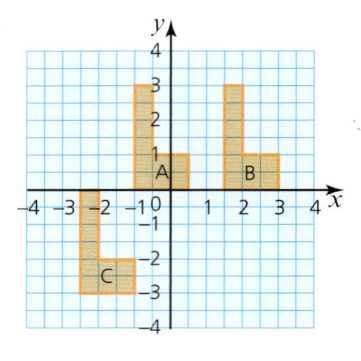

Exercise 26.6 Copy the diagrams for questions 1–6 and draw the object. Translate the object by the vector given in each case and draw the image in its new position. (Note: A bigger grid than the one shown may be needed.)

1. Vector = $\begin{pmatrix} 3 \\ 5 \end{pmatrix}$

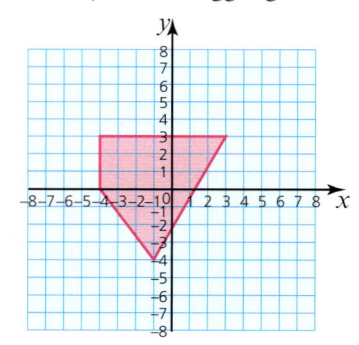

2. Vector = $\begin{pmatrix} 5 \\ -4 \end{pmatrix}$

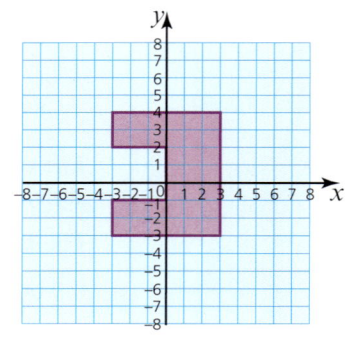

Enlargement

3

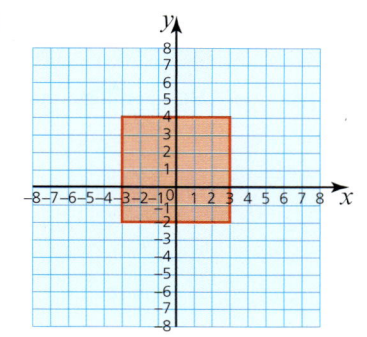

Vector = $\begin{pmatrix} -4 \\ 4 \end{pmatrix}$

4

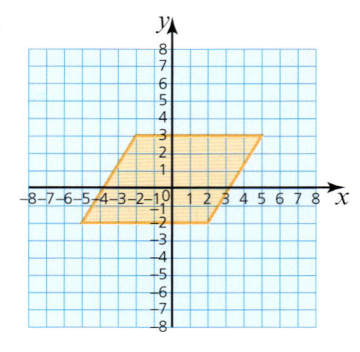

Vector = $\begin{pmatrix} -2 \\ -5 \end{pmatrix}$

5

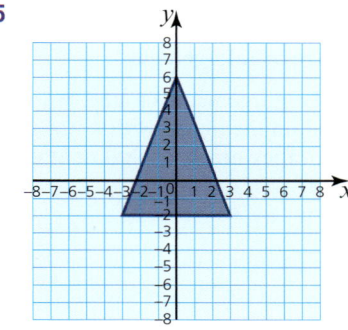

Vector = $\begin{pmatrix} -6 \\ 0 \end{pmatrix}$

6

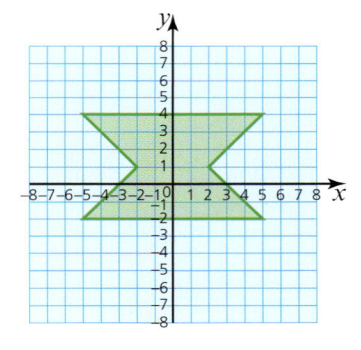

Vector = $\begin{pmatrix} 0 \\ -1 \end{pmatrix}$

Enlargement

When an object is enlarged, the result is an image which is mathematically similar to the object but is a different size. The image can be either larger or smaller than the original object. To describe an enlargement, two pieces of information need to be given: the position of the **centre of enlargement** and the **scale factor of enlargement**.

26 TRANSFORMATIONS

Worked examples

1 In the diagram, triangle ABC is enlarged to form triangle $A'B'C'$.

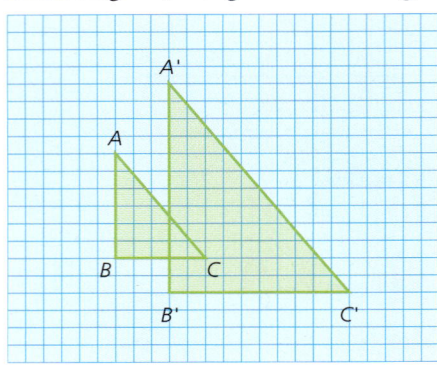

   a Find the centre of enlargement.

   The centre of enlargement is found by joining corresponding points on the object and on the image with a straight line. These lines are then extended until they meet. The point at which they meet is the centre of enlargement O.

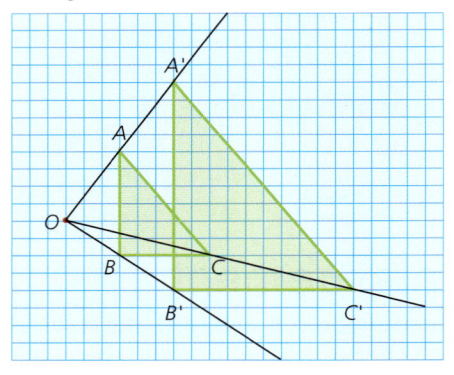

   b Calculate the scale factor of enlargement.

   The scale factor of enlargement can be calculated in two ways. From the previous diagram it can be seen that the distance OA' is twice the distance OA. Similarly, OC' and OB' are twice OC and OB respectively, so the scale factor of enlargement is 2.

   Alternatively, the scale factor can be found by considering the ratio of the length of a side on the image to the length of the corresponding side on the object, i.e.:

   $$\frac{A'B'}{AB} = \frac{12}{6} = 2$$

   So the scale factor of enlargement is 2.

Enlargement

2 In the diagram, rectangle $ABCD$ undergoes a transformation to form rectangle $A'B'C'D'$.

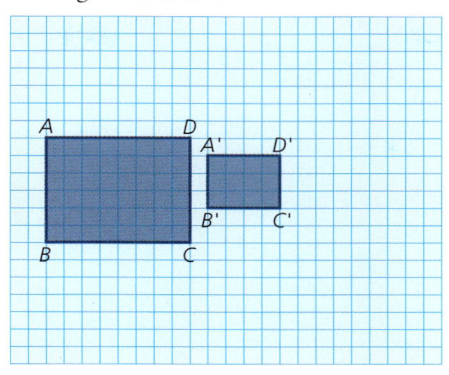

a Find the centre of enlargement.

By joining corresponding points on both the object and the image, the centre of enlargement is found at O:

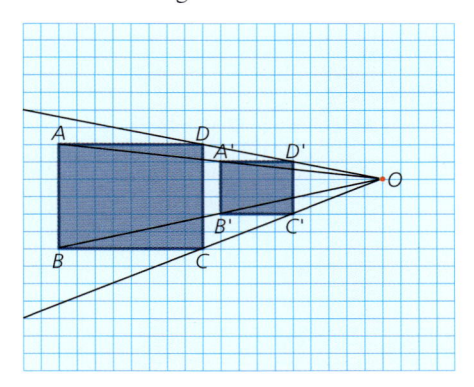

b Calculate the scale factor of enlargement.

The scale factor of enlargement $\dfrac{A'B'}{AB} = \dfrac{3}{6} = \dfrac{1}{2}$

Note

If the scale factor of enlargement is greater than 1, then the image is larger than the object. If the scale factor lies between 0 and 1, then the resulting image is smaller than the object. In these cases, although the image is smaller than the object, the transformation is still known as an enlargement.

26 TRANSFORMATIONS

Exercise 26.7 For questions 1–5, copy the diagrams and find:
  a the centre of enlargement
  b the scale factor of enlargement.

1

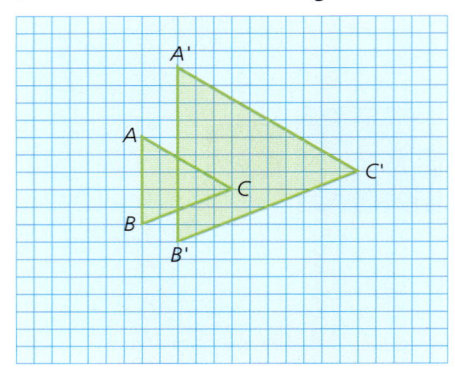

2

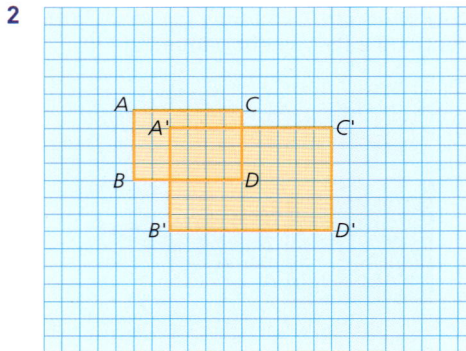

3

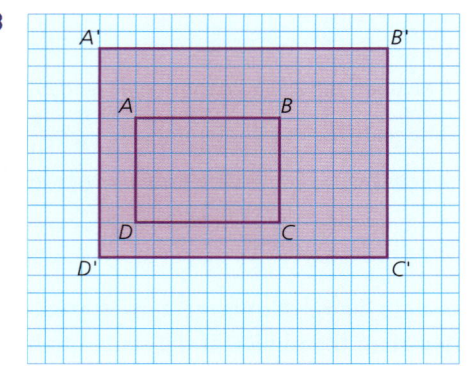

Enlargement

Exercise 26.7 (cont)

4.

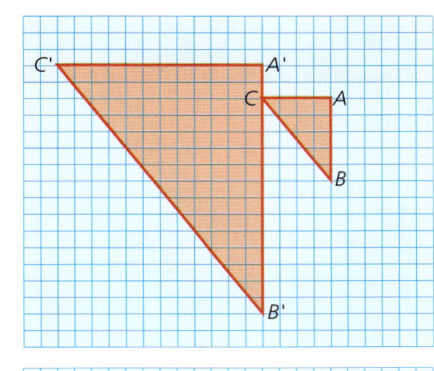

5.

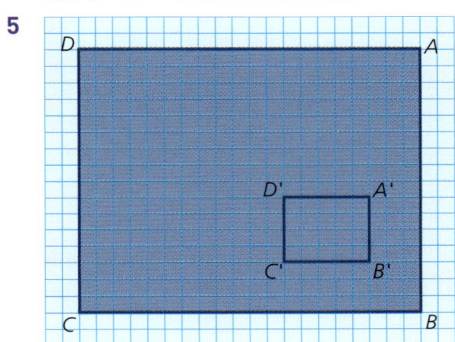

Exercise 26.8

For questions 1–4, copy the diagrams. Enlarge the objects by the scale factor given and from the centre of enlargement shown. (Note: Grids larger than those shown may be needed.)

1. scale factor 2

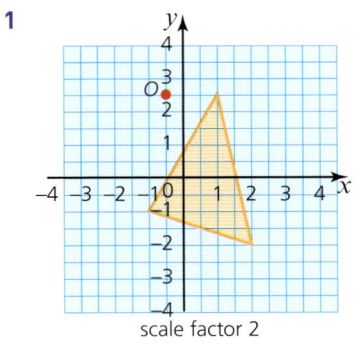

2. scale factor 2

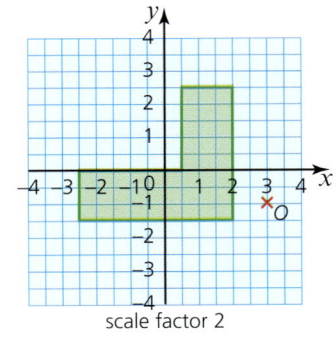

3. scale factor 3

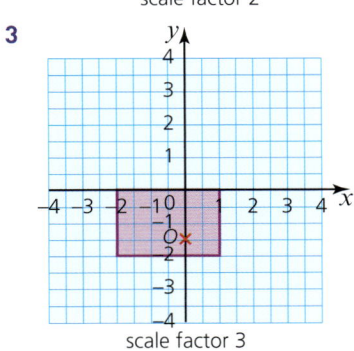

4. scale factor $\frac{1}{3}$

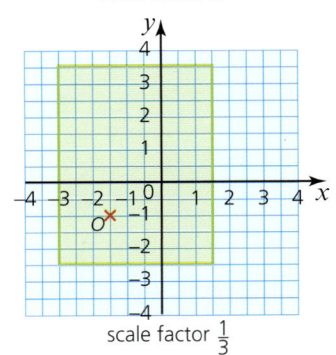

305

26 TRANSFORMATIONS

Student assessment 1

1. Copy the diagram and rotate the object 90° anticlockwise about the origin.

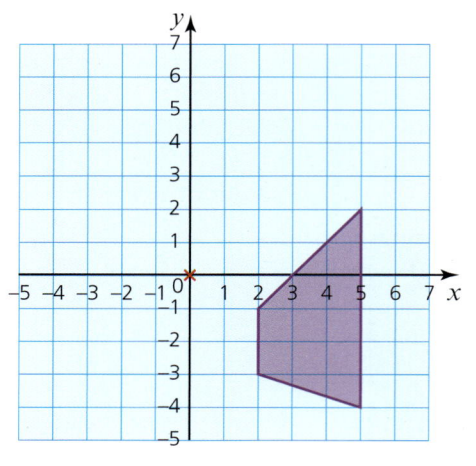

2. Write down the column vector of the translation which maps:
   a rectangle A to rectangle B
   b rectangle B to rectangle C.

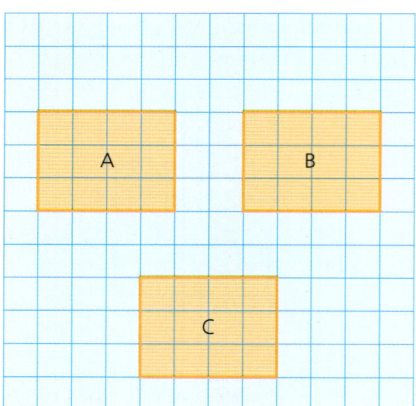

3. Enlarge the triangle by scale factor 2 and from the centre of enlargement O.

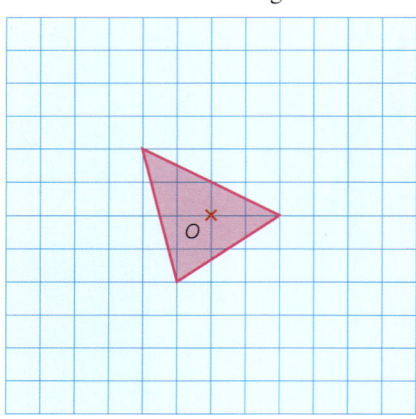

4. Enlarge the shape below by a scale factor of $\frac{1}{3}$ and from the centre of enlargement O.

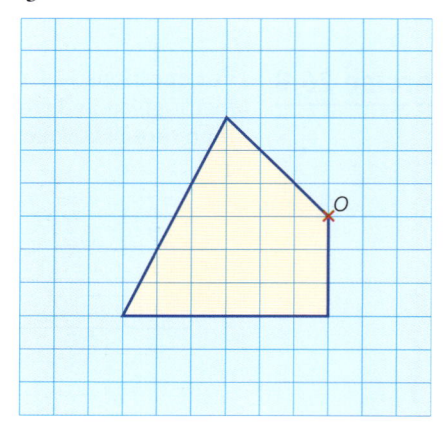

Mathematical investigations and ICT 7

A painted cube

A $3 \times 3 \times 3$ cm cube is painted on the outside, as shown in the left-hand diagram below:

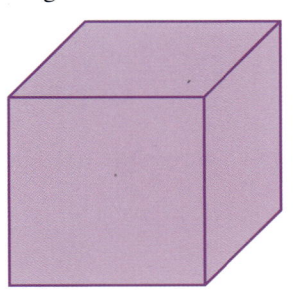

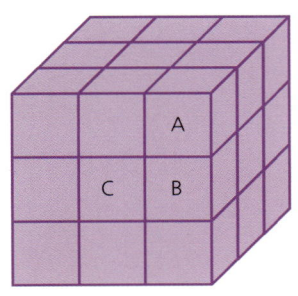

The large cube is then cut up into 27 smaller cubes, each $1\,\text{cm} \times 1\,\text{cm} \times 1\,\text{cm}$, as shown on the right.

$1 \times 1 \times 1$ cm cubes with 3 painted faces are labelled type A.

$1 \times 1 \times 1$ cm cubes with 2 painted faces are labelled type B.

$1 \times 1 \times 1$ cm cubes with 1 face painted are labelled type C.

$1 \times 1 \times 1$ cm cubes with no faces painted are labelled type D.

1
  a How many of the 27 cubes are type A?
  b How many of the 27 cubes are type B?
  c How many of the 27 cubes are type C?
  d How many of the 27 cubes are type D?

2 Consider a $4 \times 4 \times 4$ cm cube cut into $1 \times 1 \times 1$ cm cubes. How many of the cubes are type A, B, C and D?

3 How many type A, B, C and D cubes are there when a $10 \times 10 \times 10$ cm cube is cut into $1 \times 1 \times 1$ cm cubes?

4 Generalise for the number of type A, B, C and D cubes in an $n \times n \times n$ cube.

5 Generalise for the number of type A, B, C and D cubes in a cuboid l cm long, w cm wide and h cm high.

MATHEMATICAL INVESTIGATIONS AND ICT 7

Triangle count

The diagram below shows an isosceles triangle with a vertical line drawn from its apex to its base.

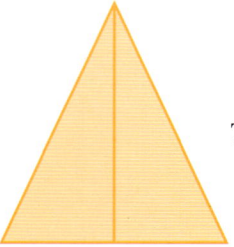

There is a total of 3 triangles in this diagram.

If a horizontal line is drawn across the triangle, it will look as shown:

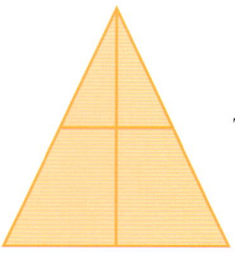

There is a total of 6 triangles in this diagram.

When one more horizontal line is added, the number of triangles increases further:

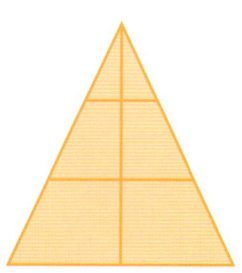

1. Calculate the total number of triangles in the diagram above with the two inner horizontal lines.
2. Investigate the relationship between the total number of triangles (t) and the number of inner horizontal lines (h). Enter your results in an ordered table.
3. Write an algebraic rule linking the total number of triangles and the number of inner horizontal lines.

ICT activity

In this activity, you will be using a geometry package to investigate enlargements.

1. Using a geometry package, draw an object and enlarge it by a scale factor of 2. An example is shown below:

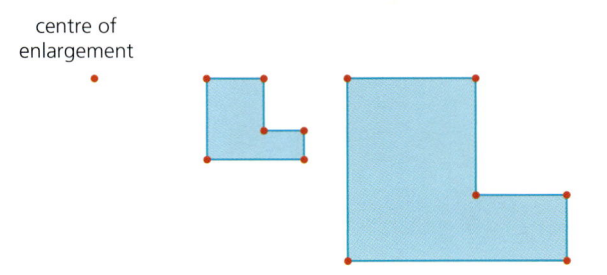

   centre of enlargement

2. Describe the position of the centre of enlargement used to produce the following diagrams:

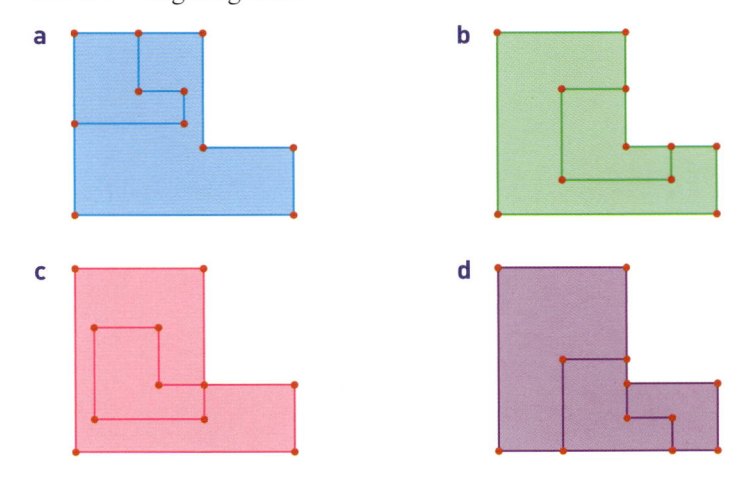

   a

   b

   c

   d

3. Move the position of the centre of enlargement to test your answers to Q.2 above.

TOPIC 8
Probability

Contents
Chapter 27 Probability (C8.1, C8.2, C8.3)

Learning objectives

C8.1
1. Understand and use the probability scale from 0 to 1.
2. Calculate the probability of a single event.
3. Understand that the probability of an event not occurring = 1 – the probability of the event occurring.

C8.2
1. Understand relative frequency as an estimate of probability.
2. Calculate expected frequencies.

C8.3
Calculate the probability of combined events using, where appropriate:
- sample space diagrams
- tree diagrams
- Venn diagrams.

The development of probability

Probability was first discussed in letters between the French mathematicians Pierre de Fermat and Blaise Pascal in 1654. Christiaan Huygens, a Dutch mathematician, gave the earliest known scientific treatment of the subject in 1657. By the early eighteenth century, probability was regarded as a branch of mathematics. Swiss mathematician Jakob Bernoulli published his book, *Ars Conjectandi* (*The Art of Conjecturing*), in 1713; this included work on permutations and combinations and other important concepts. French mathematician Abraham de Moivre published his book, *The Doctrine of Chances*, in 1718, in which he explained probability theory.

Blaise Pascal (1623–1662)

27 Probability

Probability is the study of chance, or the likelihood of an event happening. However, because probability is based on chance, what theory predicts does not necessarily happen in practice.

Theoretical probability

A **favourable outcome** refers to the event in question actually happening. The **total number of possible outcomes** refers to all the different types of outcome you can get in a given situation. Generally:

Probability of an event = $\dfrac{\text{number of favourable outcomes}}{\text{total number of equally likely outcomes}}$

If the probability = 0, the event is impossible.
If the probability = 1, the event is certain to happen.

If an event can either happen or not happen then:

Probability of the event not occurring = 1 − the probability of the event occurring

→ Worked examples

Although probabilities are written here as fractions, they could also be expressed as decimals or percentages.

1. An ordinary, fair dice is rolled. Calculate the probability of getting a six.

   Number of favourable outcomes = 1   (i.e. getting a 6)

   Total number of possible outcomes = 6   (i.e. getting a 1, 2, 3, 4, 5 or 6)

   Probability of getting a six = $\dfrac{1}{6}$

   Probability of not getting a six = $1 - \dfrac{1}{6} = \dfrac{5}{6}$

2. An ordinary, fair dice is rolled. Calculate the probability of getting an even number.

   Number of favourable outcomes = 3   (i.e. getting a 2, 4 or 6)

   Total number of possible outcomes = 6   (i.e. getting a 1, 2, 3, 4, 5 or 6)

   Probability of getting an even number = $\dfrac{3}{6} = \dfrac{1}{2}$

3. Thirty students are asked to choose their favourite subject out of Maths, English and Art. The results are shown in the table below:

	Maths	English	Art
Girls	7	4	5
Boys	5	3	6

   A student is chosen at random.

a What is the probability that it is a girl?

Total number of girls is 16.

Probability of choosing a girl is $\frac{16}{30} = \frac{8}{15}$.

b What is the probability that it is a boy whose favourite subject is Art?

Number of boys whose favourite subject is Art is 6.

Probability is therefore $\frac{6}{30} = \frac{1}{5}$.

c What is the probability of **not** choosing a girl whose favourite subject is English?

There are two ways of approaching this:

Method 1:

Total number of students who are not girls whose favourite subject is English is $7 + 5 + 5 + 3 + 6 = 26$.

Therefore, probability is $\frac{26}{30} = \frac{13}{15}$.

Method 2:

Total number of girls whose favourite subject is English is 4.

Probability of choosing a girl whose favourite subject is English is $\frac{4}{30}$.

Therefore the probability of **not** choosing a girl whose favourite subject is English is:

$$1 - \frac{4}{30} = \frac{26}{30} = \frac{13}{15}.$$

The probability scale

Exercise 27.1 Draw a line about 15 cm long. At the extreme left put 0, and at the extreme right put 1. These represent impossible and certain events, respectively.

Try to estimate the chance of the following events happening and place them on your line:

a You will watch TV tonight.
b You will play sport tomorrow.
c You will miss school one day this month.
d You will be on a plane next year.
e You will learn a new language one day.
f You will have a visitor at school today.

The likelihood of the events in Exercise 27.1 varies from person to person. Therefore, the probability of each event is not constant. However, the probability of some events, such as the result of throwing dice, spinning a coin or dealing cards, can be found by experiment or calculation.

The line drawn in Exercise 27.1 is called a **probability scale**.

The scale goes from 0 to 1.

A probability of 0 means the event is impossible.

A probability of 1 means it is certain.

27 PROBABILITY

Exercise 27.2

1 Copy the probability scale:

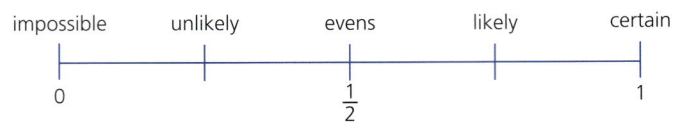

```
impossible   unlikely    evens      likely     certain
|------------|-----------|----------|----------|
0                       1/2                    1
```

Mark on the probability scale the probability that:
a a day chosen at random is a Saturday
b a coin will show tails when spun
c the Sun will rise tomorrow
d a woman will run 100 metres in under 10 seconds
e the next car you see will be silver.

2 Express your answers to Q.1 as fractions, decimals and percentages.

Exercise 27.3

1 Calculate the probability, when rolling an ordinary, fair dice, of getting:
a a score of 1   b a score of 2, 3, 4, 5 or 6
c an odd number   d a score less than 6
e a score of 7   f a score less than 7.

2 a Calculate the probability of:
  i   being born on a Wednesday
  ii not being born on a Wednesday.
b Explain the result of adding the answers to **ai** and **ii** together.

3 250 balls are numbered from 1 to 250 and placed in a box. A ball is picked at random. Find the probability of picking a ball with:
a the number 1   b an even number
c a three-digit number   d a number less than 300.

4 In a class there are 25 girls and 15 boys. The teacher takes in all of their books in a random order. Calculate the probability that the teacher will:
a mark a book belonging to a girl first
b mark a book belonging to a boy first.

5 26 tiles, each lettered with one different letter of the alphabet, are put into a bag. If one tile is taken out at random, calculate the probability that it is:
a an A or P   b a vowel   c a consonant
d an X, Y or Z   e a letter in your first name.

6 A boy was late for school 5 times in the previous 30 school days. If tomorrow is a school day, calculate the probability that he will arrive late.

7 a 3 red, 10 white, 5 blue and 2 green counters are put into a bag. If one is picked at random, calculate the probability that it is:
  i   a green counter   ii a blue counter.
b If the first counter taken out is green and it is not put back into the bag, calculate the probability that the second counter picked is:
  i   a green counter   ii a red counter.

The probability scale

8 A circular spinner with an arrow at its centre, has the numbers 0 to 36 equally spaced around its edge. Assuming that it is unbiased, calculate the probability of the spinner landing on:
- **a** the number 5
- **b** not 5
- **c** an odd number
- **d** zero
- **e** a number greater than 15
- **f** a multiple of 3
- **g** a multiple of 3 or 5
- **h** a prime number.

9 The letters R, C and A can be combined in several different ways.
- **a** Write the letters in as many different orders as possible.

If a computer writes these three letters at random, calculate the probability that:
- **b** the letters will be written in alphabetical order
- **c** the letter R is written before both the letters A and C
- **d** the letter C is written after the letter A
- **e** the computer will spell the word CAR.

10 A normal pack of playing cards contains 52 cards. These are made up of four suits of 13 cards: hearts, diamonds, clubs and spades. The cards are labelled Ace, 2, 3, 4, 5, 6, 7, 8, 9, 10, Jack, Queen and King. The hearts and diamonds are red; the clubs and spades are black.

If a card is picked at random from a normal pack of cards, calculate the probability of picking:
- **a** a heart
- **b** not a heart
- **c** a 4
- **d** a red King
- **e** a Jack, Queen or King
- **f** the Ace of spades
- **g** an even numbered card
- **h** a 7 or a club.

Exercise 27.4

1 Zuri conducts a survey on the types of vehicle that pass her house. The results are shown in the table:

Vehicle type	Car	Lorry	Van	Bicycle	Motorbike	Other
Frequency	28	6	20	48	32	6

- **a** How many vehicles passed her house?
- **b** A vehicle is chosen at random from the results. Calculate the probability that it is:
  - **i** a car
  - **ii** a lorry
  - **iii** not a van.

2 In a class, data is collected about whether each student is right-handed or left-handed. The results are shown in the table:

	Left-handed	Right-handed
Boys	2	12
Girls	3	15

- **a** How many students are in the class?
- **b** A student is chosen at random. Calculate the probability that the student is:
  - **i** a girl
  - **ii** left-handed
  - **iii** a right-handed boy
  - **iv** not a right-handed boy.

27 PROBABILITY

Exercise 27.4 (cont)

3 A library keeps a record of the books that are borrowed during one day. The results are shown in a chart:

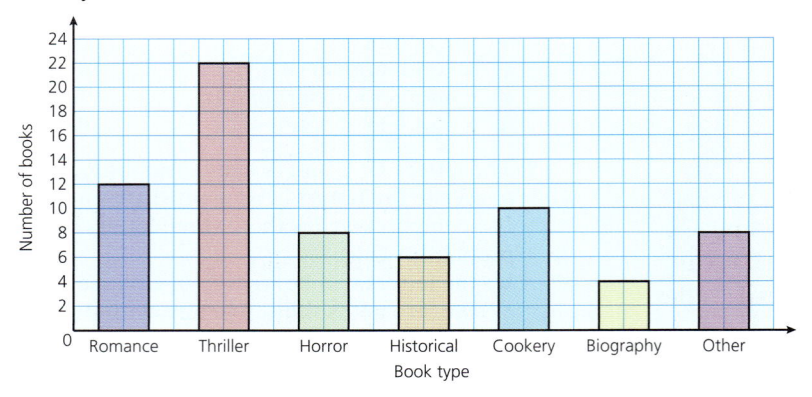

[Bar chart showing Number of books by Book type: Romance 12, Thriller 22, Horror 8, Historical 6, Cookery 10, Biography 4, Other 8]

   a How many books were borrowed that day?
   b A book is chosen at random from the ones borrowed. Calculate the probability that it is:
      i a thriller   **ii** a horror or a romance
      iii not a horror or a romance   **iv** not a biography.

Tree diagrams

When more than two combined events are being considered, two-way tables cannot be used. Another method of representing information diagrammatically is needed. **Tree diagrams** are a good way of doing this.

➡ Worked examples

1 If a coin is tossed three times, show all the possible outcomes on a tree diagram, writing each of the probabilities at the side of the branches.

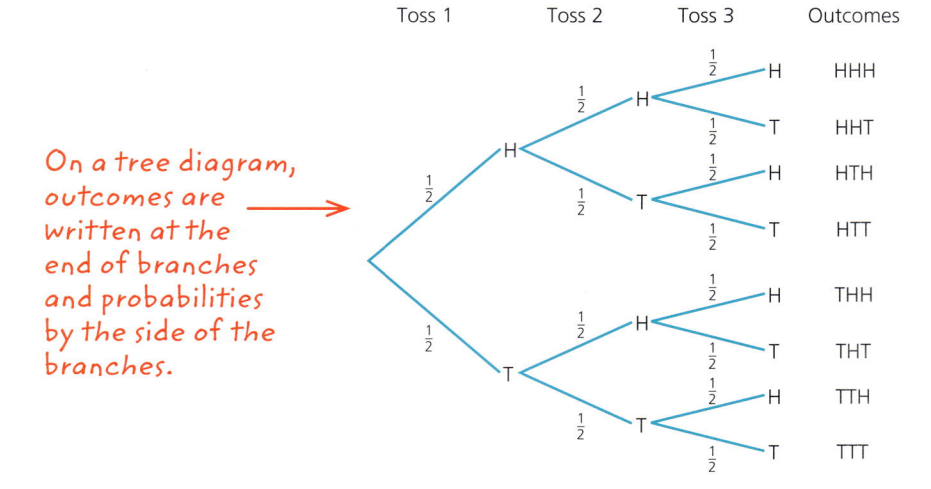

[Tree diagram with Toss 1, Toss 2, Toss 3, Outcomes. All branches labelled $\frac{1}{2}$. Outcomes: HHH, HHT, HTH, HTT, THH, THT, TTH, TTT]

On a tree diagram, outcomes are written at the end of branches and probabilities by the side of the branches.

Tree diagrams

Note

Although P( ) is not on the Core syllabus, it is an efficient way of describing the probability of something, i.e. P(HHH) can be read as 'the probability of getting three heads'.

2. What is the probability of getting three heads?
   To calculate the probability of getting three heads, multiply along the branches:
   $P(HHH) = \frac{1}{2} \times \frac{1}{2} \times \frac{1}{2} = \frac{1}{8}$

3. What is the probability of getting two heads and one tail in any order?
   The successful outcomes are HHT, HTH, THH.
   $P(HHT) + P(HTH) + P(THH) = \left(\frac{1}{2} \times \frac{1}{2} \times \frac{1}{2}\right) + \left(\frac{1}{2} \times \frac{1}{2} \times \frac{1}{2}\right) + \left(\frac{1}{2} \times \frac{1}{2} \times \frac{1}{2}\right) = \frac{3}{8}$
   Therefore, the probability is $\frac{3}{8}$.

4. What is the probability of getting at least one head?
   This refers to any outcome with one, two or three heads, i.e. all of them except TTT.
   $P(\text{at least one head}) = 1 - P(TTT) = 1 - \frac{1}{8} = \frac{7}{8}$
   Therefore, the probability is $\frac{7}{8}$.

5. What is the probability of getting no heads?
   The only successful outcome for this event is TTT.
   Therefore, the probability is $\frac{1}{8}$.

Exercise 27.5

Note

A palindromic number reads the same forwards and backwards, for example, 121, 232 or 333.

1. **a** A computer uses the numbers 1, 2 or 3 at random to print three-digit numbers. Assuming that a number can be repeated, show on a tree diagram all the possible combinations that the computer can print.
   b Calculate the probability of getting:
   i the number 131   **ii** an even number
   iii a multiple of 11   **iv** a multiple of 3
   v a multiple of 2 or 3   **vi** a palindromic number.

2. **a** A family has four children. Draw a tree diagram to show all the possible combinations of boys and girls. [Assume that the probability of having a girl is the same as the probability of having a boy.]
   b Calculate the probability of getting:
   i all girls   **ii** two girls and two boys
   iii at least one girl   **iv** more girls than boys.

3. **a** A netball team plays three matches. In each match the team is equally likely to win, lose or draw. Draw a tree diagram to show all the possible outcomes over the three matches.
   b Calculate the probability that the team:
   i wins all three matches
   ii wins more times than it loses
   iii loses at least one match
   iv either draws or loses all the three matches.
   c Explain why it is not very realistic to assume that the outcomes are equally likely in this case.

317

27 PROBABILITY

Exercise 27.5 (cont)

4 A spinner is split into quarters.
   a If it is spun twice, draw a tree diagram showing all the possible outcomes.
   b Calculate the probability of getting:
      i   two greens
      ii   a green and a blue in any order
      iii no whites.

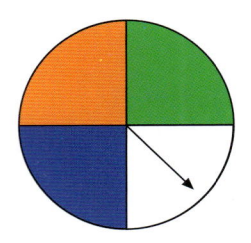

Tree diagrams for unequal probabilities

In each of the cases considered so far, all of the outcomes have been assumed to be equally likely. However, this may not be the case.

Worked examples

In winter, the probability that it rains on any one day is $\frac{5}{7}$.

1 Using a tree diagram, show all the possible combinations for two consecutive days. Write each of the probabilities by the sides of the branches.

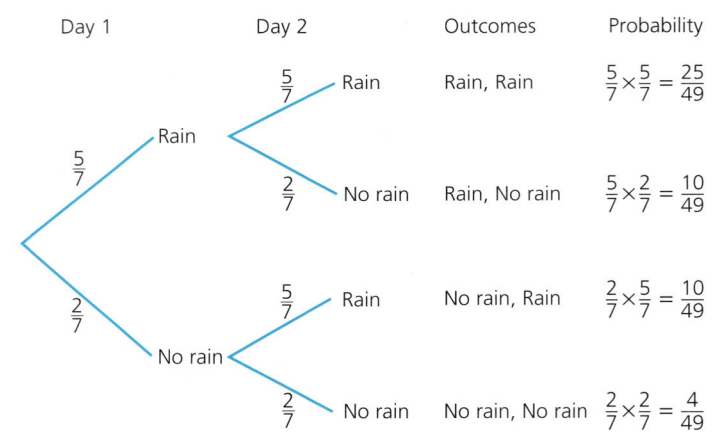

Day 1	Day 2	Outcomes	Probability
Rain ($\frac{5}{7}$)	Rain ($\frac{5}{7}$)	Rain, Rain	$\frac{5}{7} \times \frac{5}{7} = \frac{25}{49}$
Rain ($\frac{5}{7}$)	No rain ($\frac{2}{7}$)	Rain, No rain	$\frac{5}{7} \times \frac{2}{7} = \frac{10}{49}$
No rain ($\frac{2}{7}$)	Rain ($\frac{5}{7}$)	No rain, Rain	$\frac{2}{7} \times \frac{5}{7} = \frac{10}{49}$
No rain ($\frac{2}{7}$)	No rain ($\frac{2}{7}$)	No rain, No rain	$\frac{2}{7} \times \frac{2}{7} = \frac{4}{49}$

The probability of each outcome is found by multiplying the probabilities for each of the branches. This is because each outcome is the result of calculating the fraction of a fraction.

2 Calculate the probability that it will rain on both days.
   This is an outcome that is $\frac{5}{7}$ of $\frac{5}{7}$.
   $P(R, R) = \frac{5}{7} \times \frac{5}{7} = \frac{25}{49}$

3 Calculate the probability that it will rain on the first day but not the second day.
   $P(R, NR) = \frac{5}{7} \times \frac{2}{7} = \frac{10}{49}$

4 Calculate the probability that it will rain on at least one day.
   The outcomes which satisfy this event are (R, R), (R, NR) and (NR, R).
   Therefore, the probability is $\frac{25}{49} + \frac{10}{49} + \frac{10}{49} = \frac{45}{49}$.

Venn diagrams

Exercise 27.6

1. A board game involves players rolling a dice. However, before a player can start, he or she needs to roll a six.
   a. Copy and complete the tree diagram to show all the possible combinations for the first two rolls of the dice.

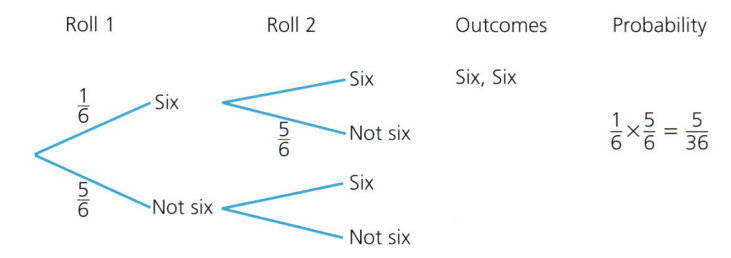

   Roll 1   Roll 2   Outcomes   Probability

   $\frac{1}{6}$ Six — Six → Six, Six $\frac{1}{6} \times \frac{5}{6} = \frac{5}{36}$
   $\frac{5}{6}$ Not six
   $\frac{5}{6}$ Not six — Six
   Not six

   b. Calculate the probability of:
      i. getting a six on the first throw
      ii. starting within the first two throws
      iii. starting on the second throw
      iv. not starting within the first three throws
      v. starting within the first three throws.
   c. Add the answers to Q.1b **iv** and **v**. What do you notice? Explain your answer.

2. In Italy, $\frac{3}{5}$ of the cars are made abroad. By drawing a tree diagram and writing the probabilities next to each of the branches, calculate the probability that:
   a. the next two cars to pass a particular spot are both Italian
   b. two of the next three cars are from overseas
   c. at least one of the next three cars is Italian.

3. The probability that a morning bus arrives on time is 65%.
   a. Draw a tree diagram showing all the possible outcomes for three consecutive mornings.
   b. Label your tree diagram and use it to calculate the probability that:
      i. the bus is on time on all three mornings
      ii. the bus is late the first two mornings
      iii. the bus is on time two out of the three mornings
      iv. the bus is on time at least twice.

4. Light bulbs are packaged in boxes of three. 10% of the bulbs are found to be faulty. Calculate the probability of finding two faulty bulbs in a single box.

Venn diagrams

You saw in Chapter 10 how Venn diagrams can be used to represent sets. They can also be used to solve problems involving probability.

27 PROBABILITY

→ Worked examples

1 In a survey, students were asked which was their favourite subject.

   15 chose English.

   8 chose Science.

   12 chose Mathematics.

   5 chose Art.

   What is the probability that a student chosen at random will like Science the best?

   This can be represented on a Venn diagram:

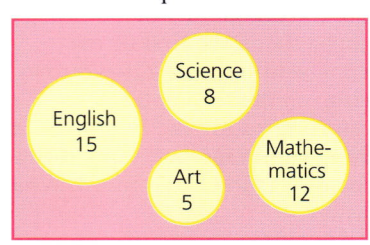

   [Venn diagram showing: English 15, Science 8, Art 5, Mathematics 12]

   There are 40 students, so the probability is $\frac{8}{40} = \frac{1}{5}$.

2 A group of 21 friends decide to go out for the day to the local town. 9 of them decide to see a film at the cinema and 15 of them go for lunch.

   a Draw a Venn diagram to show this information if set A represents those who see a film and set B represents those who have lunch.

   $9 + 15 = 24$; as there are only 21 people, this implies that 3 people see the film and have lunch. This means that $9 - 3 = 6$ only went to see a film and $15 - 3 = 12$ only had lunch.

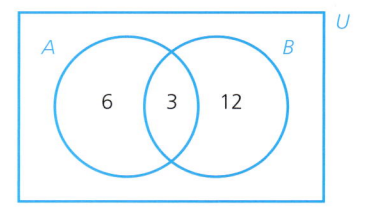

   [Venn diagram with sets A and B in universe U: A only = 6, intersection = 3, B only = 12]

   b Determine the probability that a person picked at random only went to the cinema.

   The number who only went to the cinema is 6, therefore the probability is $\frac{6}{21} = \frac{2}{7}$.

Relative frequency

Exercise 27.7

1. In a class of 30 students, 20 study French, 18 study Spanish and 5 do not study either language.
   a Draw a Venn diagram to show this information.
   b What is the probability that a student chosen at random studies both French and Spanish?

2. In a group of 35 students, 19 take Physics, 18 take Chemistry and 3 take neither. What is the probability that a student chosen at random takes:
   a both Physics and Chemistry
   b Physics only
   c Chemistry only?

3. 108 people visited an art gallery. 60 liked the pictures, 53 liked the sculpture and 10 did not like either. What is the probability that a person chosen at random liked the pictures but not the sculpture?

Relative frequency

A football referee always uses a special coin. She notices that out of the last 20 matches the coin has come down heads far more often than tails. She wants to know if the coin is fair, i.e. if it is as likely to come down heads as tails.

She decides to do a simple experiment by tossing the coin lots of times. Her results are shown in the table:

Number of trials	Number of heads	Relative frequency
100	40	0.4
200	90	0.45
300	142	
400	210	
500	260	
600	290	
700	345	
800	404	
900	451	
1000	499	

The relative frequency = $\frac{\text{number of successful trials}}{\text{total number of trials}}$

In the 'long run' (i.e. after a large number of trials), did the coin appear to be fair?

27 PROBABILITY

> **Note**
> The greater the number of trials, the better the estimated probability or relative frequency is likely to be. The key idea is that increasing the number of trials gives a better estimate of the probability, and the closer the result obtained by experiment will be to that obtained by calculation.

Exercise 27.8

1. Copy and complete the table on page 321. Draw a graph with 'Relative frequency' as the y-axis and 'Number of trials' as the x-axis. What do you notice?

2. Conduct a similar experiment using a dice to see if the number of sixes you get is the same as the theory of probability would make you expect.

3. Make a hexagonal spinner. Conduct an experiment to see if it is fair.

4. Ask a friend to put some coloured beads in a bag. Explain how you could use relative frequency in an experiment to find out what fraction of each colour are in the bag.

Worked examples

1. There is a group of 250 people in a hall. A girl calculates that the probability of randomly picking someone that she knows from the group is 0.032. Calculate the number of people in the group that the girl knows.

$$\text{Probability} = \frac{\text{number of favourable results }(F)}{\text{number of possible results}}$$

$$0.032 = \frac{F}{250}$$

$$250 \times 0.032 = F$$

$$8 = F$$

The girl knows 8 people in the group.

2. A boy enters 8 short stories into a writing competition. His father knows how many short stories have been entered into the competition, and tells his son that he has a probability of 0.016 of winning the first prize (assuming all the entries have an equal chance). How many short stories were entered into the competition?

$$\text{Probability} = \frac{\text{number of favourable results}}{\text{number of possible results }(T)}$$

$$0.016 = \frac{8}{T}$$

$$T = \frac{8}{0.016}$$

$$T = 500$$

So, 500 short stories were entered into the competition.

Relative frequency

Exercise 27.9

1. Mikki calculates that he has a probability of 0.004 of winning the first prize in a photography competition if the selection is made at random. If 500 photographs are entered into the competition, how many photographs did he enter?

2. The probability of getting any particular number on a spinner game is given as 0.04. How many numbers are there on the spinner?

3. A bag contains 7 red counters, 5 blue, 3 green and 1 yellow. If one counter is picked at random, what is the probability that it is:
   a yellow
   c blue or green
   e not blue?
   b red
   d red, blue or green

4. Luca collects marbles. He has the following colours in a bag: 28 red, 14 blue, 25 yellow, 17 green and 6 purple. If he picks one marble from the bag at random, what is the probability that it is:
   a red
   c yellow or blue
   e not purple?
   b blue
   d purple

5. The probability of Hanane randomly picking a marble of one of the following colours from another bag of marbles is:

   blue 0.25   red 0.2   yellow 0.15   green 0.35   white 0.05

   If there are 49 green marbles, how many of each other colour does he have in his bag?

6. There are 6 red sweets in a bag. If the probability of randomly picking a red sweet is 0.02, calculate the number of sweets in the bag.

7. The probability of getting a bad egg in a batch of 400 is 0.035. How many bad eggs are there likely to be in a batch?

8. A sports arena has 25 000 seats, some of which are VIP seats. For a charity event, all the seats are allocated randomly. The probability of getting a VIP seat is 0.008. How many VIP seats are there?

9. The probability of Juan's favourite football team, Harts Utd, winning 4–0 is 0.05. How many times are they likely to win by this score in a season of 40 matches?

27 PROBABILITY

Student assessment 1

1 An octagonal spinner has the numbers 1 to 8 on it as shown:

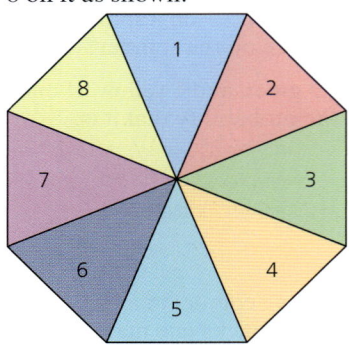

    What is the probability of spinning:
    a a 7
    b not a 7
    c a factor of 12
    d a 9?
    e If the spinner is spun 640 times, calculate the expected number of times it would land on the 7 or 8.

2 180 students in a school are offered the chance to attend a football match for free. If the students are chosen at random, what is the chance of being picked to go if the following numbers of tickets are available?
    a 1   b 9   c 15
    d 40   e 180

3 A bag contains 11 white, 9 blue, 7 green and 5 red counters. What is the probability that a single counter drawn will be:
    a blue   b red or green
    c not white?

4 A bag contains only red, blue and green marbles. There are 320 marbles in total. The probability of randomly picking a red marble is 0.4, while the probability of picking a blue marble is 0.25.
    a Calculate the probability of picking a green marble.
    b How many marbles of each colour are there?

5 Students in a class conducted a survey to see how many friends they have on a social media site. The results were grouped and are shown in the pie chart (right).

    Number of friends on social media site
    More than 400: 8
    None: 2
    1–100: 4
    101–200: 6
    201–300: 12
    301–400: 8

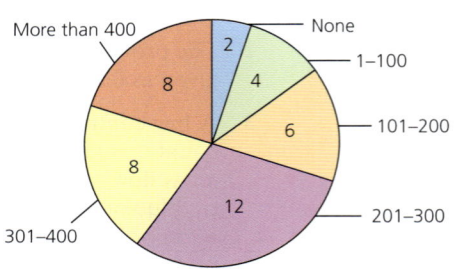

    A student is chosen at random. What is the probability that he/she:
    a has 101–200 friends on the site
    b has friends on the site
    c has more than 200 friends on the site?

6 a If I enter a competition and have a 0.00002 probability of winning, how many people entered the competition?
    b What assumption do you have to make in order to answer part a?

7 A large bag contains coloured discs. The discs are either completely red (R), completely yellow (Y) or half red and half yellow. The Venn diagram below shows the probability of picking each type of disc.

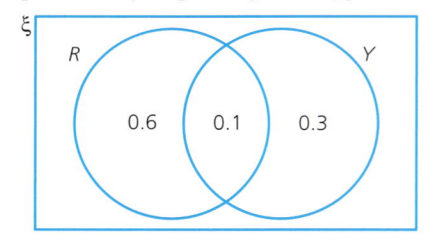

    R: 0.6, intersection: 0.1, Y: 0.3

    If there are 120 discs coloured completely yellow, calculate:
    a the number of discs coloured completely red
    b the total number of discs in the bag.

8 A cricket team has a 0.25 chance of losing a game. Calculate, using a tree diagram if necessary, the probability of the team achieving:
    a two consecutive wins
    b three consecutive wins
    c ten consecutive wins.

Mathematical investigations and ICT 8

Probability drop

A game involves dropping a red marble down a chute. On hitting a triangle divider, the marble can bounce either left or right. On completing the drop, the marble lands in one of the trays along the bottom. The trays are numbered from left to right. Different sizes of game exist; the four smallest versions are shown below:

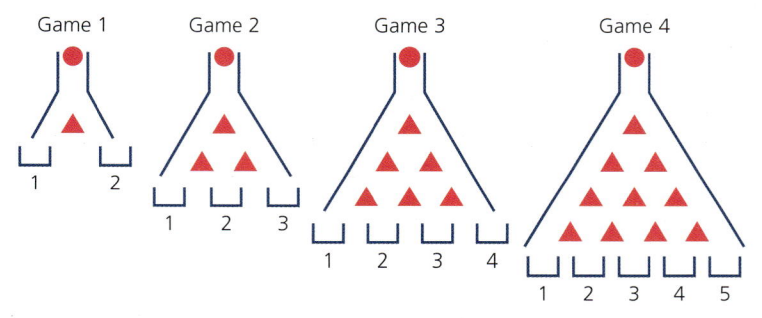

To land in tray 2 in the second game above, the marble can travel in one of two ways. These are: Left–Right or Right–Left. This can be abbreviated to LR or RL.

1 State the different routes the marble can take to land in each of the trays in the third game.
2 State the different routes the marble can take to land in each of the trays in the fourth game.
3 State, giving reasons, the probability of a marble landing in tray 1 in the fourth game.
4 State, giving reasons, the probability of a marble landing in each of the other trays in the fourth game.
5 Investigate the probability of the marble landing in each of the different trays in larger games.
6 Using your findings from your investigation, predict the probability of a marble landing in tray 7 in the tenth game (11 trays at the bottom).

MATHEMATICAL INVESTIGATIONS AND ICT 8

Dice sum

Two ordinary dice are rolled and their scores added together. Below is an incomplete table showing the possible outcomes:

		\multicolumn{6}{c}{Dice 1}
		1	2	3	4	5	6
Dice 2	1	2			5		
	2						
	3				7		
	4				8		
	5				9	10	11
	6						12

1 Copy and complete the table to show all possible outcomes.
2 How many possible outcomes are there?
3 What is the most likely total when two dice are rolled?
4 What is the probability of getting a total score of 4?
5 What is the probability of getting the most likely total?
6 How many times more likely is a total score of 5 compared with a total score of 2?

Now consider rolling two 4-sided dice, each numbered 1–4. Their scores are also added together.

7 Draw a table to show all the possible outcomes when the two 4-sided dice are rolled and their scores added together.
8 How many possible outcomes are there?
9 What is the most likely total?
10 What is the probability of getting the most likely total?
11 Investigate the number of possible outcomes, the most likely total and its probability when two identical dice are rolled together and their scores added, i.e. consider 8-sided dice, 10-sided dice, etc.
12 Consider two m-sided dice rolled together and their scores added.
  a What is the total number of outcomes, in terms of m?
  b What is the most likely total, in terms of m?
  c What, in terms of m, is the probability of the most likely total?
13 Consider an m-sided and n-sided dice rolled together, where $m > n$.
  a In terms of m and n, deduce the total number of outcomes.
  b In terms of m and/or n, deduce the most likely total(s).
  c In terms of m and/or n, deduce the probability of getting a specific total out of the most likely total(s).

ICT activity

For this activity, you will be testing the fairness of a spinner that you have constructed.

1. Using card, a pair of compasses and a ruler, construct a regular hexagon.
2. Divide your regular hexagon into six equal parts.
3. Colour the six parts using three different colours, as shown below:

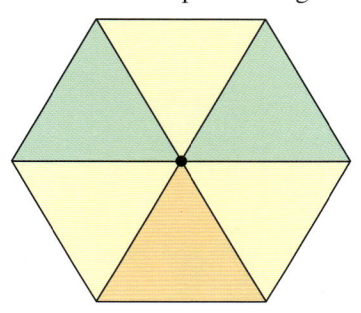

4. Calculate the theoretical probability of each colour. Record these probabilities as percentages.
5. Carefully insert a small pencil through the centre of the hexagon to form a spinner.
6. Spin the spinner 60 times, recording your results in a spreadsheet.
7. Using the spreadsheet, produce a percentage pie chart of your results.
8. Compare the actual probabilities with the theoretical ones calculated in Q.4. What conclusions can you make about the fairness of your spinner?

TOPIC 9
Statistics

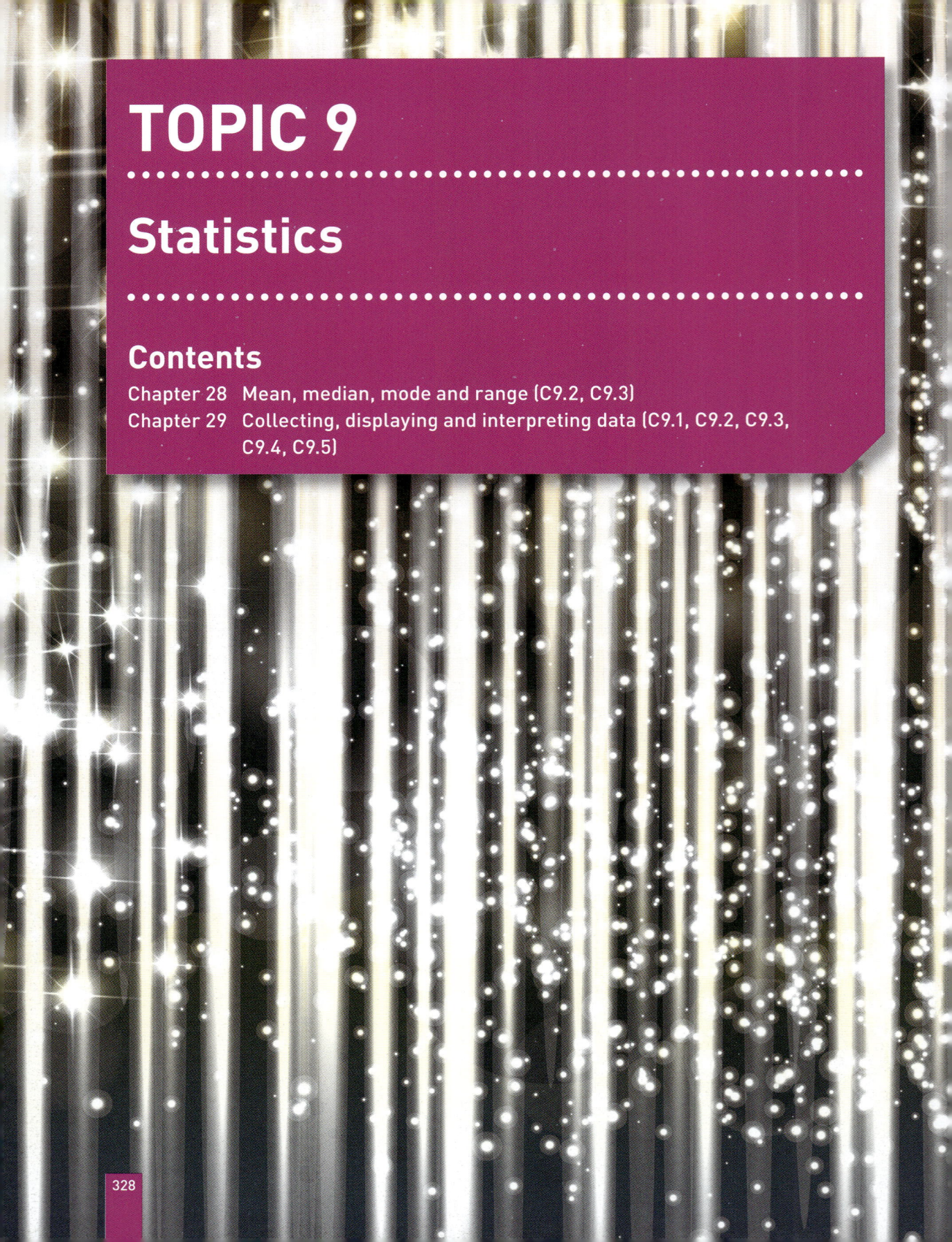

Contents

Chapter 28 Mean, median, mode and range (C9.2, C9.3)
Chapter 29 Collecting, displaying and interpreting data (C9.1, C9.2, C9.3, C9.4, C9.5)

Learning objectives

C9.1
Classify and tabulate statistical data.

C9.2
1 Read, interpret and draw inferences from tables and statistical diagrams.
2 Compare sets of data using tables, graphs and statistical measures.
3 Appreciate restrictions on drawing conclusions from given data.

C9.3
Calculate the mean, median, mode, and range for discrete data and distinguish between the purposes for which these are used.

C9.4
Draw and interpret:
a bar charts
b pie charts
c pictograms
d stem-and-leaf diagrams
e simple frequency distributions.

C9.5
1 Draw and interpret scatter diagrams.
2 Understand what is meant by positive, negative and zero correlation.
3 Draw by eye, interpret and use a straight line of best fit.

The development of statistics

The earliest writing on statistics was found in a ninth-century book entitled *Manuscript on Deciphering Cryptographic Messages*, written by Arab philosopher al-Kindi (801–873) who lived in Baghdad. In his book, he gave a detailed description of how to use statistics to unlock coded messages.

The *Nuova Cronica*, a fourteenth-century history of Florence by Italian banker Giovanni Villani, includes much statistical information on population, commerce, trade and education.

Florence Nightingale (1820–1910) was a famous British nurse who treated casualties in the Crimean War (1853–1856). By using statistics she realised that most of the deaths that occurred were not as a result of battle injuries but from preventable illnesses afterwards such as cholera and typhoid. By understanding these statistics, Florence Nightingale was able to improve the sanitary conditions of the injured soldiers and therefore reduce their mortality rates.

Early statistics served the needs of states – *state-istics*. By the early nineteenth century, statistics included the collection and analysis of data in general. Today, statistics are widely used in government, business, and natural and social sciences. The use of modern computers has enabled large-scale statistical computation and has also made possible new methods that are impractical to perform manually.

28 Mean, median, mode and range

Average

'**Average**' is a word which, in general use, is taken to mean somewhere in the middle. For example, a person may describe themselves as being of average height. A student may think they are of average ability in maths. Mathematics is more exact and uses three principal methods to measure average.

Key points:
- The **mode** is the value occurring the most often.
- The **median** is the middle value when all the data is arranged in order of size.
- The **mean** is found by adding together all the values of the data and then dividing that total by the number of data values.

> **Note**
>
> In a set of data, there can be more than one mode or in fact, there might not be a mode at all.

Spread

It is often useful to know how spread out the data is. It is possible for two sets of data to have the same mean and median but very different spreads.

The simplest measure of spread is the **range**. The range is simply the difference between the largest and smallest values in the data.

Worked examples

1. a Find the mean, median and mode of the data given:

    1, 0, 2, 4, 1, 2, 1, 1, 2, 5, 5, 0, 1, 2, 3

    $$\text{Mean} = \frac{1+0+2+4+1+2+1+1+2+5+5+0+1+2+3}{15}$$

    $$= \frac{30}{15}$$

    $$= 2$$

    Arranging all the data in order and then picking out the middle number gives the median:

    0, 0, 1, 1, 1, 1, 1, ②, 2, 2, 2, 3, 4, 5, 5

    The mode is the number which appeared most often.

    Therefore the mode is 1.

   b Calculate the range of the data.

    Largest value = 5

    Smallest value = 0

    Therefore the range = 5 − 0 = 5

Spread

2 a The bar chart shows the score out of 10 achieved by a class in a maths test. Calculate the mean, median and mode for this data.

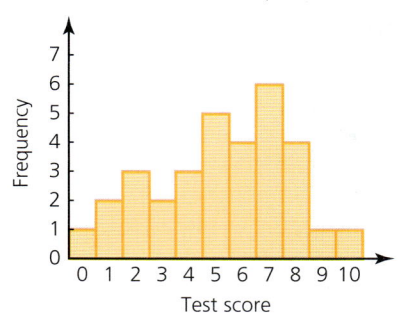

Transferring the results to a frequency table gives:

Test score	0	1	2	3	4	5	6	7	8	9	10	Total
Frequency	1	2	3	2	3	5	4	6	4	1	1	32
Frequency × score	0	2	6	6	12	25	24	42	32	9	10	168

> **Note**
> This frequency table also shows the **frequency distribution** of the test scores.

From the total column, we can see the number of students taking the test is 32 and the total number of marks obtained by all the students is 168.

Therefore, the mean score = $\frac{168}{32}$ = 5.25

Arranging all the scores in order gives:

0, 1, 1, 2, 2, 2, 3, 3, 4, 4, 5, 5, 5, 5, 5, 6, 6, 6, 6, 7, 7, 7, 7, 7, 7, 8, 8, 8, 8, 9, 10

Because there is an even number of students, there isn't one middle number. There is a middle pair.

Median = $\frac{(5 + 6)}{2}$

= 5.5

The mode is 7 as it is the score which occurs most often.

b Calculate the range of the data.

Largest value = 10

Smallest value = 0

Therefore the range = 10 − 0

= 10

Exercise 28.1

1 Calculate the mean and range of each set of numbers:
  a 6 7 8 10 11 12 13
  b 4 4 6 6 6 7 8 10
  c 36 38 40 43 47 50 55
  d 7 6 8 9 5 4 10 11 12
  e 12 24 36 48 60
  f 17.5 16.3 18.6 19.1 24.5 27.8

28 MEAN, MEDIAN, MODE AND RANGE

Exercise 28.1 (cont)

2 Find the median and range of each set of numbers:
   a 3 4 5 6 7
   b 7 8 8 9 10 12 15
   c 8 8 8 9 9 10 10 10 10
   d 6 4 7 3 8 9 9 4 5
   e 2 4 6 8
   f 7 8 8 9 10 11 12 14
   g 3.2 7.5 8.4 9.3 5.4 4.1 5.2 6.3
   h 18 32 63 16 97 46 83

3 Find the mode and range of each set of numbers:
   a 6 7 8 8 9 10 11
   b 3 4 4 5 5 6 6 6 7 8 8
   c 3 5 3 4 6 3 3 5 4 6 8
   d 4 3 4 5 3 4 5 4
   e 60 65 70 75 80 75
   f 8 7 6 5 8 7 6 5 8

Exercise 28.2

In Q.1–5, find the mean, median, mode and range for each set of data.

1 A hockey team plays 15 matches. The number of goals scored in each match was:
   1, 0, 2, 4, 0, 1, 1, 1, 2, 5, 3, 0, 1, 2, 2

2 The total score when two dice were thrown 20 times was:
   7, 4, 5, 7, 3, 2, 8, 6, 8, 7, 6, 5, 11, 9, 7, 3, 8, 7, 6, 5

3 The ages of girls in a group are:
   14 years 3 months,   14 years 5 months,
   13 years 11 months,   14 years 3 months,
   14 years 7 months,   14 years 3 months,
   14 years 1 month

4 The number of students present in class over a three-week period was:
   28, 24, 25, 28, 23, 28, 27, 26, 27, 25, 28, 28, 28, 26, 25

5 An athlete keeps a record in seconds of her training times for the 100 m race:
   14.0, 14.3, 14.1, 14.3, 14.2, 14.0, 13.9, 13.8,
   13.9, 13.8, 13.8, 13.7, 13.8, 13.8, 13.8

6 The mean mass of 11 players in a football team is 80.3 kg. The mean mass of the team plus a substitute is 81.2 kg. Calculate the mass of the substitute.

7 After eight matches, a basketball player had scored a mean of 27 points. After three more matches his mean was 29. Calculate the total number of points he scored in the last three games.

Exercise 28.3

1 Two dice were thrown 100 times. Each time, their combined score was recorded and the results put into the table:

Score	2	3	4	5	6	7	8	9	10	11	12
Frequency	5	6	7	9	14	16	13	11	9	7	3

Calculate the mean score.

Spread

2. An ordinary dice was rolled 60 times. The results are shown in the table:

Score	1	2	3	4	5	6
Frequency	12	11	8	12	7	10

Calculate the mean, median, mode and range of the scores.

As there are three types of average, it is important to consider which is most appropriate to use for a particular situation. Using the wrong one can give a misleading impression.

Unfortunately, sometimes people want to mislead and deliberately use the least appropriate type of average.

➜ Worked example

60 flowering bushes were planted. At their flowering peak, the number of flowers per bush was counted and recorded. The results are shown in the table:

Flowers per bush	0	1	2	3	4	5	6	7	8
Frequency	0	0	0	6	4	6	10	16	18

a Calculate the mean, median, mode and range of the number of flowers per bush.

Mean = $\frac{(1 \times 0) + (2 \times 0) + (3 \times 6) + (4 \times 4) + (5 \times 6) + (6 \times 10) + (7 \times 16) + (8 \times 18)}{60} = 6\frac{1}{3}$

Median: As there are 60 bushes, the median bush is midway between the 30th and 31st bush.

This falls in the 7 flowers per bush category. Therefore the median is 7.

Mode: The number of flowers per bush with the highest frequency is 8. Therefore the mode is 8.

Range = 8 − 3 = 5

b Which of the mean, median and mode would be most useful when advertising the bush to potential buyers? Justify your answer.

As the mode is the larger of the three averages, it is likely that this is the value that an advertiser would use.

Note

Unusual results in a data set (known as **outliers**) can be much bigger or smaller than the rest of the data. These outliers would affect a mean score, but not a median score.

Exercise 28.4

1. A group of 7 students sit a spelling test. They try to spell 10 words. The number of spellings they each got right is listed below.

   2   2   6   7   8   9   10

   a One of the students tells the group that they haven't done very well as the average score was 2.
   Comment on the accuracy of the student's statement.
   b Which average is more representative of their results? Justify your answer.

2. A 100 m sprinter records her race times. The times taken for her last 8 races are given below.

Race	1	2	3	4	5	6	7	8
Time (s)	12.2	12.2	12.1	11.9	12.3	11.8	12.3	12.9

333

28 MEAN, MEDIAN, MODE AND RANGE

Exercise 28.4 (cont)

To be selected for her country, her average race time should be no slower than 12.2 seconds.
She believes she has been selected, but is told that the statistics show that she hasn't.
Explain how the different conclusions are possible.

3 A shoe manufacturer records the size and number of shoes he sells of a particular style. The data is shown in the table below.

Shoe size	38	39	40	41	42	43	44
Number sold	10	2	3	1	2	3	10

  a Calculate the mean, median and modal sizes of shoes sold.
  b He wants to manufacture the average shoe size as he thinks this will reduce waste. He decides to manufacture only size 41 as it is closest to the mean size.
  Explain why this is not the most appropriate average to take.
  c Which measure of average should he use? Justify your answer.

Student assessment 1

1 Find the mean, median, mode and range of each of the following sets of numbers:
  a 63 72 72 84 86
  b 6 6 6 12 18 24
  c 5 10 5 15 5 20 5 25 15 10

2 The mean mass of 15 players in a rugby team is 85 kg. The mean mass of the team plus a substitute is 83.5 kg. Calculate the mass of the substitute.

3 An ordinary dice was rolled 50 times. The results are shown in the table:

Score	1	2	3	4	5	6
Frequency	8	11	5	9	7	10

  Calculate the mean, median and mode of the scores.

4 The bar chart shows the marks out of 10 for an English test taken by a class of students.
  a Calculate the number of students who took the test.
  b Calculate for the class:
    i   the mean test result
    ii the median test result
    iii the modal test result.

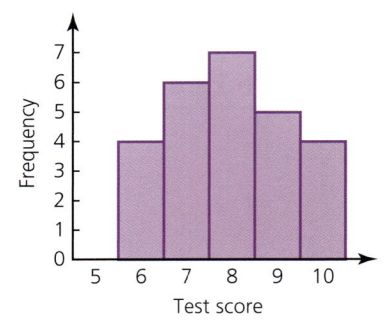

5 A javelin-thrower keeps a record of her best throws over 10 competitions. These are shown in the table:

Competition	1	2	3	4	5	6	7	8	9	10
Distance (m)	77	75	78	86	92	93	93	93	92	89

Find the mean, median, mode and range of her throws.

29 Collecting, displaying and interpreting data

Tally charts and frequency tables

The figures in the list below are the numbers of chocolate buttons in each of 20 packets of buttons:

35 36 38 37 35 36 38 36 37 35

36 36 38 36 35 38 37 38 36 38

The figures can be shown on a tally chart:

Number	Tally	Frequency
35	||||	4
36	⦉||	7
37	|||	3
38	⦉|	6

When the tallies are added up to get the frequency, the chart is usually called a **frequency table**. The information can then be displayed in a variety of ways.

Pictograms

● = 4 packets, ◕ = 3 packets, ◐ = 2 packets, ◔ = 1 packet

Buttons per packet	Frequency
35	●
36	●◕
37	◕
38	●◐

Note that the circle symbol ● was used to represent a value of 4 as it could easily be divided to represent the numbers 3, 2, or 1. It is therefore important to choose an appropriate shape for a pictogram.

29 COLLECTING, DISPLAYING AND INTERPRETING DATA

> **Note**
>
> When a bar chart is showing categorical data (such as favourite subjects) rather than numerical data, there are gaps between the bars.

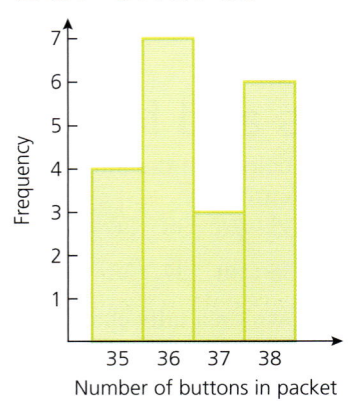

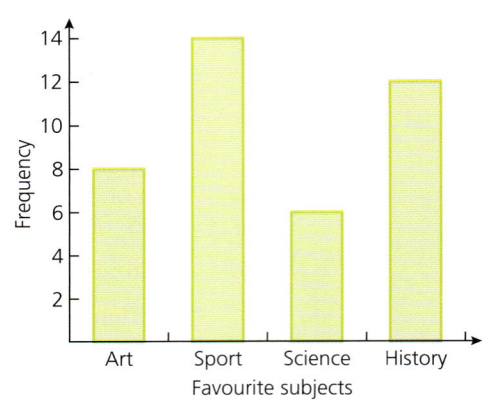

Bar charts

The height of each bar represents the frequency. Therefore, the width of each bar must be the same. To avoid producing a misleading graph, the frequency axis should always start at zero.

Stem-and-leaf diagrams

Discrete data is data that has a specific, fixed value. A stem-and-leaf diagram can be used to display discrete data in a clear and organised way. It has an advantage over bar charts as the original data can easily be recovered from the diagram.

The ages of people on a coach transferring them from an airport to a ski resort are as follows:

22 24 25 31 33 23 24 26 37 42
40 36 33 24 25 18 20 27 25 33
28 33 35 39 40 48 27 25 24 29

Displaying the data on a stem-and-leaf diagram produces the following graph:

```
1 | 8
2 | 0 2 3 4 4 4 4 5 5 5 5 6 7 7 8 9
3 | 1 3 3 3 3 5 6 7 9
4 | 0 0 2 8
```

Key
2 | 5 represents 25

A key is important so that the numbers can be interpreted correctly.

In this form the data can be analysed quite quickly.

- The youngest person is 18.
- The oldest is 48.
- The modal ages are 24, 25 and 33.

As the data is arranged in order, the median age can also be calculated quickly. The middle people out of 30 will be the 15th and 16th people. In this case the 15th person is 27 years old and the 16th person is 28 years old. Therefore, the median age is 27.5.

Back-to-back stem-and-leaf diagrams

Stem-and-leaf diagrams are often used as an easy way to compare two sets of data. The leaves are usually put 'back-to-back' on either side of the stem.

Continuing from the example given above, consider a second coach from the airport taking people to a golfing holiday. The ages of these people are shown below:

43	46	52	61	65	38	36	28	37	45
69	72	63	55	46	34	35	37	43	48
54	53	47	36	58	63	70	55	63	64

The two sets of data displayed on a back-to-back stem-and-leaf diagram are shown below:

```
       Golf                          Skiing
                        1 | 8
                    8 | 2 | 0 2 3 4 4 4 5 5 5 6 7 7 8 9
      8 7 7 6 6 5 4 | 3 | 1 3 3 3 3 5 6 7 9
      8 7 6 6 5 3 3 | 4 | 0 0 2 8
          8 5 5 4 3 2 | 5 |
        9 5 4 3 3 3 1 | 6 |
                  2 0 | 7 |    Key: 5 |3| 6 represents 35 to the left and 36 to the right
```

From the back-to-back diagram it is easier to compare the two sets of data. This data shows that the people on the bus going to the golf resort tend to be older than those on the bus going to the ski resort.

Pie charts

Data can be displayed on a **pie chart** – a circle divided into sectors. The size of the sector is in direct proportion to the frequency of the data.

29 COLLECTING, DISPLAYING AND INTERPRETING DATA

Worked examples

1. In a survey, 240 English children were asked to vote for their favourite holiday destination. The results are shown on the pie chart.

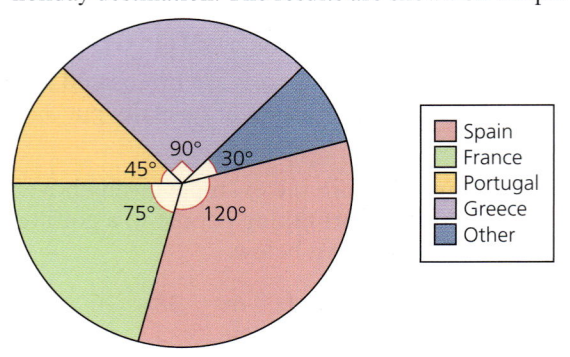

   Calculate the actual number of votes for each destination.

   The total 240 votes are represented by 360°.

   It follows that if 360° represents 240 votes:

   There were $240 \times \frac{120}{360}$ votes for Spain

   so, 80 votes for Spain.

   There were $240 \times \frac{75}{360}$ votes for France

   so, 50 votes for France.

   There were $240 \times \frac{45}{360}$ votes for Portugal

   so, 30 votes for Portugal.

   There were $240 \times \frac{90}{360}$ votes for Greece

   so, 60 votes for Greece.

   Other destinations received $240 \times \frac{30}{360}$ votes

   so, 20 votes for other destinations.

   Note: It is worth checking your result by adding them:

   $80 + 50 + 30 + 60 + 20 = 240$ total votes

2. The table shows the percentage of votes cast for various political parties in an election. If a total of 5 million votes were cast, how many votes were cast for each party?

Party	Percentage of vote
Social Democrats	45%
Liberal Democrats	36%
Green Party	15%
Others	4%

Pie charts

The Social Democrats received $\frac{45}{100} \times 5$ million votes

so, 2.25 million votes.

The Liberal Democrats received $\frac{36}{100} \times 5$ million votes

so, 1.8 million votes.

The Green Party received $\frac{15}{100} \times 5$ million votes

so, 750 000 votes.

Other parties received $\frac{4}{100} \times 5$ million votes

so, 200 000 votes.

Check total:

2.25 + 1.8 + 0.75 + 0.2 = 5 (million votes)

3 The table shows the results of a survey among 72 students to find their favourite sport. Display this data on a pie chart.

Sport	Frequency
Football	35
Tennis	14
Volleyball	10
Hockey	6
Basketball	5
Other	2

72 students are represented by 360°, so 1 student is represented by $\frac{360}{72}$ degrees. Therefore the size of each sector can be calculated as shown:

Football	$35 \times \frac{360}{72}$ degrees	i.e. 175°
Tennis	$14 \times \frac{360}{72}$ degrees	i.e. 70°
Volleyball	$10 \times \frac{360}{72}$ degrees	i.e. 50°
Hockey	$6 \times \frac{360}{72}$ degrees	i.e. 30°
Basketball	$5 \times \frac{360}{72}$ degrees	i.e. 25°
Other sports	$2 \times \frac{360}{72}$ degrees	i.e. 10°

29 COLLECTING, DISPLAYING AND INTERPRETING DATA

Check total:

175 + 70 + 50 + 30 + 25 + 10 = 360

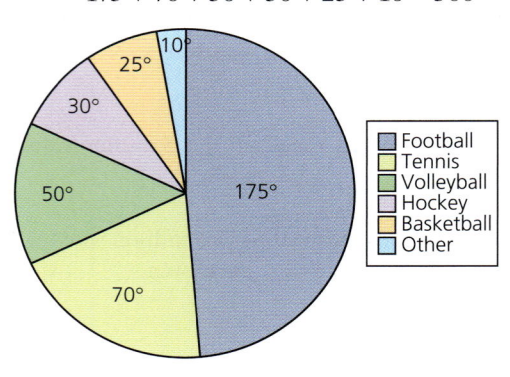

Exercise 29.1

1. The unfinished pie charts below show how Ayse and her brother, Ahmet, spent one day. Calculate how many hours they spent on each activity. The diagrams are to scale.

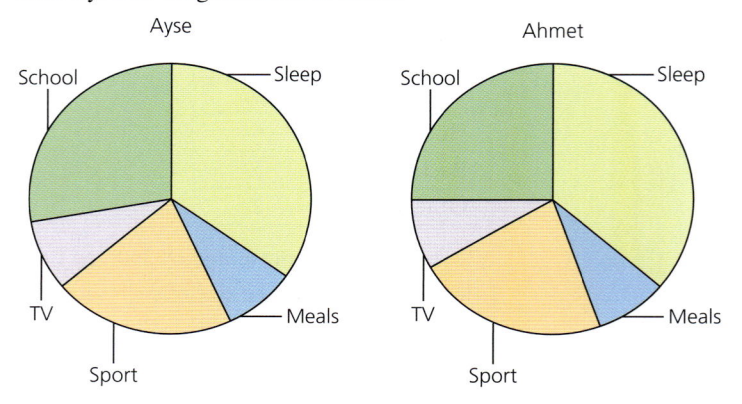

2. A survey was carried out among a class of 40 students. The question asked was, 'How would you spend a gift of $15?' The results were:

Choice	Frequency
Music	14
Books	6
Clothes	18
Cinema	2

Illustrate these results on a pie chart.

Pie charts

3 A student works during the holidays. He earns a total of $2400. He estimates that the money earned has been used as follows: clothes $\frac{1}{3}$, transport $\frac{1}{5}$, entertainment $\frac{1}{4}$. He has saved the rest.
Calculate how much he has spent on each category, and illustrate this information on a pie chart.

4 Two universities in central Asia compared the percentages of people who enrolled on different engineering courses in 2022. The results are shown in the table below.

Engineering course	University A (percentage)	University B (percentage)
Civil	22	38
Mechanical	16	8
Chemical	24	16
Electrical	12	24
Industrial	8	10
Aerospace	18	4

a Illustrate this information on two pie charts, and make two statements that could be supported by the data.
b If 3000 people enrolled on engineering courses at University B in 2022, calculate the number who enrolled on either mechanical or aerospace engineering courses.

5 A village has two leisure clubs. The ages of people in each club are:

Ages in Club 1									
38	8	16	15	18	8	59	12	14	55
14	15	24	67	71	21	23	27	12	48
31	14	70	15	32	9	44	11	46	62

Ages in Club 2									
42	62	10	62	74	18	77	35	38	66
43	71	68	64	66	66	22	48	50	57
60	59	44	57	12	–	–	–	–	–

a Draw a back-to-back stem-and-leaf diagram for the ages of the members of each club.
b For each club calculate:
  i the age range of its members
  ii the median age.
c One of the clubs is computer gaming club, and the other is the swimming club. Which club is likely to be which? Give a reason for your answer.

341

29 COLLECTING, DISPLAYING AND INTERPRETING DATA

Exercise 29.1 (cont)

Dual bar charts are also sometimes known as comparative bar charts as it is easier to compare two sets of data.

6 The birthday months of boys and girls in one class are plotted as a dual bar chart below.

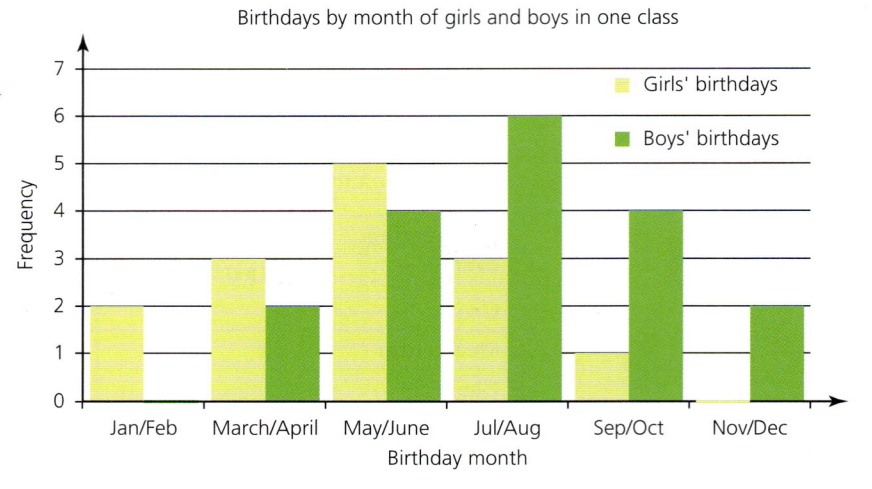

Birthdays by month of girls and boys in one class

a How many girls are there in the class?
b How many more boys than girls have their birthdays in either July or August?
c Describe the differences in the birthdays of boys and girls in the class.
d Construct a dual bar chart for the birthday months of boys and girls in your own class.

7 Two fishing boats return to port and the mass of two types of fish caught by each boat is recorded. The quantities are shown in the composite (stacked) bar chart below.

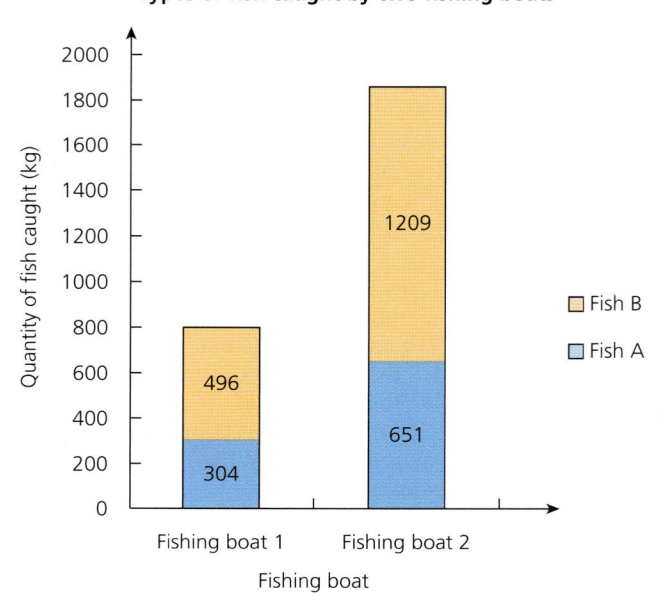

Types of fish caught by two fishing boats

342

a Which boat caught the most of fish type A?
b Assuming only the two types of fish were caught, which boat's catch had a higher percentage of fish type A? Show your working clearly.
c The above stacked bar chart shows the quantity of fish in kg on the vertical axis.
Construct a stacked bar chart comparing the catches of both boats, but with percentages on the vertical axis.

Scatter diagrams

Scatter diagrams are particularly useful because they can show us if there is a **correlation** (relationship) between two sets of data. The two values of data collected represent the coordinates of each point plotted. How the points lie when plotted indicates the type of relationship between the two sets of data.

➡ Worked example

The heights and masses of 20 children under the age of 5 were recorded. The heights were recorded in centimetres and the masses in kilograms. The data is shown in a table:

Height	32	34	45	46	52
Mass	5.8	3.8	9.0	4.2	10.1
Height	59	63	64	71	73
Mass	6.2	9.9	16.0	15.8	9.9
Height	86	87	95	96	96
Mass	11.1	16.4	20.9	16.2	14.0
Height	101	108	109	117	121
Mass	19.5	15.9	12.0	19.4	14.3

a Plot a scatter diagram of the above data.

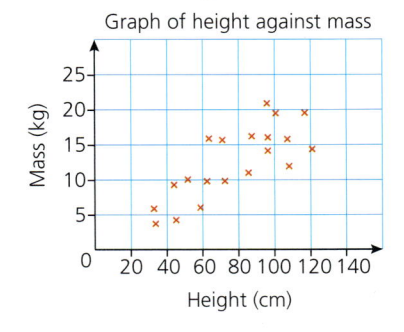

343

29 COLLECTING, DISPLAYING AND INTERPRETING DATA

b Comment on any relationship you see.

The points tend to lie in a diagonal direction from bottom left to top right. This suggests that as height increases then, in general, mass increases too. Therefore there is a **positive correlation** between height and mass.

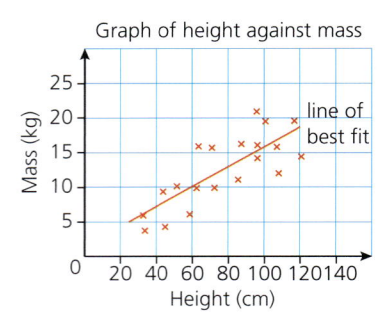

c If another child was measured as having a height of 80 cm, approximately what mass would you expect him or her to be?

We assume that this child will follow the trend set by the other 20 children. To deduce an approximate value for the mass, we draw a **line of best fit**. This is done by eye and is a solid straight line which passes through the points as closely as possible, as shown. The line of best fit can now be used to give an approximate solution to the question. If a child has a height of 80 cm, you would expect his or her mass to be in the region of 14 kg.

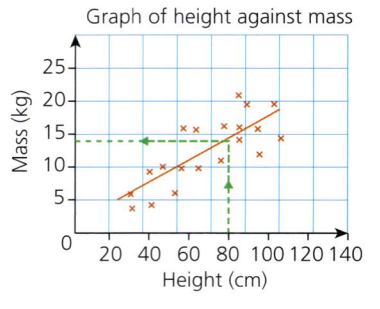

d Someone decides to extend the line of best fit in both directions because they want to make predictions for heights and masses beyond those of the data collected. The graph is shown below.

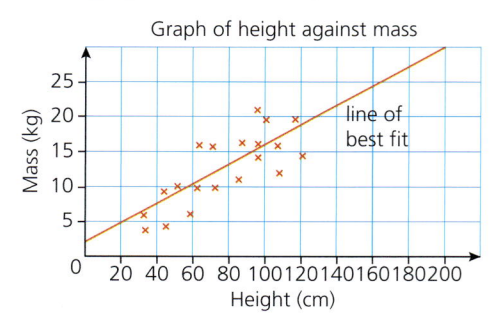

Explain why this should not be done.

The line of best fit should only be extended beyond the given data range with care. In this case it does not make sense to extend it because it implies at one end that a child with no height (which is impossible) would still have a mass of approximately 2 kg. At the other end it implies that the linear relationship between height and mass continues ever upwards, which of course it doesn't.

Types of correlation

There are several types of correlation, depending on the arrangement of the points plotted on the scatter diagram.

> **Note**
>
> This syllabus only requires the use of positive, negative or zero correlation.

A **strong positive correlation** between the variables x and y. The points lie very close to the line of best fit. As x increases, so does y.

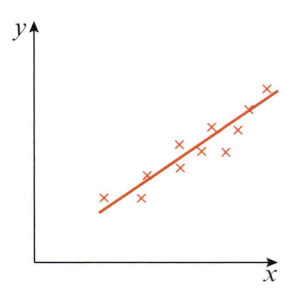

A **weak positive correlation**. Although there is direction to the way the points are lying, they are not tightly packed around the line of best fit. As x increases, y tends to increase too.

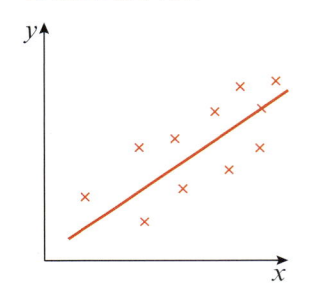

A **strong negative correlation**. The points lie close around the line of best fit. As x increases, y decreases.

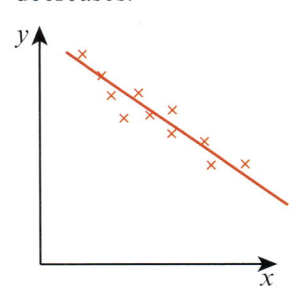

A **weak negative correlation**. The points are not tightly packed around the line of best fit. As x increases, y tends to decrease.

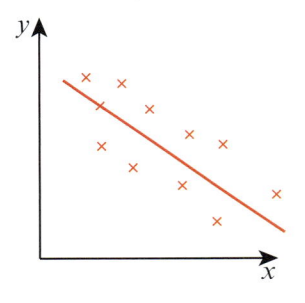

No correlation. As there is no pattern to the way in which the points are lying, there is no correlation between the variables x and y. As a result there can be no line of best fit.

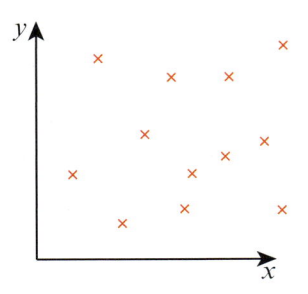

29 COLLECTING, DISPLAYING AND INTERPRETING DATA

Exercise 29.2

1 State what type of correlation you might expect, if any, if the following data was collected and plotted on a scatter diagram. Give reasons for your answers.
   a A student's score in a Maths exam and their score in a Science exam.
   b A student's hair colour and the distance they have to travel to school.
   c The outdoor temperature and the number of cold drinks sold by a shop.
   d The age of a motorcycle and its second-hand selling price.
   e The number of people living in a house and the number of rooms the house has.
   f The number of goals your opponents score and the number of times you win.
   g A child's height and the child's age.
   h A car's engine size and its fuel consumption.

2 A website gives average monthly readings for the number of hours of sunshine and the amount of rainfall in millimetres for several cities in Europe. The table is a summary for July:

Place	Hours of sunshine	Rainfall (mm)
Athens	12	6
Belgrade	10	61
Copenhagen	8	71
Dubrovnik	12	26
Edinburgh	5	83
Frankfurt	7	70
Geneva	10	64
Helsinki	9	68
Innsbruck	7	134
Krakow	7	111
Lisbon	12	3
Marseilles	11	11
Naples	10	19
Oslo	7	82
Plovdiv	11	37
Reykjavik	6	50
Sofia	10	68
Tallinn	10	68
Valletta	12	0
York	6	62
Zurich	8	136

   a Plot a scatter diagram of the number of hours of sunshine against the amount of rainfall. Use a spreadsheet if possible.
   b What type of correlation, if any, is there between the two variables? Comment on whether this is what you would expect.

Types of correlation

3 The United Nations keeps an up-to-date database of statistical information on its member countries. The table shows some of the information available:

Country	Life expectancy at birth (years, 2005–2010) Female	Life expectancy at birth (years, 2005–2010) Male	Adult illiteracy rate (%, 2009)	Infant mortality rate (per 1000 births, 2005–2010)
Australia	84	79	1	5
Barbados	80	74	0.3	10
Brazil	76	69	10	24
Chad	50	47	68.2	130
China	75	71	6.7	23
Colombia	77	69	7.2	19
Congo	55	53	18.9	79
Cuba	81	77	0.2	5
Egypt	72	68	33	35
France	85	78	1	4
Germany	82	77	1	4
India	65	62	34	55
Israel	83	79	2.9	5
Japan	86	79	1	3
Kenya	55	54	26.4	64
Mexico	79	74	7.2	17
Nepal	67	66	43.5	42
Portugal	82	75	5.1	4
Russian Federation	73	60	0.5	12
Saudi Arabia	75	71	15	19
South Africa	53	50	12	49
United Kingdom	82	77	1	5
United States of America	81	77	1	6

a By plotting a scatter diagram, decide if there is a correlation between the adult illiteracy rate and the infant mortality rate.
b Are your findings in part **a** what you expected? Explain your answer.
c Without plotting a graph, decide if you think there is likely to be a correlation between male and female life expectancy at birth. Explain your reasons.
d Plot a scatter diagram to test if your predictions for part **c** were correct.

29 COLLECTING, DISPLAYING AND INTERPRETING DATA

Exercise 29.2 (cont)

4 Kris plants 10 tomato plants. He wants to see if there is a relationship between the number of tomatoes the plant produces and its height in centimetres.
The results are presented in the scatter diagram. The line of best fit is also drawn.
   a Describe the correlation (if any) between the height of a plant and the number of tomatoes it produced.
   b Kris has another plant grown in the same conditions as the others. If the height is 85 cm, estimate from the graph the number of tomatoes he can expect it to produce.
   c Another plant only produces 15 tomatoes. Estimate its height from the graph.
   d Kris thinks he will be able to make more predictions if the height axis starts at 0 cm rather than 50 cm and if the line of best fit is then extended. By re-plotting the data on a new scatter graph and extending the line of best fit, explain whether Kris' idea is correct.

5 The table shows the 15 countries that won the most medals at the 2016 Rio Olympics. In addition, statistics relating to the population, wealth, percentage of people with higher education and percentage who are overweight for each country are also given.

Country	Olympic medals			Population (million)	Average wealth per person ($000's)	% with a higher education qualification	% adult population that is overweight	
	Gold	Silver	Bronze				Male	Female
U.S.A.	46	37	38	322	345	45	73	63
U.K.	27	23	17	65	289	44	68	59
China	26	18	26	1376	23	10	39	33
Russia	19	18	19	143	10	54	60	55
Germany	17	10	15	81	185	28	64	49
Japan	12	8	21	127	231	50	29	19
France	10	18	14	664	244	34	67	52
S. Korea	9	3	9	50	160	45	38	30
Italy	8	12	8	60	202	18	66	53
Australia	8	11	10	24	376	43	70	58
Holland	8	7	4	17	184	35	63	49
Hungary	8	3	4	10	34	24	67	49
Brazil	7	6	6	208	18	14	55	53
Spain	7	4	6	46	116	35	67	55
Kenya	6	6	1	46	2	11	17	34

348

Surveys

A sports scientist wants to see if there is a correlation between the number of medals a country won and the percentage of overweight people in that country. She plots the number of gold medals against the mean percentage of overweight people; the resulting scatter graph and line of best fit is:

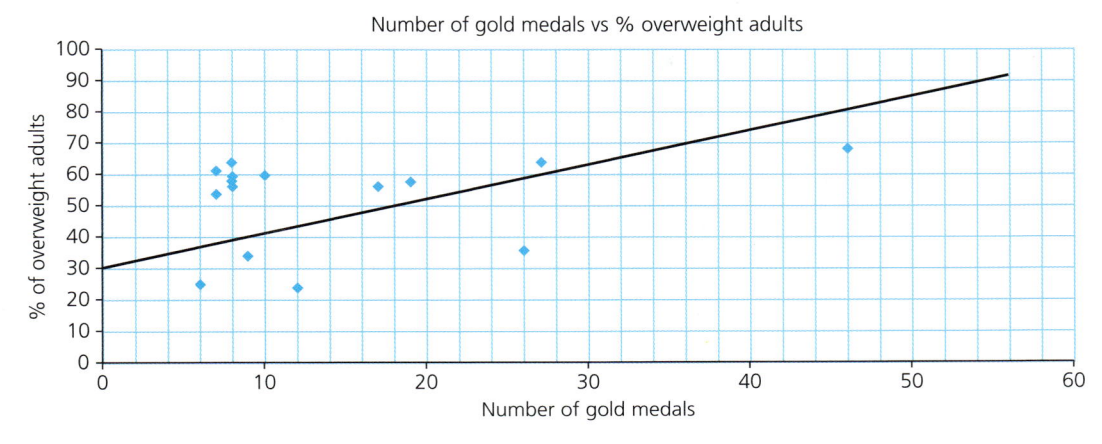

Number of gold medals vs % overweight adults

a Describe the type of correlation implied by the graph.
b The sports scientist states that the graph shows that the more overweight you are the more likely you are to win a gold medal. Give two reasons why this conclusion may not be accurate.
c Analyse the correlation between two other sets of data presented in the table and comment on whether the results are expected or not. Justify your answer.

Surveys

A survey requires data to be collected, organised, analysed and presented.

A survey may be carried out for interest's sake, for example, to find out how many cars pass your school in an hour. A survey could be carried out to help future planning – information about traffic flow could lead to the building of new roads, or the placing of traffic lights or a pedestrian crossing.

Exercise 29.3

1 Below are some statements, some of which you may have heard or read before. Conduct a survey to collect data which will support or disprove one of the statements. Where possible, use pie charts to illustrate your results.
   a Magazines are full of adverts.
   b If you go to a football match, you are lucky to see more than one goal scored.
   c Every other car on the road is white.
   d Most retired people use public transport.
   e Children today do nothing but watch TV.
   f Newspapers have more sport than news in them.
   g More people prefer to drink coffee than tea.

29 COLLECTING, DISPLAYING AND INTERPRETING DATA

Exercise 29.3 (cont)

    h Nobody walks to school anymore.
    i Nearly everybody has a computer at home.
    j Most of what is on TV comes from America.

2 Below are some instructions relating to a washing machine in English, French, German, Dutch and Italian. Analyse the data and write a report. You may wish to comment upon:
    i the length of words in each language
    ii the frequency of letters of the alphabet in different languages.

ENGLISH

ATTENTION

Do not interrupt drying during the programme.

This machine incorporates a temperature safety thermostat which will cut out the heating element in the event of a water blockage or power failure. In the event of this happening, reset the programme before selecting a further drying time.

For further instructions, consult the user manual.

FRENCH

ATTENTION

N'interrompez pas le séchage en cours de programme.

Une panne d'électricité ou un manque d'eau momentanés peuvent annuler le programme de séchage en cours. Dans ces cas arrêtez l'appareil, affichez de nouveau le programme et après remettez l'appareil en marche.

Pour d'ultérieures informations, rapportez-vous à la notice d'utilisation.

GERMAN

ACHTUNG

Die Trocknung soll nicht nach Anlaufen des Programms unterbrochen werden.

Ein kurzer Stromausfall bzw. Wassermangel kann das laufende Trocknungsprogramm annullieren. In diesem Falle Gerät ausschalten, Programm wieder einstellen und Gerät wieder einschalten.

Für nähere Angaben beziehen Sie sich auf die Bedienungsanleitung.

ESTONIAN

TÄHELEPANU

Ärge katkestage kuivatamist programmi ajal.

Sellel masinal on temperatuuri turvatermostaat, mis lõikab veeummistuse või voolukatkestuse korral kütteelemendi välja.

Juhul kui see peaks juhtuma, lähtestage programm uuesti enne uue kuivamisaja valimist. Täiendavate juhiste saamiseks vaadake kasutusjuhendit.

MALAY

PERHATIAN

Jangan ganggu pengeringan semasa program.

Mesin ini menggabungkan termostat keselamatan suhu yang akan dipotong keluarkan elemen pemanas sekiranya berlaku penyumbatan air atau kegagalan kuasa.

Sekiranya ini berlaku, tetapkan semula atur cara sebelum memilih a masa pengeringan selanjutnya. Untuk arahan lanjut, rujuk manual pengguna.

Student assessment 1

1 The areas of four countries are shown in the table. Illustrate this data as a bar chart.

Country	Nigeria	Republic of the Congo	South Sudan	Kenya
Area in 10 000 km^2	90	35	70	57

2 The table gives the average time taken for 30 pupils in a class to get to school each morning, and the distance they live from the school.

Distance (km)	2	10	18	15	3	4	6	2	25	23	3	5	7	8	2
Time (min)	5	17	32	38	8	14	15	7	31	37	5	18	13	15	8
Distance (km)	19	15	11	9	2	3	4	3	14	14	4	12	12	7	1
Time (min)	27	40	23	30	10	10	8	9	15	23	9	20	27	18	4

a Plot a scatter diagram of distance travelled against time taken.
b Describe the correlation between the two variables.
c Explain why some pupils who live further away may get to school more quickly than some of those who live nearer.
d Draw a line of best fit on your scatter diagram.
e A new pupil joins the class. Use your line of best fit to estimate how far away from school she might live if she takes, on average, 19 minutes to get to school each morning.

3 A class of 27 students was asked to draw a line 8 cm long with a straight edge rather than with a ruler. The lines were measured and their lengths to the nearest millimetre were recorded:

```
8.8   6.2   8.3   8.1   8.2   5.9   6.2   10.0  9.7
8.1   5.4   6.8   7.3   7.7   8.9   10.4  5.9   8.3
6.1   7.2   8.3   9.4   6.5   5.8   8.8   8.1   7.3
```

a Present this data using a stem-and-leaf diagram.
b Find the range of the lengths of the lines drawn.
c Calculate the median line length.
d Calculate the mean line length.
e Using your answers to parts **b**, **c** or **d**, comment on whether students in the class underestimate or overestimate the length of the line and how accurate they were.

Mathematical investigations and ICT 9

Reading age

Depending on their target audience, newspapers, magazines and books have different levels of readability. Some are easy to read and others more difficult.

1. Decide on some factors that you think would affect the readability of a text.
2. Write down the names of two newspapers which you think would have different reading ages. Give reasons for your answer.

There are established formulae for calculating the reading age of different texts.

One of these is the Gunning Fog Index. It calculates the reading age as follows:

Reading age $= \frac{2}{5}\left(\frac{A}{n} + \frac{100L}{A}\right)$ where

A = number of words
n = number of sentences
L = number of words with 3 or more syllables

3. Choose one article from each of the two newspapers you chose in Q.2. Use the Gunning Fog Index to calculate the reading ages for the articles. Do the results support your predictions?
4. Write down some factors which you think may affect the reliability of your results.

ICT activity

In this activity, you will be using the graphing facilities of a spreadsheet to compare the activities you do on a school day with the activities you do on a day at the weekend.

1. Prepare a 24-hour timeline for a weekday similar to the one shown below:

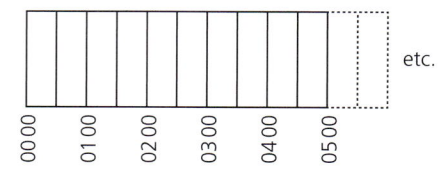

2. By using different colours for different activities, shade in the timeline to show what you did and when on a specific weekday, e.g. sleeping, eating, school, watching TV.

ICT activity

3 Add up the time spent on each activity and enter the results in a spreadsheet like the one below:

	A	B	C
1	Activity	Time spent (hrs)	
2	Sleeping		
3	Eating		
4	School		
5	TV		

4 Use the spreadsheet to produce a fully labelled pie chart of this data.

5 Repeat steps 1–4 for a day at the weekend.

6 Comment on any differences and similarities between the pie charts for the two days.

Glossary

= = means is equal to. For example, 3 + 4 = 7.

≠ ≠ means is not equal to. For example, 3 + 4 ≠ 8.

> > means is greater than. For example, 8 > 3 + 4.

< < means is less than. For example, 3 + 4 < 8.

⩾ ⩾ means is greater than or equal to. For example, $x \geq 5$ means x is any number greater than or equal to 5.

⩽ ⩽ means is less than or equal to. For example, $x \leq 5$ means x is any number less than or equal to 5.

A ∩ B A ∩ B means all the elements that belong to BOTH set A and set B. A ∩ B denotes the elements that are in the intersection of A and B on a Venn diagram.

A ∪ B The union of sets A and B, A ∪ B, is all the elements that belong to EITHER set A OR set B OR both sets.

n(A) The number of elements in set A.

ξ The universal set, ξ, for any particular problem is the set which contains all the possible elements for that problem.

12-hour clock 12-hour clock is when the day is split into two halves 'am' and 'pm. The times before 12 noon are written using am and times after 12 noon are written as pm.

24-hour clock 24-hour clock is when the time is given as the number of hours that have passed since midnight. The hours part of the time is given two digits. For example, 01 30 is 1.30 am and 13 30 is 1.30 pm.

accuracy The accuracy of a measurement tells you how close the measurement is to the true value. For example, if you measure a pencil correct to the nearest centimetre, your measurement will be within 0.5 cm of the true measurement.

acute angle An acute angle lies between 0° and 90°.

acute-angled isosceles triangle An acute-angled isosceles triangle has two equal angles and two sides of equal length, and all three angles are less than 90°.

acute-angled triangle In an acute-angled triangle, all three angles are less than 90°.

addition Addition is one of the four operations: addition, subtraction, multiplication and division. It means to find the total or sum of two or more numbers or quantities.

adjacent In a right-angled triangle, the adjacent is the side which is next to the angle.

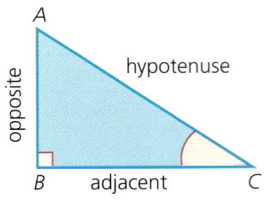

alternate angles Alternate angles are formed when a line crosses a pair of parallel lines. Alternate angles are equal. Look for a Z shape.

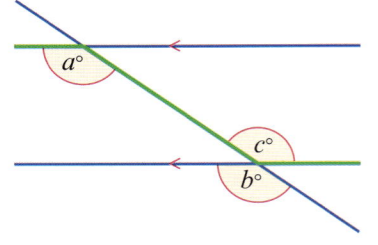

altitude The altitude of a triangle is the perpendicular height.

angles at a point The angles at a point add up to 360°.

angles on a straight line The angles on a straight line add up to 180°.

apex The apex of a pyramid is the point where the triangular faces of the pyramid meet.

arc An arc is part of the circumference of a circle between two radii. When the angle between the two radii of length r is ϕ, then: arc length = $\frac{x}{360} \times 2\pi r$

area The area of a shape is the amount of surface that it covers. Area is measured in mm², cm², m², km², etc.

area of a circle The area, A, of a circle of radius r is: $A = \pi r^2$

area of a parallelogram The area, A, of a parallelogram of base length b and perpendicular height h is: $A = bh$

area of a rectangle The area, A, of a rectangle of length l and breadth b is: $A = lb$

area of a trapezium The area, A, of a trapezium is: $A = \frac{1}{2}h(a+b)$

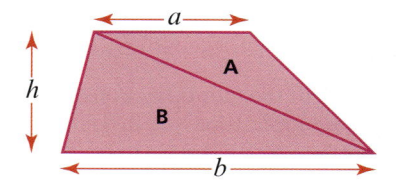

area of a sector The area of a sector is given by: $\frac{x}{360} \times \pi r^2$

area of a triangle The area, A, of a triangle of base b and perpendicular height h is: $A = \frac{1}{2}bh$

average An average is a measure of the typical value in a data set. There are three measures: mean, mode and median.

average speed average speed = $\frac{\text{total distance}}{\text{total time}}$

back bearing If the bearing of B from A is given, then the back bearing is the bearing of A from B. It is the bearing that takes you from B back to A. The back bearing is in the reverse direction to the original bearing – it represents the direction of the return journey. (*See* bearing)

bar chart A bar chart is a chart that uses rectangular bars to display data. The height of each bar represents the frequency.

base The base of a triangle is one of its sides. Any side can be the base, but the height must be measured perpendicular to the chosen base.

basic pay Basic pay is the fixed pay that an employee is given for working a certain number of hours.

basic week A basic week is the fixed number of hours that an employee is expected to work each week.

bearing A bearing is a direction. It is the angle measured clockwise from North. Bearings are given as 3 figures so, for example, for an angle of 45° the three-figure bearing is 045°.

bonus A bonus is an extra payment that is sometimes added to an employee's basic pay.

breadth The breadth of a rectangle is the measure of its shortest side.

centre of enlargement The centre of enlargement is a specific point about which an object is enlarged.

centre of rotation The centre of rotation is a specific 'pivot' point about which an object is rotated.

chord A chord is a straight line that joins two points on the circumference of a circle.

circumference The circumference is the perimeter of a circle.

circumference of a circle The circumference, C, of a circle of radius r is: $C = 2\pi r$

common difference The common difference, d, is the difference between one term and the next in an arithmetic sequence.

complementary angle Two angles which add together to total 90° are called complementary angles.

composite bar chart A composite bar chart shows the bars stacked on top of each other.

compound interest Compound interest is interest that is paid not only on the principal amount, but also on the interest itself. So the amount of interest earned each year increases.

complement The complement of set A is the set of elements which are in ξ but not in A. The complement of A is written as A'.

compound measure A compound measure is one made up of two or more other measures.

compound shape A compound shape is a shape that can be split into simpler shapes.

cone A cone is a like a pyramid, but with a circular base.

congruent Congruent shapes are exactly the same shape and size – they are identical.

construction A construction is an accurate drawing made using a ruler and a pair of compasses.

conversion graph A conversion graph is a straight-line graph used to convert one set of units to another.

correlation Correlation is the relationship between two sets of data.

corresponding angles Corresponding angles are formed when a line crosses a pair of parallel lines. Corresponding angles are equal. Look for an F shape.

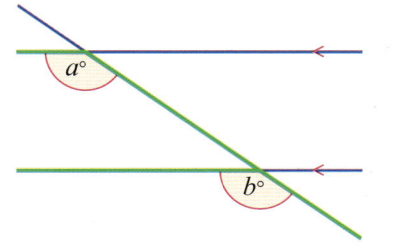

cosine The cosine of an angle, cos x, in a right-angled triangle is the ratio of the adjacent side to the hypotenuse: $\cos x = \frac{\text{length of adjacent side}}{\text{length of hypotenuse}}$

cost price The cost price is the total amount of money that it costs to produce a good or service, before any profit is made.

cube number A cube number is the result when an integer is multiplied by itself twice. The cube numbers are 1, 8, 27, 64, 125, ...

cube root The cube root of a number is the number which when multiplied by itself twice gives the original number. The inverse of cubing is cube rooting. For example, the cube root of 27 is 3 (as 3 × 3 × 3 = 27). The symbol $\sqrt[3]{}$ is used for the cube root of a number, so $\sqrt[3]{27} = 3$.

cuboid A cuboid is a prism with a rectangular cross-section.

cylinder A cylinder is a three-dimensional shape with a constant circular cross-section.

decagon A decagon is a 10-sided polygon.

decimal A decimal is a number with digits after the decimal point. It is a number which is not an integer.

decimal fraction A decimal fraction is a fraction between 0 and 1 in which the denominator is a power of 10 and the numerator is an integer.

decimal place The decimal place is the number of digits after the decimal point. For example, 3.2 has 1 decimal place and 5.678 has 3 decimal places.

denominator The denominator is the bottom line of a fraction; it tells you how many equal parts the whole is divided into. For example, $\frac{3}{8}$ has a denominator of 8, so the 'whole' has been divided into 8 equal parts.

density Density is a measure of the mass of a substance per unit of its volume. It is calculated using the formula: density = $\frac{mass}{volume}$

depreciate When the value of something decreases over a period of time, it is said to depreciate.

diameter A diameter is a straight line which passes through the centre of a circle and joins two points on the circumference.

direct proportion Two quantities are in direct proportion when one quantity increases as the other increases.

directed number A directed number is a number that is positive or negative. A number has size (magnitude) and its sign (+ or −) tells you which *direction* to move along a number line from 0 in order to reach that number.

discount An item sold at 10% discount is 10% cheaper than the full selling price.

discrete data Discrete data is numerical data that can only take on certain values, usually whole numbers. For example, the number of peas in a pod is discrete data.

distance between two points The distance, d, between two points (x_1, y_1) and (x_2, y_2) is:
$$d = \sqrt{(x_1 - x_2)^2 + (y_1 - y_2)^2}$$

division Division is one of the four operations: addition, subtraction, multiplication and division. To divide one number by another means to find how many times one number goes into another number, for example,
20 ÷ 5 = 4
5 ÷ 20 = 0.25

double time Overtime is often paid at a higher rate. When overtime is paid at twice the basic pay, it is called double time.

dual bar chart A dual bar chart shows the bars side by side.

element An object or symbol in a set is called an element.

elevation An elevation is a two-dimensional view of a three-dimensional object. A side elevation is the view from one side of the object and the front elevation is the view from the front.

elimination method The elimination method is a method for solving simultaneous equations. One of the unknowns is eliminated by either adding or subtracting the pair of equations.

enlargement An enlargement changes the size of an object. When a shape is enlarged, the image is mathematically similar to the object but is a different size. Note: the image may be larger or smaller than the original object.

equation An equation says that one expression is equal to another. For example, 6 + 4 = 16 − 6. When an expression contains an unknown, it can be solved. For example, the solution to the equation $x + 4 = 16 - x$ is $x = 6$.

equation of a straight line The equation of a straight line can be written in the form $y = mx + c$, where m is the gradient of the line and the y-intercept is at $(0, c)$.

equilateral triangle An equilateral triangle has three equal angles (all 60°) and three sides of equal length.

equivalent fraction Equivalent fractions have the same decimal value. For example, $\frac{3}{5} = 0.6$ and $\frac{9}{15} = 0.6$, so $\frac{3}{5}$ and $\frac{9}{15}$ are equivalent.

estimate / estimation Estimation is a way of working out the approximate answer or estimate to a calculation. The numbers in the calculation are rounded (usually to 1 significant figure) so that the calculation is easier to work out without a calculator. Estimation is useful for checking a calculation.

evaluate Evaluate means to work out the value of something.

expand Expand means to multiply out or remove the brackets.

exterior angle The exterior angle of an n-sided regular polygon = $\frac{360°}{n}$.

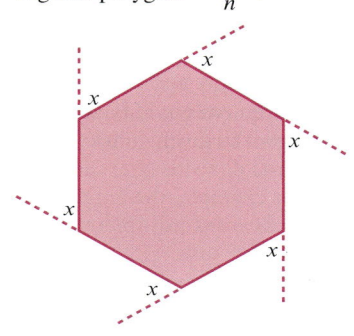

factor A factor of a number divides into that number exactly. For example, the factors of 18 are 1, 2, 3, 6, 9 and 18.

factorise Factorise means to remove common factors and write an equivalent expression using brackets. For example, $2x - 6$ factorises to give $2(x - 3)$.

favourable outcome A favourable outcome refers to the event in question (for example, getting a 6 when a dice is thrown) actually happening.

fraction A fraction represents a part of a whole.

frequency Frequency is the number of times a particular outcome happens.

frequency table A frequency table shows the frequency of each data value in a data set.

gradient Gradient is a measure of how steep a line is. The gradient of the line joining two points on a line is:

gradient = $\frac{\text{vertical distance between two points}}{\text{horizontal distance between two points}}$

gradient-intercept form The gradient-intercept form of the equation of a straight line is the form $y = mx + c$, where m is the gradient and c is the y-intercept.

gross earnings Gross earnings are the total earnings *before* all the deductions such as tax, insurance and pension contributions are made.

grouped frequency table A grouped frequency table is a method of displaying a large data set so that it is easier to handle.

height The height of a triangle is the perpendicular distance from its base to its third vertex.

highest common factor The highest common factor (HCF) of two numbers is the greatest integer that divides exactly into both numbers. For example, the highest common factor of 6 and 15 is 3.

hyperbola The graph of a reciprocal function in the form $y = \frac{k}{x}$, where k is a constant, is a hyperbola.

hypotenuse The hypotenuse is the longest side of a right-angled triangle.

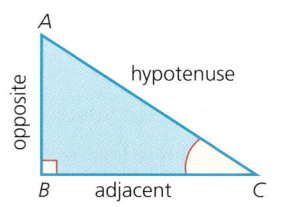

image When an object undergoes a transformation, the resulting position or shape is the image.

improper fraction In an improper fraction, the numerator is more than the denominator. For example, $\frac{8}{3}$ is an improper fraction.

index The index is the power to which a number is raised. For example, in 4^3 the power (or index) is 3 and so $4^3 = 4 \times 4 \times 4$.

inequality An inequality says that one expression is not equal to a second expression. For example, $x + 2 < 8$ or $7 > 6$

integer An integer is a positive or negative whole number (including zero). The set of integers is $\{..., -3, -2, -1, 0, 1, 2, 3, ...\}$.

interest Interest is the money added by a bank to a sum deposited by a customer. Interest is also the money charged by a bank for a loan to a customer. It can be either simple interest or compound interest (see separate entries).

interior angle The sum of the interior angles of an n-sided polygon is $180(n - 2)°$.

intersection The intersection of two sets is the elements that are common to both sets. It is represented by the symbol ∩.

inverse proportion Two quantities, x and y, are in inverse proportion when the product of the two quantities xy is constant, i.e. when an increase in one quantity causes a decrease in the second quantity.

irrational number An irrational number is any number (positive or negative) that cannot be written as a fraction. Any decimal which neither terminates nor recurs is irrational. The square root of any number other than square numbers is also irrational. Some examples of irrational numbers are π, $\sqrt{2}$ and $\sqrt{10}$.

irregular polygon An irregular polygon is a polygon that does not have equal sides or equal angles.

isosceles trapezium An isosceles trapezium is a quadrilateral with the following properties:
- one pair of parallel sides
- the other pair of sides are equal in length
- two pairs of equal base angles
- opposite base angles add up to 180°.

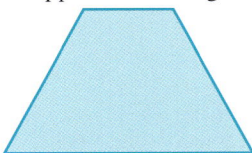

isosceles triangle An isosceles triangle has two equal angles and two sides of equal length.

kite A kite is a quadrilateral with the following properties:
- two pairs of equal sides
- one pair of equal angles
- diagonals which cross at right angles.

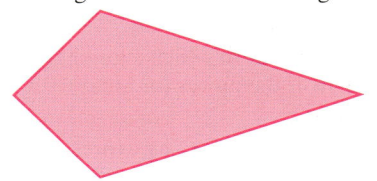

laws of indices The laws of indices are:
- $a^m \times a^n = a^{m+n}$
- $a^m \div a^n$ or $\frac{a^m}{a^n} = a^{m-n}$
- $(a^m)^n = a^{mn}$
- $a^1 = a$
- $a^0 = 1$
- $a^{-m} = \frac{1}{a^m}$
- $a^{\frac{1}{n}} = \sqrt[n]{a}$
- $a^{\frac{m}{n}} = \sqrt[n]{(a^m)}$ or $\left(\sqrt[n]{(a)}\right)^m$

length The length of a rectangle is the measure of its longest side.

line A line is a one-dimensional object with length but no width. It has infinite length.

line of best fit A line of best fit is a straight line that passes as close as possible to as many points as possible on a scatter diagram.

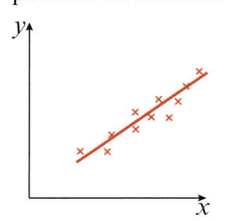

line of symmetry A line of symmetry divides a two-dimensional shape into two congruent (identical) shapes.

line segment A line segment is part of a line.

linear equation The graph of a linear equation is a straight line. The highest power of the variable is 1.

linear function The graph of a linear function is a straight line.

loss When an item is sold for less than it cost to make, it is sold at a loss: loss = cost price – selling price

lower bound Measurement is only approximate; the actual value of a measurement could be half the rounded unit above or below the given value. The lower bound is the least possible value that the true measurement could be. For example, the length of a pencil is 15.5 cm to the nearest millimetre. So the lower bound is 15.5 cm – 0.5 mm = 15.45 cm. The actual length, l, of the pencil is greater than or equal to 15.45 cm, so $15.45 \leq l$.

lowest common multiple The lowest common multiple (LCM) of two numbers is the lowest integer that is a multiple of both numbers. For example, the lowest common multiple of 6 and 15 is 30.

lowest terms or simplest form A fraction is in its lowest terms when the highest common factor of the numerator and denominator is 1. In other words, the fraction cannot be cancelled down any further. For example, $\frac{30}{45} = \frac{6}{9} = \frac{2}{3}$, so $\frac{2}{3}$ is a fraction in its lowest terms.

magnitude Magnitude means size.

mean The mean is found by adding together all of the data values and then dividing this total by the number of data values. The mean is one of the three ways to measure an average.

median The median is the middle value when the data set is organised in order of size. The median is one of the three main ways to measure an average.

metric units of capacity 1 litre (l) = 1000 millilitres (ml)   1 ml = 1 cm³

metric units of length 1 kilometre (km) = 1000 metres (m)   1 metre (m) = 100 centimetres (cm)   1 centimetre (cm) = 10 millimetres (mm)

metric units of mass 1 tonne (t) = 1000 kilograms (kg)   1 kilogram (kg) = 1000 grams (g)   1 gram (g) = 1000 milligrams (mg)

mirror line The mirror line is the line in which an object is reflected.

mixed number A mixed number is made up of a whole number and a proper fraction. For example, $2\frac{3}{8}$ is a mixed number.

mode The mode is the value occurring most often in a data set. The mode is one of the three main ways to measure an average.

multiple The multiple of a number is the result when you multiply that number by a positive integer. For example, the multiples of 6 are 6, 12, 18, 24, 30, …

multiplication Multiplication is one of the four operations: addition, subtraction, multiplication and division. Multiplication is repeated addition, so 3 multiplied by 4 means 3 + 3 + 3 + 3.

natural number A natural number is a whole number (integer) that is used in counting and starts at zero. The set of natural numbers is {…, –3, –2, –1, 0, 1, 2, 3, …}.

net A net is a two-dimensional shape which can be folded up to form a three-dimensional shape.

net pay Net pay is sometimes called 'take-home' pay. It is the money left *after* all the deductions such as tax, insurance and pension contributions are made.

negative correlation Two quantities have negative correlation if, in general, one decreases as the other increases.

negative number A negative number is any number less than 0.

no correlation Correlation is the relationship between two sets of data. If there is no correlation, then there is no relationship between the two data sets. In a scatter graph showing no correlation, there is no pattern in the plotted points.

numerator The numerator is the top line of a fraction. It represents the number of equal parts of the whole. For example, $\frac{3}{8}$ has a numerator of 3, so there are 3 equal parts and each part is equal to $\frac{1}{8}$ of the 'whole'.

obtuse angle An obtuse angle lies between 90° and 180°.

obtuse-angled triangle In an obtuse-angled triangle, one angle is greater than 90°.

octagon An octagon is an 8-sided polygon.

opposite In a right-angled triangle, the opposite side is the one which is opposite the angle.

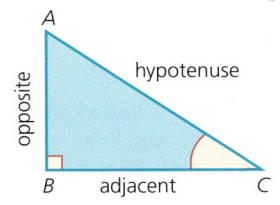

order of operations When a calculation contains a mixture of brackets and/or the operations (×, ÷, + and –), the order that the operations should be carried out in is:
- First work out any …   Brackets and Indices
- … then carry out any …   Multiplication and Division
- … finally   Addition and Subtraction

When a calculation contains operations of equal priority (e.g. + and –, or × and ÷), work from left to right. For example, 10 – 7 + 2 = 3 + 2 = 5.

order of rotational symmetry The order of rotational symmetry is the number of times a shape, when rotated about a central point, fits its outline during a complete revolution of 360°.

origin The origin is the point at which the *x*-axis and the *y*-axis meet.

overtime Overtime is any hours worked in excess of the basic week.

parabola The graph of a quadratic function is a parabola.

parallel A pair of parallel lines can be continued to infinity in either direction without meeting. Parallel lines have the same gradient.

parallelogram A parallelogram is a quadrilateral with the following properties:
- two pairs of parallel sides
- opposite sides are equal
- opposite angles are equal.

pentagon A pentagon is a 5-sided polygon.

per cent (%) Per cent means parts per 100.

percentage A percentage is the number of parts per 100.

percentage interest (or interest rate) Interest is earned on a fixed percentage of the principal. The interest rate gives the percentage interest earned.

percentage loss percentage loss = $\frac{\text{loss}}{\text{cost price}} \times 100\%$

percentage profit percentage profit = $\frac{\text{profit}}{\text{cost price}} \times 100\%$

perimeter The perimeter of a shape is the distance around the outside edge of the shape. Perimeter is measured in mm, cm, m, km, etc.

perimeter of a rectangle The perimeter of a rectangle of length *l* and breadth *b* is: 2*l* + 2*b*

perpendicular Two lines are perpendicular if they meet at right angles. The product of the gradients of two perpendicular lines is –1.

pictogram A pictogram is a chart that uses pictures or symbols to display data.

pie chart A pie chart is a circular chart divided into sectors that is used to display data. The area of each sector is proportional to the frequency.

piece work Piece work is when an employee is paid for the number of articles made (rather than the time spent working).

plan A plan of an object is a scale diagram of the view from above the object, looking directly down on the object.

point A point is an exact location or position.

polygon A polygon is a two-dimensional shape made up of straight lines.

population density Population density is a measure of the population per unit of area. It is calculated using the formula: population density $= \frac{\text{population}}{\text{Area}}$

positive correlation Two quantities have positive correlation if, in general, one increases as the other increases.

positive number A positive number is any number greater than 0.

power For example, in 4^3 the power is 3 and so $4^3 = 4 \times 4 \times 4$.

pressure Pressure is a compound measurement and is measured in Pascals (Pa) or N/m^2: Pressure $= \frac{\text{Force}}{\text{Area}}$

prime factor A prime factor of a number is any factor of that number that is also a prime. For example, the prime factors of 60 are 2, 3 and 5.

prime number A prime number is a number with exactly two factors: one and itself. The prime numbers are 2, 3, 5, 7, 11, … Note: 1 is not a prime number as it only has one factor.

principal The principal is the amount of money deposited by a customer in a bank account.

prism A prism is a three-dimensional object with a constant cross-sectional area.

probability Probability is the study of chance. The probability of an event happening is a measure of how likely that event is to happen. Probability is given on a scale of 0 (an impossible event) to 1 (a certain event): probability $= \frac{\text{number of favourable outcomes}}{\text{total number of equally likely outcomes}}$

probability scale A probability scale is a scale that indicates how likely an event is, ranging from impossible to certain.

profit When an item is sold for more than it cost to make, it is sold at a profit: profit = selling price − cost price

proper fraction In a proper fraction, the numerator is less than its denominator. For example, $\frac{3}{8}$ is a proper fraction.

pyramid A pyramid is a three-dimensional shape. It has a polygon for a base and the other faces are triangles which meet at a common vertex, called the apex.

Pythagoras' theorem Pythagoras' theorem states the relationship between the lengths of the three sides of a right-angled triangle. Pythagoras' theorem is: $a^2 = b^2 + c^2$

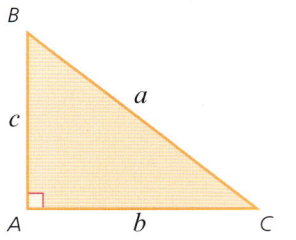

quadratic equation A quadratic equation can be written in the form $y = ax^2 + bx + c$, where a, b and c are constants.

quadratic function A quadratic function is in the form $y = ax^2 + bx + c$, where a, b and c are constants.

quadrilateral A quadrilateral is a 4-sided polygon.

radius A radius is a straight line which joins the centre of a circle to a point on the circumference.

range Range is a measure of the spread of a data set. The range is the difference between the largest and smallest data values.

rate Rate is a ratio of two measurements, usually the second measurement is time. For example, water flows through a pipe at a rate of 1 litre per second or a computer programmer types at a rate of 30 words per minute.

ratio A ratio is the comparison of one quantity with another.

ratio method The ratio method is used to solve problems involving direct proportion by comparing the ratios. For example, a bottling machine fills 500 bottles in 15 minutes. How many bottles will it fill in 90 minutes?

$$\frac{x}{90} = \frac{500}{15} \text{ so } x = \frac{500 \times 90}{15} = 3000$$

3000 bottles are filled in 90 minutes.

rational number A rational number is any number (positive or negative) that can be written as a fraction. All integers and all terminating and recurring decimals are rational numbers.

real number The real numbers are all the rational and irrational numbers. So any integer, fraction or decimal is a real number.

reciprocal The reciprocal of a number is 1 divided by that number. So the reciprocal of 4 is $1 \div 4 = \frac{1}{4} = 0.25$ and the reciprocal of $\frac{1}{5}$ is $1 \div \frac{1}{5} = 5$.

reciprocal function A reciprocal function is in the form $y = \frac{k}{x}$, where k is a constant.

rectangle A rectangle is a quadrilateral with the following properties:
- two pairs of parallel sides
- opposite sides are equal
- four equal angles (each 90°).

recurring decimal A recurring decimal has digits that repeat forever. For example, $\frac{2}{9} = 0.2222\ldots = 0.\dot{2}$ and $\frac{415}{999} = 0.415415415415\ldots = 0.\dot{4}1\dot{5}$.

reflection A reflection is a 'flip' movement in a mirror line. The mirror line is the line of symmetry between the object and its image.

reflex angle A reflex angle lies between 180° and 360°.

region A region is a part of a graph, shape or Venn diagram.

regular polygon A regular polygon has all sides of equal length and all angles of equal size.

relative frequency relative frequency $= \frac{\text{number of successful trials}}{\text{total number of trials}}$

rhombus A rhombus is a quadrilateral with the following properties:
- two pairs of parallel sides
- four equal sides
- opposite angles are equal
- diagonals which cross at right angles.

right angle A right angle is 90°.

right-angled triangle In a right-angled triangle, one angle is 90°.

roots (of an equation) The root(s) of an equation are the value(s) of x when $y = 0$. On a graph, these are the values of x where the curve crosses the x-axis.

rotation A rotation is a 'turning' movement about a specific point known as the centre of rotation.

rotational symmetry A shape has rotational symmetry if, when rotated about a central point, it fits its outline more than once in a complete turn.

round or rounding Rounding is a way of rewriting a number so it is simpler than the original number. A rounded number should be approximately equal to the unrounded (exact) number and be of the same order of magnitude (size). Rounded numbers are often given to 2 decimal places (2 d.p.) or 3 significant figures (3 s.f.), for example.

sample space diagram A sample space diagram shows all the possible outcomes of an experiment.

scale A scale on a drawing shows the ratio of a length on the drawing to the length on the actual object.

scale factor of enlargement The scale factor of enlargement is the ratio between corresponding sides on an object and its image.

scalene triangle In a scalene triangle, none of the angles are of equal size and none of the sides are of equal length.

scatter diagram A scatter diagram is a graph of plotted points which shows the relationship between two variables.

sector A sector is the region of a circle enclosed by two radii and an arc.

segment A segment is an area of a circle formed by a line (chord) and an arc.

selling price The selling price is the total amount of money that an item is sold for.

semicircle A semicircle is made when a circle is cut into two congruent halves. A semicircle is half a circle.

sequence A sequence is a collection of terms arranged in a specific order, where each term is obtained according to a rule.

set A set is a well-defined group of objects or symbols.

significant figures The first significant figure of a number is the first non-zero digit in the number. The second significant figure is the next digit in the number, and so on. For example, in the numbers 78 046 and 0.0078 046 the first significant figure is 7, the second significant figure is 8 and the third significant figure is 0.

similar Two shapes are similar if the corresponding angles are equal and the corresponding sides are in proportion to each other.

simple interest Simple interest is calculated only on the principal (initial) amount deposited in an account. When simple interest is earned, the amount of interest paid is the same each year.

simple interest $= \frac{\text{principal} \times \text{time in years} \times \text{rate percent}}{100}$

simplest form or lowest terms A fraction is in its simplest form when the highest common factor of the numerator and denominator is 1. In other words, the fraction cannot be cancelled down any further. For example, $\frac{30}{45} = \frac{6}{9} = \frac{2}{3}$, so $\frac{2}{3}$ is a fraction in its simplest form.

simultaneous equations Simultaneous equations are a pair of equations involving two unknowns.

sine The sine of an angle, sin x, in a right-angled triangle is the ratio of the side opposite the angle and the hypotenuse.

$$\sin x = \frac{\text{length of opposite side}}{\text{length of hypotenuse}}$$

speed speed = $\frac{\text{distance}}{\text{time}}$ When the speed is not constant: average speed = $\frac{\text{total distance}}{\text{total time}}$

sphere A sphere is a three-dimensional shape which is a ball.

square A square is a quadrilateral with the following properties:
- two pairs of parallel sides
- four equal sides
- four equal angles (90°)
- diagonals which cross at right angles.

square number A square number is the result when an integer is multiplied by itself. The square numbers are 1, 4, 9, 16, 25, …

square root The square root of a number is the number which when multiplied by itself gives the original number. The inverse of squaring is square rooting. Every number has two square roots, for example, the square root of 9 is 3 (as 3 × 3 = 9) and −3 (as −3 × −3 = 9). The symbol $\sqrt{}$ is used for the positive square root of a number, so $\sqrt{9}$ = 3.

standard form Standard form is a way of writing very large or very small numbers. A number in standard form is written as $A \times 10^n$, where $1 \leq A \leq 10$ and n is a positive or negative integer. Examples of numbers in standard from are 5×10^3 and 2.7×10^{-18}.

stem-and-leaf diagram A stem-and-leaf diagram is a diagram where each date value is split into two parts – the 'stem' and the 'leaf' (usually the last digit). The data is then grouped so that data values with the same stem appear on the same line.

straight line A straight line is the shortest distance between two points.

subject The subject of a formula is the single variable (often on the left-hand side of a formula) that the rest of the formula is equal to. For example, in $C = 2\pi r$, C is the subject and in $a^2 + b^2 = c^2$, c^2 is the subject.

substitute / substitution Substitution is replacing the variables (letter symbols) in an expression or formula with numbers.

substitution method The substitution method is a method for solving simultaneous equations, where one unknown is made the subject of one of the equations, and then this expression is substituted into the second equation.

subtraction Subtraction is one of the four operations: addition, subtraction, multiplication and division. It means to take one number away from another.

supplementary angle Two angles that add together to total 180° are called supplementary angles.

surface area of a cuboid The surface area of a cuboid of length l, width w and height h is: surface area = $2(wl + lh + wh)$

surface area of a cylinder The surface area of a cylinder of radius r and height h is: surface area = $2\pi r(r + h)$

surface area of a sphere The surface area of a sphere is $4\pi r^2$.

tally table A tally table is table where the frequencies of each outcome are recorded using marks like ||| for 3 or |||| for 5.

tangent The tangent to a curve at a point is a straight line that just touches the curve at that point. The gradient of the tangent is the same as the gradient of the curve at that point.

tangent (x) The tangent of an angle, tan x, in a right-angled triangle is the ratio of the sides opposite and adjacent to the angle.

$$\tan x = \frac{\text{length of opposite side}}{\text{length of adjacent side}}$$

term Each number in a sequence is a called a term.

terminating decimal A terminating decimal has digits after the decimal point that do not continue forever. For example, 0.123 and 0.987654321.

term-to-term rule A term-to-term rule describes how to use one term in a sequence to find the next term.

three-figure bearing A three-figure bearing is a measure of the direction in which an object is travelling. North is 000° and South is 180°.

time and a half Overtime is often paid at a higher rate. When overtime is paid at 1.5 × basic pay, it is called time and a half.

total number of possible outcomes The total number of possible outcomes refers to all the different types of outcomes one can get in a particular situation.

transformation A transformation changes either the position or size of an object, such as translation, rotation, reflection and enlargement.

translation A translation is a sliding movement. Each point on the object moves in the same way to its corresponding point on the image, as described by its translation vector.

translation vector A translation vector describes a translation in terms of its horizontal and vertical movement. For example, the translation vector $\begin{pmatrix} 2 \\ -3 \end{pmatrix}$ describes a translation of 2 units right and 3 units down.

trapezium A trapezium is a quadrilateral with one pair of parallel sides.

travel graph A travel graph is a diagram showing the journey of one or more objects on the same pair of axes. The vertical axis is distance and the horizontal axis is time.

triangle A triangle is a 3-sided polygon.

triangular numbers The triangular numbers are the numbers in the sequence 1, 3, 6, 10, 15, etc., where the difference between terms increases by 1 each time. The formula for the nth triangular number is: $\frac{1}{2}n(n+1)$

union The union of two sets is everything that belongs to EITHER or BOTH sets. It is represented by the symbol $\cup$.

unitary method The unitary method is used to solve problems involving direct proportion by first finding the value of a single unit. For example, 5 pens cost $8. Work out the cost of 7 pens.

5 pens cost $8

1 pen costs $8 ÷ 5 = $1.60 (the cost of 1 unit)

So 7 pens cost $1.60 × 7 = $11.20

universal set The universal set for any particular problem is the set which contains all the possible elements for that problem. It is represented by the symbol ξ.

upper bound Measurement is only approximate; the actual value of a measurement could be half the rounded unit above or below the given value. The upper bound is the greatest value up to which the true measurement can be. For example, the length of a pencil is 15.5 cm to the nearest millimetre. So, the upper bound is the measurement up to, but not equalling, 15.5 cm + 0.5 mm = 15.55 cm. Therefore, the actual length, l, of the pencil is less than 15.55 cm, so $l < 15.55$.

Venn diagram A Venn diagram is a diagram comprising of overlapping circles, which is used to display sets.

vertex (plural: vertices) A vertex of a shape is a point where two sides meet.

vertically opposite angles Vertically opposite angles are formed when two lines cross. Vertically opposite angles are equal.

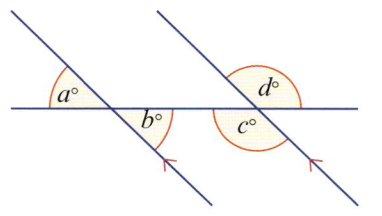

volume (capacity) The volume of a 3D solid is the amount of space the solid fills.

volume of a cylinder The volume of a cylinder of radius r and height h is given by: $volume = \pi r^2 h$

volume of a cone The volume of a cone with height h and a base of radius r is given by: $volume = \frac{1}{3}\pi r^3 h$

volume of a prism The volume of a prism is given by: volume = area of cross-section × length

volume of a pyramid The volume of pyramid is given by: volume = $\frac{1}{3}$ × area of base × perpendicular height

volume of a sphere The volume of a sphere is given by: $volume = \frac{4}{3}\pi r^3$

***x*-axis** The *x*-axis is the horizontal axis on a graph.

***y*-axis** The *y*-axis is the vertical axis on a graph.

Index

Numbers
24-hour clock 84

A
accuracy, degree of 18
activities spreadsheet 352–3
acute-angled triangles 209
acute angles 178
addition of fractions 39–40
adjacent side 275
algebra
    development of 101
    expanding a pair of brackets 104
    expanding a single bracket 102
    factorising 104
    rearranging formulae 107
    substitution 105–6
algebraic indices 109–11
al Khwarizmi 101
angles
    alternate 206–7
    co-interior 209
    corresponding 206–7
    measuring 188–9
    at a point 202
    of polygons 216–17, 224
    of quadrilaterals 213–15
    in a semi-circle 218
    on a straight line 202
    supplementary 178, 209
    between a tangent and a radius 219
    of triangles 209–11
    types of 178
    vertically opposite 205
approximation 16
    estimation 18–19
    rounding 16–17
    upper and lower bounds 20–1
arc length 250–1
arcs 180
area
    of a circle 241–3
    of compound shapes 237
    converting between units 231–2
    of a parallelogram 238–9
    of a rectangle 234–5
    of a sector 252–3
    of a trapezium 239–40
    of a triangle 236
    see also surface area
Aryabhata 271
asymptotes 147
averages 330–1, 333
average speed 86

B
back bearings 273
back-to-back stem-and-leaf diagrams 337
bar charts 336
    composite (stacked) 342
    dual (comparative) 342
bearings 272–3
Bellavitis, Giusto 295
Bernoulli, Jakob 311
Bolzano, Bernhard 295
bonuses 71
brackets 29, 37
    expanding a pair of brackets 104
    expanding a single bracket 102

C
calculators 27
    brackets 29
    order of operations 28
capacity, units of 231
Cardano, Girolamo 101
centre of enlargement 301–3, 308
centre of rotation 297
chequered boards investigation 153
chords 180
circles 180
    arc length 250–1
    area of a sector 252–3
    associated angles 218–19
    circumference and area 241–3
circumference of a circle 180, 241–2
co-interior angles 209
compass points 272
complementary angles 178
complement of a set 90
compound interest 76–8
compound measures 56–8
compound shapes 237
cones
    surface area 263–4
    volume 259–61
congruent shapes 183–4
constructing a triangle 191–2
conversion graphs 133
coordinates 157–8
    equation of a straight line 166, 170–2
    gradient of a straight line 160–3
correlation 343–4
    types of 345
corresponding angles 206–7
cosine (cos) 281
cube numbers 5, 10–11, 130
cube roots 11, 12
cuboids
    surface area 244–5
    volume 247
currency conversion 70
    graphs 133
    ICT activity 99
cylinders
    surface area 244–5
    volume 247

D
data displays
    bar charts 336, 342
    pictograms 335
    pie charts 337–40
    scatter diagrams 343–5
    stem-and-leaf diagrams 336–7
    tally charts and frequency tables 335
decimal fractions 34
decimal places (d.p.) 17
decimals 34
    changing to fractions 42–3
    percentage and fraction equivalents 45

de Moivre, Abraham 311
denominator 32
density 56-7
depreciation 80
Descartes, René 295
diameter 180
dice sum investigation 326
directed numbers 12
direct proportion 51-3
discounts 48
discrete data 336
distance-time graphs 135-7
distance travelled 134
division 36-7
division of fractions 41
dodecagons 181

E

elements of a set 89
elimination method, simultaneous equations 119-20
enlargement 301-3
  ICT activity 308
equation of a straight line 166, 170-1
  parallel lines 171-2
equations
  construction of 114-15, 118
  exponential 110-11
  linear 112
  quadratic 145-6, 155
  simultaneous 119-22, 142, 154-5
equilateral triangles 210
equivalent fractions 38-9
estimation 18-19
Euclid 177
exponential equations 110-11
exterior angles, sum of 217

F

factorising 104
factors 5-6
favourable outcomes 312
Fermat, Pierre de 295, 311
football leagues investigation 98
formulae (singular: formula)
  rearranging 107
  subject of 107
fountain borders investigation 223

fractions 32
  addition and subtraction 39-40
  changing to decimals 42
  changing to percentages 35
  decimal 34
  equivalent 38-9
  multiplication and division 41
  percentage and decimal equivalents 45
fractions of an amount 32
frequency tables 335
functions
  linear 140-1, 147-8
  quadratic 143-4, 148-50
  reciprocal 146-7
  recognising and sketching 147-50

G

geometry, historical development 177
gradient of a straight line 160-3
  parallel lines 171-2
graphs
  conversion 133
  linear functions 140-1, 147-8
  quadratic functions 143-4, 148-50
  reciprocal functions 146-7
  sketching functions 147-50
  solving quadratic equations 145-6, 155
  solving simultaneous equations 142, 154-5
  travel 135-7
gross earnings 71

H

Harrison, John 157
height (altitude) of a triangle 179, 236
heptagons 181
hexagons 181
highest common factor (HCF) 6
house of cards investigation 153
Huygens, Christiaan 311
hyperbolas 146-7
hypotenuse 275

I

ICT activities
  activities spreadsheet 352-3
  angles of polygons 224
  currency conversion 99
  enlargements 308
  quadratic equations 155
  simultaneous equations 154-5
  spinner 327
  step patterns 98-9
  trigonometric ratios 293
images 296
improper fractions 32, 33
indices (singular: index) 61
  algebraic 109-10
  exponential equations 110-11
  negative 63, 110
  positive 62, 109
  standard form 63-7
  zero 62, 110
inequalities 24-5
integers 4
interest
  compound 76-8
  simple 74-6
interior angles, sum of
  polygons 216-17
  quadrilaterals 215
  triangles 211
intersection of sets (∩) 90-1
inverse proportion 55
investigations 95
  chequered boards 153
  dice sum 326
  football leagues 98
  fountain borders 223
  house of cards 153
  metal trays 269
  mystic roses 95-7
  painted cube 307
  plane trails 174
  primes and squares 98
  probability drop 325
  Pythagoras' theorem 291
  reading age 352
  stretching a spring 154
  tiled walls 224
  towers of Hanoi 292
  triangle count 308
irrational numbers 7-8
isosceles triangles 210

K

Khayyam, Omar 101
kites 214

L

laws of indices 62
length, units of 229
linear equations 112
linear functions 140-1
    sketching 147-8
lines of best fit 344
lines of symmetry 198
long division 37
loss 79-80
lowest terms (simplest form) 38-9

M

mass, units of 230
mean 330-1, 333
measurement
    of angles 188-9
    metric system 228-31
    SI units 227
    of straight lines 188
median 330-1, 333
metal trays investigation 269
metric system 228-31
mirror lines 296
mixed numbers 32, 33, 40
Möbius, August 295
mode 330-1, 333
money
    compound interest 76-8
    currency conversion 70, 99
    personal and household finance 71-2
    profit and loss 79-80
    simple interest 74-6
multiples 7
multiplication 36
    of fractions 41
mystic roses investigation 95-7

N

natural numbers 4
negative correlation 345
negative indices 63, 110
net pay 71
nets 194
nonagons 181
nth term of a sequence 128
number line, inequalities 24-5

numbers
    historical development 3
    types of 4-5, 7-8
numerator 32

O

obtuse-angled triangles 210
obtuse angles 178
opposite side 275
ordering 24
order of operations 28, 37
order of rotational symmetry 200
origin 158
outliers 333
overtime 71

P

painted cube investigation 307
parabolas 143-4
    sketching 148-50
parallel lines 180
    angles formed within 206-7, 209
    equations of 171-2
parallelograms 213
    area 238-9
Parimala, Raman 101
Pascal, Blaise 311
pentagons 181
percentage increases and decreases 48
percentage interest 74
percentage profit and loss 80
percentages 35, 45-6
    expressing one quantity as a percentage of another 47
    fraction and decimal equivalents 45
    of a quantity 46
perimeter of a rectangle 234
perpendicular lines 179
pictograms 335
piece work 72
pie charts 337-40
plane trails investigation 174
P() notation 317
points, angles at 202
polygons 181
    sum of exterior angles 217
    sum of interior angles 216-17

population density 57, 58
positive correlation 344, 345
positive indices 62, 109
powers 8-9, 10-12
    see also indices
prime factors 5-6
prime numbers 4
primes and squares investigation 98
principal 74
prisms, volume 247-8
probability 312-13
    historical development 311
    relative frequency 321
    tree diagrams 316-18
    Venn diagrams 319-20
probability drop investigation 325
probability scale 313-14
profit 79-80
proper fractions 32
proportion
    direct 51-3
    inverse 55
protractors 188-9
pyramids
    surface area 259
    volume 257-8
Pythagoras' theorem 282-3
    investigation 291

Q

quadratic equations, graphical solution 145-6, 155
quadratic functions 143-4
    sketching 148-50
quadrilaterals
    sum of interior angles 215
    types of 213-14

R

radius 180
range of data 330-1
ratio method, direct proportion 51-3
rational numbers 7-8
ratios, dividing a quantity in a given ratio 54
reading age investigation 352
rearranging formulae 107
reciprocal functions 146-7
reciprocals 4, 41
rectangles 213

area 234–5
   perimeter 234
reflection 296
reflex angles 178
relative frequency 321
rhombuses 213
right-angled triangles 209
   Pythagoras' theorem 282–3
   trigonometric ratios
      275–81
right angles 178
roots 9, 11–12
roots of an equation 145
rotation 297
rotational symmetry 200
rounding 16–17

S

scale drawings 192–3
scale factor of enlargement
   301–3
scale factors, of enlargement
   182
scalene triangles 210
scales 159
scatter diagrams 343–5
sectors of a circle 180
   area 252–3
segments of a circle 180
semi-circle, angle in 218
sequences 126
   common types 129–31
   nth term of 128
   term-to-term rules 126–7
sets 89–90
   problem solving with 92–3
   Venn diagrams 90–1
short division 36
shortest distance between two
   points 179
significant figures (s.f.) 17
similar shapes 182
simple interest 74–6
simplest form (lowest terms)
   38–9
simultaneous equations 119
   elimination by multiplication
      121–2
   elimination method 119–20
   graphical solution 142,
      154–5
   substitution method 120–1

sine (sin) 279
SI units 227
sketching functions
   linear 147–8
   quadratic 148–50
speed 56, 57–8, 134
   average 86
spheres
   surface area 256
   volume 254–5
spinner activity 327
spreadsheets
   activities 352–3
   angles of polygons 224
   currency conversion 99
   spinner activity 327
springs, extension of 154
square numbers 5, 8–9, 129
square roots 9–10
squares 213
standard form
   adding and subtracting 66
   multiplying and dividing 65
   negative indices and small
      numbers 67
   positive indices and large
      numbers 63–4
statistics
   averages 330–1, 333
   data displays 335–45
   spread of data 330–1
stem-and-leaf diagrams
   336–7
step patterns ICT activity 98–9
straight line graphs 140–1
   sketching 147–8
straight lines 160
   angles on 202
   equation of 166, 170–2
   gradient of 160–3
   measuring 188
subject of a formula 107
substitution 105–6
substitution method,
   simultaneous equations
   120–1
subtraction of fractions 39–40
supplementary angles 178, 209
surface area
   of a cone 263–4
   of a cuboid and a cylinder
      244–5

   of a pyramid 259
   of a sphere 256
symmetry
   lines of 198
   rotational 200

T

tally charts 335
tangent (tan, trigonometric
   ratio) 275–6
tangents to a circle 180
   associated angles 219
term-to-term rules, sequences
   126–7
Thales of Miletus 177
tiled walls investigation 224
time 84, 86
   relationship to speed and
      distance 134
towers of Hanoi investigation
   292
transformations 296
   enlargement 301–3, 308
   reflection 296
   rotation 297
   translation 299
translation 299
translation vectors 299
trapeziums 214
   area 239–40
travel graphs 135–7
tree diagrams 316–17
   for unequal probabilities
      318
triangle count investigation
   308
triangles 181
   area 236
   construction of 191–2
   height (altitude) of 179,
      236
   sum of interior angles 211
   types of 209–10
triangular numbers 130–1
trigonometric ratios 275
   cosine (cos) 281
   ICT activity 293
   sine (sin) 279
   tangent (tan) 275–6
trigonometry, historical
   development 271
turning points 149

U

union of sets (∪) 91
unitary method, direct proportion 51–3
universal set 89–90
upper and lower bounds 20–1

V

vectors 299
    historical development 295
Venn diagrams 90–1
for probability problems 319–20
vertex of a triangle 236
vertically opposite angles 205
volume
    of a cone 259–61
    converting between units 232
    of a prism 247–8
    of a pyramid 257–8
    of a sphere 254–5

X

x-axis 158

Y

y-axis 158

Z

zero index 62, 110